Conflict Resolution and its Context

Law, Governance and Technology Series

VOLUME 18

Series Editors:
POMPEU CASANOVAS, *UAB Institute of Law and Technology,*
Bellaterra, Barcelona, Spain

GIOVANNI SARTOR, *University of Bologna (Faculty of Law-CIRSFID) and*
European University Institute, Bologna, Italy

Scientific Advisory Board:

For further volumes:
http://www.springer.com/series/8808

Davide Carneiro • Paulo Novais • José Neves

Conflict Resolution and its Context

From the Analysis of Behavioural Patterns to Efficient Decision-Making

Davide Carneiro
CCTC/Department of Informatics
University of Minho
Braga
Portugal

Paulo Novais
CCTC/Department of Informatics
University of Minho
Braga
Portugal

José Neves
CCTC/Department of Informatics
University of Minho
Braga
Portugal

ISSN 2352-1902   ISSN 2352-1910 (electronic)
ISBN 978-3-319-37757-5   ISBN 978-3-319-06239-6 (eBook)
DOI 10.1007/978-3-319-06239-6
Springer Cham Heidelberg New York Dordrecht London

Springer is part of Springer Science+Business Media (www.springer.com)

To the ones we never forget

Foreword

In June 2007, I attended the 11th international conference on Artificial Intelligence and Law, held at the Stanford University Law School. As well as presenting two papers, Gray et al. (2007) and Zeleznikow et al. (2007), I gave a three-hour tutorial with my colleague Arno Lodder from Vrije Universiteit Amsterdam and organized a full day workshop on Online Dispute Resolution at the offices of E-Bay in San Jose, California. Arno and I had just published a paper in the Harvard Negotiation Law Review (Lodder and Zeleznikow 2005) and were preparing a book on the topic, to be published by Cambridge University Press.

For me, my participation at the conference was my first major involvement in the growing area of Online Dispute Resolution. There had been papers on the issue of Technology and Dispute Resolution in the late 1990s, such as Bordone (1998). By the early 2000s we had books being published on the topic – for example Katsh and Rifkin (2001) and Rule (2002).

I had initially been interested in the use of machine learning to model reasoning in discretionary legal domains. Our work in mimicking the reasoning of Australian Family court judges led us to closely examine negotiation processes and subsequently the use of technology to support alternative forms of dispute resolution (Bellucci and Zeleznikow 2006). But this work did not focus upon the use of the World Wide Web for dispute resolution. Indeed the associated software Family Winner[1] was primarily designed to operate upon personal computers.

In retrospect, the most important result of my attendance at the conference at Stanford University was my meeting two researchers and scholars at the University of Minho in Braga Portugal – Francisco Andrade a lawyer and Paulo Novais a computer scientist. Save for a brief trip to Lisbon in 2004, I had not been to Portugal and knew little about the significant research being conducted by Portuguese academics. This situation would soon change.

During that first week of June 2007, Paulo, Francisco, Arno and I spent much time discussing Online Dispute Resolution opportunities. Francisco had a keen

---

[1] See https://www.youtube.com/watch?v=YOZczuvrou4 last accessed 4 March 2014.

interest in Portuguese Labour Law. He and Paulo wanted to build ODR systems to support negotiation in Portuguese Labour Law. As a result, a prototype, UMCourt has been developed.

Since 2007, I have been able to meet the University of Minho group on a number of occasions. I visited Braga in October 2008 (when I gave a keynote address at the Group Decision and Negotiation Conference in Coimbra) and June 2013, whilst Paulo spent a week with me in Melbourne in September 2010. We also met at international conferences on Artificial Intelligence and Law (Barcelona 2009; Pittsburgh 2011) and the annual JURIX conferences (Florence 2008; Liverpool 2010; Bologna 2013). During my trips to Braga I was able to meet with Prof. José Neves. Since 2010, I have been fortunate to meet with Davide Carneiro, Dr. Novais' superb PhD student and now his postdoctoral fellow.

Over the last 7 years I have been able to observe the excellent research performance of the ODR group at the University of Minho. They have conducted significant research on:

1. ADR processes – BATNAs, WATNAs, ZOPA
2. Artificial Intelligence in ODR
3. ODR architectures
4. Information retrieval in ODR
5. Measuring emotions in ODR

The culmination of this research has led to the development of a prototype of a communication environment which assesses contextual information from the parties in an autonomous way. Hardware and software has been developed to assess the level of stress displayed by the competing parties in a negotiation. This information is conveyed through the communication medium in real time, making it richer and increasing the efficiency of the communication process.

Such information can also prove very useful to mediators in offline environments. Because of a need to engage in ethical processes, the information is only gathered with the consent of the disputants. It is being used by mediators to enhance the support and advice they provide to the disputing parties.

The ultimate goal of the University of Minho research is to build a transparent computational environment that can support the conflict resolution system with the provision of meaningful context information.

This excellent book is the culmination of their important research. I highly commend it to you.

John Zeleznikow
Professor of Information Systems,
Laboratory of Decision Support and
Dispute Management, College of Business,
Victoria University, Melbourne, VIC, Australia

References

Bellucci, Emilia, and John Zeleznikow. 2006. Developing negotiation decision support systems that support mediators: A case study of the Family_Winner system. *Journal of Artificial Intelligence and Law*, 13(2): 233–271.

Bordone, Robert. 1998. Electronic online dispute resolution: A systems approach – Potential, problems, and a proposal. *The Harvard Negotiation Law Review* 3: 175.

Gray, P., X. Gray, and J. Zeleznikow. 2007. Decision negotiating logic: For richer or poorer. In *Proceedings of eleventh international conference on artificial intelligence and law*, ed. R. Winkels. ACM Press, Palo Alto, CA, USA.

Katsh, E., and Janet Rifkin. 2001. *Online dispute resolution: Resolving conflicts in Cyberspace*. San Francisco: Jossey-Bass..

Lodder, A., and J. Zeleznikow. 2005. Developing an online dispute resolution environment: Dialogue tools and negotiation systems in a three step model. *The Harvard Negotiation Law Review* 10: 287–338.

Rule, C. 2002. *Online dispute resolution for businesses*. San Francisco: Jossey-Bass.

Zeleznikow, J., E. Bellucci, U.J. Schild, G. Mackenzie. 2007. Bargaining in the shadow of the law – Using utility functions to support legal negotiation. In *Proceedings of the 11th international conference on Artificial intelligence and law*, 237–246, ACM.

Preface

This book results of several years of applied research in the intersection of Artificial Intelligence and The Law, undertaken by a multi-disciplinary team. During these years, our aim has always been to study, address and solve actual problems in the domain of Conflict Resolution, especially the one carried out with the support of the new information technologies. The book provides an overview of the current challenges in this field. It addresses some of these challenges, from a technological point of view, by detailing tools developed by the authors over the last years. Finally, the book focuses on the context of a conflict, how it can be characterized and how it can be efficiently used by conflict managers to improve their decision-making processes. It is suited for students, legal practitioners, conflict managers or the general public with interest in conflict, its context and its resolution.

In carrying out this research work, nonetheless, we have not been alone. Therefore, we would like to acknowledge the important input that stemmed from casual conversations, insightful ideas, informed opinions and the concrete cooperation in this research effort of:

- John Zeleznikow, whose expertise in Artificial Intelligence and its application to support decision-making in the legal field contributed constantly and significantly towards the improvement of the research carried out over these years
- Marta Poblet, for her insightful and realistic views on mediation and its real-world challenges
- Francisco Andrade, our ever-present legal expert
- António Caballero and José Carlos Montoya, for their technological input to this work, at first sight so unrelated to theirs, and their hospitality
- Our students of the Master Courses in Law and Informatics and in Informatics Engineering, with whom we had always fruitful discussions about this work and its implications

- The members of the ISLab, who make up a rich environment to work in
- The Editors of this Series, Pompeu Casanovas and Giovanni Sartor, for their support during the publication process
- The anonymous people that participated in the studies carried out and described in this book

Braga, Portugal   Davide Carneiro
                                                                                              Paulo Novais
                                                                                              José Neves

Acknowledgements

This work is part-funded by ERDF – European Regional Development Fund – through the COMPETE Programme (operational programme for competitiveness) and by Portuguese National Funds through the FCT – *Fundação para a Ciência e a Tecnologia* (Portuguese Foundation for Science and Technology) within project FCOMP-01-0124-FEDER-028980 (PTDC/EEI-SII/1386/2012).

Acknowledgements

This work is part-funded by ERDF – European Regional Development Fund through the COMPETE Programme (operational programme for competitiveness) and by Portuguese National Funds through the FCT – Fundação para a Ciência e a Tecnologia (Portuguese Foundation for Science and Technology) within project FCOMP-01-0124-FEDER-037281 (FTDC/EEI-SII/1386/2012).

Abbreviations

ADR	Alternative dispute resolution
AI	Artificial intelligence
BATNA	Best Alternative to a Negotiated Agreement
CBR	Case-based reasoning
DSS	Decision support system
IE	Intelligent environment
IM	Instant messaging
IT	Information technologies
KR	Knowledge retrieval
MAS	Multi-agent system
MDA	Model driven architecture
MLATNA	Most Likely Alternative to a Negotiated Agreement
ODR	Online dispute resolution
OWL	Web Ontology Language
RbS	Rule-based systems
SIEJ	*Sistema de Informaçao das Estatísticas da Justiça* (Justice Statistics Information System)
SOA	Service oriented architecture
TIARAC	Telematics and Artificial Intelligence in Alternative Conflict Resolution
UML	Unified Modelling Language
WATNA	Worst Alternative to a Negotiated Agreement
XMI	XML Metadata interchange
ZOPA	Zone of possible agreement

Contents

Part I Online Dispute Resolution and Its Context

1 Introduction 3
   1.1   Introduction 3
   References 9

2 Traditional and Alternative Ways to Solve Conflicts 11
   2.1   Introduction 11
   2.2   Litigation in Courts 15
   2.3   Current State of Judicial Systems 16
   2.4   Alternative Dispute Resolution 20
         2.4.1   Negotiation 22
         2.4.2   Mediation 24
         2.4.3   Arbitration 26
         2.4.4   Conciliation 28
   2.5   Online Dispute Resolution 28
         2.5.1   Inside a Typical ODR Process 30
         2.5.2   Classifying ODR Systems 31
   2.6   Conclusion 34
   References 35

3 Advantages and Disadvantages of Avoiding the Courtroom 39
   3.1   Introduction 39
   3.2   The Traditional Alternatives 40
   3.3   The Online Alternatives 43
   3.4   Media Richness in ODR 48
   3.5   Cause and Effect Analysis 51
   3.6   Conclusion 57
   References 58

4   Artificial Intelligence in Online Dispute Resolution   61
   4.1   Introduction   61
   4.2   Classical Sub-fields of AI and the Law Research   64
         4.2.1   Decision Support Systems   64
         4.2.2   Expert Systems   66
         4.2.3   Knowledge-Based Systems   67
         4.2.4   Intelligent Interfaces   68
         4.2.5   Case-Based Reasoning   70
         4.2.6   Multi-agent Systems   72
         4.2.7   Legal Ontologies   73
         4.2.8   Rule-Based Systems   74
         4.2.9   Evolutionary Computation   75
   4.3   Projects on the Intersection of AI and the Law   76
         4.3.1   Rule-Based Legal Decision-Making Systems (LDS) . . .   76
         4.3.2   EXPERTIUS   77
         4.3.3   SmartSettle   77
         4.3.4   Family_Winner   78
         4.3.5   ALIS   78
         4.3.6   PERSUADER   79
   4.4   New Fields, New Possibilities   79
         4.4.1   Sense, Reason, Act   82
         4.4.2   AmI Projects   84
         4.4.3   Intelligent Environment for Conflict Resolution:
                A Scenario   87
   4.5   The Current State of Artificial Intelligence and ODR   89
   4.6   Conclusion   89
   References   92

5   Context and Its Importance   97
   5.1   Introduction   97
   5.2   Different Contextual Dimensions   99
         5.2.1   Verbal   99
         5.2.2   Social   99
         5.2.3   Historical   100
         5.2.4   Physical   101
         5.2.5   Psychological   101
         5.2.6   Symbolical   102
         5.2.7   Relational   103
         5.2.8   Situational   103
         5.2.9   Cultural   104
         5.2.10 Digital   104
   5.3   Context-Aware Computing   105
   5.4   Harnessing Content and Context   106
   5.5   Contextualizing Conflicts   109

	5.5.1	Delimiting the Conflict	109
	5.5.2	Past Cases	111
	5.5.3	Conflict Handling Style	112
	5.5.4	Stress	112
	5.5.5	Fatigue	113
	5.5.6	Level of Escalation	113
5.6	Conclusion		113
References			115

Part II   Technological Framework

6   An Agent-Based Architecture for a Second Generation ODR Tool 121
6.1	Introduction		121
6.2	Identifying Useful Abstract Concepts		123
6.3	Identifying Abstract Processes		124
	6.3.1	Information Retrieval	124
	6.3.2	Generation of Solutions	126
	6.3.3	Negotiation	127
	6.3.4	Generation of Strategies	129
	6.3.5	Generic Conflict Resolution Model	130
6.4	Software Agents		131
	6.4.1	Coordination and Control Layer	133
	6.4.2	Rules Layer	133
	6.4.3	Data Layer	133
	6.4.4	Knowledge Layer	134
	6.4.5	Context Layer	134
	6.4.6	Application Layer	135
6.5	An Abstract Architecture to Solve Specific Problems		135
6.6	Conclusion		138
References			139

7   Information Retrieval 141
7.1	Introduction		141
7.2	Information Retrieval Approaches		144
7.3	Information Retrieval in UMCourt		145
	7.3.1	Preliminary Considerations	147
	7.3.2	Parsing and Indexing	148
	7.3.3	Case Structure	149
	7.3.4	The CBR Process Model	150
7.4	Conclusion		160
References			160

8   The Conflict Resolution Process   163
      8.1   Introduction   163
      8.2   Using Negotiation and Mediation to Improve CBR
             Efficiency   166
             8.2.1   Mediation   167
             8.2.2   Guided Negotiation   169
      8.3   An Evolutionary Approach to Conflict Resolution   172
             8.3.1   A Closer Overview of Evolutionary Algorithms   172
             8.3.2   Using Genetic Algorithms to Create Solutions for
                      Conflict Resolution   174
      8.4   Conclusion   183
      References   185

Part III   Context Acquisition in Online Dispute Resolution

9   A Framework for Developing Sensible Environments   189
      9.1   Introduction   189
      9.2   Traditional Approaches on Context Acquisition   190
      9.3   A Systematic Behavioral Analysis of a Living Organism   193
             9.3.1   Acquiring Contextual Features from Behavioral
                      Analysis   195
             9.3.2   Acting on the Environment   202
      9.4   Conclusion   203
      References   204

10   Inferring Conflict Resolution Styles   207
      10.1   Introduction   207
      10.2   From the Computation of the Utility to the Classification
             of the Personal Conflict Resolution Style   211
      10.3   Studying the Relationship Between Stress and Conflict
             Resolution Style   215
      10.4   A Sensible and Dynamic Conflict Resolution Model   217
      10.5   Conclusion   220
      References   221

11   Stress in Conflict Resolution   223
      11.1   Introduction   223
      11.2   A Multi-modal View on Stress   224
      11.3   Common Stressors   228
      11.4   A study on the Effects of Stress   229
             11.4.1   Real-Time Assessment of Stress   231
      11.5   Conclusion   237
      References   239

Part IV   Conclusions and Future Directions

12   Analysis of Practical Results 243
    12.1   Concerning Information Retrieval 243
        12.1.1   Efficiency 244
        12.1.2   Efficacy 247
    12.2   Concerning Conflict Handling Styles 249
    12.3   Concerning Stress 252
        12.3.1   Preliminary Data Analysis 252
        12.3.2   Classifiers 260
    12.4   Conclusion 265

13   Concluding Remarks and Future Thoughts 269
    13.1   On the Use of Case-Based Reasoning in the Legal Context 269
    13.2   On the Use of Negotiation/Mediation for Conflict
           Resolution 271
    13.3   On the Relationship Between Personal Conflict Handling
           Styles and Stress 272
    13.4   On the Assessment of Stress 273
    13.5   Future Lines 274
    References 279

List of Figures

Fig. 2.1   Average duration of the litigation processes in Portuguese first
instances courts between 2001 and 2010 19

Fig. 3.1   The main causes and effects identified in the current state of
judicial systems 52

Fig. 3.2   The main problems and their causes identified in current
Online Dispute Resolution tools 54

Fig. 3.3   A general view of the main problems identified in the field of
conflict resolution, their causes and the potential solutions to
address them 55

Fig. 6.1   Activity diagram depicting the sequence of main activities
needed to implement the process of information retrieval 125

Fig. 6.2   Activity diagram depicting the sequence of main activities
needed to implement the process of generating solutions,
using a nature-inspired approach 126

Fig. 6.3   Activity diagram depicting the sequence of main activities
needed to implement the negotiation process 128

Fig. 6.4   Activity diagram depicting the sequence of main activities
needed to implement the assisted negotiation process.
This model is especially suited for scenarios in which parties
are unable or unwilling to generate solutions 129

Fig. 6.5   Activity diagram depicting the sequence of main activities
needed to implement a generic conflict resolution model.
It can be seen as a high-level composition of the previously
depicted models 131

Fig. 6.6   Diagram depicting the layered nature of the architecture,
with the organization of the software agents according to their
functionalities. Lines between agents depict important
communication paths. More than one instance of some
agents may exist simultaneously 132

Fig. 6.7   Hierarchical nature of the architecture in which the
complexity of providing specific services is hidden.
Each agent forwards the request to more specific agents.
Domain coordinators (e.g. *CoordinatorL*) are used to implement
more complex activities involving more than one service (the
computation of the BATNA requires the use of a single service
from a single agent) 138

Fig. 7.1   Indexed cases can be organized by means of association rules;
i.e., all the cases for which a given rule is enforced successfully
belong to the same category 149

Fig. 7.2   Representing an N-dimensional case 150

Fig. 7.3   Representing a case database as a matrix 150

Fig. 7.4   The CBR model 152

Fig. 7.5   The output of a typical case retrieval process 154

Fig. 7.6   Visualization of a typical communication between agents for
retrieving similar cases 155

Fig. 7.7   Visual representation of the information retrieved for a given
case. It includes several past cases, displayed in the space
according to their degree of similarity to the current case and
their utility for a given party 157

Fig. 7.8   The *CBR* process as part of a higher-level dispute resolution
process 159

Fig. 8.1   A simple visual interface of the blackboard status
(*upper image*), and the content of a reply (*lower image*) 167

Fig. 8.2   The several consecutive phases of the mediation process 168

Fig. 8.3   The information needed to guide a negotiation process 170

Fig. 8.4   A negotiation process coordinated by the blackboard agent 170

Fig. 8.5   Under this approach a population of size *s* is represented
as a set of chromosomes with a cardinality of *s* 175

Fig. 8.6   A prototype of the interface used to configure the genetic
algorithm, including information about the parties, the issues
and the weight of each genetic operator 176

Fig. 8.7   The first ten generations of a run of the algorithm, showing
only the best solutions generated 181

Fig. 8.8   A jump: when the state of another party is worsening,
the mediator may select a solution from the species of that
party in the next round 182

Fig. 8.9   A walk: when the state of the party improves or worsens
slightly or when the negotiation is proceeding acceptably,
the mediator is able to move up or down the tree in order to
select solutions that are similar in terms of fitness 182

Fig. 8.10   A dynamic negotiation model; this picture depicts a high level
            view of a dynamic negotiation setting that is able to adapt
            strategies and propose different solutions according to changes
            in the process of negotiation. The input for the adaptation is
            information describing the state of the parties (e.g. emotional
            arousal, level of stress and personal conflict handling style)   184
Fig. 9.1   Some of the devices that make up the environment   196
Fig. 9.2   Interface of the INT3 framework, a multilevel framework for
            intelligent multisensory monitoring and activity
            interpretation   198
Fig. 9.3   The layered architecture of the environment   201
Fig. 10.1   The distribution of the different styles in terms of their degree
            of assertiveness and cooperation   209
Fig. 10.2   The space that defines the personal conflict resolution styles in
            function of the utility of the proposals and the values of the
            BATNA, BATNA and ZOPA   212
Fig. 10.3   The evolution of the conflict resolution style of a party in
            10 rounds following the approach presented and the styles
            depicted by Thomas and Kilmann   215
Fig. 10.4   The setting in which the participants took part in the
            negotiation competition   217
Fig. 10.5   A high level view of the dynamic conflict resolution archetype.
            With information detailing the emotional arousal, level of
            stress or conflict handling style, the mediator is able to adapt
            his posture in real-time, resulting in a dynamic process that
            uses as input the state of the parties   219
Fig. 10.6   Screenshots of Android interfaces that provide interaction
            with the conflict resolution platform while, at the same time,
            providing information about interaction patterns   219
Fig. 11.1   The stress recognition model described in this chapter.
            It includes two main groups of aspects: predictive and
            diagnostic. Predictive aspects are the ones that can be
            estimated from the background or context of the individual.
            Diagnostic aspects are the ones that can be observed and
            measured and have a relationship with the level of stress   226
Fig. 11.2   Screenshots of the game interface in which the user must
            perform mental calculations and memorization of
            intermediary results while under stress   232
Fig. 11.3   Quantifying the similarity between two distributions of
            data by measuring the overlap of their confidence intervals   233
Fig. 11.4   Example of the working of the nearest neighbor algorithm
            by a majority vote: in this case the *green dot* (new instance)
            would be classified as "stressed" (the class of the *red dots*)
            (Color figure online)   234

Fig. 11.5   (a) Ten different touch patterns from users: touches can be
             composed of a different number of touch events. The *orange
             lines* depict touches classified as "calm" whereas the *blue
             lines* belong to touches classified as "stressed". (b) Fitting a
             polynomial curve (*blue curve*) to a given touch (*orange line*)
             (Color figure online) 236
Fig. 11.6   The proposed concept of a Conflict Resolution Environment is
             central in this book: the user's context is acquired from sensors
             placed in the environment of the user. This allows to build a
             contextualized representation of his actions, supporting the
             conflict resolution and the mediator in taking better actions 238
Fig. 12.1   Summary of the performance of the pre-selection task using
             association rules for 100 requests generated randomly 245
Fig. 12.2   Summary of the performance of the pre-selection task using the
             Template Retrieval technique for 155 requests generated
             randomly 246
Fig. 12.3   Summary of the performance of the evaluation task using
             the Cosine Similarity technique for 99 requests generated
             randomly 247
Fig. 12.4   Summary of the performance of the evaluation task using
             the Nearest Neighbor algorithm for 48 requests generated
             randomly 247
Fig. 12.5   Summary of the performance of the "Get Complete Info"
             task for 55 requests generated randomly 248
Fig. 12.6   The output of a self-assessment request for the pre-select
             action 248
Fig. 12.7   Histograms depicting the distribution of the styles used by
             the parties: the *red line* represents data from the stressed phase
             while the *green line* represents data from the calm phase.
             The X axis represents the ordinal rank of the conflict handling
             styles as defined in Table 12.1. In a calm state the users
             evidence more cooperative styles (color figure online) 250
Fig. 12.8   Evolution of the values proposed during the negotiation
             when under stress (a) and without stress (b). The *red line*
             depicts the values proposed by the manufacturer while the
             blue line depicts the values proposed by the retailer. It is
             possible the see that under stress the values proposed vary
             faster: the parties achieve a similar result in only half the
             rounds (color figure online) 252
Fig. 12.9   Different styles of the lines used to depict the different
             groups of the data collected. These styles will be used in the
             remaining of this book 253

Fig. 12.10   Histograms of data from the module of the acceleration
             concerning two different users. The difference between the
             baseline data and the stressed data (and its subgroups) is
             clearly visible: the data from stressed users has more
             variability, i.e., stressed users move their hands more or
             in more sudden ways 254
Fig. 12.11   Histograms of two different individuals concerning the
             maximum intensity of the touch. These two histograms
             show the tendency observed in most of the data: stressed
             individuals touch the screen with more intensity 255
Fig. 12.12   Histograms of two participants of the study concerning
             the average intensity of the touch. As with almost every
             participant, the average intensity of the touch increases with
             increased levels of stress 256
Fig. 12.13   Results of movement detection on a non-stressed user.
             Row (a) shows input images, row (b) shows binarized
             and filtered movement and row (c) shows the amount of
             movement detected 256
Fig. 12.14   Results of movement detection on a stressed user.
             Row (a) shows input images, row (b) shows binarized
             and filtered movement and row (c) shows the amount of
             movement detected 257
Fig. 12.15   An example of how the amount of movement generally varies
             with the amount of stress: higher stress is related to a smaller
             amount of movement. (a) Range of the values of movement for
             each dataset. (b) Average and standard deviation for the
             different datasets for a specific user 257
Fig. 12.16   Histograms of two different participants concerning the
             duration of their touches. This feature does not have a
             homogeneous behavior: some stressed participants have
             shorter touches while others have longer ones 258
Fig. 12.17   Box-and-Whisker plot denoting the distribution of the scores
             for a given participant, in different levels of stress (a).
             The same data is shown in (b). Although the several
             distributions are visually different, these differences are not
             statistically significant. However, the general tendency is that
             participants under stress tend to have worse performances 259
Fig. 12.18   This plot shows the percentage of touches on target in the five
             different analysis for all the participants 260
Fig. 12.19   Box-and-whisker diagram detailing the sample accuracies
             of the classifiers trained for the acceleration feature 261

Fig. 12.20   Box-and-whisker diagram detailing the sample accuracies
              of the classifiers trained for the movement feature 261
Fig. 12.21   Box-and-whisker diagram detailing the sample accuracies
              of the classifiers trained for the maximum touch intensity
              feature 262
Fig. 12.22   Box-and-whisker diagram detailing the sample accuracies
              of the classifiers trained for the average touch intensity
              feature 263
Fig. 12.23   Box-and-whisker diagram detailing the sample accuracies
              of the classifiers trained for the touch duration feature 264
Fig. 12.24   J48 pruned tree generated by the algorithm. This tree can be
              used to classify touches in real time as stressed ("yes" leaves)
              or not stressed ("no" leaves) 265
Fig. 12.25   Percentage of users that reveal significant differences between
              baseline and stressed data considering a first order analysis
              (Setting 1) and second order analysis (Setting 2) 266
Fig. 12.26   The evolution of the level of stress for a given user. The *red
              dashed line* represents the level of stress, the *orange dashed line*
              represents the quality of the information and the remaining
              lines represent the contribution of each parameter for the
              level of stress computed (color figure online) 267
Fig. 13.1   Percentage of users that reveal significant differences between
              baseline and stressed data considering a first order analysis
              (Setting 1) and a second order analysis (Setting 2) 273

Part I
Online Dispute Resolution and Its Context

Chapter 1
Introduction

Abstract Conflicts emerge naturally and daily from our constant social interactions. While conflicts exist also in other species, the more refined ways we Humans have to resolve them is one of the things that distinguishes us. Conflicts and approaches to their resolution have indeed evolved significantly over time, with technology providing a valuable contribution in the last decades. Artificial Intelligence, in particular, has been providing this field with new approaches to old problems, alleviating the work of legal practitioners and the participation of the parties in such procedures. This book covers these issues in some detail, touching aspects such as the definition of software architectures for conflict resolution platforms or the several ways in which sub-fields of Artificial Intelligence can improve conflict resolution. A particular emphasis is placed on the analysis of the behavior of the parties and their context to better frame the conflict and enrich the decision-making process. This first chapter provides an overview of the topic and of the book.

1.1 Introduction

In our complex society, in which interactions of different types grow at an increasing rate, conflicts are inevitable. To a large extent, this increase in the number of interactions is due to the emergence of the Internet and all related technologies, which, among other things, allow individuals to enter into contracts and electronic transactions at an amazing speed, often giving little time for weighted considerations. Moreover, due to the increasing rights of individuals, more and more actions and events are likely to constitute valid reasons to start a judicial process.

Indeed, the traditional forum for conflict resolution is the courtroom. In such spaces a judge or a jury listens to the arguments of the parties, attends to their interpretation of the law and then makes a decision stating who wins, who loses and how much is won or lost. Thus, it comes as no surprise that courtrooms are seen as highly competitive milieus, in which parties fight each other in search for the maximization of their individual gain. Moreover, courts are concerned primarily with the "blind" application of legislation or prior rulings, following strict and inflexible processes in which the role of the parties is severely limited. Other issues can obviously be pointed out that account for disadvantages of litigation in court, namely that it can be a lengthy, non-private, costly and highly wearing process.

Legitimated by these issues, alternative approaches to solve conflicts started to emerge some decades ago. These include methods such as negotiation, mediation or arbitration, conducted by independent practitioners and law experts, outside the sphere of influence of governmental entities. Due to this independence from governmental bodies, such processes can be more flexible and less formal, giving more space to creativity and out of the box solutions. Another major difference is that these alternative methods focus on inter-cooperation rather than on the notion of winner-looser. Indeed, the aim is to reach an outcome that, given the restrictions and characteristics of the case, can be deemed by both parties as fair and acceptable. Thus, parties are encouraged to communicate, to make their objectives, desires or worries clear, to put everything they have on the table, so that the best possible solution can be achieved. This more cooperative model generally results in a better preservation of interpersonal relationships, which is paramount for reaching an agreement.

More recently, as in many other fields, technological tools started to be used to support these alternative approaches. In the simpler cases, technology is used to support the neutral's work in managing documentation, scheduling sessions or keeping contact with the parties. In more innovative approaches, technology can be used to generate strategies, suggest outcomes, compile relevant information or even conduct automated negotiation processes.

Undoubtedly, one field that plays here a major role is Artificial Intelligence. Indeed, the interest on the intersection of Artificial Intelligence and legal reasoning is not new, touching application fields such as automated negotiation, reasoning, argumentation, language processing, data mining or models of legal procedures (Palmirani et al. 2012). As will be seen in this book, many research efforts took on sub-fields of Artificial Intelligence to develop innovative tools for the legal domain, including Multi-agent Systems, Ontologies or Expert Systems.

Nonetheless, we are now witnessing the emergence of a new trend in what concerns our interaction with technology. We are now moving towards a paradigm in which technology is embedded in almost every device, seamlessly surrounding us. More and more we are required to do less explicit interactions as applications and devices learn our preferences, infer our activities and proactively provide contextualized functionalities. This is a common philosophy in recently emerged domains such as Context-aware Computing or Ambient Intelligence.

Such new ideas and approaches have, however, not been used so far in the context of conflict resolution, despite the appealing possibilities. In this book we explore the idea of intelligent environments for conflict resolution, in an approach based on the most recent developments of some sub-fields of Artificial Intelligence.

The resulting environment is sensible to the state of the parties and to their context, providing valuable information to more traditional technological tools such as the ones used for communication, generation of solutions or definition of strategies. Indeed, we envision an environment in which the level of stress of the parties, the level of escalation of the conflict, the personal conflict handling style, signs of fatigue or the emotional arousal of the parties is taken as input in the decision making processes, whether it is conducted by Human experts or by machines.

Indeed, human experts frequently take these variables into account when conducting such processes in the presence of the parties (e.g. making a pause when parties become too stressed or tired, preventing them to regret bad decisions later). This, however, becomes harder when the process is conducted online, as in many of current conflict resolution processes. Indeed, the aim is to provide the mediators and other practitioners with such valuable information, which is absent in online procedures.

It is our conviction that a mediator should not be a cold outsider that simply examines facts and decides upon them. In fact, being able of reading the parties' feelings about the subjects may be a very important skill for really understanding how important each subject is for the parties, as Langer (2005) points out. In all of this, the mediator's communication skills and an efficient communication medium are paramount. In fact, and as will be seen further ahead in this book, communication is so important for conflict resolution that it is the lack of this efficient communication framework, observed in some of the current technology-supported conflict resolution approaches, that motivates the whole work.

One can, evidently, argue that such decisions in conflict resolution processes should be taken objectively and rationally. We do not argue otherwise, obviously. Under this point of view, subjective information such as the one mentioned has apparently no place in the decision making process. However, emotions and other subjective aspects have a very important weight in our decision-making mechanisms (Damásio 1994). These same mechanisms become impaired and perform poorer when they have to work without access to this information. At the time of making or accepting an offer the party is unaware of how the other parties feel about the issue: are they stressed? Are they calm? Are they in the verge of abandoning the process? Questions like these are crucial in the moment of making decisions and are very hard to answer using current mostly text-based ODR tools.

This is the main challenge that this book sets out to address. Thus, a guiding line can be drawn that spans the whole book. It starts in the more traditional tools from the spectrum of Artificial Intelligence, that allow to compile useful information for the parties involved in the conflict resolution, whether it is undertaken online or face-to-face. It ends with the most innovative aspects, in what concerns the compilation of information regarding the parties' context in a non-invasive way, through behavioral biometrics, and the providing of this information to improve decision-making processes.

In more detail, this chapter constitutes the first one of the book and provides a general overview of the book and a brief description of each of the remaining chapters.

The definition of conflict and its different forms is put forward in Chap. 2. This chapter also introduces the two main different approaches on conflict resolution: litigation in court and the so-called alternative methods. The current state of judicial systems is analyzed in a general way and the Portuguese situation is analyzed in particular, as an example of the state of affairs in most of the developed countries. This serves as the background that supports the emergence of the so-called Alternative Dispute Resolution methods. The most popular of these alternative methods are analyzed in detail, focusing on their differences when compared to litigation. The later emergence of dispute resolution methods undertaken online is also addressed in this chapter. It contextualizes the growth of the so-called Online Dispute Resolution and classifies its different forms.

However, even these online methods are not without disadvantages, as will be seen in Chap. 3. This chapter is dedicated to the detailed analysis of both Alternative and Online Dispute Resolution methodologies. This analysis considers the advantages and disadvantages of both approaches when compared to each other and to litigation in court. Particular emphasis is given to the interesting duality that resides on the use of online communication tools for conflict resolution. They significantly facilitate meetings and information exchange between the disputants. However they do it with a potentially significant cost that is proportional to the richness of the communication mean. We clearly address the drawbacks of online communication, namely in what concerns the loss of contextual modalities of communication such as our body language. These aspects are analyzed in detail before advancing to a systematic analysis of the main problems identified in litigation and its alternatives, their main causes and their potential solutions. The solutions put forward in Chap. 3 will then be addressed individually in different chapters of the book.

A step forward in the line of the book is taken in Chap. 4, which is dedicated to the relationship between Artificial Intelligence and conflict resolution. Several classical sub-fields of Artificial Intelligence are analyzed in detail, placing the emphasis on how each of these fields improves or could improve technology-supported conflict resolution. This is complemented with an analysis of current ODR commercial providers and research projects, which supports the statement that there are still opportunities to be explored. Particularly, the chapter looks at the recent field of Ambient Intelligence and how its key features could be used to develop environments for conflict resolution. A scenario is laid out that allows to grasp the potential advantages of such approach. This chapter thus starts to unveil the possibilities that recent technological advances may provide to the field of conflict resolution, in an introduction to a topic that will be thoroughly addressed during the remainder of the book.

The last issue addressed in the first part of this book is the one of context and its importance. The interest on harnessing and using accessory information that can better describe an event, action, place or situation has recently given birth to the field of Context-aware Computing. This field aims at the development of applications that can, autonomously, acquire such knowledge from their users' surroundings in order to provide services that, at that time and given the user's state, make sense. Already typical applications include the search for a nearby restaurant in a mobile phone (using as input the user's current location, preferences and budget) or specialized search engines that use as input the field in which the user is working (acquired from recently open documents) to better target search results. Indeed, the possibilities are immense and context can truly expand the functionalities of current applications. Nevertheless, in what concerns conflict resolution, such techniques are not yet being explored. Thus, this chapter ends with the identification of the types of contextual information that could result interesting to fully comprehend a conflict and the hinges of its resolution.

The second part of the book opens with the description of an agent-based architecture that can support an innovative conflict resolution platform, UMCourt, and continues by detailing its major components and functionalities. Specifically, this first chapter focuses on how an agent-based architecture that provides its functionalities across different legal domains, in a highly-modular and transparent way can be developed. To accomplish it we first identify which concepts and processes would be interesting, from the point of view of the parties, during the resolution of the conflict. Then, we determine which of these exist in different legal domains, i.e., concepts that are valid and encode the same notions independently of the domain of the dispute. Finally, we describe a hierarchic agent-based structure to implement such vision that results in a number of advantages, which are enumerated in the conclusions. UMCourt and its services were initially developed for the domain of Case Law, in which past cases establish the ruling for similar cases in the future. Nonetheless, given that the notion of past cases makes sense in Statutory Law as well (although past cases do not make a binging precedent, they do exist), the same services can be considered in this domain all the same.

Chapter 7 describes the Information Retrieval services that the architecture implements, which also constitute the backbone of a range of other higher-level services. The main objective of the approach described in this chapter is indeed to compile information for the parties so that they can more realistically frame their objectives and build a clear notion about their chances in the dispute. To accomplish it, the retrieval methods implemented provide information about potential outcomes as well as their likeliness and utility, boundary values, and adaptation techniques. This same information, by being structured in nature, can also be used by higher-level services of the platform to support the management of negotiation processes, the generation of solutions or strategies or simply to better frame a given dispute. This is detailed in the following chapters. The services related to Information Retrieval can thus be seen as central in the conflict resolution platform described in this book.

The book continues by taking a step forward in the conflict resolution process, i.e., into the actual tasks parties undergo when trying to achieve an outcome. Particularly, Chap. 8 details two different methods for generating solutions for a given conflict. Indeed, the generation of solutions is one of the most important aspects when seeking to solve a conflict, although parties often find it difficult to come up with mutually satisfactory and fair solutions. The chapter presents an approach relying on case-based reasoning and another one relying on genetic algorithms, each one with characteristics of their own. Both are meant to create solutions, either by observing past similar cases or by following a creative nature-inspired approach. These solutions are created to be used by the mediator or by the parties, at the time of designing a strategy or proposing an outcome. They are also meant to be used by the actual conflict resolution platform, to implement some intelligent behaviors. As described in the following chapters, we are particularly interested in devising platforms that can manage conflicts autonomously, taking as input the evolving state of the parties and a list of possible solutions.

The accurate analysis of the state of the parties is, indeed, one of the most important responsibilities of a mediator. If the mediator is able to do so, he will be in a better position to understand the parties' decisions, actions and worries and will, therefore, be able to more effectively help them. Failing to do so may result on misunderstandings and poor communication, ultimately resulting on the potential failure of the conflict resolution process. As stated before, the actions of the mediator in this domain are largely limited in an online environment. With this concern in background, Chap. 9 details the development of an environment that is sensible to these indicators and is able to provide knowledge to the mediator that allows him to quantify the state of the parties. All in all, with the use of the proposed environment the mediator is in a better position to understand the state of the parties and, thus, to take better decisions. Moreover, the environment also encompasses the possibility of actually influencing the environment, at several levels, in order to induce desirable states on the environment or on its users.

The book continues by detailing the processes through which such contextual information is acquired. Specifically, Chap. 10 details how the personal conflict resolution style of each participant is classified. Indeed, this feature is among the most important ones when it comes to understanding the state of the parties in a negotiation process: knowing how they tend to behave before a conflict can help the mediator to plan ahead or avoid potential negative situations. The chapter starts with a brief overview of several models for classifying the behavior of the parties before a conflict. It then details how the personal conflict handling style is inferred without the use of questionnaires, through the analysis of the messages exchanged between the parties and the values of their proposals when compared to the boundary values of the case. It also looks into the non-invasive analysis of the level of stress during a negotiation or mediation process and how stress relates to personal conflict handling styles.

The following chapter is also dedicated to the generation of knowledge to characterize the parties and their environment. However, it focuses on the acquisition of data that can be used to characterize the level of stress of the users of a technological environment equipped with devices such as computers, smartphones or video cameras. As in many other scenarios in our lives, stress significantly conditions our actions, reactions and behaviors, being a recurrent reason for performance failure, hasty decisions or threats to interpersonal relationships. Thus being, the monitoring of the level of stress in a conflict resolution process can be seen as fundamental as weighted decisions and good interpersonal relationships are paramount. Following the approach and philosophy first detailed in Chap. 9, this chapter proposes, once again, a non-intrusive approach to the problem. With the knowledge generated, the mediator can have a more precise idea about the state of the parties while solving the dispute, despite the fact that they are not in a face-to-face setting. This is truly the key aspect of this approach: the access to information that is present in a face-to-face scenario, in an online one. This chapter concludes the third part of the book, dedicated to detail of sensible environments.

Concerning the two previously mentioned chapters, an important distinction must be highlighted. While Chap. 10 focuses on the relationship between stress and conflict handling style, Chap. 11 looks at the analysis of stress in a general way. Together, the two chapters describe a way of assessing the level of stress of the parties in more generic scenarios (e.g. while they are doing routine tasks such as exchanging or analyzing information) and while they are involved in the actual negotiation process, an especial and potentially stressful moment. The two approaches, when combined, result in the continuous ability to monitor the level of stress, allowing a mediator to, for example, prepare ahead for a negotiation session that may start with an increased level of escalation.

The fourth and final part of the book is dedicated to the analysis of the results and the concluding remarks. Chapter 12 analyses a wide range of results, including the efficiency and efficacy of information retrieval methods, the classification of conflict handling styles, and the quantification of stress. It provides thorough description that will allow to understand how each study was designed and conducted and the main results attained. The book ends with Chap. 13, in which the concluding remarks are put forward. Namely, conclusions address the use of CBR in the legal context, the use of automated methods for negotiation or mediation, the relationship between personal conflict handling styles and stress, and the assessment of stress from behavioral patterns. A significant part of the chapter is dedicated to the analysis of future lines in this field, addressing a number of interesting issues that must be considered in a near future in order for the envisioned second generation of Online Dispute Resolution platforms to become true.

References

Damásio, A. 1994. *Descartes' error: Emotion, reason, and the human brain*. New York: Putnam Publishing. Hardcover: ISBN 0-399-13894-3.
Langer, A. 2005. *The importance of mediators, bridge builders, wall vaulters and frontier*. Forli: Una Città.
Palmirani, M., U. Pagallo, P. Casanovas, and G. Sartor (eds.). 2012. *AI approaches to the complexity of legal systems. Models and ethical challenges for legal systems, legal language and legal ontologies, argumentation and software agents*. International workshop AICOL-III, held as Part of the 25th IVR Congress, Frankfurt am Main, Germany, 15–16 August 2011. Revised selected papers. Lecture notes in computer science 7639, Springer 2012. ISBN 978-3-642-35730-5.

Chapter 2
Traditional and Alternative Ways to Solve Conflicts

Abstract The existence of conflicts is universal, old and indissoluble from our sense of civilized and evolved species. Since conflicts must be seen as natural and inevitable, focus should be placed on efficient ways to avoid and solve them. This chapter introduces the notion of conflict and its different shapes. It moves on to introduce the two main approaches to conflict resolution: litigation in the courtroom and alternative methods. The advantages and disadvantages of each one are presented, with the latter being detailed in its different forms. The chapter highlights the need for alternative approaches in face of the current disadvantages of litigation, namely in what concerns its inefficiency. However, its alternatives are also not without disadvantages. These are hence also analyzed in detail. Specifically, a first view on the drawbacks of current online alternatives is put forward in what concerns the lack of the contextual richness of face-to-face interaction. This lays the ground for the following chapters.

2.1 Introduction

Recently, Harvard evolutionary biologist Professor David Haig brought forward a controversial theory defending that conflicts in our life start while we are still in the womb (Haig 2010). According to the author, these parent-offspring or offspring-offspring conflicts may result in a wide range of behavioral and psychological disorders, including Tourette syndrome, autism or depression. Conflicts are present in our lives since our conception to our passing. Similarly to any other living organism, we live with and solve conflicts on a daily basis, frequently in a natural and unconscious way. However, whereas other living organisms face conflicts that are mostly related to their biologic imperatives, we Humans face far more complex ones, which can be organized into four categories (Kennedy 1998).

Intrapersonal conflicts constitute the simplest form of conflict in terms of the number of parts involved. These conflicts happen within ourselves, when we face situations in which contradictory values or convictions must be weighted and a decision or action, based on them, taken. Most of these conflicts are generated by:

- A contradiction between our preconceived notions and observed evidence or facts;
- Abstract social values that can be hard to define, understand and live by;
- Uncertainty when taking binding and important decisions; and
- A contradiction between inner values. Although these conflicts are not so *"visible"* as open conflicts or confrontation with other individuals, they happen frequently and have a constant effect in our daily living.

For a more in-depth analysis of intrapersonal conflicts please refer to (Lauterbach 1991), in which this type of conflicts is seen as one of the issues that affects life stress and emotions.

Interpersonal conflicts are the most *"classical"* type of conflict. They constitute a conflict between two or more individuals, and can be seen as a struggle between interdependent parties (Bergmann and Volkema 1994). It exists when parties acknowledge the existence of incompatible goals, scarce resources, and interference from others in achieving their objectives (Burton 1990). According to this definition it can also be concluded that a conflict only exists when the parties become aware of it. Consequently, one party may also perceive a conflict while the other does not. Interpersonal conflicts may emerge from many different scenarios, including conflicts of values, interests or relationship conflicts, and at different levels of affiliation (e.g. at work, among friends, within the family). Clearly, this will be the type of conflict in which this book focuses. For a better understanding of interpersonal conflicts and their relationship with stress, cognition, and behavioral responses, please see (Bergmann and Volkema 1994), who studied conflicts in the workplace or (Sillars and Parry 1982), who studied conflicts between roommates.

Two other types of conflict can be identified, more complex in the dynamics of their interactions. Intragroup conflicts take place between individuals that belong to a same group, i.e., those individuals often share interests, cultural aspects, objectives and other identifying characteristics. In such cases, the resolution of the conflict may be crucial for the maintenance of good group dynamics. Two of the most common types of conflict within a group are relationship conflicts (i.e. when two or more individuals have conflicting values or views) and task conflicts (i.e. when the tasks or objectives of the individuals within the organization clash). Jehn (1995) analyzes in detail this topic in the context of organizations, looking at both the advantages and disadvantages of conflict at the different levels of the organization.

Finally, intergroup conflicts emerge when two or more groups, with their own culture, objectives or beliefs, take actions that go against each other's values. Such conflicts are socially complex since they involve an arbitrary large number of individuals, behaving under the frame of social groups. Some of the most visible examples include sports teams, ethnic groups, gangs or religious groups. These conflicts may take place at a regional level or span entire countries or even wider regions. Bar-Tal (2011) examines intergroup conflicts, especially those conflicts involving very large groups in different parts of the globe, touching aspects such as the motivation behind the members of the group, the sense of solidarity and unity or the pressure exerted on leaders.

Conflicts can indeed be very heterogeneous in their form, characteristics, origin and outcome. We must therefore clearly define conflict the way it is seen in this book. Conflicts with the inner self will not be considered in this book, nor will conflicts involving large groups of people. The tools and approaches described rather focus on conflicts involving small relatively small groups of people, tendentiously two or three. In that sense, the following definition of conflict, as it is viewed in this book, can be put forward:

A conflict is a conscious, open and mutually perceived opposition of interests or positions between two or more individuals, concretized through actions or words, that represents a significant threat to at least one of the parties' needs, interests, beliefs or activities.

While conflicts involving humans are far more complex than the ones observed in any other species, our refined ways of solving them are what distinguish us from them. Gavin Kennedy goes as far as stating that conflict resolution mechanisms are one of the bases for civilization, and thus one of the key characteristics that distinguish us from any other animal (Kennedy 1998). In fact, faunae were not ever observed negotiating over food, territory or a mate. Instead, organisms use violence or the threat of violence to get what they want. We, as the creatures that we are, still have this basic way of solving conflicts that, in some situations, may try to emerge. However, a healthy and balanced individual is able to control such impulses and rely on more subtle approaches to resolve the conflict.

In fact, the art of solving conflicts is quite a classic and old one. Foremost, conflicts are natural and emerge as a consequence of our complex society, in which individuals focus on the maximization of their own gain, sometimes disregarding the others'. The concept of conflict and its resolution has traditionally been addressed by Social Sciences. However, in the last decades this field also started to be approached by Information Sciences. The intersection of these two fields is of large interest as it combines all the established theory about conflict resolution with computational power, new methodologies and support tools for problem solving.

Despite the negative connotation generally associated to conflicts, these should not be regarded as necessarily negative. In fact, they can even be positive for the group of individuals or the organization in which they take place.

Jehn (1995), after studying the structure of 105 work groups and management teams, shows that conflict can be positive in an organization, depending on the type of conflict and the structure of the group in terms of task type, task interdependence, and group norms. From a cognitive perspective, Baron (1991) adds other factors that influence how positive a conflict can be: the impact of strong negative emotions on cognition, stereotype-driven thinking, and attributional processes. Moreover, the author suggests techniques for modifying conflict situations so that they are more likely to result in positive effects. In more general terms, a positive outcome in a conflict may result in the improvement of the quality of the decisions taken as the involved parties make an effort to search for solutions that might not have been visible at first sight. In the process, parties are stimulated to take part in the process, with an effort on being creative and imaginative. When this is conducted in a positive manner, the parties move closer towards their goals and together build a more energetic climate, with increased synergy and cohesion, and a more propitious environment for new ideas, alternatives and solutions. At a personal level a conflict and its resolution allows individuals to test their positions and beliefs and, ulti- mately, makes them define themselves, who they are, what they value and what they want. Evidently, a conflict that is poorly managed and becomes negative will have opposite effects.

Whatever the case, the fact is that conflicts are universal and, sooner or later, will have to be faced. In that sense, there is a need for conflict resolution processes that can minimize, manage and hopefully settle them.

The ideal conflict resolution process is one in which the parties are better at the end of the course of action than they were at the beginning, i.e., not only in terms of what they gained or loose, but also in terms of the quality of their interpersonal relationships. This should be the focus of any conflict resolution process.

Although the term conflict/dispute resolution is from time to time used to describe Alternative Dispute Resolution (ADR) (Brown and Marriott 2012) methods, in a broad sense it marks out a process in which two or more parties engage in order to situate their differences. Conflict resolution may be divided into two main tendencies, namely Judicial Dispute Resolution and Alternative Dispute Resolution.

The most common form of Judicial Dispute Resolution is litigation, opposing a plaintiff and a defendant. The legal system has the coercive power to enforce an outcome. This means that at the end of the process, the parties are bound to the decision of the court, although in some cases parties may appeal to other instances. Outcomes are decided either by a judge, a jury or a combination of both, taking into account the facts presented by the parties and the application of The Law. All these processes are very formal and are defined by rules established by a legislature.

Alternatively, extra-judicial dispute resolution methods aim to avoid going into a court. They are being adopted by many countries as a first attempt to solve a dispute before advancing to litigation. These methods include arbitration, collaborative law or mediation, and are generally managed by non-governmental institutions, whose powers may vary from simple advice to an active role on the achievement of the outcome. The steady development of this alternative trend on conflict resolution is due to a perception of greater flexibility, lower costs and faster outcome when compared to litigation (Brown and Marriott 2012).

This chapter briefly describes what does it means to solve a conflict in court, focusing afterwards on the current state of judicial systems. Then it moves on to describe thoroughly the alternatives to the courtroom.

2.2 Litigation in Courts

Litigation is the process that states the means by which a lawsuit is conducted through court. This process is more or less well-defined and generally includes a minimum number of participants. The plaintiff is the individual who brings the charge; and the defendant is the one against whom the charge is brought. The plaintiff claims to have incurred loss as a result of a defendant's actions, and thus demands a legal or equitable remedy. In litigation the defendant is mandatorily required to respond to the complaint and must therefore present himself to court and take the necessary steps in his defense. In this process the parties have the right to attorneys that may represent them, who are called litigators.

A litigation process takes place in a sequence of steps that are more or less general in common law judicial systems. It starts with the plaintiff presenting his claim and asking for damages or equitable relief from the defendant. In this phase, generally called pleading, it is important that the plaintiff:

- Selects the proper venue with the proper jurisdiction;
- Access basic legal and factual bases; and
- Correctly identifies the defendant. It is then the responsibility of the court to contact the defendant, informing him about the nature of the lawsuit, the identification of the plaintiff, the time limits and his rights to counterclaims.

Then, litigants are encouraged to clearly state what the lawsuit is about. This may include actions such as disclosure of evidence or exchange of information and facts in a structured manner. The main objective is to clarify the nature of the claim and its characteristics and avoid unexpected events later on the process.

Following this phase of exploration, the process advances to judgment. At this point, litigants may bring forth witnesses and evidence. At the end a judge or jury will render a decision, based on his interpretation of the evidence and the legal norms.

Later, once the process is finished, either litigant may have the right to appeal, which can be used when they feel that there has been some procedural error. These appeals follow similar processes as the ones being described. At the end, the court has the power to enforce the outcome, namely by making the defendant pay a monetary award if the judgment is for the plaintiff. If the defendant fails to pay, the court has the power to seize defendant's assets.

For a number of reasons, analyzed in detail in the following chapter, litigation in court is nowadays synonym to a number of significant disadvantages, which in part result in the increase use of alternative methods. These disadvantages essentially revolve around the inefficiency of courtrooms, at different instances or courts, and results in conflict resolution processes that take longer and cost more than they should, ultimately pushing disputants away.

2.3   Current State of Judicial Systems

Among other reasons, the increasing rights of defendants and the general improvement of the access to government services resulted in a significant increase in the number of claims filed in court. This results in a relative long time to solve each case, which in fact has also repercussions on its costs. This has been a reality for decades and many studies have been conducted to analyze the current efficiency of the judicial systems and how it could be improved. The general conclusion of these studies is that courts around the world are in a state of crisis, dealing with backlogs and inefficiencies caused mostly by an explosion in litigation (Fix-Fierro 2004), in some cases as severe as to rouse lawmakers, politicians, scholars, business leaders, and citizens to petition for substantial reformation of the judicial system (Farhang 2010).

Defining efficiency, particularly in the scope of conflict resolution institutions, is thus the first step. It can be outlined from different interpretations or assessments. However, all of them revolve around some key symptoms perceived by the society in general, including unnecessary delays within the process, unnecessary steps (e.g. procedures mandated by The Law, policy or tradition that are deemed counter-productive or constitute duplication), unproductive activities (e.g., unproductive court hearings, people turning up for a court case that does not take place), failed or aborted prosecutions or the exorbitant costs associated with certain types of trials or procedures (Dandurand 2009). Efficiency can also be described clearly from an economic standpoint, including the costs of providing justice, measured in terms of both the private expenditures (borne by the parties to the dispute) as well as any external price associated with providing a particular level of justice (borne by members of the society who are not parties to the dispute).

With respect to this matter, Héctor Fix-Fierro points out a few noteworthy ideas. Indeed, one must be aware that the concept of efficiency is not central or does not come first in conflict resolution, i.e., other more important values exist in legal decision-making, as it is subject to all kinds of constraints, local conditions and concrete negotiations with other values and interests (Fix-Fierro 2004). For instance, before being quick a courtroom must be fair, i.e., decision-making focuses on the nature of the decision, rather than the time spent making it. Nevertheless, the author agrees that the efficiency of courts should be improved as these general perceptions of overload, inefficiency, delay and the like, although relative and subjective, have repercussions on the societies' view about the judicial system, resulting in a sense of crisis in the administration of justice.

Inefficiency in judicial systems may stem from different causes. Djankov et al. (2003) point out three different principles, each one supported by different authors. The former one supports that efficiency in the courtroom as in other institutions, is directly affected by the level of richness and education of the population (Demsetz 1967). This belief states the fixed costs of setting up institutions only become socially worth paying when the demand for them – largely driven by the level of economic development – becomes high enough, i.e., while a poor society may rely on informal dispute resolution, a richer one trusts on more complex contracts and needs more complex judicial systems to resolve disputes. A poor population will not use complex or advanced mechanisms, thus there will be no demand to make them viable. Similarly, a better-educated population both raises the efficiency of courts (more educated workers are able to work in more efficient ways and with more efficient tools), and the demand for them. According to this principle, judicial systems in richer and more educated countries tend to be more efficient.

The second principle considers the incentives of the stakeholders throughout the conflict resolution process to be one key factor for efficiency. Its main view on the problem is that judges, lawyers and litigants that have weak incentives (such as a low salary or lack of incentive plans for meeting performance objectives) or wrong ones (such as accepting bribes) will not care about delays since they gain nothing by working faster or better (Buscaglia and Dakolias 1999).

Djankov et al. (2003) propose a latest principal or belief stating that the performance of courts is determined by how the law regulates their operation (which the authors call procedural formalism). The authors begin by pointing out that legal systems heavily regulate dispute resolution, relying on lawyers and professional judges, regimenting the steps that the disputants must follow, regulating the collection and presentation of the evidence, insisting on legal justification of claims and judges' decisions or giving predominance to written submissions. In line with this view, one must enquire to what extent such formalisms matter with respect to the value of simple disputes resolution, i.e., should all cases, independently of their complexity, follow the same stages? To support this view the authors analyze the procedures used to solve two specific disputes in 109 countries and their estimated duration to achieve a conclusion. Indeed, abstract procedures are related to longer duration of dispute resolution, i.e., such formalisms lead to a poorer enforceability of contracts, higher corruption, as well as less honesty, consistency, and fairness of the system. Moreover, the authors found no evidence that procedural formalisms secures justice.

Following a similar view, Posner points out the effect of oral arguments on the delay of the process (Posner 1996). Oral arguments generally have a fixed duration. Judges must be present and eventually travel some distance to get to the proper location, which adds to the time expended. While oral arguments can play an important role in the decision process of judges, they are costly, and there are cases in which they are unnecessary (e.g. in cases that are frivolous, hinge on issues that have already been decided, or are adequately presented in a written record, such that oral arguments would not provide additional information). Thus, legal systems must have the flexibility to decide on the aspects of the procedural formalism that are indeed necessary and significant.

One of the biggest concerns is related with the often-poor collaboration and coordination between the several agencies involved, including police, prosecutors, judiciary or defense (Dandurand 2009). Each of these agencies may have different priorities, technological platforms, objectives (which may not be compatible), procedures or culture, which adds to the effort of coordination. As an example, the police's primary function is not to support courtroom processes but to be "on the streets" promoting law and order. In fact, police forces even search for ways to prevent crime, thus decreasing the use of judicial systems. Moreover, each of these entities may have a different perception of what efficiency is.

There are also cases in which cooperation is hampered by poor data sharing mechanisms, which in some countries still rely heavily on inefficient paper transactions. This results in more costly processes and duplication of effort, as files are photocopied and couriered back and forth.

Christensena and Szmer (2012) refer to a relatively wide group of additional causes for courtroom inefficiency. The root cause, as expected, is the increasing workloads of courtrooms, often due to the reluctance to appoint more judges (Lindquist et al. 2007), which leads to bureaucratization. Bureaucratization, in turn, has an effect on factors like the use of support staff and judge collegiality, which are thought to influence process, outcomes (Lindquist et al. 2007) and costs. The diversity (e.g. ideological, tenure or law school quality) of a jury panel can lead to conflict (i.e. reduced collegiality) (Pelled et al. 1999) or to longer disposition times (Cauthen and Latzer 2008), which result in less efficient decision-making processes. The increasing number of cases, associated with the reluctance to appoint more judges, has an effect on the workload of judges. This increased request for throughput, often stressful, may lead to a burnout, which significantly decreases the performance indicators and the quality of the work (Bakker et al. 2004). Another factor that can be related to efficiency is the experience of the legal practitioners. Cohen (2002) goes as far as implying that efficiency is a function of the judge's expertise, since judges must learn a relatively comprehensive set of applicable rules and The Law and its application to the cases factual data. Thus, experienced judges may be in a better position to take better judgments and in time.

Concretely, we have analyzed the Portuguese reality in what concerns the efficiency of its judicial system, taking it as an example of what takes place in so many countries. Portugal is no exception to the above symptoms and litigation is generally seen by society as an inefficient process, in which key issues stand for the high costs and long wait for the way out of processes. Courts are currently clogged due to the amount of cases, most of which involving claims of relatively low value. Thus, the Portuguese legal system can be seen as an example of the current state of affairs.

Several performance indicators of the Portuguese judicial system are analyzed, once compiled from the Portuguese legal statistics consultation system, available online – SIEJ.[1] If we consider the average duration of the processes in first instances courts between 2001 and 2010, it is possible to conclude that there was a substantial rise, being the larger one in Civil Justice, from 20 months in 2001 to 29 months in 2010. This trend was continuous until 2007 (33 months), and then gradually

---

[1] The web-site of the SIEJ is available online at http://www.siej.dgpj.mj.pt (Accessed on September 2013).

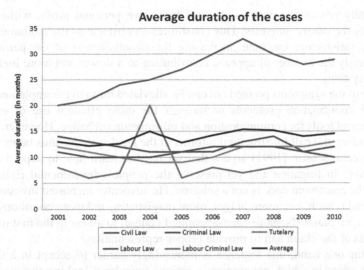

Fig. 2.1 Average duration of the litigation processes in Portuguese first instances courts between 2001 and 2010

reversed. In average, considering the different areas under analysis, each process takes 10–15 months until its end. Figure 2.1 depicts the data considered.

This relatively high duration time of the processes has as its main consequence an upsurge in the number of pending ones. In fact, the congestion rate for the Portuguese judicial courts in 2009 was of 253.3 %, i.e., for each process that was concluded, 235.3 were pending.[2] According to the same source, there are currently more than 1.7 million pending processes. This represents an increase of 2.2 % compared with the numbers of 2011, in which there were 1.666.348 pending processes. The trend is not recent: in 2007 and 2008 the number of pending processes grew from 1.541.239 to 1.504.553. Contradictorily enough, Portugal was in 2008 the third country in the European Union[3] with the best judge/attorney-to-population ratio, only beaten by Poland and Germany (de L'Europe 2010). According to the same study, the current pending cases would take 430 days to conclude, assuming that there are no new processes in the meantime.

One could argue that processes are nowadays more complex and include much more information or that defendants have more rights and attorneys have a larger scope of intervention. However, the truth is that nowadays the most trivial act of our life is likely to end in a court, independently of the issue. Moreover, courtrooms are not the most efficient environments for conflict resolution by themselves, i.e., they are generally highly competitive milieus, in which parties and their representatives

---

[2] Source: Portuguese Directorate-General for Justice Policy – Ministry of Justice, PORDATA.

[3] The following countries were considered in this study: Germany, Austria, Belgium, Denmark, Scotland, Spain, Finland, France, England and Wales, Italy, Norway, The Netherlands, Poland, Portugal, Sweden and Switzerland.

will blindly pursue the maximization of their own personal profit, without any regard for the others' interests. This constitutes an obstacle to the attainment of a mutually satisfactory outcome, increasing the dissatisfaction of the parties and consequently the number of appeals, contributing to a slower and more inefficient judicial system.

Some of the symptoms pointed out can be alleviated through the implementation of better coordination protocols or through the more efficient use of existing technological tools for communication and information exchange. However, others are far graver and call for structural reforms in the legal systems, thus being harder to implement. Mastro (1991) argues that we need to learn how to cope with this *"explosion"* in litigation and yet preserve the people's fundamental rights, i.e., closing the courtroom door is not a solution. He advocates increased investment in the judicial branch, i.e., more judges, more magistrates, and more courthouses; for indigent civil plaintiffs, more court-appointed counsel to assess in the first instance the merits of the claim and to provide proper representation.

One the one hand, this sentence is increasingly harder to accept in a time of financial crises in which government's actions have been looking the other way around, i.e., towards a decrease in the expenses in the services being provided. However, on the other hand, the same sentence points out an alternative that, given the current economic scenario, is potentially more sustainable and viable, i.e., *"more court-appointed counsel to assess in the first instance the merits of the claim"*, which undoubtedly may include the appointment of alternative methods prior to litigation. Such potential alternatives are described next.

2.4 Alternative Dispute Resolution

Abraham Lincoln once stated the following: "Discourage litigation, persuade your neighbor to compromise where you can. Point out to them how the nominal winner is often the loser... in expenses and waste of time". This sentence sums up, in a few words, key factors that may lead one individual into engaging in an alternative conflict resolution process, i.e., in a courtroom, the outcome may not be all favorable, despite winning the case. Additional aspects must be considered in litigation that can have a significant impact, including the time spent and all the costs of the process. ADR methods for problem solving address exactly these issues (Brown and Marriott 2012).

Historically, the use of ADR methods has faced some resistance, which it still faces nowadays in some arenas. As Redfern (2011) points out, many parties and lawyers do not fully appreciate the working of these alternative methods, i.e., many of them have spent their whole professional lives within the realm of litigation and are now uncomfortable or opposed to the commerciality, informal nature and apparent lack of strict rules of ADR. There are also lawyers who are not comfortable with the empowering of their clients, i.e., they do not acknowledge that the point of view or the eventual strategy of the client may have interesting insights and find it more comfortable to pursue the far more familiar and controlled path of the litigation process. Ultimately, a more competitive lawyer may also have as objective to retain the case for as long as possible rather than settling it in an early stage using an alternative method.

Notwithstanding, ADR methods have being used and adopted by both legal systems and parties as the first step to attempt to solve a dispute. There are even countries in which parties are encouraged or required to try some kind of mediation before advancing into court. Taking as an example the United States of America (USA), numerous laws firms and companies have committed by themselves to use ADR prior to litigation. Mediation is also mandatory in a number of USA states, including California, Florida, Oregon, and Texas (Barbieri, Gina Lea 2011).

At a European level, the European Parliament and its Council recently approved measures towards the encouragement of the use of extra-judicial procedures (Directive 2008/52/EC of the European Parliament and of the Council on Certain Aspects of Mediation in Civil and Commercial Matters). This directive specifically states *"A court before which an action is brought may, when appropriate and having regard to all the circumstances of the case, invite the parties to use mediation in order to settle the dispute. The court may also invite the parties to attend an information session on the use of mediation if such sessions are held and are easily available."* (art. 5, (1)). Moreover, article 9 states that *"Member States shall encourage, by any means which they consider appropriate, the availability to the general public, in particular on the Internet, of information on how to contact mediators and organizations providing mediation services"*. This directive places the responsibility to inform about extra-judicial approaches on the member states and their courts.

Prior to this European directive, the United Kingdom had already amended its civil procedure rules, introducing the use of alternative dispute resolution procedures where appropriate, and empowering the courts to order the stay of proceedings pending the use of ADR (Barbieri, Gina Lea 2011).

All these actions by part of the governments evidence the potential benefits of the use ADR methods, even from the standpoint of the judicial systems. These actions may even become mandatory considering the current phase of generalized crisis in the courtrooms due to the impracticable and increasing amount of pending cases. Following such methods, governments expect to decrease the number of cases that actually need to be solved by means of a traditional court.

Concerning the disputant parties, the main reason in the acceptance and use of ADR relies on the expectation of smaller times and costs for the conclusion of the processes. Parties also tend to choose ADR mechanisms as they are usually associated to less exposure than traditional ones. The last but not the least is that the mediator may be chosen by the parties and agreed upon, instead of being appointed by a courtroom, which increases the parties' confidence and satisfaction.

One may be faced with many different types of ADR procedures, classified according to their objectives, terms or duration. Some of the less frequent or known approaches include the so-called minor trials and fact-finding procedures. In a minor trial there is a session that usually lasts for a day or less, in which the lawyers of each side present their cases to representatives of the parties who have authority to settle the dispute. In general, the parties hire a mediator to preside over the minor trial. The parties meet to try to negotiate a settlement. In a fact-finding procedure, the facts relevant to a controversy are determined. Other procedures exist, some of them far more used and common, particularly in civil law cases. These include negotiation, mediation, arbitration or conciliation, which will be analyzed in detail in the following sub-sections.

2.4.1 Negotiation

Negotiation (Raiffa 2002) is a collaborative and informal process by means of which the parties communicate and, without any external influence, try to achieve an outcome that can satisfy both. Negotiation is widely used in the most different arenas, such as legal proceedings, divorces, parental disputes or hostage situations. It is a non-binding process, which means that the parties are not legally obliged to comply with the outcome. There are many ways of organizing the several negotiation techniques. From the perspective of Walton and McKersie (1991), negotiation can be classified as distributive or integrative.

In the distributive approach, one looks at the items in dispute as something that can be divided and distributed by the parties in an attempt to maximize their satisfaction. A good example can be a divorce process in which the parties sit down to divide the assets. There are a fixed number of items, each one with a given value, and they will be divided applying understandings such as fairness and equality. Another well-known process of distributive negotiation is the one that goes on between unions and executives, where the resources are scarce and include wages, work hours and other working conditions. In this process, unions defend the interests of the workers, thus trying to maximize the income and optimize working conditions. On the other hand, managers try to maximize the profit of the company. The conjoint point is that the company needs the workers and the workers need the job, so it is around that matter that the negotiation will develop.

This type of negotiation is also characterized by the fact that what one part wins, the other loses, i.e., if the workers earn a higher wage, the company will lack the same value, thus decreasing the profit. In game theory, these scenarios are known as zero-sum games, depicting a situation in which a participant's gain (or loss) of utility is exactly balanced by the losses (or gains) of the utility of the other partaker. If the total gains of the contestants are added up, and the total losses are subtracted, they will sum to zero (Raghavan 1994). Two central perceptions here are the ones of utility and resistance (Zeleznikow and Bellucci 2004). Utility denotes the value that a given item being negotiated has to a party, while resistance denotes the willingness of a party to change its notion of utility. A good negotiator usually tries to convince the opponent that certain items do not really have the value that they are being given by the opponent. The negotiator will succeed if the opponent adopts a low profile concerning a given item, and if he does, it will be easier for the negotiator to win or he will at least be in a better position for the rest of the negotiation process (Jennings et al. 2001). Accordingly, utility functions can be formalized that help to understand how each party values the items being distributed therefore predicting possible outcomes and the evolution of the negotiation process (Zeleznikow and Bellucci 2004).

In integrative negotiation, the problem is expected to have more solutions than the ones visible at a first sight. In this type of problems, the parties try to bring to the conciliation table as much interests as possible, so that there are even more valuable items to negotiate. When the parties are increasing the value of what they put on the table, they take into account their interests, which include their needs, fears, concerns, and desires. This type of negotiation is also known as interest-based as the parties try to combine their interests, and find topics in which they may meet. By doing so, more satisfactory outcomes are achieved. This makes integrative negotiation more desirable than the distributive one.

In order to illustrate the difference between these two types of negotiation let us consider the following situation: *"Two old ladies have a dispute because of an orange. They both want the last orange that is in the fruiter. If they resolve the dispute using the distributive approach they will split the orange in two equal parts and each one will get half of the orange. If, on the other hand, they use the integrative approach, each one will state what they want, listen to what the other part wants and try to reach an outcome that would satisfy both"*. In this example, one of the ladies wanted to eat the orange while the other just wanted the peel for making a tea. By following and integrative approach, each one gets what they wanted and the outcome is optimum. A dominant perception here is the one of Pareto efficiency (Fudenberg and Tirole 1983). In these problems, this discernment denotes a state of allocation of resources in which it is impossible to make any individual better off, without making at least one individual worse off. In the given example, the solution obtained with the integrative approach would have been a Pareto efficient one, as no better solution could have been achieved.

An important aspect, as may be seen from the example, relies on the identification and the justification of the interests of each party, so that each one can understand them. If there is good will and each one understands the position of the others, in terms of their interests, desires and fears, it will be easier to reach a better outcome. This process eventually leads to what is known in game theory as a win-win game, i.e., all the parties are better at the end of the negotiation process than when it started.

Although these two approaches when analyzed in this way may be seen as conflicting, they may be used conjointly as introduced by Lax and Sebenius (1986). In fact, even in an integrative approach the items have eventually to be split up. The joint use of these two approaches has the advantage of creating a relationship of trust between the parties when they are increasing the values of their items, so that when they get to the phase of splitting them, everyone knows the interests and fears of the opponents, which makes it easier to divide the items in a fair fashion and reach a common agreement.

In general, a negotiated procedure can be organized in four steps although, given the informal and flexible nature of negotiation, these may vary:

- Identification of interests – definition of the key issues in dispute, and separation of what is an interest and what is a position;
- Alternative scenarios – definition of alternative scenarios not considered by the parties that may yet meet their underlying interests;
- Refining – after the establishment of one or more baseline acceptable scenarios, the process moves forward to the combination or refining of scenarios in order to meet their interests as much as possible; and
- Outcome – final step in the negotiation process in which a final scenario is selected via consensus.

2.4.2 Mediation

Mediation (Brown and Marriott 2012) refers to a form of alternative dispute resolution in which the parties in dispute are guided by an independent mediator, also known as the third party, which tries to guide the process to an outcome that may satisfy both parties. In this approach, like in negotiation, the parties decide about the outcome instead of it being imposed by someone else, but with the added assistance of the mediator. This third party is chosen by both the parties and has no authority for deciding on the outcome of the dispute, but only to guide and assist them throughout it. This should be done by maintaining the parties focused on the subject of the dispute, and by facilitating all the interaction and communication between them. Mediators are hence key persons as their skills and aptitudes may represent the success or failure of the dispute resolution process.

In fact, the mediator is often in a difficult position, i.e., he lacks the power to impose a solution but must, nevertheless, lead disputants into an agreement. To achieve this, besides substantive expertise and a keen and analytical eye, certain communicational skills are fundamental in order to establish the necessary and fundamental rapport. The mediator must be able to win the parties' trust: only in this way may the parties be guided into accepting a solution that is probably not the best one possible nor the one hoped for. Moreover, a mediator should be able to listen, have problem-solving skills and be creative in it, separate personal feelings from the issues under consideration, maintaining an image of neutrality and be assertive while maintaining a strong physical presence, marked by honesty, dignified behavior and respect for the parties.

He should provide strategic advices in the correct time with the objective of easing the process without forgetting to maintain its neutrality. For this purpose it is imperative that the mediator will work under different angles and assessments, recognizes the expectations and frustrations of the parties, and react to them. It is also important that he shows the ability to calm down the parties when needed and, at the same time, support and encourage them to reach a satisfactory outcome. Thus a mediator must have, above all, good communication skills so that his ideas are correctly transmitted to the parties. A mediator should not be a cold outsider that simply examines facts and decides upon them. In fact, being able of reading the parties feelings about the subjects under dispute, it is also very important for him to understand how significant each subject is for the parties (Langer 2005).

In all of this, the mediator's communication skills and an efficient communication medium are paramount. In fact, and as will be seen further ahead, communication is so important for conflict resolution that it is the lack of this efficient framework, observed in some of the current technology-supported conflict resolution approaches, that inspires the whole book.

From a mediator's perspective, the process is organized into a more or less stable sequence of steps, namely:

- Opening – the discussion is officially opened and the process is outlined. The mediator establishes contact with both parties and brings them into his laps. He introduces the parties to the event and pictures how the process will take place;
- Scope definition – the parties must agree on the scope of the process, as well as on each one's objectives and roles;
- Definition of an agenda – mediation usually consists of a series of meetings. Parties must agree and commit to their frequency, schedule and location;
- Rules – despite the informality, mediation follows some basic rules and principles. In this phase, the ground rules are established (e.g. one person speaks at a time, the mediator may interrupt a party);
- Breaking down the problem – in this phase all the parties present their viewpoints, perceptions of the issues, and reasons for the dispute. Here, the mediator must be able to identify the key issues in dispute, the claim and the expectations of each party. Then he must separate what is an interest from what is a position, pointing out when positions are unrealistic, unfair or simply an obstacle to the process. The mediator must also be proactive in helping people to express their concerns, ensuring that they go through all the issues;
- Identify common interests – after careful hearing of the parties, the mediator should identify any points of agreement;
- Potential outcomes – the mediator is responsible for devising potential outcomes and their alternatives or variations, in a constant attempt to bridge the gap among the parties; and
- Outcome – agreement and documentation of a solution concerning the dispute or other decisions agreed upon by the parties.

The clients often prefer approaches based on mediation to others (Sussman 2009). One of the most chief concerns is the fact that mediation, when conducted in a positive way, often reaches better results for the disputants. This happens because parties have an active role in the definition of the outcome, whereas in other approaches they may not have it. Unlike negotiation, when two parties seek mediation as a way to solve their dispute, they are often more willing to reach a solution. The simple fact of agreeing in a common mediator and granting him the authority for conducting the process is a sign of good will and determination in achieving a solution for the problem. Disputants following this approach are usually more willing to work together than against each other. Moreover, the slightly more structured nature of mediation and the existence of the character of the mediator are often seen as positive by the parties, as they feel an increased sense of security and confidence on the whole process.

Likewise to negotiation, mediation is generally a non-binding process in the sense that the parties have no legal obligations between them at the end of the process. However, more recently, binding forms of mediation have been emerging. Their finality is similar to that of binding arbitration, with the added advantage of allowing the parties to work together, with the assistance of a mediator, to come to an acceptable agreement. At the end, the parties sign a legally binding contract establishing the terms agreed upon during the mediation and each one's obligations. This form of dispute resolution can be placed somewhat between traditional mediation and arbitration.

Mediation is a tool often used in a wide range of cases ranging from a mother trying to calm down two brothers that are fighting over a toy car to conflicts between countries (Zartman 2007). One of the most widely known examples is the one of the U.S. mediating the Israeli-Palestinian conflict in the Middle East, with the objective of achieving a long lasting armistice (Feste 1991).

2.4.3   Arbitration

As in mediation, in arbitration (Bennett 2002) the two parties also use a third independent and neutral entity for solving a dispute. However, this entity has generally no active role on assisting the parties throughout the process. In this approach, the mediator or arbitrator simply hears the parties and, based on the facts presented, takes a decision without influencing the parties during their presentations, i.e., it can be stated that the arbitrator acts as both judge and jury. The outcome of an arbitration process is also singular as it may be binding or non-binding.

In the binding forms of arbitration the conciliators' decision is final and cannot be disputed or appealed. At the end, an enforceable arbitration award is issued, with legal validity, expressing the decision of the settlement. Parties are thus bound to this decision whether they find it fair and acceptable or not. Such a contract does not exist in non-binding forms of mediation. In these forms, the arbitrator makes a determination of the rights of the parties to the dispute, but this willpower is not binding upon them. Thus, the award is actually an advisory and expert opinion of the arbitrator's view of the respective merits of the parties' cases, and is by no means enforceable, i.e., the role of the arbitrator becomes closer to the one of the mediator in mediation. The main difference is that, while a mediator assists the parties during the process in an attempt to reach a middle-ground compromise, the arbitrator will remain out from the settlement process, *"merely"* giving a determination of liability and, if appropriate, an indication of the damages to be matured.

As the decision of the third party may be definitive and binding, its role in the process is even more important than in mediation. In fact, the arbitrator's relevance can be compared to the one of a judge or a jury in a litigation process in court.

Disputants find a number of advantages in the use of arbitration. Like with other alternative approaches to conflict resolution, the time spent and the cost of these processes can be significantly smaller than in courts. Efficient conflict resolution processes are valued particularly by companies that see their efforts hindered by slow and costly litigation procedures (Buhring-Uhle and Kirchhof 2006). Another factor that definitively contributes to minimize the time being spent has to do with the growing number of arbitration service providers. Its confidentiality when compared to litigation is also seen as a positive factor.

Powered by these advantages, the use of arbitration has been growing steadily. One particular area of success is in the field of international commercial disputes (Varady et al. 2006), in which parties seek a solution for disputes arising from international commercial agreements and other international relationships (Buhring-Uhle and Kirchhof 2006). Here, in particular, parties desire to avoid the uncertainties and potential costs of the local practices associated with litigation in national courts, while relying on the commercial expertise of arbitrators. Another advantage of arbitration in this domain concerns the language of the proceedings. In arbitral proceedings the language of arbitration may be chosen, whereas in judicial proceedings the official language of the country of the competent court will be automatically used, which may result disadvantageous for some of the parties. Companies involved in international disputes also find it advantageous that there are limited avenues for appeal of an arbitral award. This can be advantageous in the sense that it limits the duration of the dispute and any associated liability.

However, at the same time, this can also be seen as a disadvantage in the sense that the parties waive their rights to access the courts and to have a judge or jury decide the case, even if they do not find the award fair, making it hard to overturn an eventual erroneous decision. Other disadvantages can still be pointed out. One of the most significant is that sometimes an individual, when entering into a contract, does not know that the only way of solving an eventual dispute is through a binding arbitration process, without the possibility to go into court (Moses 2008). This may represent a serious threat to the parties' rights. This is even worse in scenarios in which parties have to pay for the arbitration service they are *"forced"* to use. Contrary to courts, the right to an attorney is not always granted. Thus, sometimes, parties that cannot afford one end up without any legal representative.

The arbitration process may, from an abstract perspective, be organized in the following number of steps:

- Initialization – at the beginning of the process, the parties must provide their personal data as well as a preliminary statement of their claims, including their value. They may also have to, if applicable, pay some initial fee;
- Definition of rules – previously to begin the process, parties must agree on its terms, particularly on the arbitrator or arbitral tribunal. If no agreement can be

reached at this state, and arbitrator or arbitrator tribunal may be appointed by the
arbitration institution or service;

- Proceedings – the actual proceedings take place before the arbitrator or arbitrator
  tribunal. At this stage each party has the opportunity to present its case; and
- Award – the arbitrator or the arbitrator tribunal issues an award, usually in the
  form of a document that should be signed by the parties. On the other hand, at the
  end of the process the parties may have to pay some kind of fee.

2.4.4 Conciliation

A process of conciliation is an approach on conflict resolution by means of which a
conciliator meets the parties separately, and aims at the resolution of their differences. The conciliator should be an expert with skills that allow him to lower
tensions between the parties as a first step for finding common ground. Then, he
should communicate effectively with the parties in order to understand all the issues
that generated the dispute. Subsequently, the conciliator should be able to provide
technical assistance to the parties as needed, so that they should have access to
reliable evidences in order to take the right decisions. Finally, the conciliator should
explore all the potential paths for solutions and, at the end, achieve a mutually
acceptable settlement.

When compared to the previously depicted methods, conciliation has some
dissimilarities. It is different from arbitration in that conciliation is a non-binding
process, and the conciliator has usually no legal authority, i.e., the conciliator
cannot seek evidence or call witnesses, nor endorse an enforceable award. When
compared to mediation, conciliation is also different. In fact, while in mediation the
mediator tries to find ways to maximize the mutual gain by bringing as much
interests to the table as possible, in conciliation the mediator will try to seek for
concessions. Another major difference is that during conciliation parties seldom
meet in person, i.e., conciliation is generally more suited for parties that have an
already ruined personal relationship, and whose joint presence would constitute an
obstacle to the resolution of the conflict.

2.5 Online Dispute Resolution

In the move to a global society based on computers, new needs emerged in the field
of ADR. As disputes can now take place between virtually any two entities
regardless of their location, it would be impracticable for them, despite all the
good will, to use an ADR mechanism. In fact, despite the inexistence of a designated court in ADR, and despite the fact that the parties can choose the location for
the dispute resolution to take place, there is still the need for a physical location, so
that the parties can meet and carry on the proceedings.

With the integration of new communication technologies into our daily lives, ADR procedures began to change, giving birth to what is nowadays known as Online Dispute Resolution (ODR) (Lodder and Thiessen 2003; Katsh and Rifkin 2001). This new model for dispute resolution aims at being an online alternative to litigation. It can however expand the possibilities of already traditional ADR approaches, with the introduction of virtual entities with enhanced abilities and increased communication possibilities (Larson 2006). ODR became possible thanks to technologies such as Instant Messaging, Electronic Mail, videoconference, forums, mailing lists and, more recently, video presence. Using these technologies parties can communicate remotely, in a synchronous or asynchronously way, instead of communicating in the physical presence of each other.

However, every major technological shift raises questions and new issues that should always be analyzed with care. Technologies can, on the one hand, be used as a simple tool for ADR. In this approach ODR results much similar to ADR, except for the fact that the parties are not in the physical presence of one another, but are communicating through a telematics medium. The most common image is the one of two parties in different parts of the globe, an eventual third party with a mediator or arbitrator role in another location, all of them communicating via IM or video conference. Technologies, in this simpler approach, have no active role; they act only as a facilitator for the process.

In a different course of action, technologies can be seen as a fourth party that assists the mediator (Katsh 2002). Although not having here an active role, these tools can assist the mediator or arbitrator in taking the right decisions or planning the right strategy. In this field the most important technology is that of Expert Systems. They can provide the third party with knowledge about past cases and their outcomes, about the legal norms that apply or even about other issues. Technologies may entail the use of decision support systems that guide the parties through the course of action, or simple tools for storing and managing the information about the case.

On the other hand, technologies can be used as party representatives. In this approach parties do not have the main or the most active role on the process. Instead, they make use of software agents that represent them and act on their behalf. In this arena, the most common systems are automated systems and intelligent agents. These systems know the objectives of the part they are representing and have the ability to define a strategy that they will follow to achieve these objectives. They may be designed and configured to act like the party they represent or to act in an even better and efficient way. For a more in-depth discussion, Andrade et al. (2007) examine, in a general sense, the implications of software agents with legal personality and representation while Fasli looks at the specific field of e-Commerce and how software agents can be used to act on behalf of the user to sign commercial contracts.

We may even think of computer systems that are indeed the third party. In this more radical approach, there is no human deciding on the outcome or guiding the parties in their way to achieve it. There is, instead, a system that performs this major role. Li et al. (2013) describe an approach on automated negotiation as a way to take optimal decisions in distributed systems, that can be seen as a recent example. This usually involves an electronic mediator or arbitrator, acting as the coordinator of the process. It should have skills for communicating with the parties and understanding their desires and fears, and have the ability to decide the best strategy to follow in each scenario. This is evidently the hardest approach to follow, since it is not easy to provide a computer system with the decision and planning abilities of a human expert as well as the ability to perceive the emotions and desires of the parties involved. It must also be acknowledged that humans are in general reluctant in relying in machines to take the binding decisions that power their lives as Davenport and Harris discuss (2005).

ODR is a relatively new approach to dispute resolution since the technologies it builds in are also recent. It has, however, known a fast growth in its use given its advantages (Krause 2007), which are further discussed in the following chapter.

2.5.1 Inside a Typical ODR Process

An ODR process may, in general, be organized according to a sequence of phases (Lodder and Zeleznikow 2005; Chiti and Peruginelli 2002). A first one where a party contacts an ODR provider with the intention of starting an online dispute resolution process. This party must, in this phase, provide information about the other parties. The system must then inform all the intervenient, put them into contact and determine if they are willing to participate on the dispute resolution process. If all the parties agree, the system moves into the next phase in which it tries to gather as much information about the problem as possible.

In this phase, the parties are asked about all the details of the dispute, including eventual monetary values involved, as well as documents or items that can act as evidence or facts that are essential to the case. It is therefore very important that the system understands the expectations of the parties and how they feel about each subject under discussion. This is probably the most challenging phase for a completely autonomous ODR system, i.e., without human intervention.

Then, the system may enter into the last phase, in which the data collected in the previous one is analyzed. This is the key phase in the ODR process. To conduct this analysis, the expert acting as the neutral may consider past known similar cases, legal norms and other information. In the last phase a decision or strategy is generated and the parties are informed. In this phase, the effectiveness of the algorithms and strategies used is reflected in terms of the success or failure of the process. This may later be used for improving the strategies and algorithms for future iterations.

2.5.2 Classifying ODR Systems

ODR systems can be categorized according to the way they assist the parties in a dispute resolution process (Thiessen and Zeleznikow 2004):

- *Information systems* – this type of ODR system simply provides information that can be useful for the parties when working out a solution for the dispute. This information may comprise the norms of a given country concerning the domain of the dispute, information about the parties, about the status of the process, among others. Examples of these systems are **Scenario Builder** that can automatically generate web pages with information relevant for assisting parties in an ODR process, and **Notgoodenough.org** that provides its customers with an online space for the share of experiences and information, along with information on its web page, radio spots, TV and print media;
- *Blind Bidding* – the systems included in this category aim at the automation of simple purely monetary questions. This may include cases like divorces without children, failed buy or sell operations. Parties make confidential bids and the system is responsible for deciding when a possible agreement point has been reached. An example of such systems is **CyberSettle**, which is a fast and simple way of solving small disputes. Its conception is based on the elimination of the personal and sentimental matters and the reduction of problems to purely economic ones. Besides that, this service includes facilitators that by phone will communicate with the parties to try to conduct the process to a successful outcome. The company claims to have handled over 200,000 transactions over the past 10 years, and facilitated over $1.6 billion in settlements;
- *Document management* – these systems include facilitators working online or offline with parties, providing services for the creation and management of contracts and other structured documents. The clients of these systems are usually individuals with some difficulty in creating documents that need to meet a specific standard or structure. **Netdocuments** is an online service for document management that allows documents to be uploaded, accessed and shared with other persons from any part of the world. Another example is **Negoisst**, which is a project from the Electronic Negotiation Group, founded by the German Research Foundation. It is an electronic negotiation support system that covers semi-structured communication as well as document management and decision support. The key characteristic of the system is the integration of these components. This system was tested in the 3rd Annual International eNegotiation Tournament in November 2003, with a simulated case of a classic Union-Management dispute;
- *Automated Negotiation* – The systems under this category rely on advanced optimization algorithms that try to find the optimum solution for complex problems. These systems generally work by asking the user their preferences about the items in dispute, i.e., a quantification of how much they want each item. They can be used in a variety of different cases, ranging from divorces on which people need to agree on who gets what, to unions and managements trying

to agree on wages and working conditions for the workers of a given company. Examples are Zeleznikow's **Familly_Winner**, which produces an outcome to divorce cases after the parties have provided as input how much they want each item in dispute. **Inspire** is a system for simple negotiations in which the preferences of the users are provided as satisfaction graphs. After an agreement is reached the system generates suggestions to improve the satisfaction of the parties, which may or may not be accepted by them. Another well-known example is **SmartSettle**, an online tool that empowers negotiators and allows for faster and less stressing negotiations to take place between parties from any point of the world;

- *Customized Systems* – these are custom systems built for specific purposes or requisites. Some scenarios have unique characteristics that are not fit by any existing system and specific ones have to be developed. A good example is the one of transactions in **eBay**. In this service, users can sell and buy goods directly between one another, and many disputes arise every day due to the most diverse cases, i.e., damaged objects, wrong objects, no delivery, delay, just to name a few. For dealing with cases that involve small amounts of money, **eBay** developed its own mediator that tries to put the two parties into contact and solve the dispute. For higher amounts, services like the ones once provided by **SquareTrade** can be used. This company was the first online dispute resolution service to address e-commerce disputes. Much of this process was automated but, in case the automation failed, the services of a human mediator were also provided. This company discontinued its dispute resolution services in early 2008, and now focus only on extended warranties for electronic devices;

- *Virtual Mediation Rooms* – these systems are very similar to traditional mediation, except that the meetings take place in virtual rooms using tools such as instant messaging, video conference or email. The mediator will try to work out a favourable outcome without meeting the parties, by means of these communication technologies. One of such environments is **ECODIR**, which stands for *"Electronic Consumer Dispute Resolution"* and helps consumers and businesses prevent or solve their complaints and disputes online. An important note is that this is a free service and it is funded by the European Union. It provides services for communication between the parties through the web site and, if requested, mediation services. Another example is the **Mediation Room**, which is a very flexible online space for the mediation of disputes;

- *Arbitration Systems* – these systems are equivalent to traditional arbitration services except for the fact that they are provided online. In this approach, human arbitrators work from any point of the world solving cases with the help of communication technologies like email, telephone or instant messaging. An example of an online arbitration services provider is the **American Arbitration Association** which offers these services globally. Although the association provides other dispute resolution means like mediation, arbitration may ultimately be the only solution. Another service provider is **Mediation Arbitration Resolution Services** which provides arbitration and other services based on technologies like videoconference with the objective of providing a service as similar as possible to the traditional services, but with the advantages associated to online tools.

ODR systems can also be classified according to their degree of autonomy, as first or second generation. First generation ODR systems describe systems that nowadays are generally implemented. The main idea behind these systems is that the human beings remain the central pieces in the planning and decision making process. Because of that, human mediators are carefully chosen according to their skills, aptitudes and previous cases they participated in, since they will have a determinant role in the process. Electronic tools are evidently used, but are seen as no more than tools, without any autonomy or major role. Their only purpose is to assist the parties and make the management of the information and communications between them easier. In first generation ODR, the main technologies used are instant messaging, forums, video and phone calls, videoconference, mailing lists and more recently videopresence. Agent-based technologies may be used, but have no active role or autonomy. These systems are common nowadays and are usually supported by a web page. They represent a first necessary step before a more autonomous role of intelligent systems appears.

The second generation of ODR systems is essentially defined by a more active role of technology. It is no longer used for the mere role of putting the parties into contact and making access to information easier. It goes beyond that and is used for idea generation, planning, strategy definition and decision making processes. Humans have in this generation a secondary role, whether they are one of the parties in dispute or the mediator. They will be represented by intelligent agents that will have the autonomy for representing the intentions and desires of the humans. These agents try to behave and pursue the same objectives that the humans that they represent do. The technologies used in this new generation of ODR systems will comprise not only the communication technologies used nowadays, but also an umbrella of scientific fields such as Artificial Intelligence, Mathematics or Philosophy.

The evolution towards second-generation ODR systems has been slow. It is, on the one hand, difficult to emulate in software agents the complex cognitive processes that human expert use. On the other hand, there is always a sense of reluctance when software agents are to be empowered with the autonomy to take decisions on their own. This might even be the main barrier to this evolution, as one would be more prone to disagree with an unfavorable outcome if it was decided by a computer system instead of being decided by a human expert.

Although the path to this second generation of ODR is set and the technologies needed are already more or less known and explored, there is still a long way for reaching it, most likely because of our reluctance to be replaced by computer systems and the consequences of it. It is expected that ODR tools slowly move towards this new generation, giving small but solid paces, bringing it closer to reality.

2.6 Conclusion

According to the matters endorsed here, parties facing a conflict can use different resolution methods. The most traditional form of conflict resolution is litigation in court. It is a long-established process, controlled by the judicial system, i.e., it can be seen as a somehow safe approach. Parties generally have the notion that their rights are defended, i.e., courtrooms grant the right to a legal representative, even if the parties cannot afford one, and the right to several appeals that may be used when parties disagree with the outcome. However, presently, litigation in courts presents a considerable number of disadvantages.

Litigation in court is a very expensive and slow process. Even a minor case may take more than 1 year to meet a conclusion. Moreover, these processes are open to the general public and may be the subject to media coverage. This is not always desired by the parties, which would often rather choose privacy over public exposure. Another negative aspect is related with the social image of the courtroom itself. People see a courtroom as a place of conflict rather than a place to solve conflicts. In a courtroom parties take up opposite positions, they acquire the notion that what one wins the other loses. This does not promote a cooperative resolution of the differences, nor does it foster the interpersonal relationships, which are fundamental for the success of the process. All this results in a mentally and emotionally wearing process, connoted with negativity.

Propelled by these disadvantages, alternative methods for conflict resolution started to emerge. Approaches such as negotiation, mediation or arbitration became the most widely used. These approaches, despite their differences, have the same objective: to be a more efficient path to solve a conflict than the courtroom. Moreover, they share a considerable number of advantages. Alternative processes for conflict resolution are not dependent on the loads of the courtrooms or on the formality of their processes, i.e., they are more dependent on the availability of the parties, thus being more time-efficient. There is also the general notion that alternative methods are cheaper. They are also much more dynamic and flexible, allowing to adapt to the needs of the parties. Contrary to litigation, they tend to be private processes, taking place only in the presence of the third party who, besides being impartial, commits to maintain secrecy.

However, a still more significant advantage when compared to litigation is that the conflict resolution environment itself, the place where the parties meet, is far more favorable for conflict resolution. In fact, alternative methods focus on improving the communication and the relationships, on searching for mutually satisfactory solutions rather on maximizing individual gain. This is fundamental for the achievement of successful outcomes.

With the technological evolution, a natural step forward was the gradual involvement of technology in these processes. ADR methods gradually started to incorporate technology, whether for simply facilitating communication or information management or, later, to support the generation of solutions or the compilation of useful information. This brought along some many new advantages but also some new issues and challenges, which will be analyzed in the following chapters.

Specifically, this book places a particular emphasis on the lack of contextual information of ODR tools. In fact, these tools can give origin to *"cold"* environments, where emotional response and other important aspects of our interaction mechanisms play a reduced role. One may, evidently, argue that such decisions should be taken objectively; and they should. However, emotions and other aspects have a very important weight in our decision-making mechanisms (Damásio 1994). Thus, these same mechanisms become impaired when they have to work without access to this information. At the time of making or accepting an offer, a party is unaware of how the other parties feel about the issue; i.e., are they stressed? Are they calm? Are they in the verge of abandoning the process? Questions like these are crucial in the moment of making decisions, and are very hard to answer using current mostly text-based ODR tools.

The lack of contextual information that would allow parties to take better decisions is due to the low richness of the media used to communicate, mostly text-based. In fact, it results difficult to convey emotions and other aspects of our rich communication processes using text only, something that we do intuitively and unconsciously when we are face-to-face. A significant part of this book will focus on how current communication mechanisms can be improved in order to convey this information to the parties and the mediator, so that better and more informed decisions may be taken.

References

Andrade, F., P. Novais, J. Machado, and J. Neves. 2007. Contracting agents: Legal personality and representation. *Artificial Intelligence and Law* 15(4): 357–373.
Bakker, A.B., E. Demerouti, and W. Verbeke. 2004, Spring. Using the job demands-resources model to predict burnout and performance. *Human Resource Management* 43(1): 83–104.
Barbieri, Gina Lea. 2011. *Alternative dispute resolution center manual: Guide for practitioners on establishing and managing ADR centers.* Investment Climate Advisory Services. Washington, DC: World Bank.
Baron, R.A. 1991. Positive effects of conflict: A cognitive perspective. *Employee Responsibilities and Rights Journal* 4(1): 25–36.
Bar-Tal, D. 2011. *Intergroup conflicts and their resolution: A social psychological perspective.* New York: Psychology Press.
Bennett, S.C. 2002. *Arbitration: Essential concepts.* New York: ALM Publishing.
Bergmann, T.J., and R.J. Volkema. 1994. Issues, behavioral responses and consequences in interpersonal conflicts. *Journal of Organizational Behavior* 15: 467–471. doi:10.1002/job. 4030150510.
Brown, H., and A. Marriott. 2012. *ADR: Principles and practice*, 3rd ed, 868 pages. London: Sweet & Maxwell. ISBN 978–0414044791.
Buhring-Uhle, C., and G.L. Kirchhof. 2006. *Arbitration and mediation in international business,* 2nd ed. Alphen aan den Rijn: Kluwer Law International.
Burton, J. 1990. *Conflict: Resolution and prevention.* New York: St Martin's Press.

Buscaglia, E., and M. Dakolias. 1999. *Comparative international study of court performance indicators*. Washington, DC: Legal Department, The World Bank.

Cauthen, J.N.G., and B. Latzer. 2008. Why so long? Explaining processing time in capital appeals. *Justice System Journal* 29(3): 298–312.

Chiti, G., and G. Peruginelli. 2002. Artificial intelligence in alternative dispute resolution. In *Proceedings of LEA 2002. Workshop on the law of electronic agents*, 97–104. Bologna: CIRSFID.

Christensena, R.K., and J. Szmer. 2012. Examining the efficiency of the U.S. courts of appeals: Pathologies and prescriptions. *International Review of Law and Economics* 32(1): 30–37.

Cohen, J.M. 2002. *Inside appellate courts: The impact of court organization on judicial decision making in the United States Courts of Appeal*. Ann Arbor: University of Michigan Press.

Damásio, A. 1994. *Descartes' error: Emotion, reason, and the human brain*. New York: Putnam Publishing. Hardcover: ISBN 0-399-13894-3.

Dandurand, Y. 2009. *Addressing inefficiencies in the criminal justice process*. International Centre for Criminal Law Reform and Criminal Justice Policy, University of British Columbia. Available online at https://www.library.yorku.ca/find/Record/2338349. Accessed on April 2013.

Davenport, T.H., and J.G. Harris. 2005. Automated decision making comes of age. *MIT Sloan Management Review* 46(4): 83.

de L'Europe, C. 2010. The European Commission for the efficiency of justice: Evaluation of European judicial systems, rapport 2010 (donnees 2008). Available online at http://www.coe.int/t/dghl/cooperation/cepej/evaluation/default_en.asp

Demsetz, H. 1967. Towards a theory of property rights. *American Economic Review* LVII: 347–359.

Djankov, S., R. La Porta, F. Lopez-de-Silanes, and A. Shleifer. 2003. Courts. *The Quarterly Journal of Economics* 118(2): 453–517. doi:10.1162/003355303321675437.

Farhang, S. 2010. *The litigation state: Public regulation and private lawsuits in the United States*. Princeton: Princeton University Press. ISBN 9780691143828.

Feste, K.A. 1991. *Plans for peace: Negotiation and the Arab-Israeli conflict*. New York: Praeger Publishers.

Fix-Fierro, Héctor. 2004. *Courts, justice and efficiency: A socio-legal study of economic rationality in adjudication*. Oxford/Portland: Hart Publishing Ltd., 268 pp. ISBN 1-84113-382-5.

Fudenberg, D., and J. Tirole. 1983. *Game theory*. Cambridge: MIT Press.

Haig, D. 2010. Colloquium papers: Transfers and transitions: Parent offspring conflict, genomic imprinting, and the evolution of human life history. *Proceedings of the National Academy of Sciences of the United States of America* 107(Suppl): 1731–1735.

Jehn, K.A. 1995. A multimethod examination of the benefits and detriments of intragroup conflict. *Administrative Science Quarterly* 40: 256–282.

Jennings, N.R., P. Faratin, A.R. Lomuscio, S. Parsons, C. Sierra, and M. Wooldridge. 2001. Automated negotiation: Prospects, methods and challenges. *International Journal of Group Decision and Negotiation* 10(2): 199–215.

Katsh, E. 2002. Online dispute resolution: The next phase. *Lex Electronica* 7(2), Printemps/Spring 2002. http://www.lex-electronica.org/articles/v7-2/katsh.htm

Katsh, E., and Janet Rifkin. 2001. *Online dispute resolution: Resolving conflicts in cyberspace*. San Francisco: Jossey-Bass.

Kennedy, G. 1998. *The new negotiating edge: The behavioral approach for results and relationships*. London: Nicholas Brealey Publishing.

Krause, J. 2007. Settling it on the web. New technology, lower costs enable growth of online dispute resolution. *American Bar Association Journal* 93: 42–46.

Langer, A. 2005. *The importance of mediators, bridge builders, wall vaulters and frontier*. Forli: Una Città.

Larson, D.A. 2006. Technology Mediated Dispute Resolution (TMDR): A new paradigm for ADR. *Ohio State Journal on Dispute Resolution* 21: 629.

Lauterbach, W. 1991. Intrapersonal conflict, life stress, and emotion. In: Charles Donald Spielberger, Irwin G. Sarason, Jan Strelau, John M. Brebne (eds.), *Stress and anxiety*, vol. 85, 85–100. New York: Hemisphere.

Lax, D.A., and J.K. Sabenius. 1986. *The manager as negotiator: Bargaining for cooperative and competitive gain*, 29–45. New York: Free Press.

Li, M., Q.B. Vo, K. Ryszard, S. Ossowski, and G. Kersten. 2013. Automated negotiation in open and distributed environments. *Expert Systems with Applications* 40: 6195–6212.

Lindquist, S.A., W.L. Martinek, and V.A. Hettinger. 2007. Split decisions: Explaining mixed outcomes on the United States Courts of appeals. *Law and Society Review* 41(2): 429–456.

Lodder, A., and E. Thiessen. 2003. The role of artificial intelligence in online dispute resolution. In *Workshop on online dispute resolution at the international conference on artificial intelligence and law*, Edinburgh, UK.

Lodder, A.R., and J. Zeleznikow. 2005. Developing an online dispute resolution environment: Dialogue tools and negotiation support systems in a three-step model. *Harvard Negotiation Law Review* 10: 287.

Mastro, R.M. 1991. The myth of the litigation explosion. *Fordham Law Review* 60: 199. Available at: http://ir.lawnet.fordham.edu/flr/vol60/iss1/6. Accessed on April 2013.

Moses, M.L. 2008. *The principles and practice of international commercial arbitration*. Cambridge: Cambridge University Press.

Pelled, L.H., K.M. Eisenhardt, and K.R. Xin. 1999. Exploring the black box: An analysis of work group diversity, conflict, and performance. *Administrative Science Quarterly* 44(1): 1–28.

Posner, R.A. 1996. *The Federal courts: Challenge and reform*, 2nd ed. Cambridge, MA: Harvard University Press.

Raghavan, T.E.S. 1994. Zero-sum two-person games. In *Handbook of game theory 2*, ed. R.-J. Aumann and S. Hart, 735–759. Amsterdam: Elsevier. ISBN 0-444-89427-6.

Raiffa, H. 2002. *The art and science of negotiation*. Cambridge, MA: Harvard University Press.

Redfern, M. 2011. *The elephant in the room – Should pre-litigation mediation be mandatory?* LEADR kon Gres 2011, Brisbane, Australia.

Sillars, A., and D. Parry. 1982. Stress, cognition, and communication in interpersonal conflicts. *Communication Research* 9(2): 201–226.

Sussman, E. 2009. Why mediate? The benefits of mediation over direct negotiation and litigation. *TDM* 1. www.transnational-dispute-management.com

Thiessen, E., and J. Zeleznikow. 2004. Technical aspects of online dispute resolution challenges and opportunities. In *Proceedings of the third annual forum on online dispute resolution*, ed. Melissa Conley Tyler, Ethan Katsh, and Daewon Choi. Melbourne, Australia.

Varady, T., J.J. Barcelo, and A.T. Von Mehren. 2006. *International commercial arbitration*, 3rd ed. St. Paul: West Group Publishers.

Walton, R.E., and R.B. McKersie (eds.). 1991. *A behavioral theory of labor negotiations: An analysis of a social interaction system*. Ithaca: Cornell University Press.

Zartman, I.W. 2007. *Negotiation and conflict management: Essays on theory and practice*. London: Routledge.

Zeleznikow, J., and E. Bellucci. 2004. Building negotiation decision support systems by integrating game theory and heuristics. *Artificial Intelligence and Law* 7: 2–3. Dordrecht: Springer.

Chapter 3
Advantages and Disadvantages of Avoiding the Courtroom

Abstract Currently, there are two main trends from which parties involved in a conflict can choose to resolve it. On the one hand, parties can choose to initiate a litigation process in a courtroom, making their stands before a judge or a jury and having these establishing an outcome. On the other hand, parties can go for alternative approaches such as negotiation, mediation or arbitration, either in their traditional forms or through an electronic mean, with the assurance that they will undergo a more flexible process, with emphasis on building empathy and searching for mutually satisfactory solutions. This chapter focuses particularly on these alternative means: their advantages and their disadvantages. It does so in a systematic manner, pointing out the current causes for the identified problems and ending with the enumeration of a series of potential solutions for these problems. One particular issue addressed is the one of Media Richness and how the current lean communication means are hindering conflict resolution processes conducted online. The solutions pointed out will be addressed individually in the upcoming chapters.

3.1 Introduction

Judicial systems, in general, are becoming increasingly ineffective, facing the need of considering the new adaptive models of organizational efficiency, either in terms of cost or time. Either the more traditional or the present technology-based alternatives to conflict resolution try to, in some way or another, overcome the main problems of the courtroom, i.e., aim to be less expensive, quicker and friendlier. Still, they also present some insufficiencies or flaws.

Traditional alternatives to litigation try to bring the parties into an agreement under a constructive form of cooperation, possibly with the help of a mediator that may even try to point out the eventual barriers and the potential solutions. Despite

D. Carneiro et al., *Conflict Resolution and its Context*, Law, Governance and
Technology Series 18, DOI 10.1007/978-3-319-06239-6_3,
© Springer International Publishing Switzerland 2014

taking place outside the formal circuit of the courtroom, parties still meet at specific times and places.

Technology-based alternatives, on the other hand, tend to break with physical and temporal constraints, allowing the parties to meet in a virtual setting, possibly in an asynchronous way. This significantly increases the flexibility of the process and reduces costs, mostly the ones associated with traveling and the usage of spaces. However, this departing from the current practice should always be analyzed with care, with all their shortcomings weighted against their advantages.

Avoiding the courtroom, either to use a traditional approach or a technology-based one has its pros and cons, which should be taken into consideration in a case-by-case base. However, in a general way, the advantages surpass the disadvantages, which may explain the increasing use of alternative methods for conflict resolution, as has been evidenced in the last decades.

This chapter provides a thorough revision of the advantages and disadvantages of avoiding the courtroom. It ends with a systematic cause-and-effect analysis of both litigation in court and its alternatives. A set of answers is put forward to tackle the main problems being identified. The viability and validity of these results will then be addressed in detail, in the remaining chapters of the book.

3.2 The Traditional Alternatives

Traditional Alternative Dispute Resolution (ADR) methods aim to support the disputant parties into settling their differences, or at least a part of them, without resorting to judicial practices. Avoiding litigation has its advantages and disadvantages.

The main and more general differences between judicial processes and alternative methods are that the latest take place in a more informal and less competitive environment (Eisen 1998). In fact, in a courtroom, there is usually a competitive atmosphere, in which each party will focus on maximizing his own gain. This evidently has repercussions not only on the quality of the outcomes, that normally do not maximize mutual gain, but also on the willingness of the parties to comply with them. The atmosphere is different when using alternative methods, i.e., both parties agreed on using a specific method, being willingly engaged in it, tending to be more open to cooperate in order to solve their differences. This constructive environment is paramount for the success of the conflict resolution process and, ultimately, it works for the best interest of both parties. The mediators give an important contribution to this positive environment; indeed, they are experts on understanding the parties, their fears and objectives, and generally focus on improving the relationship between them, knowing that cooperation is fundamental for the success of the process. With the necessary skills, the mediator may encourage parties to reach an agreement by enabling them to communicate more effectively through the rephrasing of their arguments. Judges, on the other hand, focus mostly on solving the conflict, simply listening to the parties and issuing an outcome.

Such differences between judicial processes and the alternative ones are also visible on the type of proceedings carried out, i.e., while in courtrooms there are clearly the figures of the *winner* and the *looser*, in alternative methods the focus is on the broadening of the degrees of freedom in order to achieve win-win scenarios (Thiessen and McMahon 2000). This is only possible due to two factors:

- The flexibility of ADR methods, which allow for remedies that are not available in a courtroom; and
- The empowerment of the parties, which are encouraged to freely express their views, fears and desires.

In general, ADR is also less expensive and faster than litigation. Judicial processes involve a large number of costs that include court fees, documentation fees, advocate's fees or costs associated with the use of lawyer's services. On the other hand, although ADR methods may involve some costs, these tend to be significantly smaller than the ones of the judicial process. This allows for the consideration of more ordinary claims that are not viable in litigation, resulting in a fairer access to justice.

Concerning its promptness, ADR methods are generally less time-consuming than the judicial ones. On the one hand this is related to the number of appeals that parties are entitled to enforce in the courtroom, which may end up dragging the case for months or years. Undoubtedly, this is the result of the valuable rights of the defendants. Nevertheless, it slows down the whole judicial system. In ADR, on the other hand, methods tend to be quicker due to a number of reasons. First of all, since there are few people involved in the process, the scheduling of meetings results easier and faster. Indeed, given the number of pending cases, access to the court-room's spaces and services is highly competitive. Meetings in the context of ADR do not need to take place in a special space nor require the use of specific and limited services. Moreover, these meetings are also not so tightly bounded by the physical or temporal constraints, regarding the use of these spaces. All these factors result in an easier and more flexible scheduling practice, in which the disputants mutually agree rather than in one that may be imposed on them.

Privacy is another issue in which judicial processes and alternative methods differ. Judicial processes are, in general, public events, freely attended by the public with coverage by the media, bringing to the public domain aspects of cases that the disputant parties might wish to keep to themselves. On the contrary, alternative processes are strictly confidential, being confined to the space of the room, where no public or media is present.

Another advantage worth mentioning is the sense of control that the parties have in ADR methods. In a judicial litigation everything is imposed, from the dates of the proceedings to the jury, judge or even the outcome. On the contrary, in an ADR process, parties may decide on the experts guiding or managing the process, on the condition that they agree on the ADR provider. This not only empowers the sense of control of the parties, but also represents a point of agreement that may foster future ones. Furthermore, disputants may even choose the extent of the process, the set of rules used or the application or not of morals or ethics values. Finally, in some forms of ADR parties may even participate on or jointly define the outcome, which significantly increases their satisfaction and their willingness to comply with it. This power of control may also result in having qualified experts, i.e., while in judicial processes the judges are more generalist and may lack expertise in a specific field, in ADR parties may choose and agree on an expert with a specialization in the domain of the issue under consideration.

Nevertheless, alternative methods also carry along some disadvantages that should be discussed and taken into attention, given their possible consequences. One of the most important is the potential for unequal bargain power. This is common in cases in which one party surpasses the role of the other or when one of the parties has a dominant character. Traditional scenarios include cases of divorce, especially when there is domestic violence, or cases of employers versus employees. The risk here is that one of the parties is able to influence the other, ultimately controlling the process and leading to an outcome that is not deemed fair. In such cases courtrooms might better defend the weakest party.

Another issue about the use of mediators or other conflict managers is that, sometimes, such experts lack the legal background of judges, and may therefore not take the best decisions or actions from a legal standpoint, independently of their expertise on the domain or on managing conflicts.

The flexible nature of ADR and its more informal model may also result in drawbacks. Predicting the unfolding of a given conflict resolution process or event, as well as its outcome, is fairly difficult. The lack of the notion of precedence, so present in the courtroom, may make it difficult for the parties to understand their different possibilities and the implications to each one, sometimes resulting in a sense of insecurity and unknowing. More worrying, however, is that this informal model may lead to solutions that would not have been deemed in the courtroom. In face of this, some authors argue that government should play an active role in this world of private dispute resolution, in order to have outcomes within the boundaries of The Law (Thornburg 2001).

Another potential disadvantage worth mentioning is related with the fact that most forms of ADR are not legally binding, i.e., the parties are not forced to comply with the outcome, even if they agree with it. The main strategy of alternative methods to counter this drawback relies on the fomenting of good interpersonal relationships, on achieving the possible and consensual outcome, and on pointing out that going to court would not comprise better results for any of the parties. However, interpersonal trust and satisfaction with the results so far achieved are not enough to assure the enforceability of the verdict, i.e., a party may just reach the end of the process and ignore the outcome, maintaining the conflict. Ultimately, it may be worsened by the need to solve the case in court, with the consequent increase in costs, and the possibility of the court over-run the previous decision.

Depending on the nature of the cases, alternative methods might simply not be the best approach. In fact, these methods generally focus on cases that belong to the traditional distributive monetary problems. They do not tend to, for example, enforce a party to take or refrain from taking a given action.

Given this view on the differences between judicial processes and traditional ADR methods, it is clear that there are advantages of the latest over the former. However, there are also some drawbacks. The fruition of these alternative methods, nevertheless, shows that the advantages are noteworthy, i.e., not only disputant parties are, in general, more open to such approaches, but there are also judicial systems that encourage or even force parties to engage in an alternative processes before moving into the courtroom. Such methods may, thus, be seen as a potentially efficient alternative to litigation in courts, holding more satisfactory outcomes for the parties involved.

3.3 The Online Alternatives

The emergence of technology-based conflict resolution mechanisms may be seen as predictable, in line with many other developments with effects in our daily life. Nevertheless, technological progress that encompasses changes as significant as the ones endorsed here should always be analyzed with caution (Friedman 1997). Online methods of conflict resolution, as much as the traditional ones, have their fair number of advantages and disadvantages when compared to judicial processes or even to the traditional alternatives (Bordone 1998).

One of the first advantages worth mentioning is that ODR methods generally take place under the use of intuitive and easy to use technological tools. These user-friendly interfaces build up an environment far friendlier than courtrooms, allowing parties to think more creatively, without the pressing constraints imposed by the courtroom, the figure of the judge or the public. Desirably, parties must interact with intuitive interfaces that hide the eventual complexity of the models being used, reducing it to a sequence of well-defined and clear actions. This eventually increases the satisfaction of the parties in solving their disputes online, as they feel that it is a more transparent and controlled process.

Another major advantage of ODR against judicial processes or even against ADR is its availability. In judicial processes the evolution of the process is dependent on the limited availability of the courtroom's services. In ADR it is still limited by the availability of the elements involved, although to a smaller degree, since there are fewer services and stakeholders involved, being also more flexible. Nonetheless, in ODR these constraints are further diminished, since ODR platforms are available online, around the clock. Parties may therefore view information related to their cases, submit or edit documents or consult the state of their processes at any time.

Still related with the use of online communication frameworks, ODR also inherits the advantages of asynchronous communication. In fact, it may be sometimes hard, even in ADR methods, for the parties to agree on meeting hours, namely due to incompatible schedules. ODR tools facilitate this process by providing means of synchronous and asynchronous communication. Moreover, this communication may take place from virtually any place in the world. This brings along one of the most significant advantages of ODR when compared to ADR or judicial processes: parties do not need to travel to specific physical locations in order to solve a conflict. This has a significant and direct impact on the overall costs of the conflict resolution process (Krause 2007), especially in the increasing cases in the domain of worldwide e-commerce (Hang 2001).

Still concerning this topic, there are other costs that are significantly reduced in ODR approaches (Hörnle 2003), namely the ones associated with the transport of documents and materials or the rent of a facility to conduct the process.

In the previous section it was stated that ADR methods were generally conducted in an environment that fomented cooperation between the parties. The same applies to ODR. On the one hand, by being behind a computer screen instead of being in front of the intimidating presence of a judge, the party is able to feel less pressure and think more freely. In these conditions people tend to be more disposed to participate on the process, being at the same time able to be more creative. On the other hand, since the parties are not in physical contact, they tend to be more focused on the subject under discussion than on the opponent, i.e., more focused on the facts than on the personal feelings. There are even cases where the parties refuse to sit around the same table, a situation that may endorse this approach as the more appropriate to solve the dispute in a civilized way. Furthermore, when parties are by themselves, and not in the presence of others that may have a bad influence on them (e.g. such as the relations in the cases of domestic violence), they also tend to speak more freely and without fearing the consequences. The neutrality of the ODR environment must also be seen as positive. Courtrooms, and sometimes ADR approaches, suffer from the so-called "home court advantage", in which there is a feeling that a party is better defended because it is, for instance, in its own country or in its cultural milieu, and the others not (Victorio 2001).

Another advantage is a consequence of the application of ODR tools, specifically when asynchronous communication methods are used. In a courtroom, as well as in an ADR process, once the disputant parties portrayed something, there is no way back. Indeed, the parties may utter words or take actions that may be regretted later, a consequence of their states of stress or emotional conditions. Undeniably, under ODR approaches, parties have the opportunity to reflect more and end up making better decisions. This is due to the fact that the parties, under these circumstances, have more time to think about what they are going to do or say than if they were in the presence of their panelists: parties can write down a message, review it or change it before sending it or they can also discard it. Communication processes thus tend to be more rational, well-thought rather than impulsive. This is more notorious when asynchronous communication mechanisms like forums or email are being used.

Also worth considering is the fact that all the communication processes are or can be recorded for future use, being even possible to use them as a proof. A skilled mediator may study these communication processes to understand which party is being uncooperative or unrealistic, which party is hindering the process or placing obstacles, even if in an unconscious way. The mediator may use these records as a way to improve the conflict resolution process by pointing out potential problems in their communication processes or by better identifying the parties' interests.

All the potential of computer-based tools must also be mentioned (Goodman 2003). When the conflict resolution process is moved onto the virtual sphere, there is a wide range of possibilities that emerge, being the most interesting ones those that emerge from the areas of Artificial Intelligence or Game Theory. Besides support for communication, ODR approaches may include additional tools aimed at better informing the parties and facilitating the conflict resolution process as a whole. These tools may include, among others, the generation and management of formal documents, the generation of potential and valid solutions, the definition of the boundary outcomes for a specific case, the compilation of past similar cases, the automated distribution of assets, the suggestions of strategies or lines of attack, among others. In fact, these tools may, to some extent, address some of the drawbacks of ADR. Specifically, in ADR it can be somehow difficult to estimate outcomes given the lack of the notion of precedence: each ADR process is isolated; none is based on the outcome of others. With the use of such tools, that might draw information from judicial processes, parties may become more aware of their actual possibilities, giving them a more realistic view of the whole conflict resolution process in which they are engaged.

Summarizing, ODR tools can be a more accessible, fast, economic and transparent way of solving disputes. However, the factors that in some cases constitute an advantage of ODR may also constitute disadvantages. If, in some scenarios, moving from a paper-based process to an online one brings it closer to people, there are others in which that does not necessarily happen. This is especially true for population groups who do not have access or that do not have the necessary training for efficiently using such tools. This clearly results in undesired inequalities in the access to justice. Evidently, adequate training can be provided in such cases, although such a solution is far from optimal: there is the pressure to learn to use a new tool as well as the time spent on doing it.

Furthermore, if it is true that in most of the developed countries the technologies needed for using ODR tools are inexpensive and widely available, there are others realities, especially in developing countries or other poor areas, in which this is not necessarily true. This too may represent a source of dissimilarity and inhibit parties from using ODR tools.

There are, however, other potential inhibitors to the use of online methods for conflict resolution. A particularly important one is the notion of trust. Social interactions have always been based on the trust between the participants: from simple conversations between friends to the design of contracts. Geographical proximity, prior acquaintance or a brief talk allows building a notion of trust. This is however not possible or at least not so effective online. Thus, people often place more trust on the traditional courtrooms, which may be seen, which have a physical location and are run by "real" people that may be addressed in a formal or informal manner. ODR methods, as other online experiences, should thus comply with standards, be certified by trustworthy entities and be completely and utterly clear about the whole procedure (Shneiderman 2000). The lack of this sense of trust may make agreements more difficult to reach, and ultimately move disputants away from alternative methods.

More than a disadvantage, Information Security in ODR systems must be seen as a major concern given the sensibility of this domain. A few key issues can be pointed out that are by no means specific to ODR tools, but inherited from Information Systems and Online Communication Systems.

First of all, there is the need to ensure that information shared and stored online remains confidential, i.e., that it will not be disclosed to unauthorized individuals or systems. Information is generally more secure in an online device than printed on a paper. However, this can be quickly inverted with negative consequences that are worsened by the velocity at which information can nowadays be copied and transmitted: if an authorized individual gains access to the credentials of the information owner, this information can quickly be copied from and to any location in the world, whereas in the paper scenario this would not be so straightforward.

The integrity of the information stored online should also be taken into consideration. In fact, in modern data storage and management systems, it is fairly easy for someone with access to the system to make changes. These changes can result in accuracies or inconsistencies. Additionally, changes made can easily go undetected or overwrite older versions of documents, making it difficult or even impossible to revert, if necessary. In paper-based conflict resolution, these issues are generally easier to control.

Another concern in information security is the one of availability. It has been mentioned as an advantage the fact that ODR systems are always available around the clock. Nevertheless, the risk of an online system to be offline is always present, either from an internal error, a problem on a communication channel or even attacks such as denial-of-service. This type of attack is an attempt to make a machine or network resource unavailable to its intended users, generally by saturating the target machine with requests to the point that it cannot respond to legitimate traffic, or it responds so slowly that is rendered essentially unavailable. In this sense, paper-based approaches are more robust and are often preferred by more conservative people, since paper and the pencil never fail.

The issue of authenticity should also be considered, especially in such legal domains. In a courtroom, a great deal of importance is placed on authenticating documents, on ensuring that a given document or item is genuine. This becomes more difficult in ODR at several levels. Firstly, there is the need for mechanisms that can ensure that a given document is authentic. However, this raises further questions: when we make a digital copy of a document, which is in logical terms completely identical to the original, does the issue of genuinely still applies? How can we establish the difference? Is this difference even relevant when the documents are exactly the same? Still of a more serious concern, there must be mechanisms to ensure that each party is who they claim to be. While in a courtroom this is fairly easy, it may be difficult to ensure the same online, once it is subject to problems such as identity theft. Generally digital signatures and public key encryption are used to address these problems. A digital signature is a mathematical approach for demonstrating the authenticity of a digital message or document. It can be used not only to authenticate an individual but also to ensure that it was actually the individual who sent a communication or transaction. Public key encryption, on the other hand, refers to a cryptographic system that requires two separate but mathematically linked keys to implement. One of these keys is secret and the other is public. They are used to encrypt and decrypt texts and only with access to both of them can this be performed. The public key may be published without compromising security, while the private key must not be revealed to anyone not authorized to read the messages.

Finally, one last concern particularly important in the legal domain is the one of non-repudiation. There is the need to ensure that a party cannot deny having sent a transaction or a communication after having effectively sent them. Nor can parties refuse to comply with their obligations to the contracts that they agreed on and their terms, nor refuse to accept that they agreed on such terms. Generally, to avoid such problems, all the transactions and communications are stored for further analysis, if necessary.

Security in ODR systems, as in any other information systems, will always go down to a balancing of risks versus measures to counter them, with the negative costs and implications of this measure, i.e., ultimately the safest would be to disconnect the information system from the network. Nonetheless, this would also render it useless in the context of ODR.

The lack of the physical presence of the parties is also consensually pointed out as a disadvantage in the literature. Katsh and Rifkin (2001) state that online interactions cannot match the richness of the face-to-face sessions that are at the heart of offline mediation. Goodman (2003) points out another interesting factor, namely that people that solve conflicts online are often strangers to each other and the lack of the personal connection makes it more difficult for them to communicate effectively. Thompson and Nadler (2002) examined how people negotiate over email and, in particular, how the outcomes of these processes differ from the traditional face-to-face bargaining. The authors conclude that negotiations conducted over email are more likely to fail than traditional ones. The reason pointed out is its dearth of physical, social, and vocal cues, often leading to misunderstandings, ambiguous messages, and unnecessary impasses. The authors show that this can be improved with a prior phase of preparation in which the parties engage in a getting-to-know-you phone conversation, setting off a chain reaction of goodwill that allows parties to be more cooperative and creative. Similar conclusions are achieved by Swaab and Swaab (2007) in which the authors point out that it is difficult to establish social rapport with the lack of nonverbal cues, causing the parties to be impolite and to show little concern for their counterparts.

However, there are also cases in which the physical separation of the parties is a constraint or even a requirement. Lodder and Zeleznikow (2005) point out that the lack of presence in ODR can result in an advantage in cases in which the parties have a history of violent conflict, the costs of being in the same room are exorbitant, parties are in different time zones, or parties cannot agree upon a joint meeting.

A particularly interesting aspect to consider here, derived from the physical separation of the parties and the consequent use of technological tools to enable communication, is the one of the richness of the media in online communication. In fact, there is here a complex duality of advantages and disadvantages that needs a more exhaustive analysis. If on the one hand one does not feel intimidated by not speaking in front of a jury or an opponent and may speak truer, it also becomes easier to lie online since there is not the presence of a figure of authority. One even more important issue is the one of the body language. Mehrabian (1980) states that most of the meaning that we derive from a face-to-face conversation comes from other aspects than the words spoken, namely the tone of voice, the loudness, the facial expressions and body gestures.

Evidently, all this information produced in a given context that makes up a conversation is lost when technologies like IM, email, forums or similar are used. Goodman (2003) analysis this issue in the particular context of conflict resolution to conclude that assessing feelings, confronting emotions, and empathizing with each other, which are crucial for a successful mediation, are rather difficult when parties communicate via computer screens. From the point of view of mediators, there is the generalized feeling that they are unable to make full use of their skills when in a virtual milieu (Eisen 1998). Online, the mediator feels almost "powerless" without the ability to use his own physical personhood to act on the parties, to make them at ease and to create an inter-personal environment that fosters problem-solving tasks (Katsh et al. 2000).

A solution for this problem would be to use more recent technologies like videoconference or TelePresence, which are more similar to a face-to-face conversation, although that is neither always possible nor desirable. The key idea is to place the emphasis on transmitting how things are said instead of just what is said. These issues, given their complexity, are analyzed in more detail in the following section.

Similarly to ADR, it can be concluded that ODR presents its own advantages and disadvantages. Many of the advantages identified directly address drawbacks from ADR or from judicial processes, which make ODR methods an increasingly appealing way to solve conflicts, together with their reduced costs and time efficiency. On the other hand, many of the drawbacks identified are inherited from generic online communication tools. Hence, their diminishing is dependent on further development on technological areas such as Communications, Security or Distributed Systems.

3.4   Media Richness in ODR

In a pursuit of better remote communication frameworks, our society relies more and more in Virtual Environments (VEs). When resolving conflicts there is a trend to increase the use of telematics means. However, one must enquire to which extent are the VEs a suitable tool for conflict resolution.

Blascovich and Loomis (2002) define VEs as synthetic sensory information systems that lead to perceptions of environments and their contents as if they were not synthetic. In other words, VEs may be seen as simulated environments that, in some way, try to look like the real environments being simulated, with the aim of implementing some kind of interaction scenario. Typical fields of application of VEs include teaching in classrooms, informal learning, distance learning, business, e-commerce, gaming, real-life simulation or conflict resolution. However VEs, as they are seen nowadays, may still not be a suitable replacement for traditional face-to-face communication. In fact, a VE is frequently regarded as "cold", with emotions and other traces of our complex interaction modalities playing little to no role at all. The degree of the use of these modalities can be used to classify the richness of the communication mean.

In this scope, Richard L. Daft and Robert H. Lengel (1984) introduced the theory of Media Richness. Their aim was to define a model to classify a communication mean according to its ability to reproduce the information sent over it. Four features are identified upon which the communication medium is classified: the ability to handle multiple information cues simultaneously; the ability to facilitate rapid feedback; the ability to establish a personal focus; and the ability to use natural language. Based on this, the authors organized some of the most common communication means in use, according to their efficiency in "passing the message" (Daft et al. 1987).

Unaddressed documents such as bulk mail or posters where deemed as the leaner mediums of communication, followed closely by written addressed documents such as letters or email. In increasing order efficiency the authors put 2-way radio, telephone, video conferencing and face-to-face communication.

The first aspect worthy of note here is that most of the ODR approaches nowadays are based on text-based communication tools such as e-mail or chat, which are among the leaner mediums of communication. According to Newberry (2001), although text-based chats have a high feedback, they have low support for multiple cues, message tailoring or emotions. E-mails are still leaner since their rating in the feedback criteria is even lower. One could argue in favor of the use of video-based communication approaches, which are far richer. Nevertheless, there are cases in which such is not possible, due to technological constraints, privacy issues, or others. It can even not be desirable, particularly in the ODR domain, in cases in which the parties are not event willing to see each other or when seeing each other may foster the conflict. Thus, other alternatives should be contemplated.

One of the most important aspects to consider here is that of body language. People, in their day-to-day interactions (unconsciously) rely on body language to express themselves in a richer way. Mehrabian (1980) concludes that in a face-to-face communication there are three key elements: the words, the tone of voice and the non-verbal behavior. The author also concludes that the non-verbal elements are particularly important for communicating feelings and attitudes, stating that they account for the majority of the information transmitted, i.e., the way words are said is more important than the words themselves.

In a related line of research, Dodds et al. (2011) concludes that the lack of gestural information from both speaker and listener limits successful communication in VEs. The authors experimentally prove not only that body language is very important for transmitting information but also central to perceive feedback from that transmission, i.e., to perceive if the communication is being successful or a different approach should be followed. Both the lack of feedback from the environment and meaningful content are also pointed out as a drawback by other researchers (Campbell 1997; Marucci et al. 2001).

To deal with this issue, several approaches may be followed. Alsina-Jurnet and Gutiérrez-Maldonado (2010) investigated the influence of some user features, namely test anxiety, spatial intelligence, verbal intelligence, personality and computer experience – on the sense of presence. Also, Rehm et al. (2008) dealt with the idea of the analysis of the user's behavior and interpretations regarding the cultural background, utilizing accelerometers to uncover the user's cultural background by analyzing his/her patterns of gestural expressivity in a model based on cultural dimensions. Jaimes and Sebe (2007) describe the concept of multi-modal interaction as a way to communicate between humans and computers using more than one modality or communication channel (e.g., speech, gesture or writing).

Also important is the affective aspect of communication (Beale and Creed 2009; Hudlicka 2003). Emotions appear in almost all models of human communication (e.g., facial expression, gestures, voice tone, respiration, skin temperature). Moreover, the message also changes depending on the emotions: once again, the most important is not what is said, but how it is said. As noted by Picard (2000), affect recognition is most likely to be accurate when it combines multiple modalities, information about the user's context, situation, goal, and preferences.

The importance of stress must also be considered. Evidently, stress is a key factor in interpersonal communication, as it is in virtually any other aspect of our lives. However, current approaches on VEs lack stress models that can support it. This constitutes an obstacle to effective communication between the participants. In fact, research on stress applied to VEs does not exist. Moreover, stress is also a very important indicator for a mediator to understand the state of the parties and perceive when actions should be taken to maintain a healthy communication between the parties. Letting stress levels escalate may ruin the conflict resolution process.

The loss of this information in virtual settings makes it hard for the intervening parties to understand the thoughts of each other. In fact, when communicating online, people tend to forget that there is another person behind the screen on the other side. In that sense, there is a disinhibiting effect and people tend to forget about the other's feelings and simply do not worry too much about the consequences of the words they utter and the actions they commit. Thus, we are more likely to offend people online.

So far, it can be concluded that communication processes in general and ODR tools in particular could profit from richer communication means. Current virtual environments for conflict resolution are largely based on text-based communication tools, which are incapable to efficiently convey important modalities of our statements such as emotions, stress level, body language, intonation, speech rhythm, among others. In the second part of this book we detail a novel approach to improve text-based communication means by including additional information in the communication channel. Conflict managers, in particular, could profit largely from this evolution since they would be able to make better-informed decisions. They would know when a party becomes too stressed or too emotional, when parties would gain more in making a pause than in continuing to communicate. This would allow implementing richer and more realistic communication processes, involving modalities that would move them from the current machine-like ones.

3.5   Cause and Effect Analysis

In a sense, this book is concerned with improving the current paradigms for conflict resolution, namely the ones based on technology. The drawbacks of conflict resolution identified in this chapter can be organized in two main groups: (1) drawbacks inherited from the current state of judicial systems and (2) drawbacks related with the current approaches on alternative conflict resolution methods.

In this section we systematically retake the main problems pointed out above and identify their main causes. Based on this, possible solutions to the problem will be considered, and will constitute the guiding line for the remaining of the book.

Concerning the issues that derive from the current state of judicial systems, the main problem may be stated as follows: they are very slow and very expensive. A list of causes and their relationships are now put forward, and are depicted in Fig. 3.1.

1. *Uncooperative environments* – Courtrooms are highly uncooperative environments in which parties have as main objective to gain their cases, at the expenses of the other side. These classical win-lose scenarios, common in the courtroom, hinder the achievement of a mutually agreeable outcome, with consequences on cause (2);

2. *Numbers of appeals* – Defendants have the right to appeals, which is a manifestation of their increasing rights. However, it is also one of the major causes for the low throughput of courtrooms, as each appeal adds to the amount of time needed and costs associated to resolve a case, with outcomes being delayed further;

3. *Increasing new cases* – Currently every minor action is liable to end up in court, independently of the costs involved. A significant amount of these processes involves small-value claims resulting from the number of exponentially increasing e-Commerce transactions. Unfortunately, the time to conclude the process is not proportional to the value of the claim;

4. *Increasing rights* – Defendants have increasing rights, which is undoubtedly the reflection of a positive evolution of the legal systems. Nonetheless, this also contributes to the aggravation of the problems of judicial systems, mainly when concerned with points (5) and (6);

5. *Complexity of legal systems* – Legal systems are becoming increasingly complex due to the increase in the number and complexity of rules, the existence of

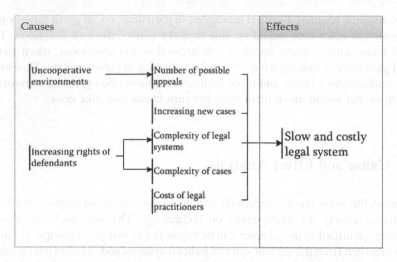

Fig. 3.1 The main causes and effects identified in the current state of judicial systems

several ways to do similar things, the use of specialist terms and specialized language, the rapid appearance of new concepts or the increasing amount of information in each case, just to name a few. This makes the analysis of each individual claim more complex, costly and lengthy;

6. *Complexity of cases* – Each legal process is becoming increasingly complex due to a need for a more precise specification of each word, decision or rule used. The emergence of new (legally challenging) concepts and the easiness with which proof is managed and presented electronically also adds to this problem;

7. *Costs of legal practitioners* – Although the legal system and some of the parties may divide the costs of a legal process, they still tend to be significant. They include the costs of the whole court staff (e.g., clerk, administration, security, legal staff, support staff, court reporter), solicitor fees, disbursements, lawyer services (generally paid hourly), document management or transportation, among others;

Concerning the issues related with the current approaches on online dispute resolution, other problems have been identified:

1. *Richness of online communication* – Depending on the communication mean, communicating online poses new challenges, as the lack of contextual information (e.g., body language or associated functional answers), which may threaten the efficiency of the communication process. Misunderstandings are frequent and are particularly frightening in the legal domain as they can result in harmed relationships;

2. *Info-exclusion* – The lack of training in the generic use of technological tools poses an obstacle to the use of ODR mechanisms. Complex or unfriendly user interfaces are other common deterrents that can result in an unbalance between the parties when using the ODR tool;

3. *Costs of ODR* – The use of ODR is generally cheaper than litigation, but it is not necessarily inexpensive. Besides the fees to use a given ODR service, additional costs may exist such as the cost of the access to the technology (e.g., internet, computer), particularly significant in developing countries;
4. *Security, privacy, data protection and identity* – These issues are not specifically related to ODR but rather result from the use of online communication methods and online tools. Nevertheless, they reasonably constitute one important concern in a field such as the legal one;
5. *Rudimentary access to information* – ODR tools frequently have data access methods that are tightly coupled with the data representation layer, providing no abstraction, making it difficult for the parties to efficiently understand and manage the data;
6. *Rudimentary conciliation methodologies* – Conciliation methodologies in ODR frequently place emphasis on human factors and depend significantly on the parties' decisions and judgment. This lack of a formal structure may result in a sense of disorganization as well as in longer processes and less successful processes;

These problems are rooted in a number of concrete causes, which are described next and depicted in Fig. 3.2.

1. *Lack of body language* – Body language is one of the most important communication modalities. Our gestures, our posture, our attitudes or our facial expressions provide the necessary framework for our interlocutors to correctly understand our own words. The lack of this information significantly hinders communication;
2. *Lack of contextual factors* – There are other modalities involved in communication besides the ones mentioned in (1). These modalities include the physiological response of our body, the rhythm of the speech, the tone of the voice or the accentuation. The lack of such modalities in online communication negatively affects it;
3. *Lack of training* – Even today there are people who are ill at ease with the use of the technological tools that support ODR. This factor, as well as the lack of specific training or support in using a given tool, may make it difficult for parties to efficiently use an ODR environment;
4. *Non-intuitive interfaces* – Many ODR tools available nowadays still rely largely on traditional web forms and static pages as an interface for information. This may pose an obstacle, mainly when they are not adapted to the specific context or to the needs/characteristics of the users;
5. *Cost of access to technology* – There are costs associated to the use of technological solutions that, although not dependent on the ODR approach, are inherent to their use. These costs may include the costs of the hardware necessary as well as the costs of using the necessary telecommunication channel (e.g., internet or a telephone service provider);
6. *Fee for using tools* – Although ODR tools tend to be less expensive than traditional litigation, their use may be subject to a fee (fixed or per unit of

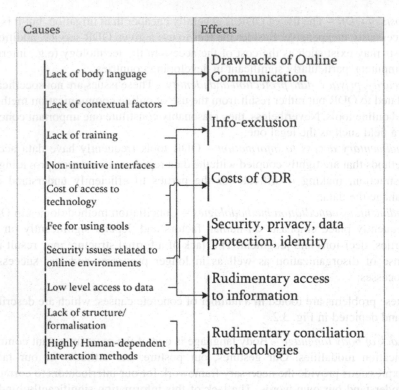

Fig. 3.2 The main problems and their causes identified in current Online Dispute Resolution tools

time), which may amount to a significant sum. Moreover, the use of conciliation services mediated by a neutral mediator also tends to have an associated
fee;

7. *Information security in online environments* – The sheer fact of communicating
online rises issues related, namely, to online identity (how am I sure that I am
talking to whom I think I am?), privacy (how do I know that my information
would not be accessed by someone who should not access it?) or data protection (how do I know that my personal data will not be available to anyone
else?). Although these issues are transversal, they are particularly worrying in
the legal domain;

8. *Low level access to data* – Data representation models tend to be very close to
the data layer. Representing information as it is stored, without abstraction
methods, makes it difficult for parties to efficiently understand and manage it;

9. *Lack of structure/formalization* – Many ODR processes, despite taking place in
online environments, are still largely unstructured. This informal approach,
largely human-based, which on the one hand results from the flexible nature of
ODR, may also result in difficulties for taking decisions, for managing information and for following some desirable line of attack or strategy;

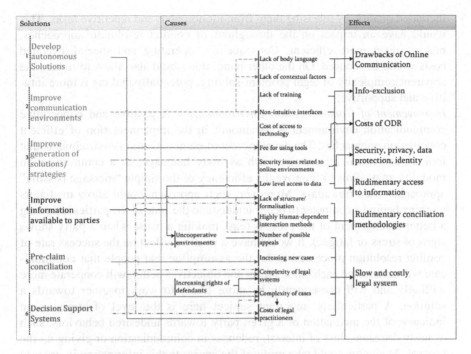

Fig. 3.3 A general view of the main problems identified in the field of conflict resolution, their causes and the potential solutions to address them

10. *Highly human-dependent interaction methods* – Interaction methods in ODR tools still rely largely on natural language and on the rhythm or pace that the participants impose. Moreover, they focus too much on subjective issues such as the parties' personal views on the problem. This hampers the use of tools to support conciliation;

The current main problems in judicial litigation and ODR as well as their causes have been put forward. The issues mentioned were compiled from a revision of the current state of the art in the legal systems as well as from an analysis of several commercial ODR providers and research projects.

Based on this study, several solutions that would contribute to the improvement of the current state of affairs are put forward. These solutions constituted the foundation for the definition and steering of the work detailed in this book. A brief description of each potential solution is given below. Each one tackles one or more of the causes described, thus tackling the problems associated to such causes, as depicted in Fig. 3.3.

1. *Development of autonomous solutions* – The development of technological solutions that may, to some extent, alleviate the work of human practitioners could have positive effects on the efficiency of the legal systems. On the one hand, it could allow for legal practitioners to work more efficiently and with

increased quality, by releasing them from monotonous and repetitive tasks. This would have an impact on the throughput of conflict resolution approaches, making them more efficient. Consequently, operating and specialist-related costs would be reduced. On the other hand, this would also allow to reduce the apparent complexity of legal problem-solving, potentially making it more intuitive and supportive;

2. *Improvement of Communication Environments* – A positive and cooperative communication environment is paramount in the implementation of efficient conciliation approaches. The development of communication environments that look at contextual information such as body language, as a communication modality, may allow to improve the efficiency of the simple "message passing" approaches used nowadays. Moreover, such approach would allow mediators working behind a computer to better understand the state of the parties, allowing a better management of the process (e.g., making a pause when a party shows signs of stress or fatigue). It would have a positive effect on the success rate of conflict resolution processes, under the assumption that people that communicate will understand each other's fears and objectives better, will cooperate more willingly and will consequently be more likely to work together towards a solution. A particularly important subject here is the level of stress as an indicator of the inclination of a given party towards undesired behaviors, such as hasty decisions, loss of interest, rudeness in communication or giving up the process. Mediators could take profit of the access to this information in order to better manage the process;

3. *Improve generation of solutions/strategies* – Not infrequently, the main obstacles to conflict resolution reside within the parties themselves. The generation of solutions, which is often the responsibility of the parties (especially in alternative conflict resolution approaches), is an example of a potential problem, since most of us are not familiar with the action of devising a solution for a given problem (or we are simply not willing to), namely when it includes complex issues with complex relationships. The definition of a potentially successful strategy may be even more challenging. Nevertheless, these two features are central in the conflict resolution process. Tools to support them are necessary, and may improve the quality of the solutions/strategies used;

4. *Improve information available to parties* – In order for an individual to take good decisions he/she must be able to analyze different courses of action, weight their possible outcomes, decide on one over the others and learn from the consequences of that choice. This can nevertheless be challenging without the right amount of information with a minimum level of quality. The lack of these conditions implies that individuals take decisions based on incomplete or poor information, being most likely far from optimum. Tools for compiling information are thus needed and may provide concise and useful data for the parties involved in a conflict resolution process to take realistic and weighted decisions, that will be more likely to be accepted by other parties;

5. *Pre-claim conciliation* – Currently many of the processes pending in courtrooms involve small-value claims that can nevertheless make their way through

different courts by means of consecutive appeals, making judicial processes inefficient. The parties should see pre-claim conciliation as a potential way to a faster and cheaper resolution of their differences. Successful alternative conflict resolution methods could thus not only improve the satisfaction of the parties by allowing them to solve their problems more efficiently, but also contribute to the decrease the main problem of litigation currently;

6. *Decision Support Systems* – Decisions in the legal domain are frequently multi-issue, multi-value and multi-party with complex relationships between these variables, generally hardly to understand at a first sight. Parties thus need support in analyzing their possible choices in real time and understand the relationship between them and their consequences. Tools to support parties under this setting not only contribute to more adequate decision processes but also to induce a more structured and formal way of reasoning and taking decisions in the legal arena.

As Fig. 3.3 depicts, some causes are not addressed by the solutions proposed. In fact, the solutions described here include only the ones that will be tackled in the course of this book. Despite the need for additional solutions for many other problems, this selection was performed in order to give a more precise focus to the contents of the book. Moreover, the problems to attack were selected in order to address all the stages of a conflict, i.e., definition, management and resolution.

3.6 Conclusion

Judicial systems are nowadays facing a number of problems that promote the search for more viable alternatives. In fact, courtrooms arc highly competitive milieus in which the disputant parties are led into maximizing their individual gain at the expenses of the other. This clearly points out to win-lose scenarios, which hardly reach the best solution possible. Moreover, in this race for maximizing personal gain, important aspects for the establishment of a mutually satisfactory agreement, such as a healthy and respectful relationship between the parties, are left to secondary plans. Often, relationships at the end of a judicial process worsen. In addition, litigation processes are becoming increasingly lengthy as a result of the increasing complexity of legal systems and the number of possible appeals that parties are permitted. Finally, the resolution of a conflict in a courtroom is generally expensive, which often makes the resolution of small-value claims unviable.

In a natural response to these drawbacks, alternative methods emerged with the promise of being more flexible, more cost-efficient and less expensive. These alternatives, in their most traditional form, allow parties to meet in a space outside the sphere of the courtroom. Such spaces are generally more cooperative and may count with the support or guidance of a mediator that may allow the disputants to better understand their problems and to better define strategies that may lead to a solution. Focus here is not on maximizing the individual gain, as it is in the courtroom, but on maximizing the number of possible solutions and improving the communication and the relationship between the parties at all times. This results in an environment that is more positive and cooperative, which aims not only for the sheer resolution of the conflict but also for the achievement of a mutually satisfactory resolution.

With the technological evolution, these traditional alternatives started to shape around communication tools to allow parties to settle their differences independently of their location. In their simpler forms, these methods are characterized by allowing parties to exchange documents and communicate independently of time and space, significantly increasing the flexibility of the process. In their more advanced forms these methods may include technological tools aimed at supporting the disputants in higher-level tasks such as the validation of solutions, the definition of strategies or the analysis of potential outcomes. However, a potential drawback must be considered here that results from the use of telecommunication tools, in particular text-based ones, i.e., the lack of the contextual surroundings of face-to-face interactions. In fact, it becomes increasingly harder for parties to efficiently understand each other and thus to reach an agreement without the non-verbal cues that we rely on when we communicate face-to-face. This issue, in particular, will be addressed in detail later on in this book.

When looking at what has been exposed in this chapter, it results clear that the trend in the last decades has been to move away from the competitiveness of the courtroom to more flexible and friendly environments that can foster not only better solutions but also achieve them in a more time and cost efficient manner. This resulted in an increasing use of these alternative methods, making it clear that, despite the disadvantages identified, they constitute valid and viable alternatives to litigation in the courtroom.

References

Alsina-Jurnet, I., and J. Gutiérrez-Maldonado. 2010. Influence of personality and individual abilities on the sense of presence experienced in anxiety triggering virtual environments. *International Journal of Human-Computer Studies* 68(10): 788–801.

Beale, R., and C. Creed. 2009. Affective interaction: How emotional agents affect users. *International Journal of Human-Computer Studies* 67(9): 755–776.

Blascovich, J., and J. Loomis. 2002. Immersive virtual environment technology as a methodological tool for social psychology. *Psychological Inquiry* 13(2): 103–124.

Bordone, R. 1998. Electronic online dispute resolution: A systems approach – Potential, problems, and a proposal. *Harvard Negotiation Law Review* 3: 175.

Campbell, D.A. 1997. Explorations into virtual architecture: A HIT Lab gallery. *IEEE Multimedia* 1: 74–76.

Daft, R.L., and R.H. Lengel. 1984. Information richness: A new approach to managerial behavior and organizational design. In *Research in organizational behavior*, vol. 6, ed. L.L. Cummings and B.M. Staw, 191–233. Homewood: JAI Press.

Daft, R.L., R.H. Lengel, and L.K. Trevino. 1987. Message equivocality, media selection, and manager performance: Implications for information systems. *MIS Quarterly* 11: 355–366.

Dodds, T.J., B.J. Mohler, and H.H. Bülthoff. 2011. Talk to the virtual hands: Self-animated avatars improve communication in head-mounted display virtual environments. *PLoS ONE* 6(10): e25759.

Eisen, J.B. 1998. Are we ready for mediation in cyberspace? *Brigham Young University Law Review* 1305.

Friedman, G.H. 1997. Alternative dispute resolution and emerging online technologies: Challenges and opportunities. *Hastings Communications & Entertainment Law Journal* 19: 695.

Goodman, J.W. 2003. The pros and cons of online dispute resolution: An assessment of cyber-mediation. *Duke Law and Technology Review* 4: 1–16.

Hang, Lan Q. 2001. Online dispute resolution systems: The future of cyberspace law. *Santa Clara Law Review* 41: 837.

Hörnle, J. 2003. Online dispute resolution. In *Bernstein's handbook of arbitration and dispute resolution practice*, vol. 1, ed. John Tackaberry and Arthur Marriott. London: Sweet & Maxwell.

Hudlicka, E. 2003. To feel or not to feel: The role of affect in human–computer interaction. *International Journal of Human-Computer Studies* 59(1): 1–32.

Jaimes, A., and N. Sebe. 2007. Multimodal human-computer interaction: A survey. *Computer Vision and Image Understanding* 108(1–2): 116–134.

Katsh, E., and J. Rifkin. 2001. *Online dispute resolution: Resolving conflicts in cyberspace.* San Francisco: Jossey-Bass.

Katsh, E., J. Rifkin, and A. Gaitenby. 2000. E-commerce, e-disputes, and e-dispute resolution: In the shadow of 'eBay law'. *Ohio State Journal on Dispute Resolution* 15: 705.

Krause, J. 2007. Settling it on the web. New technology, lower costs enable growth of online dispute resolution. *American Bar Association Journal* 93: 42.

Lodder, A.R., and J. Zeleznikow. 2005. Developing an online dispute resolution environment: Dialogue tools and negotiation support systems in a three-step model. *Harvard Negotiation Law Review* 10: 287.

Marucci, L., G. Mori, F. Paterno, and F. Costalli. 2001. Design criteria for usable web-accessible virtual environments. http://www.museumsandtheweb.com/node/9254.

Mehrabian, A. 1980. *Silent messages: Implicit communication of emotions and attitudes.* Belmont: Wadsworth Publishing Company.

Newberry. 2001. Raising student social presence in online classes. In *WebNet 2001: World conference on the WWW and Internet proceedings*, Orlando, FL, 23–27 Oct 2001.

Picard, R.W. 2000. *Affective computing.* Cambridge, MA: MIT Press.

Rehm, M., N. Bee, and E. André. 2008. Wave like an Egyptian: Accelerometer based gesture recognition for culture specific interactions. In *Proceedings of the 22nd British HCI Group annual conference on people and computers: Culture, creativity, interaction*, vol. 1, BCS, Swindon, 13–22.

Shneiderman, N. 2000. Designing trust into online experiences. *Communications of the ACM* 43 (12): 57–59. New York: ACM.

Swaab, R.I., and A.D. Swaab. 2007. How to negotiate when you're (literally) far apart: The media approach. *Negotiation* 10: 7–9.

Thiessen, E.M., and J.P. McMahon. 2000. Beyond win-win in cyberspace. *Ohio State Journal on Dispute Resolution* 15: 643.

Thompson, L., and J. Nadler. 2002, Spring. Negotiating via information technology: Theory and application. *Journal of Social Issues* 58(1): 109–124.

Thornburg, E.G. 2001. Fast, cheap, and out of control: Lessons from the ICANN dispute resolution process. *Journal of Small and Emerging Business Law* 7: 191.

Victorio, R.M. 2001. Internet dispute resolution (IDR): Bringing ADR into the 21st century. *Pepperdine Dispute Resolution Law Journal* 1: 279.

Chapter 4
Artificial Intelligence in Online Dispute Resolution

Abstract Artificial Intelligence is currently an umbrella for a wide range of scientific sub-fields, with application domains that span many different areas such as aviation, city planning, traffic management or disease diagnosis, just to name a few. Knowledge-based domains are especially suited to be dealt with by approaches from Artificial Intelligence that enable to learn, infer or reason in an automated way. Thus, the intersection of Artificial Intelligence and The Law comes as no surprise. This chapter is dedicated to this intersection. It starts by analyzing a large number of classical Artificial Intelligence sub-fields, pointing out how each one can or could improve the current state of affairs in conflict resolution. Then, it focuses on one particularly interesting yet unexplored sub-field: Ambient Intelligence. A scenario of its potential uses is laid out that clearly points out the innovation considered. The chapter ends with a critical analysis of the current state of affairs in the intersection of Artificial Intelligence and The Law.

4.1 Introduction

Artificial Intelligence techniques emerged in the middle of the last century as a way to emulate features generally associated to intelligence, in machines. It is probably the most ambitious and one of the most controversial research fields in Computer Science as it aims for machines that can reason at the same or at a better level than Humans (Russell and Norvig 2002).

When looking for a definition for the term Artificial Intelligence, we can think on one of the first ones to be proposed by John McCarthy, an American computer and cognitive scientist and one of the most influent scientists in AI research: "Artificial Intelligence is the science and engineering of making intelligent machines" (John McCarthy, American scientist (1927–2011)).

D. Carneiro et al., *Conflict Resolution and its Context*, Law, Governance and
Technology Series 18, DOI 10.1007/978-3-319-06239-6_4,
© Springer International Publishing Switzerland 2014

This definition is interesting in the sense that it says many things and nothing special at the same time: it is quite generic since it depends on the definition of "intelligence", which is not consensual. In humans, intelligence is generally defined in function of a set of capabilities including, but not limited to, learning, self-awareness, communication, reasoning, abstract though or planning. The Merriam-Webster dictionary defines intelligence as "the ability to learn or understand or to deal with new or trying situations" whereas the Cambridge dictionary defines it as "the ability to learn, understand and make judgments or have opinions that are based on reason". Intelligence has also been studied in animals or in plants, where a reduced set of these capabilities also depicts intelligent behaviors.

Thus, in search for a more precise definition, it results logic that Artificial Intelligence can be defined as machines that exhibit capabilities usually associated to humans. Classical research problems in this field focus on the ability of machines to reason and take decisions, to acquire and use knowledge, to plan strategies, to perceive patterns (e.g. images, languages, sounds) and the ability to move and manipulate objects (Russell and Norvig 2009). These abilities shall be used with the objective of maximizing some gain so that the machine is better at the end of its use than it was at the beginning, i.e., it proves that the machine is not only able to recognize its present status but also to establish an objective towards the improvement of some feature, draw a plan of action or execute it.

Hereupon, Artificial Intelligence can be seen as the study and design of software agents that perceive their environment and take actions that maximize its success. Important words here are "autonomy" (the machine should take decisions without the intervention of other entities) and "proactivity" (the machine should take the initiative of changing the state of the world).

The ultimate objective of research in this field is known as Strong AI. This concept denotes the moment in time when computers will have cognitive skills similar or even better than humans (Kurzweil 2000). John Searle, when trying to distinguish between two different hypotheses of AI, coined the expression *one that could only act like he thinks and one that really thinks* (Searle 1980).

Searle named the former as the weak AI hypothesis and the latest as strong AI hypothesis. The pursuit for this not yet achieved objective of AI is based on the notions of Intelligent Agent and Multi-agent Systems (Wooldridge 1995). Strong AI, as seen by Searle, has not yet been achieved. On the other hand, there is no consensus about the minimum set of abilities for a machine to be considered intelligent at a human level, i.e., it is not enough to do better than humans in some tasks.

In 1950, Alan Turing proposed a test for determining whether a computer system is or is not exhibiting an intelligent behavior, in the form of an experiment:

> *place a person and a computer in two isolated rooms and a second person, the judge, in a third isolated room. The judge exchanges written messages with the other two participants. When the judge cannot consistently tell which one of the two interlocutors is the human and which one is the computer, then the computer is considered intelligent* (Turing 1950).

The interest in AI is increasing and it now constitutes the backbone of many applications. We may even deal with applications of AI in a daily basis without noticing it. This apparent pervasiveness is related with the fact that we get used to computers showing intelligent behaviors, and we take them as granted, not noticing that they are running AI based applications. This is called the AI effect. Hogan describes it in an intuitive way (Hogan 1998):

> "At the outset of a project, the goal is to entice a performance from machines in some designated area that everyone agrees would require "intelligence" if done by a human. If the project fails, it becomes a target of derision to be pointed at by the skeptics as an example of the absurdity of the idea that AI could be possible. If it succeeds, with the process demystified and its inner workings laid bare as lines of prosaic computer code, the subject is dismissed as "not really all that intelligent after all.""

Nevertheless, AI research has led to the development of many technologies that are nowadays in intense use, most of the times in the shadow of huge systems. These technologies are generally used to optimize knowledge-based processes, to make products easier to use with the adoption of intelligent interfaces or to automate tasks. Among the main problems addressed by AI research, it may be pointed out the work done in areas such as knowledge representation and reasoning, planning, learning, natural language processing, motion and manipulation, perception, social intelligence, feelings or creativity. These insights are being applied in a wide range of domains, including medicine, weather forecast, finance, transportation, games, aviation or The Law.

Somewhere in the 1950s, the use of technological tools to support conflict resolution processes emerged as a solid possibility. At that moment, the vision of using technology for more than mere information management or data exchange started to take place. In that flourishing era, the vision was that machines would soon possess enough intelligence and problem-solving skills to replace humans in most of the tasks, mediation or negotiation included.

The Law and AI, despite being different fields of research at first sight, are indeed particularly well suited to complement. Indeed, both aim at the definition of methodologies for decision-making or problem solving. As Bench-Capon et al. (2012) point out, both make use of semi-formal modeling, i.e., in The Law it takes the form of binding precedents and statutory rules, while in AI it takes the form of logical representations.

The use of non-human agents with autonomy for decision-making, particularly in the domain of The Law and dispute resolution, raises many questions from the legal point of view, namely the definition of the relationships between agents and the parties on behalf of whom they act or the autonomous decisions taken by agents and their behaviors (Peruginelli 2002). Nevertheless, the agent paradigm is a motivating research field that is fostering the development of new solutions for a wide range of problems and, in particular, for the legal domain.

The earlier automated systems developed for the legal domain were based on logic, and therefore relatively complex to use and very domain-specific. Only a limited number of trained specialists could use them. Consequently, there was the need to develop applications that could make use of these logical tools in a broader way. According to Oskamp et al. (1995) researchers should aim at the development of practical and intuitive applications that could be used by non-experts. It is our conviction that the best path to achieve such applications consists in the integration of concepts from AI and The Law in order to develop ODR platforms that can efficiently address the challenges that the legal domain is currently facing.

4.2 Classical Sub-fields of AI and the Law Research

It is a fact that computers are being intensively used in virtually every domain, being the legal one not an exception. However, the potential of the use of computers is not being fully exploited, being mostly relegated to basic back office tasks such as text processing, billing, agenda management or communication. Nevertheless, the role that technology plays in this field slowly begins to change as AI techniques develop. Historically, the beginning of AI & The Law research can be assigned to Bruce Buchanan and Thomas Headrick when, in 1970, published the paper *Some Speculation About Artificial Intelligence and Legal Reasoning* (Buchanan and Headrick 1970). In the meantime, research in this field rose, with the appearance of international conferences, associations and journals, revealing the growing interest of the scientific community for this area. In this section some of the branches of AI research are detailed with the objective of determining how each one can improve current dispute resolution processes and tools. Table 4.1, at the end of this section, highlights the major features of each of the technologies here presented.

4.2.1 Decision Support Systems

With the constant growth of the amount of information present in the decision processes, the need for tools that could provide support has also grown. Indeed, the new economy, along with increased competition in today's complex business environments, takes the companies to seek complementarities in order to increase their competitiveness and reduce risks (Bonczek et al. 1981). Under this scenario, planning takes a major role in a company's life. However, effective planning depends on the generation and analysis of ideas (innovative or not) and, for this reason, idea generation and management processes become a crucial tool in present days. The tools used may range from simple systems for compiling useful information from raw data, to more complex ones that make suggestions on the best strategy to be used or the fairest outcome.

Decision support systems may be used in virtually any knowledge based environment and the legal domain is not an exception (Turban 1993). In the legal arena, these are known as legal decision support systems. However, as its use is still relatively recent, there are no advanced implemented systems. Nevertheless, the ones that have been developed so far have something in common (Zeleznikow and Hunter 1994): they are rule-based. There are several reasons for this: rule-based systems are generally easy to understand and implement, there are many tools to

Table 4.1 The most interesting features of several classical sub-fields of Artificial Intelligence from the conflict resolution point of view

Technology	Major features
DSS	Compile and provide useful information
	Provide support for decision processes
	Propose actions based on the analysis of facts
ES	Model human knowledge and inference mechanisms
	Reason similarly to human experts
	Automation of "simple" tasks by applying an inference engine to knowledge
KBS	Model complex knowledge
	Represent norms and judgment under uncertainty
II	Build a layer of abstraction for complex systems
	Faster, intuitive and more efficient access to information
CBR	Reasoning processes similar to the legal ones
	Contextualized retrieval of information
	Information is organized according to meaningful attributes
MAS	Distributed problem solving
	Implement negotiation protocols
	Support for argumentation
Ontologies	Representation of legal knowledge
	Inference
	Pattern extraction
RbS	Encode knowledge, expertise and processes of human experts
	Fairly simple way of interpreting and reasoning with rules
EvoComp	Search for solutions for complex black box problems
	Broad applicability, to different legal domains

build them and legal knowledge is particularly well suited to be modeled using rules. These rules are instructions of the type *IF condition THEN conclusion*, i.e., if *condition* holds, one or more *conclusions* are derived.

Considering the complexity of the legal domain, legal decision support systems can be quite useful, specifically if one considers the huge amount of information that parties and mediators must analyze in order to take decisions. Without using any supporting tools, analyzing all this information is an inefficient process that consumes time, slowing down the legal processes.

These systems thus have the ability to analyze relevant facts provided by the parties as well as legal information such as norms or past known cases in order to take decisions. For example, Social Security Systems use them to help practitioners deciding if an unemployed individual should or should not receive a benefit; Banks use them in order to more efficiently decide if a client should be granted a loan; and Insurance Companies use them when deciding on the amount of an indemnity to be paid to an insured. In any of these cases, as well as in the legal domain, results are generally supervised by human experts. Decision support systems are not necessarily automated systems that issue outcomes. They are systems that, based on important information, issue justified recommendations and compile information that can be useful for the decision making process.

One example of a decision support systems in the legal domain is Split Up (Zeleznikow and Stranieri 1995). This is an intelligent decision support system that makes predictions about the distribution of marital property following divorce in Australia. Its main purpose was to assist judges, registrars of the Family Court of Australia, mediators and lawyers. Split Up operates as a hybrid system, combining rule-based reasoning with neural network artifacts. A more recent example in the same legal domain can be found in (Abrahams and Zeleznikow 2010), in which an agent-based negotiation decision support system for the Australian Family Law is presented.

4.2.2   Expert Systems

According to (Susskind 1987), Expert Systems can be defined as computer programs that have been constructed in such a way that they are capable of functioning at the level of (and sometimes even at a higher standard than) human experts in given fields. In that sense, such systems are designed, trained and fine-tuned by humans and must embody a depth and richness of knowledge that will allow them to perform at such levels (Hayes-Roth et al. 1983). The training can be performed using information from past cases and respective decisions provided by human experts. On the other hand, these systems can also learn while they are used, generally with the supervision of an expert that makes adjustments according to the input, expected output and verified output. Harmon and King (1985) define Expert Systems as intelligent computer programs that use knowledge and inference procedures to solve problems that are difficult enough, once they require significant human expertise for their solution. Both definitions share one common idea, i.e., Expert Systems try to mimic the human expertise and knowledge in a given domain (Jackson 1990). In that sense, it is correct to state that the knowledge necessary to perform such high level tasks as well as the inference procedures used can be seen as models of expertise of the best human experts in the field.

Expert Systems also represent a change in the programming paradigm (Forsyth 1986). While traditional computer programs are seen as procedures applied to data, Expert Systems are seen as inference engines applied to knowledge. In that sense, the two new major modules are a rich knowledge base and a powerful inference engine. However, if we want to be more specific, four main components can be identified in a fully functional Expert System (Greinke 1994): the knowledge acquisition module, the knowledge base, the inference engine and the user interface. A fully functional Expert System is expected to be able to deal with information relating to a specific domain, analyze it and generate knowledge, and then take actions and decisions based on that knowledge. Given what has been said before, it is expected that these actions and decisions resemble the ones that a human practitioner would take in a similar scenario.

Expert systems can be found in a wide range of domains, including the fields of accounting, medicine, process control, financial services, production or human resources. There are several factors that lead to a growing use of this technology.

On the one hand, Expert Systems can automate simpler tasks, releasing human experts to other higher level tasks or, eventually, allowing companies to reduce costs. On the other hand, the huge amount of information that practitioners in certain fields must deal with renders nearly impracticable a purely human work-force. This is also true in the specific case of the legal domain. In fact, legal practitioners can no longer deal with the increasing number of disputes and the information that each one requires, resulting in the well-known slowness in judicial systems. Undeniably, Expert Systems may be a tool that may help legal practitioners to deal with huge amounts of information, automating the simpler tasks and, ultimately, allow them to work more efficiently.

Particularly constructive when considering the legal domain is the ability of an Expert System to detail the reasons for a specific analysis or recommendation, i.e., its ability to explain its actions. Actually, legal expert systems generally allow the assignment of weights to factual data on a given cases. This may trigger additional actions, such as comparing a given case to the cases stored in the knowledge base or producing outcomes based on similarity metrics. However, once again, these out-comes should be regarded as merely informational, i.e., legal expert systems should be used, for example, to help judges deal more rapidly with the cases, providing guidance based on a model of the legal domain in question, that includes norms, the facts and past cases.

Following this approach, James Popple (1996) presented SHYSTER, a simpler, pragmatic approach in which the utility of a legal expert system is evaluated by reference, not to the extent to which it simulates a lawyer's approach to a legal problem, but to the quality of its predictions and of its arguments. In fact, most of the legal expert systems currently at use are fairly simple implementations, focusing, for example, on automated drafting of complex legal documents. In such systems, users are generally guided through a series of interfaces with questions, while receiving practice tips or support about the legal domain or strategies. Nevertheless, other authors argue that a purely rule-based approach is inappropriate if the Expert System is to be of use to a lawyer. Popple (1991) concludes that a better approach is obtained when rule-based methods are combined with case-based ones.

4.2.3   Knowledge-Based Systems

Knowledge is an abstract term that represents a collection of specialized facts, procedures, and judgment conventions. There are many types of knowledge and many different ways of acquiring it. Knowledge can come from a single source or it can be compiled from several ones. Depending on the domain, it can be compiled from human experts (e.g. observing the behavior of a law practitioner), sensors (e.g. a domotic environment), pictures (e.g. medical imaging), maps (e.g. finding a path), flow diagrams or historic context, just to name a few. Depending on the type and source of information, several techniques for knowledge acquisition may be used, namely human observation, scanners, pattern matching, pattern recognition or intelligent agents.

Being the field of AI & The Law a knowledge-based one, the subject of Knowledge Representation (KR), is a very important one. According to Sowa (2000), KR is a multidisciplinary subject that applies theories and techniques from three other fields: logic, ontologies and computation. Logic provides structural formalisms and rules of inference. It is used to establish the validity of arguments, as well as their redundancy or contradiction, aimed at a test of the validity of a given outcome. Ontologies define the domain of the universe of discourse, as well as the objects that subsist in such an environment. Without ontologies words have no meaning or value at all and become simple sets of characters. Computation denotes the needed support to deal with these questions from a processing perspective.

In a few words, KR is concerned with formalizing our way of thinking, i.e., how to represent a given domain with symbols. Considering the complexity of legal knowledge, the development of systems that are able to formally model knowledge is highly desirable (Brachman and Levesque 2004). These are the so-called Knowledge-based Systems.

In what concerns the legal domain, such systems are central, in particular to define a model that can deal with a heterogeneous group of information, that may include but is not limited to parties' information, norms, past cases, facts or arguments. These systems are also essential when such information is to be stored digitally in a way that will allow a fast and efficient retrieval. When knowledge is stored in a formal and well-defined way, it assists in the development of automated processes that can, for example, interpret the validity of logic arguments. The development of systems that can efficiently cope with huge amounts of knowledge is in fact one important advance from which legal practitioners may take advantage in order to deal with the current increasing number of disputes. Moreover, knowledge-based systems can be designed to deal with either statute law or case law (Popple 1991). The main motivation behind the use of Knowledge-based Systems in the legal arena is its capability of representing norms and judgment under uncertainty. In fact, systems can be developed that can produce new facts or conclusions based on knowledge.

In general, several modules can be identified in a fully functional Knowledge-based System, namely the user interface; the explanation facility that details the inference mechanism regulating the outcomes; the database with the factual information; an inference engine that decides on which rules are to be enforced, and how they are prioritized; and the knowledge acquisition module that is responsible for (possibly in an automatic way) the acquisition of knowledge from the outside world.

4.2.4 Intelligent Interfaces

Lawyers currently face a problem that has already been pointed out in this document, i.e., the ever growing amount of information that must be considered in legal problems, either in statute law or case law. On the one hand, in statute law, new statutes and treaties are making its way, making legal analysis increasingly complex. On the other hand, case law is faced with more and more disputes, which generate an exponential increase in legal rulings. The main reason for this is the process of socialization in course in terms of the use of information technology by the human beings, which not only adds to the information available but also increases the number and diversity of the disputes that must be addressed.

Ironically, the same technologies that led to the exponential availability of information also show the way to the development of tools to deal with this information, i.e., technologies such as Expert Systems, Decision Support Systems or Knowledge-based Systems are now available that can assist practitioners. Nevertheless, the adoption of these useful tools has been rather slow, wasting the theoretical advantages. A possible cause for this drawback is pointed out by Matthijssen (1995), when the author states that in legal information systems the interface-modalities do not shield the users of these systems from the internal organization of the data and the additional workload associated to the processing mechanisms, i.e., legal practitioners find a conceptual gap in this process, once they work in a given way, and legal information systems are either designed to work in a different way or are designed very closely to the internal structure of the system, providing no abstract interpretation of the decision process.

This gap can be filled with the development of the so-called Intelligent Interfaces. Therefore, it is useful for developers to be aware of the way practitioners solve legal problems. Using this information, intelligent interfaces can be developed that reflect the knowledge domain of the practitioner rather than the structure of the stored data. The main objective here is that practitioners can focus on the actual content of the legal concepts rather than on how these concepts are translated and stored in legal information systems. Intelligent Interfaces are very singular, i.e., besides making the bridge between humans and computers, they present additional features. The eternal problem addressed, present on the legal domain (as well as in any knowledge-based domain), is an efficient and effective retrieval of data (generally from a database). When the methods for retrieving information are closely related to the structure of the data, it becomes harder for a non-expert to perform efficient searches. As stated by Matthijssen (1999), to a large extent, these problems can be attributed to the limitations of the traditional boolean query mechanism used in text databases, which is difficult for users to operate. Using Intelligent Interfaces, it is possible to develop different forms of abstraction, at the user level, that make possible to personalize methods to access data, regardless its structure.

In order to implement this behavior, an intelligent interface needs specific data about the legal domain that is being addressed, as well as models for the representation of legal knowledge, its rules and processes. Additionally, the interface can also take into consideration personal preferences or user roles. Then, it can act as an intelligent intermediary between the user and the database. Using such an interface, practitioners can make use of a more intuitive and powerful tool to analyze and organize information. Possible applications include the structured publication of high amounts of information, automated organization of data according to a given criteria or automated search. Another interesting area of application is one in which the user is not completely sure of how to search or what to search. A search request may be incomplete, incorrect or inaccurate and the interface is responsible for assisting the user in reformulating the request or trying to guess what the user intentions are in terms of search. In order to fulfill these goals, the interface must be adaptive, anticipate the needs of the user, proactive and able to explain its actions.

We can also think of search engines like Google or Yahoo as intelligent interfaces. In fact, they often do successful searches although we misspell the search terms, or suggest similar words or concepts in order to make our search more accurate. Intelligent Interfaces also filter the information, deciding which is closer to what the user is looking for and which is useless. In order to do this, context information is taken into account (e.g. legal domain, past experiences, domain of expertise of the practitioner). One particular case of application of Intelligent Interfaces in the legal domain is the one of the intelligent tutors, aimed at teaching or training its users in a given area. Two examples of this are LITES, an intelligent tutoring system for legal problem solving in the domain of Dutch Civil Law (Span 1993) and the intelligent tutoring system for teaching law students to argue with cases described by Ashley and Aleven (1991).

4.2.5   Case-Based Reasoning

Case-based Reasoning (CBR) can be described as a problem solving methodology that relies on past experiences and its data to make present choices (Kolodner 1992; Aamodt and Plaza 1994). The key assumption is that if a new problem is similar to an old one, it will have a similar outcome. This procedure is commonly observed in humans and is intrinsically related with our learning processes. As an example, let us consider that some time ago, an individual left home, with a cloudy sky, and the clouds turn into rain, and he/she got wet. A few days later, before leaving the house, the same individual looks at the sky and, as it is cloudy, takes an umbrella with him/her. In general, this process involves the ability to compare two scenarios (or cases) and admit that if they are similar, they will have an identical outcome.

Consequently, the first task is to select among all the singularities that describe a case, which are the ones that are useful to determine the similarity between two cases. In many cases, it is computationally impossible or inefficient to deal with all the attributes considered in the universe of discourse and their range of possible values. Continuing with the previous example, the individual could take the decision of taking or not taking an umbrella based on different factors: the day of the weak, the weather forecast, the current weather conditions, the clothes wore and/or the distance to the local of destination. While some of these factors may make sense (e.g. the current weather conditions, the weather forecast) considering the nature of the problem, others are completely irrelevant. The first challenge is therefore to select which attributes to consider, according to the domain of the problem.

It is also essential to enquire the relative significance of each of the problem's attributes. In our previous example, it makes sense to consider both the current weather conditions and the weather forecast. However, a different weight might be given to the weather forecast attribute if the individual is more worried about the evolution of the weather conditions and not so much concerning the immediate ones. This factor may however be different, depending, for example, on the amount of time that the individual will be outside or the confidence on the weather forecast.

Generally, a CBR process is organized in four sequential phases: Retrieve, Reuse, Revise and Retain (Kolodner 1993). In the first phase, the problem is analyzed and the cases that are relevant (i.e. similar enough) are retrieved from the memory, and ordered according to a value of similarity. This measure of similarity depends on the problem domain, but generally is related to the difference of the sums of the different attributes that characterize the cases. In the Reuse phase, the solution from the previous case is mapped to the target problem, which may involve adapting the solution to some specific requirement of the new problem. This phase is necessary since, in general, there is no case in the case memory that exactly matches the attributes of the new one. In theory, it would be possible to generate as many cases as needed to cover all the different attributes. However, the size of such a case base would be impracticable. There is, hence, an implicit compromise between the amount of cases stored and the values of similarity achieved. In the third phase, the solution is tested or simulated in an attempt to determine the result of its application. It may be possible that the results are not as good as expected, which should lead to the revision of the actions taken. In the last phase, the solution adopted may be stored in the case memory, along with the description of the new case, contributing to the enrichment of the case memory.

CBR is obviously suitable to be used in the legal domain, given that the ability to predict or estimate an outcome is an important component of legal advice. A legal practitioner frequently examines past similar cases and their outcomes to try to predict the outcome of a new one. There is even a similar legal concept, i.e., the legal precedent (Landes and Posner 1976). The notion of legal precedence defines a case that establishes a rule or principle that could or should be used by practitioners when deciding on subsequent similar cases.

CBR models are, in principle, particularly useful in common law systems. Nevertheless, civil law systems (in which The Law is written by a legislature's enactment (Zweigert and Kötz 1998)) can also be approached from a case-based perspective, namely through the development of systems that target the retrieval of information with the objective of informing the users instead of producing outcomes. Considering this topic, Ashley poses the question: *"should researchers in a civil law jurisdiction pursue work on implementing AI & The Law models of case-based legal reasoning in a civil law context?"* He answers with a conclusive *"the answer may well be, "Yes"!"* (Ashley 2004).

Although still being object of research, CBR is already one of the most commonly used approaches in the development of intelligent and learning systems, for the most varied purposes. (Watson 1997) gives some examples of big enterprises like air and fraud management companies where the use of CBR is long established. Likewise, the legal field has some implementations of CBR that address specific problems. HYPO models the way attorneys argue when confronted with a case, real or hypothetical (Ashley and Aleven 1991). CATO is an intelligent learning environment, designed to help Law students learn the basic skills of argument building when dealing with a case (Aleven and Ashley 1997). More recently, (Brüninghaus and Ashley 2006) presented the Issue-Based Prediction (IBP) algorithm that combines a logical representation of subjects or matters with a CBR component for predicting and explaining the case outcomes.

4.2.6 Multi-agent Systems

Multi-agent Systems (MAS) (Wooldridge 2002) emerged from the combination of Artificial Intelligence based methodologies and techniques for problem solving with distributed computational models, generating a new area of research: Distributed Artificial Intelligence. Many different definitions for MAS have been already proposed. This chapter attempts a definition from the point of view of conflict resolution. A MAS is a group of entities (software or hardware) that make intelligent decisions in order to achieve some common goal (like proposing a solution for the parties in dispute) based on information that is shared among every agent in the system. Parunak (1997) proposes a detailed definition, based on the presupposition that a MAS is not only defined by the agents or their properties but by a triple: a set of agents, an environment and a pairing between them. One must agree with Parunak since an agent is genuinely associated with the environment, as its actions depend also on its state. As an analogy, we humans commonly look to ourselves in function of our social or geographical context, i.e., our environment and our social relationships make us who we are.

Agents materialize an appealing computational tool as they allow for a wide range of behaviors and/or functionalities to be analyzed, specified and/or implemented. In particular, there is a set of assets proposed by Wooldridge and Jennings (1995) that constitute what the authors denote as the weak notion of agent: autonomy, social ability, reactivity and pro-activeness. This vision entails that the most basic agent should, at least, operate without the direct intervention of humans and formulate its own decisions in an autonomous way; be able to interact with other agents (independently of their nature); perceive the environment and respond on time to the stimuli and; take the initiative of pursuing its goals. The same authors also proposed a stronger notion of agent that may include properties such as mobility, veracity, benevolence or rationality. This means that additionally, an agent may move between locations by means of a network, will not give false information purposely and will act in order to achieve its goals.

The main objective of the present approach is to address the complexity of intelligent behavior intra and inter communities of simple entities or agents, i.e., agents must be able to autonomously make their undemanding assessments that, once combined, may lead the communities of agents to evidence intelligent behaviors. This approach has nowadays a major role in the design of intelligent systems. Especially interesting for the legal domain is the research on argumentation theory.

In argumentation, agents debate, defend their beliefs and try to convince their peers of the rationality of their causes (Rahwan and Simari 2009). There is here an evident parallelism with the argumentation procedures that take place during dispute resolution processes. Agents may also implement negotiation techniques (Beehr et al. 1999).

In the context of MAS, negotiation refers to the modeling of human conciliation techniques so that they can be used for solving conflicts between agents. The main field of application of this modus operandi is in conflicts that arise from auctions and e-Commerce. In this specific sub-field of dispute resolution, agents may represent the parties in a negotiated settlement and try by themselves to get to an end, then suggesting it to the parts in dispute. An important analogy may also be done with negotiation procedures that take place in the legal arena, between parties that are trying to achieve a common agreement.

A different kind of added value that comes with the use of MAS, from which the legal domain may profit, is distributed problem solving. Significant virtues in the legal domain (e.g. veracity, benevolence) can also be instilled into agents, namely in the so-called emotion-based ones (Velasquez 1997). In the legal field, this kind of work may lead to the implementation of the second generation of ODR systems, with the ability to understand the feelings of the parties according to each topic of the dispute.

4.2.7   Legal Ontologies

In philosophy, ontology is the study of the nature of existence in general, i.e., ontology deals with the questions that concern the definition of a given entity, its existence, and how that entity relates to others. In computer science, ontologies are a way of formally representing knowledge in terms of concepts within a domain and the relationships between those concepts. According to Gruber (1993), ontology is a *"formal, explicit specification of a shared conceptualization"*. In order for the ontology to be understood, a shared vocabulary must be provided. This vocabulary must contain all the concepts that can be used to model the universe of discourse, i.e., the ontology must define the type of each concept as well as their properties and relations. Therefore, in ontology specification, one defines classes and subclasses of individuals as well as the properties of each individual in a class or subclass. If on top of that relationships between individuals are defined, it will be possible to infer properties, namely by inheritance.

In computer science, ontologies are nowadays paramount, mainly because they are the enablers of the so-called Semantic Web (Berners-Lee et al. 2001). The Semantic Web describes a group of methods and technologies that allow machines to understand the meaning of information on the Web, rather than simply accessing it. This is indeed the main innovation that ontologies brought along, i.e., allow machines to read, interpret and understand information. Logically, such technologies can also be used in different arenas, ranging from software engineering, biomedical informatics, library science, and information architecture.

Indeed, for complex domains such as the legal one, the advantages are considerable. For instance, by systematizing knowledge, it becomes readily available. It allows not only the extraction of rich patterns of information that otherwise would not be perceptible, but also to draw inferences. Indeed, computer models that can efficiently deal with large amounts of structured information are being object of research. Corcho et al. (2005), for example, present a methodology to build an ontology in the legal domain, following the development method METHONTOLOGY, and using the ontology engineering workbench WebODE; Visser and Bench-Capon (1998) present, compare and critique four different legal ontologies. For more interesting examples on legal ontologies, the book "Law and the Semantic Web" provides a selection of revised papers drawn from two meetings devoted to the Semantic Web and the legal domain: The International Workshop on Legal Ontologies and Web-Based Legal Information Management (Benjamins et al. 2005).

4.2.8   Rule-Based Systems

Rule-based Systems (RbS) provide, in general, the straightest way of implementing a system's intelligent behavior, i.e., they constitute the simplest form of building Artificial Intelligent based systems. Using an RbS, it is possible to encode the knowledge and skill of a human expert in a given domain in the form of IF-THEN rules, in which each rule denotes a small piece of the expert's knowledge. Rules have a left and a right hand side. On the left side there is information about facts that must be true in order for the rule to be enforced. On the right hand side, the rule contains the actions that should be carried out whenever the rule is fired. The model of execution of an RbS consists, therefore, in analyzing, on the fly, the left hand side of all rules. The rules whose left hand side is evaluated to true are placed on an execution agenda. Then, rules in the agenda will be executed, without any explicit order, and afterwards removed from the agenda. One singularity of RbS, contrasting with standard object-oriented programming, is that there is not an effecting order that can be predicted beforehand.

Thus, RbS are a way to store, interpret and manipulate knowledge about a given domain. In fact, if appropriate design strategies are followed, these systems allow for an easy access to expert knowledge. Specific rules must be changed when knowledge about the domain changes. However, this can be made simpler and safer if a proper and perceptive rule editor is made available.

If we consider specifically the legal domain, a parallel can be established between the legal corpus and other legal conceptions that may be expressed as RbS. The most obvious one is that when capturing the expertise of an expert in a given field, that expertise will become available to all. However, when representing legal rules in an RbS, some issues must be kept in mind in order to avoid some possible problems. Indeed, if one tries to encode considerable amounts of knowledge into a single RbS, the system may become inefficient, once it must search through a very large number of rules. Another possible disadvantage is that rules may not exactly implement the reasoning process used by an expert as no specific execution sequence can be dictated. Last but not the least, one must also consider the open textured nature of The Law and reasoning mechanisms being used (Popple 1991). In fact, when a judge decides on verdicts, he/she does not look only at the rules that apply in that situation. There is more information that influences the outcome, such as recurrence or intention of the defendant, information that is hard to model in such systems.

Nevertheless, RbS are broadly used in many different fields, namely in insurance companies, banks, fraud detection, e-commerce and evidently in The Law. In conclusion, these systems implement a fairly simple and efficient way of modeling knowledge and expertise of a human practitioner in a well-defined field. Such systems can be particularly useful in the legal domain, once this field is rule-based by nature, i.e., legal practitioners are usually comfortable about using such systems as they reflect their way of reasoning.

4.2.9   Evolutionary Computation

Evolutionary computation encompasses techniques that involve continuous optimization of solutions towards a global optimization of the system (De Jong 2006). Mostly, evolutionary computation is used in problems for which no derivatives are known. As the name hints, this field mimics the natural evolutionary processes that occur in nature, first pointed out by Charles Darwin (1998). Darwin's theory stated that populations evolve over the course of generations through a process of natural selection in which the fittest individuals will prevail over the less fit ones, leaving a larger and stronger number of descendants. Evolutionary computation, in itself, encompasses several different techniques. Particularly interesting in the legal domain are evolutionary algorithms, and in particular the genetic algorithms (Banzhaf et al. 1998).

Genetic Algorithms (GAs) denote a heuristic search that mimics the process of natural evolution, continuously optimizing solutions for a given problem (Banzhaf et al. 1998). GAs are usually organized in four phases, starting with the creation of random solutions for the problem, in the Initialization phase. Each of these solutions can be seen as an individual of the species. At this moment of creation, some of these solutions may already be "good enough" to solve the problem. However, this is unlikely. Generally, after this phase, an iterative process starts in which the population of solutions is improved. This process will end after a given number of generations are reached or when one or a group of solutions reaches a minimum level of fitness. In each iteration the fitness of the solutions are evaluated in order to check for the termination condition. If the condition is not satisfied, a selection of the individuals to reproduce is made.

In the selection phase, a part of the population of solutions is conveyed to give birth to the new generation of solutions. Different criteria may be used to perform the selection. However, generally, fitness-based processes are used in which the fitter solutions are more likely to be selected. Alternatively, a random group of individuals may also be selected, since evaluating the fitness of every single individual may turn into a time-consuming process. The fitness function is central in this process, i.e., it determines how good a given solution is to solve a problem. In that sense, it is problem-dependent.

Once the best individuals are selected, the genetic operators are applied, in the so-called reproduction phase. These operators will give birth to the following generation of solutions, with an expected higher fitness. The three most common operators are crossover, mutation and inheritance. The crossover operator takes two parents and produces two new offspring with some of the characteristics of the parents swapped. The mutation operator takes one parent and randomly changes some of his characteristics, thus generating a new offspring. Finally, the inheritance operator simply maintains the characteristics of the parent in the new offspring.

One of the challenges is thus to find a balance on the weight of each of these operators. Indeed, the objective of mutation is to induce novelty, to open the search space. However, if mutation is excessively used the search will hardly converge to better solutions, being lost in the search in each iteration. Similarly, if in an attempt to keep all the best solutions found so far inheritance is overused, the algorithm will converge at a slower pace or stall. This process of selection and reproduction will repeat until the termination condition is reached.

Evolutionary algorithms have currently a broad range of applications in fields such as image and signal processing systems, control, telecommunications, scheduling and timetabling, robotics or aeronautics (Cagnoni et al. 2000). Evolutionary algorithms have also been successfully used in the legal domain, with different objectives, ranging from the creation of models of ontological evolution in legal reasoning (that shape the process of change that happens to a theory as it is used by agents within a particular domain) (Priddle-Higson 2010) to the automatic extraction of specific domain knowledge (Jelasity 2000). In Chap. 8, an approach for the generation of solutions for a dispute based on GAs is detailed.

4.3   Projects on the Intersection of AI and the Law

Given that the relationship between classical AI techniques and The Law is already a long-established one, a significant number of projects and research efforts can be found in this intersection. In this section several projects are briefly described that show different ways in which classical AI methods can improve conflict resolution processes.

4.3.1   Rule-Based Legal Decision-Making Systems (LDS)

This work dates from the 1980s and was one of the first decision support systems to be developed (Waterman and Peterson 1980) in the domain of liability law, which holds responsible product distributors and manufacturers for the injuries their products may cause. The system embodied the skills and knowledge of a human expert, in the form of antecedent-consequent rules. The project had as objective the shaping of the decision-making processes of attorneys and claim adjusters involved in product liability litigation in the form of a rule-based system, so that the effects that changes in legal doctrine have in settlement strategies and practices could be studied. The authors formalized the strict-liability concept on ROSIE language, so that the defendant could or could not be considered liable.

The knowledge embodied in the system was divided into five different layers, i.e., the *formal doctrine* given in terms of rules that emerge from the legally responsible and common law; the *informal principles* depicted in terms of rules that are not explicitly expressed in The Law, but are generally agreed upon by legal practitioners; the *strategies* where the authors coded the methods used by legal practitioners to accomplish a given goal; the *subjective considerations* set in terms of rules that anticipate the subjective responses of people involved in the process; and the *secondary effects* layer set in terms of meta-rules that describe the rules interactions at the object level. The authors concluded that, despite the number of rules needed for giving shape to a specific domain and to the strategies used, the rule-based model was feasible and suited for this particular legal domain.

4.3.2   EXPERTIUS

EXPERTIUS is a decision-support system that advices Mexican judges and clerks upon the determination of whether the plaintiff is or not eligible for granting him/her a pension (on the basis of the "feeding obligation"), and if so upon the determination of the amount of that pension (Cáceres 2008). The system comprises three main modules, namely the tutorial, inferential, and financial. The tutorial module guides the user through the accomplishment of a significant amount of tasks. The inferential module evaluates a distribution based on weights that the user assigns to each piece of evidence. It determines which presuppositions are defeated and which prevail. Finally, the financial module assists the user on the calculus of the pension values.

Expert knowledge is stated in terms of three interrelated layers: a first one that stands for the expert knowledge; a second that denotes the decisions regulated by the law procedures; and a third one that keeps up a correspondence between the dialogues written as conversation and measured in terms of a confrontation pattern, and the cases that arise as a result of the decisions taken at the intermediate level.

4.3.3   SmartSettle

Thiessen's SmartSettle constitutes a decision support system that aims to find the middle ground among parties to settle disputes based on satisfaction functions acknowledged by them. Initially the parties declare their tenure to each item under dispute, either using mathematical artifacts and/or by sketching it. The assigned preferences are, however, not static as they may change during the negotiation process, resembling the adjustment of the first choices made by the parties. Besides assigning their preferences, parties must decide on what would be a constructive outcome for each one and try to merge it on a single text. During the negotiation process parties may simply exchange messages or they can rely on SmartSettle to produce suggestions according to the current state of the case, which the parties may or may not accept. When the parties reach an impasse, they may ask SmartSettle for an equal distribution of the items in dispute. It is important in this phase that the preferences are well defined since the allocation of items depends on that. A final document is then produced. All this process is supported by a web site on which the parties log in, access their personal data and perform all the actions related with the negotiation process. SmartSettle is based on the doctoral thesis of Ernest Thiessen (1993). This work resulted in a commercial ODR, whose president & CEO is Thiessen himself.

4.3.4 Family_Winner

The Family_Winner project is the result of a research effort by Zeleznikow and Bellucci and provides support on the Australian family law domain (Bellucci and Zeleznikow 2001). In order to attain this goal, the system uses game theory and heuristics (Zeleznikow and Bellucci 2003, 2004), relying on an algorithm that is an adapted version of the AdjustedWinner (Brams and Taylor 2000) one. Similarly to SmartSettle, parties must provide as input to the system their tenure to each item under dispute, a value that denotes how much they want each specific item under dispute. According to these values the system tries to assign the items to the parties, having in mind that each allocated matter may change the preferences of the parties on the other issues.

Once this is done, the parties are asked whether they agree with the distribution; if the answer is no, the system embarks on a negotiation item-by-item, starting with the item considered less controversial. This process of decomposition and division goes on until there are no more items under dispute.

4.3.5 ALIS

The Automated Legal Intelligent System (ALIS) stands for a decision support system that will provide European citizens and private companies with a transparent, fast, secure and reliable access to legal data in the field of intellectual property rights. The motivation of this project lies in the fact that the daily observation of legal systems in democratic countries or supranational institutions reveals severe problems of understanding, application and adhesion. There are different reasons for this. Firstly, there is a considerable increase in the number of laws and regulations that make it more difficult to comply with the applicable legal and regulatory framework. This complexity often generates repetitions, lacks, and contradictions within the system itself. Furthermore, legal professionals may be overwhelmed by simple cases requiring time and effort that could be better allocated to solve more complex issues that may not be dealt with only by technology. The ALIS system aims at solving these problems by providing tools for regulatory compliance, alternative dispute resolution, conflict prevention, support in law making and scientific and technologic developments.

4.3.6 PERSUADER

PERSUADER (Sycara 1993) is a framework for intelligent computer-supported conflict resolution through negotiation/mediation. The model integrates Artificial Intelligence and decision based techniques to provide enhanced conflict resolution and negotiation support in group problem solving settings. This model has been implemented in the PERSUADER, a computer program that operates in the domain of labor management disputes. The main objective of PERSUADER is to act as a mediator, facilitating the disputants' problem solving so that a mutually agreed upon settlement can be achieved. The PERSUADER embodies a general negotiation model that handles multi-agent, multi-issue, singe or repeated encounters based on an integration of Case-Base Reasoning and Multi-Attribute Utility Theory.

4.4 New Fields, New Possibilities

So far in this chapter, several classical sub-fields of AI have been analyzed. In this section, a more recent and innovative one is object of attention, the one of Ambient Intelligence (AmI). AmI is the vision of a technology that will become invisibly embedded in our natural surroundings, present whenever we need it, enabled by simple and effortless interactions, attuned to all our senses, adaptive to users, context-sensitive and autonomous (Weber et al. 2005).

AmI is a relatively new paradigm, supported by new technologies, namely Ubiquitous Computing (Weiser et al. 1999); Ubiquitous Communication (Vasilakos and Pedrycz 2006); and Intelligent User Interfaces (Riva et al. 2005).

Ubiquitous Computing refers to a model of human-computer interaction in which information processing is integrated into everyday objects and activities rather than on one single physically visible device. It is a post-desktop model in which the device is no longer the centerpiece of the interaction but cedes that position to the user, who is now placed in the center of the process. The user is now surrounded by technology that enters into his own environment rather than having him entering into the technology's one.

Alongside, Ubiquitous Communication encompasses methods for seamless communication between agents. This new paradigm of communication overcomes barriers such as location or technological differences to achieve a communication environment in which all sorts of devices are able to exchange information in an efficient manner.

Finally, Intelligent User Interfaces encompass new forms of interaction in which the computer-side has a strong knowledge about the domain as well as a model of the user. This allows the device to potentially understand the user's needs in order to optimize the interaction. Interaction with these interfaces may occur with modalities that may provide additional information about the user, namely speech or gesture recognition.

The integration of these technologies gives birth to a new AI paradigm, one in which intelligence does not lie on a highly complex algorithm running on a computer but on the constant interaction of a large number of entities, embedded seamlessly in the environment. AmI thus describes systems that are:

- Embedded – computational power no longer resides solely in large devices, with defined physical locations. It also exists in small and potentially mobile devices as well as on regular objects and appliances of the environment;
- Context-aware – the environment is able to recognize the users as well as their situational context;
- Personalized – the environment models each user and takes actions tailored to each user or group of users;
- Adaptive – the environment changes autonomously in response to changes in the users behaviours or in their environment, in a continuous attempt to improve itself; and
- Anticipatory – the environment is able to anticipate events or states of the environment, being therefore able to act accordingly.

AmI is changing the way we look at and interact with computers. This change represents, in fact, the time where computers will work on behalf of their users, instead of having their users working with them. Until now, computers have been a mere tool, doing the tasks we program them to do, when they are commanded to do so. Nothing distinguishes them from any other tool, except maybe for the fact that computers may be programmed to do a wide range of tasks.

The novelty in AmI lies in the vision of a tool that ideally does what users expect, when they expect it, the way they want, without them having to explicitly command it. Moreover, users may even not be aware that they wanted to have a particular action performed. This is the shift that is happening right now with AmI. Computers, in intelligent environments, are no longer mere tools at our disposal, but tools that learn our preferences and habits, so that they can autonomously act on our behalf. Moreover, they are getting smaller and hiding in common devices so that they pass unnoticeable at our eyes.

Physically, an intelligent environment is composed of the ambient itself (e.g. a house, a single room, a car, a school, an office) and the devices in it. These devices are common devices such as smartphones, air conditioning systems, laptops or desktops, media servers, micro-waves or a Hi-Fi system. The novelty is that these devices are all connected through a control network so that they can be controlled or control other devices from any point of the network. However, this, by itself, would only be what is nowadays known as domotics: the remote control of appliances with the objective of providing security and comfort to the users of the environment. AmI goes much further than interconnecting and providing control over a group of devices.

The key difference stems from the autonomy and the personalization of the environment. Indeed, on the one hand, AmI comprehends systems that not only provide the possibility to control devices but that actively exert that control, i.e., AmI systems have the autonomy to take decisions and act on the environment, potentially without the user's acknowledgment. On the other hand these actions must also be personalized, tailored and targeted to their users.

Indeed, the objective of an intelligent environment is, above all, to ensure the user's well-being and safety. Such environments must know the needs and the preferences of the users (Rocha et al. 2003). This information can be provided manually, when configuring the system. However, ideally, information such as routines or preferences should be learned as users do their day-to-day. Several methods can be used to infer many different types of information from the user's routines, ranging from movement patterns to preferences regarding environmental temperature or luminosity (Aztiria et al. 2010).

This is in fact one of the most interesting features of AmI, it learns from the sheer interaction with the user. Without the need for explicit and conscious actions, the system is studying the users' behaviors, learning what they use to do and when they use to do it. This feature is also at the basis of the main characteristics of AmI: personalized, dynamic, and anticipatory. AmI systems are personalized once they learn how the user behaves and what he expects from the environment (Rubel et al. 2004). In that sense, even similar systems in the beginning will evolve differently when being used by different users. AmI systems are also dynamic, once when user preferences change, the system will feel the change and will modify its rules accordingly (Bick and Kummer 2008). Finally, learning user's preferences or models of behavior allows an AmI system to start taking anticipatory actions. It is evidently interesting to model users so that when an action must be taken, that action resembles one that might have been taken by the user.

However, it results even more interesting to try and guess a future state (of the environment or of the user) to take actions accordingly in order to prevent or, if desirable, to strengthen the possibility of that state to come into place. A simple nonetheless useful example may be the one of a user that every day executes the following sequence of actions: get out of bed, move to the bathroom, move to the kitchen, turn on the coffee machine. After a few reiterations of this pattern, the system may decide to turn on the coffee machine in advance, so that the user does not have to wait for his coffee.

In order to ensure the accuracy of this learning process, an issue must be considered: the one of context-awareness. In this scope, context may range from the geographical or economical context to the historic or social one. Context helps understand the user's actions. Still considering the same example, the user may only have the aforementioned routine on weekdays. On weekends, the user might wake up later and after moving out of the bathroom, go out through the front door to a walk instead of having coffee in the kitchen. It is the context-aware nature of AmI systems that allow them to better decide on which actions to take, based not only on the user's routine or preferences but also on issues such as the current date, the weather conditions, the persons around the user and even the users' emotional or arousal states (Acampora et al. 2005).

To sum up, AmI can be defined as *"a digital environment that proactively, but sensibly, supports people in their daily lives"* (Augusto and McCullagh 2007). Sensibility comes from intelligence, much like in real life (e.g. a trained doctor may identify better than others the patient's symptoms and provide better care and even anticipate probable future scenarios). This process is improved if the doctor knows the patient's health record or their special limitations and/or needs.

Nevertheless, no AmI solution has been developed so far specifically for the legal domain. Indeed, the advantages of such a system could be significant and improve many aspects of current conflict resolution processes, namely the ones undertaken online. Further on in this book, specific features already implemented that contribute to the development of such an environment will be detailed.

4.4.1 Sense, Reason, Act

The IST Advisory Group organizes the enabling technologies of AmI in well-defined groups, namely sensing, reasoning, and acting technologies (Friedwald and Costa 2003). Indeed the lifecycle of an AmI system may be seen as a continuous repetition of sensing and perceiving the environment and its users, undertaking some reasoning procedure and acting on the environment with the objective of improving it in some way.

Sensing technologies provide the data on which every reasoning process is based. Many different types of sensors exist and are interesting from the point of view of an AmI system. These can be organized according to their target, i.e., they either sense the user and his activities or the environment. A non-exhaustive list of types of information that are interesting in an AmI context are depicted below, together with the respective sensors.

- User tracking – User tracking is one of the key issues in an AmI system. More interesting still is the identification of the user being tracked, allowing to know exactly who is where. Keeping a record of the user's locations allows understanding the activities or routines being accomplished (Storf et al. 2009). Many sensors and combinations of sensors have been used for user identification and tracking, including GPS, RFID, motion sensors, smartphones with Bluetooth, wearable tags with radio identifiers or analysis of interactions with known devices. Tracking can take place at a more specific level, with the analysis of the exact body position of the user or the activity being completed (Stikic et al. 2008). This is usually implemented with the use of accelerometers or with the adding of sensors to objects such as pressure pads on beds or chairs;

- Behavioural analysis – Understanding the behaviour of the user allows an AmI system to infer his state, i.e., given behaviours (e.g. low level of physical activity) are associated with given states (e.g. depression). The behaviour of the user can be estimated from sensors such as video cameras that allow analysing user's movement patterns and other behavioural cues. Such information can also be inferred from the interaction patterns of the user with the devices and appliances in the home;

- User state – The state of the user, encompassing emotional aspects as well as physical, is fundamental in an AmI system, given that user's comfort and security are central. For this purpose many different sensors can be used, especially physiological ones such as Galvanic Skin Response (that measures the level of skin perspiration, associated to stress), hearth rate, respiratory rate, and even more invasive ones such as Electrocardiography or Electrocardio-grams; and

- Environmental state – The state of the environment is directly linked to issues such as user's comfort, safety or productivity. In that sense, such knowledge is very valuable. The state of the environment can be evaluated from many different sources. Available sensors may provide information about the level of humidity, temperature, luminosity, noise, oxygen, magnetic field, among others.

The continuous sensing of the environment and of the user provides a flow of information that is also continuously analyzed by the reasoning module. In order for a reasoning process to be carried out, the first task is to convert the incoming data into explicit user and environment states as well as user activities. In order to act intelligently, the AmI system also needs to know the plan or objective of the user for the moment (Hein and Kirste 2008). Both tasks are generally performed through classification or other machine learning algorithms (Aztiria et al. 2010). This constant monitoring of the users' activities results in a growing knowledge about their daily life. The system can then use this knowledge to take increasingly optimized decisions, i.e., the longer the system monitors the user, the better it knows him.

Every decision taken by the environment leads to the third phase of the repeating lifecycle: the acting on the environment. From a high-level point of view, the system can act on the environment in two different ways, i.e., through the use of actuators embedded on the devices or through notifications issued to specific users. The first approach refers to behaviors such as the automatic control of curtains or window blinds, of the heating or of the lights (Friedewald et al. 2005). The second approach involves acting at the user-level through notification that may be presented in several ways, ranging from sound notifications or messages in natural language to user-friendly multimodal interfaces (Kleinberger et al. 2007). Either way, it is through these mechanisms that the AmI system actually materializes its actions and enforces its decisions, making the effects visible on the user and on the environment, restarting the cycle all over again.

4.4.2 AmI Projects

Several AmI systems are already in advanced stages of development. This section presents a few different projects that allow understanding the wide range of possibilities enabled by these technologies as well as the broad spectrum of application.

Amigo – Ambient Intelligence for the Networked Home Environment

This project was a consortium of 15 European companies who joined efforts to exploit the potential of the nowadays common home networks and improve people's lives. The idea was to take profit of the fact that currently almost all equipment comes with a network connection.

It is also common for an environment to have several networks such as the electrical, Ethernet or Wi-Fi. The Amigo project interconnects these networks, thus enabling communication between devices on different networks. Over this hardware layer, Amigo implements services so that people's environments are empowered. From any point of the house or even from outside the house, users can change house parameters, watch the surveillance cameras or set their TV to record an event. This is in fact one of the purposes of the project: to empower the environment of the user, releasing them from boring, undesired or unnecessary activities. This project used 'home laboratories' across Europe including Philips Research's 'HomeLab', France Telecom's 'Creative Studio Lab' and the Fraunhofer Institute's 'InHaus'.

ReachMedia

This project from MIT (Feldman et al. 2005) resulted in a prototype of an RFID equipped wristband to provide its users with on-the-move interaction with everyday objects. Usually, there is a significant amount of information related to the objects we deal with every day, mainly on the Internet. However, it is generally only accessible through a computer. This project aims to present their users with that information wherever they are, in real time, without driving the users' attention from what they are doing.

The wristband contains an RFID reader that reads the information from RFID tags in objects close to the hands of the user. Then, information is fetched from the Internet and presented to the user in some interface. At this moment a phone is being used to obtain the information and the user listens to what is found. A scenario of use would be a client of a bookstore grabbing some book for which he/she needs some information. When the client's hand approaches the book's RFID tag, the system beeps notifying him/her that some services are available for that specific object. For an object of the type book, there can be reviews or ratings available. The client can then choose, while flipping through the book's pages, what he/she wants to listen about that book.

The navigation is also done using the wristband. As it is equipped with accelerometers, with small gestures of the wrist, the user can navigate through the several options for the object of interest and select what to listen to. The uses for such a technology are wide. When meeting people with the same wrist, one could know what their interests are, their hobbies or what their personality is like. When shopping, one could know the characteristics of every product grabbed (e.g. the calories of alimentary products) while still walking and looking at other products instead of having to stop and read the product specification.

Telecare

The objective of the Telecare (Camarinha-Matos and Afsarmanesh 2001) project is to develop a configurable framework for assisting elder people, based on the integration of a multi-agent and a federated information management approach. The result is a group of services likely to be offered by the emerging ubiquitous computing and intelligent home appliances, which are useful for elderly people. With this approach, the project expects to address issues like elderly people being moved from their homes, providing them with autonomy and independence. To achieve these objectives, this project is based on tele-supervision and tele-assistance technologies. A virtual network is created, which connects the elderly home, the relative's office, the care or leisure centers, a virtual shop, among others. It is through this virtual community that the elderly makes use of the services. The project states that it is possible nowadays to create such a network that can provide inexpensive health care to elderly, namely thanks to the current development of internet-based infrastructures. The development of such projects is one important step towards countering the problems of ageing population and possible elderly marginalization.

PokerMetrics

PokerMetrics – Stress and Lie Detection through Non-Invasive Physiological Sensing is a project developed by MIT Media Laboratory. In this study, researchers show how simple non-invasive psychological features such as voice pitch variation, skin conductance peaks, and heart rate variability are correlated to various stressful events in Hold'em Poker tournaments. With these collected features, researchers developed simple linear models that may be used to identify stress, lies or bluffs within the context of a poker game (Sung and Pentland 2005).

MIT Project Oxygen

Project Oxygen is another research effort of MIT's Computer Science and Artificial Intelligence Laboratory. Its purpose is to develop pervasive, human-centered computing. Its architecture consists of handheld terminals, computers embedded in the environment, and dynamically configured networks which connect these devices (Rudolph 2001).

The Oxygen team describes the purpose of this project as "Bringing abundant computation and communication, as pervasive and free as air, naturally into people's lives". Since the emergence of computers, people have been required to learn how to interact with computer using their language, manipulating keyboard and mouse. This project tries to make computation human-centered. Instead of forcing users to use a computer's language, in the future, computers will be human-centered. Instead of the need to carry devices, configurable generic devices will bring computation to people whenever and wherever they might need it. As people interact with anonymous devices, they will adopt peoples' information profiles, and respect peoples' desires for privacy and security.

Computers will be available everywhere, handling peoples' goals and needs, helping humans to do more and better. The purpose of this project is that, in the future, people will interact with computers naturally, using speech and gestures to communicate their intent. They will be able to automate repetitive tasks, find information for their users without them needing to examine lines of search-engines hits, and they will enable people to work together with other people over space and time.

To support highly dynamic and varied human activities, the Oxygen system must overcome significant technical challenges. According to the authors, this system must be:

- Pervasive: it must be everywhere, with a sharing of information between all devices;
- Embedded: it must be present in peoples' world, sensing and affecting it;
- Nomadic: it must allow people to move around freely according to their needs;
- Adaptable: it must provide flexibility and spontaneity, in response to changes in user requirements and operating conditions;
- Powerful, yet efficient: it must be free from constraints imposed by hardware resources;
- Intentional: it must allow people to name services by intent, for example "the nearest TV", as opposed to by address; and

- Eternal: it must never shutdown or reboot; components may come and go, but the whole system must be available all the time.

Oxygen, through a combination of specific user and system technologies, enables pervasive, human-centered computing. Speech and vision technologies enable people to communicate with Oxygen as if they were communicating with other people, saving both time and effort.

I.L.S.A. – The Independent Lifestyle Assistant

This is an initiative from the University of Minnesota, in terms of an agent-based monitoring and support system to help elderly people live longer in their homes, by reducing caregiver weight (Haigh et al. 2006). This project has as its main objective to study the response of elderly to a monitoring computer system inside their houses and determine how such systems can help this group of people.

The researchers not only determined the main problems of elder people living unaccompanied, but also performed experiments with parts of the monitoring system in some houses in real settings.

This system is a multi-agent one that incorporates a unified sensing model, situation assessment, response planning, real-time response and machine learning.

A group of sensors was placed in each house according to what was being monitored. When information was acquired, it was sent to a central that analyzed it. (e.g. if an individual does not take the medication or if their behavior is unusual, alerts are emitted).

The main features of the system included passive monitoring, cognitive support, alerts and notifications, reports and controlling remote access to information. Clients had a portable device from where they could check their agenda, change some parameters and communicate with their caregivers.

4.4.3 Intelligent Environment for Conflict Resolution: A Scenario

As seen previously, different AmI systems and projects have already been developed, supporting their users in many different aspects. However, no AmI system for the legal domain has been developed so far. Here it is presented a fictional scenario that highlights the potential advantages of the use of such technology in the domain of conflict resolution. Some of the ideas presented in this scenario are already becoming reality and will be described in detail further ahead in this book.

John has a conflict with Carl, who is in a different country. They agreed to begin a conflict resolution process conducted online by a mediator who is also located somewhere else. John decides to try out one of the novel conflict resolution environments which supposedly provide support and empower the parties.

He gets inside the environment where the computer he is going to use to communicate with the remaining parties is already turned on. When John logs in, the system detects that this is the first time he is using such a system, so it provides a brief walkthrough of the functionalities. It is merely a general overview, specific support will be provided if and when the system detects that John is hesitating while doing some complex task.

The system also provides guidelines that outline the conflict resolution process in which john is engaged. A virtual assistant helps John to understand the singularities of his case, providing assistance in the definition of a strategy, in the assessment of his real possibilities to win the case and on the characterization of a few potential solutions and their utility. This gives John a more realistic view on his problem, making him feel more confident.

Simultaneously, the system constantly monitors John's behavior to search for undesirable emotional symptoms as well as signs of fatigue or stress. To achieve it the system constantly analyses John's interaction patterns, i.e., the way he moves the mouse, the way he uses the keyboard, the way John moves, blinks or stands and even the way John talks. Therefore, the system is able to find cues that point out how stressed or tired John is. The system does so to prevent John's emotions from escalating, which could lead to frustration or disappointment, ultimately driving him away from the process. One of the main aims of the system is thus to keep John satisfied with and interested in the process. Maintaining John calm and focused is also important for him to correctly think through every issue and take weighted decisions.

In order to maintain John with a positive attitude, the system is able to play music to John's liking and adequate to induce the necessary mood. With the same objective, the system is also able to change the paintings and the colors of the walls. It is also able to control the environmental parameters such as the luminosity and temperature, so that John is comfortable. Indeed, John is a very nervous person and the system is able to decrease the temperature when John starts sweating, making him feel not only more comfortable but also more confident. From time to time, mostly when John becomes too nervous or stressed, the system also advises him to make a pause and go to the lounge for a moment, to relax. All this makes John feel less stressed and more confident on and satisfied with the process.

The exploit of the environment is even more important when John is interacting with Carl. These moments constitute emotional peaks in which the wrong attitude or a misunderstanding may result in the failing of the process. Therefore, the AmI system constantly provides the mediator with a representation of the parties' states so that he, who is accompanying the process in real-time, may take the right decisions. Indeed, without this valuable information, the mediator would hardly know the state of the parties. If, on the other hand, the interaction was face-to-face he would be able to assess the parties' feelings, mostly through body language and other non-verbal cues.

Usually, the parties involved feel that the conflict resolution environment empowers them and allows them to be calmer and take better decisions.

4.5 The Current State of Artificial Intelligence and ODR

Having analyzed some existing research projects and commercially available ODR providers, an assessment may be done concerning the shortcomings of the current state of the art in the ODR arena. If there is a conclusion that can be drawn, it is that at the present technological developments are not being as explored as they could be. Indeed, there is a limited use of IT by legal practitioners that use it mostly for word processing, office automation, case management, and here at a rudimentary level, client and case databases, or for electronic document interchange.

Some requirements may, therefore, be pointed out. First of all, most of the existing ODR implementations rely on traditional forms for acquiring information, providing little to no assistance at all. Moreover, the visualization of information is done at a very low level, i.e., users see information in a way that is very close to how it is stored. This may be pointed out as a major disadvantage as the lack of intelligent and intuitive interfaces may represent a barrier for a wide acceptation and use of these systems. Technologies are also barely used for even the simplest forms of process automation. This automation could boost the throughput of legal institutions and practitioners by automating simple tasks that do not explicitly need human intervention. Also, very little systems use IT for knowledge management and goal achievement. The use of technologies able to handle complex models of legal information would improve information structuring and retrieval, improving the work of legal practitioners.

We conclude that IT still plays a secondary role on the ODR arena. In fact, the technologies that are more used are simply the ones required to implement traditional dispute resolution mechanisms over telecommunication systems. Consequently, current ODR systems have little to no autonomy at all and are barely automated. In a few words it can be stated that, excluding some innovative research projects, first generation ODR systems are still the rule. A research effort must thus be conducted in order to achieve the so-called second generation of ODR. The path to follow lies in the use of intelligent techniques that can enhance ODR systems with conceptions such as autonomy and proactivity.

Particularly, the use of AmI techniques could represent a breath of fresh air, opening the path to a whole new vision on the ODR field in which the notion of a conflict resolution environment becomes possible. Instead of focusing on the dispute itself, this new vision would put the disputant individuals in the center of the process, focusing on perceiving their fears, their desires, their state, allowing achieving better and more satisfactory outcomes.

4.6 Conclusion

Progress in the field of Artificial Intelligence (AI) and The Law has been slower than expected. In fact, in the excitement of the early years, it was expected that computers would soon have the skills and the computational power to take over the role of judges and attorneys. This is far from happening and, nowadays, this is not the main purpose of the work that is being pursued in this area. The main reason against sitting computers in the chairs of judges and attorneys, mainly uttered by lawyers, is that doing so is morally undesirable. However, that alone would not hold back the research being done in the area of AI and The Law; it would, at most, delay its implementation but not its development.

One of the main reasons is that computers act as simple executors of rules while the legal field requires interpretation. Let us take as example the following sentence: *"Cars may not be left in the park overnight"*. For a human interpreter it is fairly easy to conclude that this sentence refers to a parking space in which our cars cannot be left during the night. However, for a computer, many interpretational issues may take place. What is a car? Is a bus also a car? What does it mean to "leave" a car? Leave it for a few hours? Abandon it? What is a park? A parking area where to leave cars? A recreational park? And what does it mean "overnight"? From dusk to down? Is overnight defined by two specific hours?

While computers are unable to actually *interpret* norms and their framework, they will not be sufficient to make judicial systems on their own. John Searle formalized this restriction on the well-known test of the Chinese Room (Searle 1980):

> Suppose I am in a closed room and that people are passing in to me a series of cards written in Chinese, a language of which I have no knowledge; but I do possess rules for correlating one set of squiggles with another set of squiggles so that when I pass the appropriate card back out of the room it will look to a Chinese observer as if I am a genuine user of the Chinese language. But I am not; I simply do not understand Chinese; those squiggles remain just squiggles to me.

Moreover, The Law is not straightforward and may, in certain cases, even be ambiguous. The interpretation of norms frequently raises doubts among legal practitioners, potentially leading to different and clashing interpretations and, consequently, different outcomes. Thus, at a first glance, one would conclude that there is the need for a more specific and clear definition of the norms, one that would lead to unambiguous interpretations. The problem is that society and its interactions are complex, with many conflicting values and norms of conduct. This approach seems thus rather utopic. Nonetheless, let us admit that such achievement is possible, that we can define norms to the point that their interpretation is straightforward and unambiguous. It is evident that this would only be achieved by having a much larger amount of more specific norms. Would it be efficient to handle such a complex legal system? Would it be feasible to develop computer systems to handle such complexity?

Another challenge that future research in AI and The Law will face is related with the changing nature of the rules. Indeed, in civil law systems, the frequency of legislation changes is higher and higher. Moreover, as the number of cases solved by courts in common law systems increases, more and more different cases can be considered when solving a new one. Thus, another major challenge will be to deal with increasing and ever changing amount of information. From the technological point of view, for ODR systems that work in civil law domains (tendentiously rule-based), this means that whenever a legal norm changes someone will have to search the system for the rules or ontologies that implemented that norm and change them accordingly. Thus, there will be a growing effort to manage such systems and keeping them up to date without creating ambiguities. The same happens in common law domains, in which systems tend to be case-based. In these systems, the question is about whether a past case should or should not be considered after a clear trend of change in more recent cases. Here, there is also a growing effort to maintain a database of relevant information.

Somewhat against the tide, Thomas Schultz proposes an increased involvement of the government in ODR processes in order to address some of these problems and for a real take-off of these processes to happen (Schultz 2003). Indeed, the generalized thought is that the government should be kept off the internet, of which ODR is part. Self-regulation should be allowed as opposed to the imposition of norms by governments that would potentially kill internet as we know it. Shultz however thinks that the involvement of government, with its powers, could improve ODR in many ways, namely by:

- Making ODR mandatory – many parties ignore or are reluctant to use ODR systems. Defendants, especially, often do not even reply to the initial notification. Making ODR mandatory would increase its use and potentially decrease the appeal to courts;
- Accreditation – when people make the decision of starting an ODR process they must search for the appropriate provider. This may sometimes be hard as there is no central database of information that not only tells people the right choice but also that ensures people can trust such providers. A unified mechanism of accreditation, managed by the government or other recognized entity could improve this aspect;
- Online appeals – appeals after an unsuccessful ODR process take place in courtrooms. However, ODR could be given a second chance by online appeals, in a process similar to litigation but undertaken online, thus still leveraging on some of the advantages of ODR;
- Independent sources of founding – ODR providers are at the moment commercial services, generally funded by user fees or memberships. An external funding model, for example through a fund by the judicial system, could not only make ODR providers more viable but also make it more cost-efficient for the parties;
- ODR as a public service – ODR should start to be seen as a public service, equated to courtrooms, and not as a private one, as it is now. Clients see ODR services as business and this decreases their trust; and
- Enforceability – negotiation and mediation agreements are not always heeded by the parties since they are not binding. This sometimes gives the feeling of ODR as a pointless exercise. A government with the authority to enforce ODR outcomes would certainly make parties feel more trust on the process.

It may be that the intervention of the government in certain aspects would indeed improve access to ODR providers, as well as the trust of their users. Nevertheless, the generalized view is that an excessive intervention of the government in ODR procedures could potentially annihilate many of its advantages, that came to exist in the first place precisely due to its independence from government regulations (Manévy 2001).

There are evidently many challenges to be addressed in the development of AI and The Law research. It is thus not clear if the development of fully autonomous software agents that can take the role of judges and attorneys will happen or not in a near future. Nevertheless, by aiming at that ambitious objective, researchers will continue to develop useful tools that will slowly but steadily improve the legal systems, making them more efficient and, ultimately, more accessible to people. This should be the goal of future AI and The Law research, i.e., not to develop highly advanced and complex systems that barely no one will use, but to develop systems that can actually be used by individuals that have little to no knowledge at all about the legal field, essentially as support decision tools.

References

Aamodt, A., and E. Plaza. 1994. Case-based reasoning: Foundational issues, methodological variations, and system approaches. *AI Communications* 7(1): 39–59. The Netherlands: IOS Press.

Abrahams, B., and J. Zeleznikow. 2010. A multi-agent negotiation decision support system for Australian Family Law. *Frontiers in Artificial Intelligence and Applications* 212: 297–308, IOS Press. ISBN 978-1-60750-576-1.

Acampora, G., V. Loia, M. Nappi, and S. Ricciardi. 2005. Ambient intelligence framework for context aware adaptive application. In *Computer architecture for machine perception. CAMP 2005. Proceedings of the seventh international workshop* 4(6): 327–332.

Aleven, V., and K.D. Ashley. 1997. Teaching case-based argumentation through a model and examples: Empirical evaluation of an intelligent learning environment. In *Artificial Intelligence in education*, vol. 39, 87–94. IOS Press.

Ashley, K.D. 2004. *Case-based models of legal reasoning in a civil law context*. International Congress of comparative cultures and legal systems of the Instituto de Investigaciones Jurídicas. Universidad Nacional Autonoma de México, Mexico City

Ashley, K.D., and V. Aleven. 1991. Toward an intelligent tutoring system for teaching law students to argue with cases. In *Proceedings of the 3rd international conference on Artificial Intelligence and Law*, 42–52. New York: ACM.

Augusto, J.C., and P. McCullagh. 2007. Ambient intelligence: Concepts and applications. Invited Paper by the *International Journal on Computer Science and Information Systems* 4(1): 1–28.

Aztiria, A., A. Izaguirre, and J.C. Augusto. 2010. Learning patterns in ambient intelligence environments: A survey. *Artificial Intelligence Review* 34(1): 35–51.

Banzhaf, W., P. Nordin, R.E. Keller, and F.D. Francone. 1998. *Genetic programming – An introduction*. San Francisco: Morgan Kaufmann.

Beehr, M., M. d'Inverno, N.R. Jennings, M. Luck, C. Preist, and M. Schroeder. 1999. Negotiation in multi-agent systems. *Knowledge Engineering Review* 14(3): 285–289.

Bellucci, E., and J. Zeleznikow. 2001. Representations of decision-making support in negotiation. *Journal of Decision Systems* 10(3–4): 449–479.

Bench-Capon, T., et al. 2012. A history of AI and Law in 50 papers: 25 years of the international conference on AI and Law. *Artificial Intelligence and Law* 20(3): 215–319.

Benjamins, R.V., P. Casanovas, J. Breuker, and A. Gangemi. 2005. *Law and the semantic web: Legal ontologies, methodologies, legal information retrieval, and applications*. Berlin: Springer.

Berners-Lee, T., J. Hendler, and O. Lassila. 2001. The semantic web. *Scientific American* 284(5): 28–37.

Bick, M., and T. Kummer. 2008. Ambient intelligence and ubiquitous computing. In *Handbook on information technologies for education and training, Part I, Subpart 1*, ed. Heimo H. Adelsberger, Kinshuk, Jan M. Pawlowski, Demetrios G. Sampson, 79–100. Berlin/Heidelberg: Springer.

Bonczek, R.H., C.W. Holsapple, and A.B. Whinston. 1981. *Foundations of decision support systems*. New York: Academic Press Inc. ISBN 978-0121130503.

Brachman, R., and H. Levesque. 2004. *Knowledge representation and reasoning*. Amsterdam: Morgan Kaufmann.

Brams, S.J., and A.D. Taylor. 2000. *The win-win solution: Guaranteeing fair shares to everybody*. New York: W. W. Norton & Company. ISBN 978-0393320817.

Brüninghaus, S., and K. Ashley. 2006. Progress in textual case-based reasoning: Predicting the outcome of legal cases from text. In *Proceedings of the twenty-first national conference on Artificial Intelligence (AAAI-06)*, 1577–1580, Boston.

Buchanan, B.G., and T.E. Headrick. 1970. Some speculation about Artificial Intelligence and legal reasoning. *Stanford Law Review* 23(1): 40–62.

Cáceres, E. 2008. EXPERTIUS: A Mexican Judicial decision-support system in the field of family law. In *Legal knowledge and information systems*, ed. E.B.E. Francesconi, G. Sartor, and D. Tiscornia, 78–87. Amsterdam: IOS Press.

Cagnoni, S., R. Poli, G.D. Smith, D. Corne, M. Oates, E. Hart, P.L. Lanzi, E.J. Willem, Y. Li, B. Paechter, and T.C. Fogarty (eds.). 2000. *Revised papers of the EvoWorkshops 2000: EvoIASP, EvoSCONDI, EvoTel, EvoSTIM, EvoRob, and EvoFlight*, Lecture notes in computer science, vol. 1803, Edinburgh, Scotland, UK, 17 Apr 2000. Berlin/Heidelberg: Springer.

Camarinha-Matos, L., and H. Afsarmanesh. 2001. Virtual communities and elderly support. In *Advances in automation, multimedia and video systems, and modern computer science*, ed. V.V. Kluev, C.E. D'Attellis, N.E. Mastorakis. 279–284. Greece: WSES Press.

Corcho, O., M. Fernández-lópez, A. Gómez-pérez, and A. Löpez. 2005. Building legal ontologies with methontology and webode. In *Law and the semantic web*, ed. V. Richard Benjamins, Casanovas Pompeu, Breuker Joost, and Gangemi Aldo. Heidelberg: Springer.

Darwin, C. 1998. *The origin of species. Oxford world's classics*. Oxford: Oxford Paperbacks. ISBN 978-0192834386.

De Jong, K.A. 2006. *Evolutionary computation: A unified approach*. Cambridge, MA: MIT Press.

Feldman, A., E. Tapia, S. Sadi, P. Maes, and C. Schmandt. 2005. ReachMedia: On-the-move interaction with everyday object. In *Wearable computers. Proceedings of the ninth IEEE international symposium*. Ambient Intelligence Group, MIT Media Laboratory. London: Taylor & Francis.

Forsyth, R. 1986. Chapter 8: The Anatomy of expert systems. In *Artificial Intelligence: Principles and applications*, ed. M. Yazdani, 186–187. London: Chapman & Hall.

Friedewald, M., and O. Da Costa. 2003. *Science and technology roadmapping: Ambient intelligence in everyday life (AmI@ Life)*. Karlsruhe: Fraunhofer-Institut für System-und Innovationsforschung (FhG-ISI).

Greinke, A. 1994. Legal expert systems – A humanistic critique of mechanical legal inference. *Murdoch University Electronic Journal of Law* 1(4).

Gruber, T.R. 1993. A translation approach to portable ontologies. *Knowledge Acquisition* 5(2): 199–220.

Haigh, K.Z., L.M. Kiff, and G. Ho. 2006. The independent lifestyle assistant: Lessons learned. *Assistive Technology: The Official Journal of RESNA* 18(1): 87–106.

Harmon, P., and D. King. 1985. *Expert systems: Artificial Intelligence in business*. New York: Wiley.

Hayes-Roth, F., D.A. Waterman, and D.B. Lenat. 1983. *Building expert systems*. Boston: Addison-Wesley Longman Publishing Co., Inc.

Hein, A., and T. Kirste. 2008. Activity recognition for ambient assisted living: Potential and challenges. In *Proceedings of the ambient assisted living conference*, Berlin: VDE Verlag.

Hogan, J.P. 1998. *Mind matters*. Westminster: Del Rey.

Jackson, P. 1990. *Introduction to expert systems*. Boston: Addison-Wesley Longman Publishing Co., Inc.

Jelasity, M. 2000. *Towards automatic domain knowledge extraction for evolutionary heuristics*, Lecture notes in computer science, vol. 1917, 755–764. Berlin: Springer.

Kleinberger, T., M. Becker, E. Ras, A. Holzinger, and P. Müller. 2007. Ambient intelligence in assisted living: Enable elderly people to handle future interfaces. In *Universal access in human-computer interaction. Ambient interaction*, Lecture notes in computer science, vol. 4555, 103–112.

Kolodner, J.L. 1992. An introduction to case-based reasoning. *Artificial Intelligence Review* 6(1): 3–34. doi:10.1007/BF00155578.

Kolodner, J.L. 1993. *Case-based reasoning*. San Mateo: Morgan Kaufmann Publishers.

Kurzweil, R. 2000. *The age of spiritual machines: When computers exceed human intelligence*. New York: Penguin.

Landes, W.M., and R.A. Posner. 1976. Legal precedent: A theoretical and empirical analysis. *Journal of Law and Economics* 19: 249.

Manévy, I. 2001. Online dispute resolution: What future? Juriscom. Available at www.juriscom. net/uni/mem/17/odr01.pdf. Accessed on June 2013.

Matthijssen, L. 1995. An intelligent interface for legal databases. In *Proceedings of the 5th international conference on Artificial Intelligence and Law*. New York: ACM.

Matthijssen, L. 1999. *Interfacing between lawyers and computers: An architecture for knowledge-based interfaces to legal databases*, Law and electronic commerce. The Hague: Kluwer Law International.

Oskamp, A., M. Tragter, and C. Groendijk. 1995. AI and Law: What about the future? *Artificial Intelligence and Law* 3(3): 209–215.

Parunak, H.V.D. 1997. Go to the ant: Engineering principles from natural multi-agent systems. *Annals of Operations Research* 75: 69–102.

Peruginelli, G. 2002. Artificial Intelligence in alternative dispute resolution. In *Proceedings of the workshop on the Law of Electronic Agents (LEA02)*, ed. G. Sartor.

Popple, J. 1991. Legal expert systems: The inadequacy of a rule-based approach. *Australian Computer Journal* 23(1): 11–16.

Popple, J. 1996. *A pragmatic legal expert system*, Applied legal philosophy series. Aldershot: Ashgate/Dartmouth.

Priddle-Higson, A. 2010. *Computational models of ontology evolution in legal reasoning*. The University of Edinburgh. Available at http://hdl.handle.net/1842/4152.

Rahwan, I., and G. Simari (eds.). 2009. *Argumentation in Artificial Intelligence*. Heidelberg: Springer.

Riva, G., F. Vatalaro, F. Davide, and M. Alcaniz. 2005. *Ambient intelligence: The evolution of technology, communication and cognition towards the future of human-computer interaction*. Amsterdam: IOS Press.

Rocha, M., P. Cortez, and J. Neves. 2003. Adaptive learning in changing environments. In *Proceedings of 11th European Symposium on Artificial Neural Networks (ESANN'2003)*, ed. M. Verleysen. Bruges, 487–492.

Rubel, P., et al. 2004. New paradigms in telemedicine: Ambient intelligence, wearable, pervasive and personalized. In *Wearable eHealth systems for personalized health management: State of the art and future challenges*. Amsterdam: IOS Press.

Rudolph, L. 2001. Project oxygen: Pervasive, human-centric computing—An initial experience. In *Advanced information systems engineering: 13th international conference, proceedings*, ed. Klaus R. Dittrich, Andreas Geppert, and Moira C. Norrie, 1–12. Berlin/Heidelberg: Springer. ISBN 3540422153.

Russell, S., and P. Norvig. 2002. Artificial Intelligence: A modern approach, 2nd ed. Englewood Cliffs: Prentice Hall.

Russell, S., and P. Norvig. 2009. *Artificial intelligence: A modern approach*, 3rd ed, 1152 pages. Englewood Cliffs: Prentice Hall. ISBN 978–0136042594.

Schultz, T. 2003. An essay on the role of government for ODR: Theoretical considerations about the future of ODR. August ADROnline Monthly. Available at SSRN: http://ssrn.com/abstract=896678.

Searle, J.R. 1980. Minds, brains and programs. *Behavioral and Brain Sciences* 3(3): 417–457.

Sowa, J.F. 2000. *Knowledge representation: Logical, philosophical, and computational foundations*. Cambridge, MA: MIT Press.

Span, G. 1993. LITES, an intelligent tutoring system for legal problem solving in the domain of Dutch Civil law. In *Proceedings of the 4th international conference on Artificial Intelligence and Law*, 76–81. New York: ACM.

Stikic, M., T. Huynh, K. Van Laerhoven, and B. Schiele. 2008. ADL recognition based on the combination of RFID and accelerometer sensing. In *Proceedings of the 2nd international conference on pervasive computing technologies for healthcare (Pervasive health 2008)*, Tampere, Finland, January, 258–263.

Storf, H., T. Kleinberger, M. Becker, M. Schmitt, F. Bomarius, and S. Prueckner. 2009. An event-driven approach to activity recognition in ambient assisted living. In *Ambient Intelligence*, Lecture notes in computer science, vol. 5859, ed. Manfred Tscheligi, Boris de Ruyter, Panos Markopoulus, Reiner Wichert, Thomas Mirlacher, Alexander Meschterjakov, and Wolfgang Reitberger, 123–132. Berlin: Springer.

Sung, M., and A.S. Pentland. 2005. *PokerMetrics?: Stress and lie detection through non-invasive physiological sensing*. Technical report. Available at http://citeseerx.ist.psu.edu/viewdoc/summary?doi=10.1.1.153.9203. Accessed on June 2013.

Susskind, R. 1987. *Expert systems in law: A jurisprudential inquiry*. Oxford: Clarendon Press.

Sycara, K. 1993. Machine learning for intelligent support of conflict resolution. *Decision Support Systems* 10: 121–136.

Thiessen, E.M. 1993. *ICANS: An interactive computer-assisted multi-party negotiation support system*. Ph.D. dissertation, School of Civil & Environmental Engineering, Cornell University, Ithaca, Dissertation Abstracts International, 172 p.

Turban, E. 1993. *Decision support and expert systems: Management support systems*. Upper Saddle River: Prentice Hall PTR.

Turing, A.M. 1950. Computing machinery and intelligence. *Mind* 59: 433–460.

Vasilakos, A., and W. Pedrycz. 2006. *Ambient intelligence, wireless networking, and ubiquitous computing*. Boston: Artech House Publishers.

Velasquez, J.D. 1997. Modeling emotions and other motivations in synthetic agents. In *Proceedings of the national conference on Artificial Intelligence*, 10–15. Hoboken: Wiley.

Visser, P.R.S., and T.J.M. Bench-Capon. 1998. A comparison of four ontologies for the design of legal knowledge systems. *Artificial Intelligence and Law* 6(1): 27–57.

Waterman, D.A., and M. Peterson. 1980. Rule-based models of legal expertise. In *Proceedings of the first national conference on AI*, Stanford: Stanford University.

Watson, I. 1997. *Applying case-based reasoning: Techniques for enterprise systems*. San Francisco: Morgan Kaufmann.

Weber, W., J. Rabaey, and E.H.L. Aarts. (eds.). 2005. *Ambient intelligence*. vol. XIV, 374 p. Berlin/Heidelberg: Springer. ISBN 978-3-540-27139-0.

Weiser, M., R. Gold, and J.S. Brown. 1999. The origins of ubiquitous computing research at PARC in the late 1980s. *IBM Systems Journal* 38(4): 693.

Wooldridge, M. 2002. *An introduction to MultiAgent systems*. New York: Wiley.

Wooldridge, M., and N.R. Jennings. 1995. Intelligent agents: Theory and practice. *The Knowledge Engineering Review* vol. 10, 115–152. Cambridge University Press.

Zeleznikow, J., and E. Bellucci. 2003. Family_Winner: Integrating game theory and heuristics to provide negotiation support. In *Proceedings of sixteenth international conference on legal knowledge based system*, 21–30, The Netherlands.

Zeleznikow, J., and E. Bellucci. 2004. Building negotiation decision support systems by integrating game theory and heuristics. *Artificial Intelligence and Law* 7: 2–3. Dordrecht: Springer.

Zeleznikow, J., and D. Hunter. 1994. *Building intelligent legal information systems: Representation and reasoning in law*, 230–237. New York, NY: ACM.

Zeleznikow, J., and A. Stranieri. 1995. The split-up system: Integrating neural networks and rule-based reasoning in the legal domain. In *Proceedings of the 5th international conference on Artificial Intelligence and law*, 185–194. New York: ACM.

Zweigert, K., and H. Kötz. 1998. *An introduction to comparative law*, 3rd ed. Oxford: Clarendon Press.

Chapter 5
Context and Its Importance

Abstract Contextual factors allow us to fully grasp an event, situation, communication process or action. Frequently, the context in which an event takes place provides more valuable information than the event itself. This chapter addresses context and its importance from a general perspective and in the particular domain of conflict resolution. It describes many different contextual dimensions such as the verbal, social or cultural, pointing out the importance of each one to understand individuals' actions. It then moves on to the address the recent field of Context-aware Computing: the vision of computers that are sensible to contextual cues, harness it and use such information to provide better services. Several context-aware solutions are described in this chapter that point out the range of application domains. However, no such application exists in the domain of conflict resolution. While the next chapters are dedicated do describing the components of such an application, this chapter ends with the enumeration of several contextual dimensions that are of relevance to fully describe a conflict and its resolution process.

5.1 Introduction

Context defines the surroundings or the circumstances in which a given event or other occurrence takes place. It allows an observer to correctly understand and interpret the occurrence. More specific definitions of this concept require the definition of the scope of the context as well, i.e., different domains may have different definitions of context. Taking the field of linguistics as an example, context refers to information that is relevant to understanding a text. This information may be very varied and include the identity of things named in the text (e.g. people, places) as well as many other aspects such as birth dates, geographical locations, temporal location, and so on. In fact, different contexts may provide completely different interpretations for the same text.

D. Carneiro et al., *Conflict Resolution and its Context*, Law, Governance and
Technology Series 18, DOI 10.1007/978-3-319-06239-6_5,
© Springer International Publishing Switzerland 2014

We constantly rely on contextual information on our daily living, although most of the times in an unconscious way. It allows us to understand the other's actions, to better accept a harsh decision from a governing body or to perceive signs of irony during a conversation. Context is important to the point of shaping ourselves, who we are.

Indeed, our life is a process of constant learning, which changes us. The knowledge acquired during our life through this constant process comes with a strong social, cultural and physical context (Anderson et al. 1996). This bound is so strong that cognition cannot be separated from context, i.e., knowing is inseparable from activity, people, culture, language or time.

The main implication of this is that an individual shows different cognitive and reasoning processes under different contexts, i.e., the context in which he is embedded provides the symbols and values that the individual will use (Eysenck and Keane 2005). The consequence of this is that we cannot define an individual, accurately and absolutely, without making a reference to context, i.e., we cannot say to another person *"I behave like this"* and expect to really be like that all the time. Instead, we should say *"In a scenario with these conditions, I would probably behave like this"*.

As an example, it would probably never cross the mind of the reader to go out and rob a pharmacy. The reader may even think *"I'm just not that kind of person"*. However, the reader could think twice and probably even feel compelled to do it if that would be the only way of saving a loved one's life. If I knew about the true motivation behind this robbery, I would sympathize and understand the reader's actions. If I did not know of it, I would condemn it. Two key ideas can be drawn from this scenario, namely:

- context significantly changes us and who we are; and
- context helps us understand the occurrences in our life.

This chapter is dedicated to the importance of context in general and in conflict resolution processes in particular. It starts with the identification of different contextual dimensions that we constantly rely on in our decision-making processes, even in an unconscious way. It then moves on to describe how context can be acquired and dealt with by machines in a way similar to ours, allowing machines to take informed and contextualized decisions. It will be shown how this is paramount for the notion of intelligent decisions. Some examples of context-aware systems are detailed before moving on to the final part of the chapter in which a more specific issue is discussed, i.e., the one of contextualizing conflicts. In this final part, the chapter addresses which information is necessary to fully describe a conflict as well as its resolution process.

5.2 Different Contextual Dimensions

Context can take many different forms, depending on the universe of discourse. This section describes some of the contextual dimensions that an individual deals with frequently. These exist in the generic activities of daily living as well as in the specific activities related to the legal domain and conflict resolution.

5.2.1 Verbal

The verbal context includes all the information that provides the reader with material about the words of a text or a talk. This may include aspects as diverse as a geographical location, a historical reference, a political frame or the identity of objects cited, in the case of a written text. In the case of a speech, context may include the tone of voice, the speech rhythm, the identity of the persons around the speaker or even the body posture, gestures or facial expressions. These elements are particularly important when the sentence includes homographs, which mandatorily require a contextual framework for their correct interpretation. The lack of (or the intentional omission of) context can indeed change the whole nature of the sentence. This happens when someone quotes another person leaving aside contextual markers, in a way that the original meaning is distorted.

This is frequently found in politics, in which opponents quote each other out of context in order to misrepresent their positions, making them more simplistic or more extreme. It is also seen when an individual quotes an authority on a given subject out of context, in order to give the idea that said authority supports the individual's position.

When in a conflict resolution process, as much as in any other communication process, the verbal context can be the difference between a successfully perceived message and a potentially negative misunderstanding. As an example, when we communicate with someone face-to-face, we are able to perceive signs of irony and understand that the individual is making an innocent joke and is not being impolite or rude. We can do it by looking at signs such as a slight smile or the blink of an eye. However, when we remove these contextual cues by, for instance, communicating through a text-based tool, it becomes harder to detect irony and we may have doubts on how to interpret a given sentence. It is thus important that communication processes, in which the health of the interlocutors' relationship is crucial (such as the ones undertaken with the objective of solving a conflict), provide support for the exchange of the needed verbal context to correctly interpret the signs exchanged.

5.2.2 Social

The social context of an individual can be defined by objective social variables such as those of class, gender, race, availability of certain infrastructures (such as educational or leisure) or by other less objective ones such as the culture that the individual lives in and the people and institutions with whom the individual interacts (Barnett and Casper 2001). Undoubtedly, the social context of the individual significantly influences his experiences and the knowledge learnt from them, strengthening or weakening them accordingly, i.e., an experience that takes place in a positive social context is more likely to be felt as positive by the individual.

Individuals are also likely to take up habits and attitudes they witness within their social context. For example, an individual that grows in a district in which everyone litters will, most likely, follow after that behavior as it is, given his context, *"a normal thing to do"*.

The social context is thus one of the key pieces in understanding an individual as a part of the individual is taken from his social identity when growing up, i.e., the traits that he shares with the other individuals in his surroundings and that give them all the notion of group (Turner et al. 1994). However, this significant influence of the group has effects not only when the cognition of the individual is still in an early development stage but also when it is fully formed, i.e., the cognitive processes of an individual are likely to change when his social context changes. Indeed, one generally thinks and acts differently when in different environments (e.g. domestic, leisure, workplace) or in the company of different people (e.g. friends, family, coworkers) (Rogoff and Lave 1984).

In fact, and in the specific domain of conflict resolution, the social context of the individuals may allow to better evaluating him in two ways, namely:

- knowing where the individual comes from can give valuable clues about his personality and his behaviours; and
- knowing how the individual behaves around other people (with their respective role, gender or status) may allow to better understand his interactions with his counterparts.

For the reader that is interested in this topic, a recent (although consisting on an improvement of a far older one) work by Talmy Givón (2005) can be used as valuable material for further reading. In line with what has been stated so far, Givón argues that we constantly estimate and monitor the others' mental states and use that estimative as an input to adapt our interaction to them, according to our objectives. According to the author, once we know our mind we are able to estimate the others' minds, their state or their intention by means of feature association. Givón points out grammar as the evolutionary proof that we needed a mechanism to induce others to know what is in our mind, and vice-versa.

5.2.3   Historical

In general, the historical context describes the particular setting in which an idea or a past event took place. It helps to understand the true reasons, the urgency, the importance or even the timing of the event. The historical context may include political, social, cultural or economic aspects. Events that took place in a very different historical context may appear incomprehensible nowadays. However, considering their historical context, one may find that at the time they made perfect sense.

Historical context may also be of importance in a conflict resolution process. Namely, it may help in the interpretation of actions or past events relevant for the conflict, allowing understanding the true motivations or reasons of the parties. The historical context may also provide information about the past relationship of the parties, which may help the mediator to better conduct the process, i.e., were the parties related in some way? Did they know each other in the past? Were they already involved in an argument?

5.2.4 Physical

The physical context reflects the space around an event and how it influences the way the event is perceived, including the objects surrounding and involved in the event. Other features of the environment with an influence on the event are also included in its physical context, such as the furniture and how it is arranged, the type of building, inside/outside environment, the size of the room, the ornamentation, the temperature, the luminosity, the time of day, among others.

People adjust their actions according to their physical context. As an example, a political activist speaking in a rally is expected to shout, pound the podium and use inflammatory language to win the crowd. The same political activist, talking about the same topic with a small group of friends in a small bar, will need to adjust his speech since shouting and using inflammatory language in such a context would be inappropriate.

The physical context thus has a significant impact on communications, which are central in conflict resolution processes. Providing the adequate physical context for the conflict resolution process may improve the chances of success (e.g. people talking inside a small room will speak softer while doing it in a large room will make them speak louder, which may be perceived as a sign of dominance or imposing). Similarly, talking face-to-face with a co-located audience is very different from talking through video-conference. The audience may be in very different physical contexts, which calls for additional care on the part of the speaker.

5.2.5 Psychological

The psychological context of an individual or group of individuals refers to their mood, feelings and emotions. In a communicative act, the way an audience feels will influence the way the message being passed is perceived. The speaker should be able to perceive that context and adapt the speech accordingly, so that the efficiency of the communication process is increased. For example, if a teacher is lecturing a class that has been in the classroom the whole day, the psychology of the audience will be different in the morning than it will be at the end of the day. The students are more likely to be more active and focused in the morning. At the end of the day the students may be evidencing signs of boredom and fatigue and the teacher should consider adapting his speech to be lighter and of easier interpretation.

The psychological context includes feelings, thoughts, sensations, emotions and other states such as hungry, sleepy, angry, happy, impatient or frustrated. This context has a very significant impact on the way the communication process is perceived. As an example, a message with an authoritarian tone may be tolerated or be perceived as a threat if the receiver is, respectively, feeling happy or frustrated. Definitely, the ability to perceive the psychological context of the interlocutors is very important in a communication process.

Considering the conflict resolution process in particular, and given its potential emotional charge, knowledge about the interlocutors' emotional state may be very important at the time of taking decisions. As Dolan (2002) points out, emotion is central to the quality and range of everyday human experience as it influences other domains of cognition, in particular attention, memory, and reasoning. This influence is significant and has been studied in depth by many Psychologists and Neuroscientists. António Damásio (1994) points precisely how we cannot (even if we want to) leave emotions aside from our decision-making processes. Even when we think we will be objectively deciding on a given issue, all our decision-making mechanisms as well as the memories and knowledge we are retrieving to take the decision have an emotional background. Thus, as Damásio points out, we end up using emotions as shortcuts to our decisions. In fact, emotional shortcuts significantly decrease the conscious complexity of the decision-making process, making it more effective and, ultimately, possible. Interestingly enough, Damásio points many cases in which the absence of important regions of the brain responsible for emotions results in the inability to take *intelligent* decisions. Baumeister et al. (2007) more recently discusses the same issue, also pointing out that our common automatic affective responses in many daily situations remind us of past emotional outcomes and provide useful guides as to what emotional outcomes may be anticipated in the present. Given this, knowing the individual's psychological context, and the emotional one in particular, is very important in a daily basis and, especially, in the context of Conflict Resolution.

5.2.6 Symbolical

We make use of symbols on a daily basis, when driving, when doing laundry, when writing, reading or shopping. A symbol, generally represented in the form of an image, word, gesture or a sound is a simple object carrying a significant amount of complex information such as an idea, a belief, an action or a material identity.

Words are particularly interesting symbols: we use them to communicate with each other as well as in our conscious cognitive processes. However, the meaning of words is not absolute, i.e., the same word or symbol may have different meanings. Its meaning may change according to culture, place or moment in time.

Certainly, in a communication process the interlocutors should be aware of each other's cultural and social background in order to choose the appropriate set of symbols to use. Failing to do so may result in misunderstandings that can be potentially negative for the communication process.

5.2.7   Relational

The relational context defines the relationship between the individuals of a group or between the participants of a communication. It caters for the definition of the role of each individual in the group and better understand their actions. In a classroom, for example, there is the relationship student-teacher, in which students are supposed to listen to the teacher and show cooperation, while the teacher is supposed to have an authoritarian attitude. Similarly, in a conflict resolution process, parts such as mediator, disputant or counselor help to provide a first insight about the communication dynamics. Additional information may provide more clues, such as a previous relation between the disputants (e.g. marriage, friends, co-workers, employee-employer). Such information may help the mediator in better preparing the way that the conflict resolution process will be conducted.

5.2.8   Situational

The situational context refers to the immediate context that surrounds a given action or event. It includes elements such as the setting or the place in which it takes place (e.g. home, workplace, shopping center, political rally), the activity being performed (e.g. lecture, political speech, party, helping a friend), as well as other elements of the environment that can help describe the action. It includes what people participating in the event feel about it as well, and that can make the whole different in the communication process. For example, when I meet a co-worker with a higher position in the street, I may look at the situation as an encounter between two friends, thus I adopt an informal and friendly behavior. He, on the other hand, may still think of me as his hierarchically inferior, and adopt a more formal behavior. This may easily result in a friction in the communication process. If the encounter had taken place in another setting, such as the cafeteria of the workplace, I would probably have adopted a more formal posture.

Situational context is the most immediate type of context, coming first than social or cultural context, i.e., we first set our behavior in terms of the present situation, then according to the people around us and finally according to our cultural background.

5.2.9   Cultural

The cultural context includes all aspects that are part of an individual's identity that were given by or learned from a given group of people. It includes values, beliefs, meanings, rituals, thoughts, opinions, ideas and other aspects of life. When an individual embodies a given cultural context, it helps to define who he is and to understand his actions. The act of marriage, for example, is seen very differently in different cultures. Indian brides and their female friends paint their hands and feed with elaborate designs called *menhdi*, Jewish grooms break a glass under his foot, and in Zulu weddings the groom's family slaughters a cow to welcome the bride. These rituals would be misinterpreted or even deemed violent outside their cultural background.

These rules and patterns of behavior are also present in communication processes. Being familiar with them is crucial to undertake successful communication processes, essentially when the interlocutors have different cultural backgrounds. Factors related to group memberships (e.g. inaccurate and unfavorable stereotypes of members of other cultures and ethnic groups) may cause misinterpretation of the messages received from members of those groups (Gudykunst 2003).

5.2.10   Digital

In our present society, one must also consider the potential importance of the digital context of an individual when trying to understand them or their actions. The digital context may indeed be seen as a mix of both human and technical aspects, bridging the individual's behavior in the real world with its representation in the digital one. The human aspects include the ones that take place in the real world and were already addressed here, namely the user's mood, behavior, personal relationships, beliefs or actions. The technical aspects include the types of devices that the user owns, the profiles in social networks, his digital calendar schedule, or the technology usage patterns, just to name a few. Technological and human aspects are intrinsically interrelated. Nevertheless, nowadays, digital profiles can provide contextual information about an individual in a much faster way than through traditional face-to-face interactions, i.e., the digital context must be considered as one of the potential sources of information when one seeks to understand an individual.

5.3 Context-Aware Computing

Context-aware computing refers to systems that are aware of their user's state and surroundings, and that are able to adapt their behavior according to changes in their context (Satyanarayanan 2002). The knowledge about the environment or the user may be relatively simple (e.g. the network to which the device is connected, the devices in the proximity) or may be more complex and even built from assumptions about the user's current situation.

In its inception, research on user context was centered mostly on user location (Dey 2001). The hype revolved around applications that would provide services personalized according to their user's location. Nevertheless, in the last years the notion of context has been widened significantly, and now refers not only to where the user is but also to who the user is, what the user is doing, when is he doing and with who is he doing it. All this information allows the system to try to infer *why* the user is doing it and this is essential in assisting him.

These novel and increasingly complex contextual models provide the support for applications that are able to adapt interfaces, improve information retrieval techniques, target services more efficiently or use implicit user-interaction techniques (Bolchini et al. 2007).

Context-aware computing relies on three central aspects: the acquisition of the contextual information, the abstraction and understanding of the context, and the execution of activities based on the recognized context.

The acquisition of contextual information is performed tendentiously through sensors. Many devices can nowadays be used as sensors, even if they do not possess such devices in the traditional way. Here it must be established the distinction between hard and soft sensing (Acharya and Kam 2011).

"Hard" sensors refer to sensors in the traditional sense, i.e., pieces of hardware dedicated primarily to the measurement of some aspect of the physical world. This includes thermal sensors, gyroscopes, accelerometers, GPS and many others. Acquiring information from hard sensors starts with the acquisition of the raw data, the extraction of interesting features, the classification and the structuring of the data, and finally a quest of the knowledge about the universe of discourse.

"Soft" sensors, on the other hand, are sources of information about some topic, generally not read from the environment, but generated through some other indirect mean. This includes things such as reports from humans, context analysis by experts, analysis of the user's calendar (as a sensor of his availability or location), analysis of the activity of the user on the device or on the browser (as a sensor of the user's preferences or activities) or the analysis of the user's social networking habits (as a sensor of many aspects of the user's life).

As an example let us consider the average smartphone available in the market nowadays. It is frequent to find such devices equipped with sensors such as accelerometer, gyroscope, electronic compass, pressure, microphone, luminosity, GPS or multiple video-cameras. These can instantly provide a significant amount of information about the user and his surroundings. Moreover, from our increasing interactions and from the current *"always on"* culture, these devices can build an extremely accurate profile of our preferences, habits or behaviors.

Information acquired from so many different sources must be combined and most likely abstracted in order for it to be understood by the device. The field of information fusion, in computer-sciences, refers precisely to this: the combination of information from different sources into a new set of information towards reducing uncertainty (Khaleghi et al. 2013). This process of fusion may also include an abstraction process in which the perceived sensory stimuli are mapped to specific contexts, allowing a more straightforward interpretation of the environment. This also unleashes the true potential of the use of contextual information, i.e., context can be aggregated over time and over the different devices that the user interacts with, resulting in a fast and cross-domains collaborative sensing, in which the contextual profile of the user is built in a seamless, transparent and highly efficient way.

When sufficiently precise, the information can then be used to act. These actions can have as target the environment or the user himself and can take many forms, depending on the purpose and scope of the application or the environment. Some examples of context-aware applications are described further ahead in this chapter.

From an abstract point of view, contextual information related to the user can be organized into three categories, which correspond to three of the more interesting aspects in research being conducted in the field: information about the user (including his preferences, habits, emotional state or limitations), about the user's social context (including the description of the relationships with other people) and the user's activities (including current activities, preferred activities, general goals and activity profile).

Similarly, contextual information concerning the environment is also organized into three categories, i.e., information about the location (e.g. absolute or relative location), infrastructure (e.g. nearby computational resources), and information about the physical conditions (e.g. level of noise, level or light, amount of technology, number of people, air quality).

5.4   Harnessing Content and Context

Information about the user's context can be acquired from the content of the objects the user is dealing with (e.g. title or topic of an e-book being read), can be inferred from the activity being performed (e.g. nature/objective of the activity), can be provided explicitly (through social tagging, comments or bookmarks), and can be acquired from hard or soft sensors, as described above.

There are many potential advantages in using information about the user's context. It allows to find links between people that share similar contexts, to better organize information for more efficient retrieval or to develop context-enabled applications. This last issue is particularly interesting. With this new type of applications, users can have access to more information. Moreover, this information can be provided in different ways, such as Augmented Reality. This refers to a process in which a virtual layer of information is overlapped over a representation of the reality, in the screen of a smartphone (Graham et al. 2012). On the other hand, users can also profit by having access to less information, through the use of applications that filter and target the search results based on the location or preferences (Tapia et al. 2013). Contextual information also allows to more easily find links between users and the elements in their surroundings such as people with similar interests, potentially interesting restaurants or the timetable of the nearest train station.

Many applications have already been developed that build on such notions to provide high-value and innovative services. Most of them are based on learning the patterns of the users on the environment, their preferences and their habits. This is fundamental in order for personalized services to be provided (Aztiria et al. 2010).

A good example of this is Magitti: an activity-aware leisure guide running on a smartphone (Bellotti 2008). Magitti is essentially a recommendation service that has a model of the preferences of the user. This model is continuously built from his current situation or his past behaviors. The system constantly acquires information from the context of the user, namely the time, the location or recent messages exchanges with other people. This allows Magitti to infer the current user activity. With this information and the preferences model, the system is able to filter and rank information items that may be of interest, namely about nearby restaurants, stores or events. The user can then consult the guide to decide between different leisure activities.

Under a different perspective, the Hearsay service developed as part of the GLOSS project (Munro et al. 2001) allows users to pick up small notes left for them in the environment. It makes sure users will find the message only in a correct context (e.g. right person in the right place at the right time). The same approach is applied to other applications, providing a structured link between environment and behavior to improve utility and usability (Dearle et al. 2003).

Other projects have also focused on acquiring contextual information from the observation of the user. Budzik and Hammond (2000) claim that user interactions with everyday productivity applications (e.g. word processors, Web browsers) provide rich contextual information that can be leveraged to support just-in-time access to task-relevant information. Besides discussing the requirements for such systems and developing a general architecture, the authors present Watson, a system which gathers contextual information in the form of the text of the document the user is manipulating in order to proactively retrieve documents from distributed information repositories. It results in a transparent and proactive search engine, which requires no explicit interaction from the part of the user.

There is also a marked interest on the use of context-aware computing in the medical field, particularly in alleviating the tasks of medical practitioners or on supporting patients. Bardram (2004) presents the design of a context-aware pill container and a context-aware hospital bed, both of which react and adapt according to what is happening in their context. The bed has an integrated computer and a touch sensitive display, and is equipped with various RFID tags that can identify the patient lying in the bed, the clinician standing beside the bed, and various medical objects. The system is able to, among other tasks, point out the location of the correct medicine to take or verify if it is the correct patient receiving it.

On a different field, Rekimoto et al. (1998) define an innovative communication framework that incorporates Augmented Reality techniques. Users can dynamically attach newly created digital information such as voice, notes or photographs to the physical environment, through wearable computers as well as normal computers. Attached data is stored with contextual tags such as location IDs and object IDs that are obtained by wearable sensors, so the same or other wearable users can notice them when they come to the same environment. The approach implemented has a role that is similar to the one that Post-it notes play in community messaging.

A particular interest lies also on the development of context-aware systems that can be carried by the user, generally in small devices such as smartphones or video cameras. This is empowered by the functionalities and potential of current mobile devices, rich with sensors, computational power and communication capabilities. O'Hare et al. (2005) address the challenge of organizing our ever-growing collections of digital photos, consequence of the enormous rise in popularity of digital cameras. To achieve it, the authors developed the MediAssist project, which uses date/time and GPS location for the organization of personal collections. The project retrieves photos of known objects (e.g. buildings, monuments) using both location information and content-based retrieval tools from the AceToolbox, allowing to improve information search and retrieval when compared to more traditional approaches.

On a more 'out-of-the-box' approach, Ljungblad et al. (2004) present the concept of context photography. It defines a new form of looking at digital photos in which the camera captures more than just incoming light: it also captures the context in which the photo is taken. Moreover, information about the physical context gathered from various sensors visually affects pictures as they are taken (translating non-visual data into visual effects in an image), and open a new scope of possible experiences and practices. The information about the time and location of a photo can also be used to generate an abundance of related contextual metadata, using off-the-shelf and Web-based data sources (Naaman et al. 2004), such as the local daylight status or weather conditions at the time and place a photo was taken. This metadata has the potential of serving as memory cues and filters when browsing photo collections. This is important as these collections grow into the tens of thousands and span dozens of years. However, it is even more important for people with cognitive or memory impairments, as they can use these contextual cues to better recall the moments in which the photos were taken.

An important issue here is the one of trust as these new services have real effects on our routines and on our environments, and must thus be used with care. Byun and Cheverst (2002) propose the requirement of an explicit explanation about the system's decisions and adaptations to the user in order to encourage a trust relationship between the user and the context-aware system.

However, the access to users' context, together with cognitive models, opens possibilities that go much further than the support of single users. When there are preference models (including the tastes, the interests or the expertise) as well as behavioral models (including activity patterns or past actions) of the population, large-scale services can be developed. These can target areas as broad as advertising, community monitoring, group coordination, information retrieval, usability studies or even public health monitoring.

5.5 Contextualizing Conflicts

Conflicts and their resolution, as any other communication process, have a strong contextual background. Frequently, most of the meaning present in the communication process stems not from the words used but from accessory information that helps understanding the real meaning or purpose of the words. This includes aspects such as the body language, the gestures, the posture, the emotional response or the tone of voice.

The importance of context in conflict resolution has been noted in one of the earliest documents written about ODR, by Etan Katsh, in 2006:

> Context can influence the approach of the neutral, the choice of process, and the behavior and attitudes of disputants. In any environment, context can affect the kinds of disputes that are likely to arise and also affect who the parties are who are likely to be involved in the dispute. Context implicitly feeds us information about the extent or nature of the injury as well as how the injury or dispute is perceived by those involved. Context situates a dispute in a particular time and place, and we react and adjust accordingly as the parameters of the environment become clear to us.

Contextual information is indeed important for the involved parties (i.e. disputants and mediators) to perceive the conflict in its whole, with its peculiarities, subjectivities and particular views. Besides what was detailed previously, this section analyzes additional aspects that make up the contextual framework of conflict resolution processes, i.e., information that will allow the parties involved to correctly understand all the aspects of the conflict.

5.5.1 Delimiting the Conflict

One of the most challenging tasks in the resolution of a conflict is to realistically perceive the boundaries of the case, i.e., which outcome would make sense and be relatively consensual and which outcome would be nonsense. In order for a party to gain a realistic view on the conflict, it would be interesting to determine, firstly, to which extent is it reasonable to engage in a dispute resolution process, i.e., are there significant advantages against a traditional litigation? This question can be analyzed from several perspectives. On the one hand, alternative dispute resolution processes are generally faster, cheaper, more private and personalized (Brown and Marriott 2012). There is however another important factor, namely the possible outcome reached through each of the processes. The party might ask himself if he will reach a better outcome using an alternative dispute resolution process instead of litigation.

Therefore, it would be important for each party to know its BATNA – Best Alternative to a Negotiated Agreement, or the possible best outcome *"along a particular path if I try to get my interests satisfied in a way that does not require negotiation with the other party"* (Notini 2010). A party should then understand the notion of a BATNA and what role it should play in ODR. Doing so will, at least, contribute to the acknowledgement that an agreement may be disadvantageous (Klaming et al. 2004). In fact, the position of the parties may become more unclear if they are not foreseeing the possible results in case the negotiation/mediation fails: *"If you are unaware of what results you could obtain if the negotiations are unsuccessful, you run the risk of entering into an agreement that you would be better off rejecting or rejecting an agreement that you would be better off entering into"* (Goldberg et al. 2003). That is to say, the parties, by determining their BATNA would, on the one hand, become *"better protected against agreements that should be rejected"* and, on the other hand, they would be in a better condition to *"reach an agreement that better satisfy their interests"* (De Vries et al. 2005). But, besides that, a BATNA may convene additional features to the parties. For instance, it may be used as a way to put pressure on the other party, especially in dispute resolution procedures allowing the choice of going to court (De Vries et al. 2005).

However, the use of the BATNA alone is not enough to take informed decisions as parties often tend *"to develop an overly optimistic view on their chances in disputes"* (De Vries et al. 2005). This may lead parties to calculate unrealistic BATNAs, which will influence later decisions, leading even to either reject generous offers from the other parties, or to stand stubbornly fixed in some positions (De Vries et al. 2005). It is thus important to also consider the concept of a WATNA, or the Worst Alternative to a Negotiated Agreement (Notini 2010; Fisher and Ury 1981; Steenbergen 2005). A WATNA estimates the worst possible outcome along a litigation path. It can be quite relevant in the calculation of the real risks that parties will face in a judicially determined litigation, imagining the worst possible outcome for the party. At this point, a party would be aware of the best and worst scenario if the dispute is to be solved in a court.

However, it could also be interesting to consider the whole space between the BATNA and WATNA as a useful element to be taken into account for making (or accepting) a proposal. If we consider, for instance, in the labor law domain, the scenario of a worker being fired, litigation will most likely occur. Under many legal systems, a huge deal of legal parameters have to be considered, including antiquity, supplementary work, just cause for dismissal, among others. For the worker, the amounts involved are not irrelevant, i.e., being fired without good indemnities may be seen as a double sacrifice. But he might, on the other hand, receive significant financial compensation. In order to clearly see the advantages of a proposed agreement, parties should consider the spectrum between their BATNA and their WATNA. Of course, the less space there is between the BATNA and the WATNA, the less dangerous it becomes for the party not to accept the agreement (unless, of course, their BATNA is really disadvantageous). A wider space between the BATNA and the WATNA would usually mean that it can become rather dangerous for the party not to accept the ODR agreement (except in situations when the WATNA is really not inconvenient at all for the party). We can thus argue that knowledge about the space between the BATNA and the WATNA is also extremely important. This space is evidently related to the Zone of Possible Agreement proposed by Raiffa (2002). It is the zone where an agreement can be met that is acceptable to both parties.

Moreover, it would also be interesting for a party to understand the region of this space in which an outcome is more likely, i.e., if the parties are to solve the dispute through litigation, what is the most likely outcome? In fact, sticking only with the BATNA and WATNA may not be realistic as these are usually not the most likely outcomes, but merely informative values that establish boundaries. Thus, an informed party should also consider the MLATNA – Most Likely Alternative to a Negotiated Agreement (Steenbergen 2005). Using the same arguments, we can also conclude that the existence of metrics that measure the probability of each possible outcome could also be extremely useful for a party.

As a final remark, it may be said that the contextual information necessary to correctly establish the boundaries of a case includes knowledge about:

- the best possible outcome in litigation;
- the worst possible outcome in litigation;
- the space between the two previous values;
- the most likely outcome in litigation; and
- the probability of each outcome within the zone of possible agreement.

5.5.2   Past Cases

One of the best ways for someone to understand a present event that is taking place or going to take place in the future, is to analyze a similar event that took place in the past, under a similar context. A case represents a past experience, teaching a past lesson, properly contextualized (Kolodner 1993). Depending on the domain of application, a case should contain a description of the state of the world when the event occurred (i.e. the problem description), the derived solution for the problem and/or the achieved outcome (i.e. the description of the state of the world after the case occurred) (David 1991). The individual can analyze the past event, with all its characteristics and within its contextual framework to fully understand it. Then, he will be in a better position to understand a similar event that may occur in the future.

Approaches relying on this idea are used in many different fields, such as the ones to train professionals for specific situations. In medicine, for example, people are trained to reduce accidents during surgery, prescription, and general practice by a simulation of scenarios that are likely to happen in the future. This allows them to perceive the problem and its context in a controlled and calm setting, making it easier for them to deal with a similar problem in the future (Kunkler 2006).

Many other fields use similar approaches, including manufacturing systems, automobile industry, logistics or the military (Banks 2007). The analysis of past cases is also of interest in the domain of conflict resolution. Disputant parties involved in a conflict resolution process may leverage on past cases, under a similar context, to better perceive the present. This would allow the parties to calmly understand the important aspects of the past case, being better prepared to fully understand their own and gaining a more realistic and objective view on the case. For example, if a given party is too greedy but notices that the outcome he desires has never happened in the past, he may conclude that such outcome is unlikely and even unrealistic. He may then reconsider his objectives and go for a more middle-ground solution.

5.5.3   Conflict Handling Style

The conflict handling style determines the expected behavior of an individual before a conflict. Each individual has a given personal conflict handling style, which may however vary according to variables such as the identity of the other parties, the nature of the conflict, or even the level of escalation of the conflict. Knowing the conflict handling style of the parties is especially important for the mediator, who can better prepare the strategy for the resolution of the conflict. Gathering and providing evidence about the party's conflict handling style may also be used by the mediator as a way to put pressure and to lead the parties into changing an undesired behavior, i.e., a mediator may show to a party that he is being an obstacle to the successful resolution of the conflict by being too greedy or competitive.

5.5.4   Stress

Stress is a universal phenomenon that affects virtually our whole life. Low levels of stress make us soft, depressive and with lack of motivation, while continued high levels of stress may result in exhaustion and breakdowns (Carneiro et al. 2012). The resolution of a conflict may be a particularly stressful process for many reasons, including the potential emotional charge (mostly when the parties had a prior relationship that may affect the process), the significant amount of gains or losses involved or the fear of the novelty or the unknown, mostly when parties engage in such a process for the first time.

In the short-term, high levels of stress lead to clouded-mind, poor decision-making, irritability, lack of judgment or violence. Failing to control these effects may jeopardize the whole conflict resolution process and even the relationship among the parties involved. It is thus important that the mediator is able to perceive signs of stress evidenced by the parties, and act accordingly in order to mitigate its effects by performing the necessary changes in the conflict resolution process.

5.5.5 Fatigue

Fatigue is a particular feeling of tiredness in which individuals experience lack of energy, lethargy or languidness. Two main forms of fatigue can be identified: physical fatigue, which defines a temporary physical inability of a muscle to function normally, and mental fatigue, which is the temporary inability to maintain optimal cognitive performance. Both types of fatigue have their negative consequences. However, in the context of a conflict resolution process, mental fatigue may be more disturbing.

Mental fatigue may be caused by sleep deprivation, long periods of work, mental stress or overstimulation, among others. A mentally fatigued individual will have a reduced cognitive capacity, namely in terms of memory, attention and decision making. A fatigued individual participating in a conflict resolution process may take poor decisions, be unable to keep up with the process or even become irritable and uncooperative. It is therefore important that the mediator is able to detect early signs of fatigue through the behaviors and attitudes of the parties and act accordingly, namely by making pauses or by rescheduling the continuation of the process.

5.5.6 Level of Escalation

The level of escalation of a conflict describes how confrontational, violent, painful or *"less comfortable"* it is. Desirably, parties involved in a conflict must be in a cooperative and compliant state. However, in general this is not the case. If not adequately managed, the conflict may escalate to increasingly worse states, in which individuals passively or actively resist to proposals or commands, with the aggravating of the escalation potentially resulting in violence. Therefore, it is mandatory that the conflict manager is able to perceive signs of escalation of the conflict. Typically he can do so through cues such as the tone of voice, signs of inflammatory speech, gestures, body postures or the use of particular words. It is the responsibility of the mediator not only perceives these signs but to act in order to prevent the conflict to escalate further.

5.6 Conclusion

Contextual information is what allows one to fully understand an event or action. For this purpose and depending on the domain, different context types may be used. This chapter was dedicated precisely to the importance of contextual information.

Specifically, and giving the scope of the book, it has been detailed information that is important to contextualize conflicts. In fact, in order for disputant parties and mediators to fully understand the conflict, it is imperative to consider information about the boundaries of the case and about past similar cases. During a conflict resolution process is necessary to understand the attitudes and behaviors of the parties, namely their level of stress or fatigue, their conflict handling style and the level of escalation of the conflict.

These aspects are essential not only for the parties to understand each other but for the mediator to apprehend the actions and reactions of the disputants. Traditionally, the mediator acknowledges this information coming from the parties through the words exchanged but also from non-verbal cues such as the tone of voice or elements of body language. However, a problem arises when we move from traditional face-to-face conflict resolution to ODR, in which interactions are far more impersonal and deprived from the rich contextual framework that stems from our multi-modal communication.

Indeed, personality traits, conflict resolution styles, emotional intelligence and response to stress are some of the key determinants of how conflicts are resolved (Daft et al. 1987; Jordan and Troth 2004). These issues share the particularity that their effects are visible more on the attitudes and behaviours of the individuals than on the words used. In fact, when resolving a conflict face-to-face most of the information is shared not through the words spoken but by the way that the words are spoken (Mehrabian 1980).

As Rifkin puts it, in face to face mediation, the spoken words and the visual cues sparked by body language are the primary elements in the communication process. However, in the *"screen to screen"* of ODR, the written word and the visual dimensions of the computer screen constitute these elements (Rifkin 2001). This may have its advantages but certainly has disadvantages too, namely concerning the amount of contextual information that is absent. Moreover, when people communicate online, they tend to forget that there is another person behind the screen, with equivalent worries, fears and desires, i.e., it becomes easier to offend people online. This constitutes a risk for the development of interpersonal relationships, which are paramount for a successful conflict resolution process (Dodds et al. 2011; Marucci et al. 2001).

This chapter analysed the implications of the lack of contextual information in current ODR approaches. The problem addressed derives from the wide Media richness theory (Sheer and Chen 2004), in which a communication medium is evaluated by its ability to reproduce the information sent over it. Text-based chats, in use in many conflict resolution tools, are very poor by nature, since they do not convey any visual social cues such as gestures. Although richer mediums such as video-conferencing could be used, this is neither always possible nor desirable (e.g. in cases of aggression the victim often feels an inhibitor effect when *"seeing"* the aggressor) (Balvin and Tyler 2006).

To deal with this issue, in the following chapters, it will be described an approach based on the concept of Ambient Intelligence (Aarts and Grotenhuis 2011). It relies on the combined use of Ubiquitous Computing, Ubiquitous

Communication and Intelligent User Interfaces to develop context-aware computational environments that are able to seamlessly acquire information from its users and take actions that aim at the maximization of some goal (e.g. user comfort or safety, efficiency at performing a given task). Mediators, in particular, will have a much larger set of contextual information, based on which they can make better decisions.

References

Aarts, E., and F. Grotenhuis. 2011. Ambient intelligence 2.0: Towards synergetic prosperity. *Ambient Intelligence and Smart Environments* 3(1): 3–11.

Acharya, S., and M. Kam. 2011. Evidence combination for hard and soft sensor data fusion. In *Proceedings of the 14th international conference on information fusion (FUSION), 2011*. New Jersey: Piscataway. ISBN 978-1-4577-0267-9.

Anderson, J.R., L.M. Reder, and H.A. Simon. 1996. Situated learning and education. *Educational Researcher* 25(4): 5–11.

Aztiria, A., A. Izaguirre, and J.C. Augusto. 2010. Learning patterns in ambient intelligence environments: A survey. *Artificial Intelligence Review* 34(1): 35–51.

Balvin, Nikola, and Melissa Conley Tyler. 2006. Emotions in cyberspace: The advantages and disadvantages of online communication. *Organisational Psychologist*: 5–8, September 2006; U of Melbourne Legal Studies research paper no. 277. Available at SSRN: http://ssrn.com/abstract=1027510

Banks, J. (ed.). 2007. *Handbook of simulation: Principles, methodology, advances, applications, and practice*. Wiley-Interscience. ISBN 978-0471134039.

Bardram, J.E. 2004. Applications of context-aware computing in hospital work: Examples and design principles. In *SAC'04 proceedings of the 2004 ACM symposium on applied computing*, 1574–1579. New York: ACM.

Barnett, E., and M. Casper. 2001. A definition of "social environment". *American Journal of Public Health* 91(3): 465.

Baumeister, R.F., K.D. Vohs, C.N. DeWall, and L. Zhang. 2007. How emotion shapes behavior: Feedback, anticipation, and reflection, rather than direct causation. *Personality and Social Psychology Review* 11(2): 167–203.

Bellotti, V. 2008. The Magitti activity-aware leisure guide. In *Social brain forum*, Tokyo Institute of Technology, February 27, Tokyo, Japan.

Bolchini, C., C.A. Curino, E. Quintarelli, F.A. Schreiber, and L. Tanca. 2007. *A data-oriented survey of context models*. Newsletter ACM SIGMOD Record 36(4): 19–26. New York, NY: ACM.

Brown, H., and A. Marriott. 2012. *ADR: Principles and practice*, 3rd ed. London: Sweet & Maxwell. ISBN 978–0414044791.

Budzik, J., and K.J. Hammond. 2000. *IUI'00 proceedings of the 5th international conference on intelligent user interfaces*, 44–51. New York: ACM.

Byun, H.E., and K. Cheverst. 2002. Harnessing context to support proactive behaviours. In *Proceedings of ECAI workshop on AI in mobile systems*. Frontiers in Artificial Intelligence and Applications, IOS Press, The Netherlands.

Carneiro, D., J.C. Castillo, P. Novais, A. Fernández-Caballero, and J. Neves. 2012. Multimodal behavioural analysis for non-invasive stress detection. *Expert Systems with Applications* 39 (18): 13376–13389, 15 December 2012. Elsevier. http://dx.doi.org/10.1016/j.eswa.2012.05.065.

Daft, R.L., R.H. Lengel, and L.K. Trevino. 1987. Message equivocality, media selection, and manager performance: Implications for information systems. *MIS Quarterly* 11: 355–366.

Damásio, A. 1994. *Descartes' error: Emotion, reason, and the human brain.* Putnam Publishing, hardcover: ISBN 0-399-13894-3.

David, B.S. 1991. Principles for case representation in a case-based aiding system for lesson planning. In *Proceedings of the workshop on case-based reasoning*, Madison Hotel, Washington, 8–10 May.

De Vries, B.R., R. Leenes, and J. Zeleznikow. 2005. Fundamentals of providing negotiation support online: The need for developing BATNAs. In *Proceedings of the second international ODR workshop*, 59–67. Tilburg: Wolf Legal Publishers.

Dearle, A., G.N.C. Kirby, R. Morrison, A. McCarthy, K. Mullen, Y. Yang, R.C.H. Connor, P. Welen, and A. Wilson. 2003. Architectural support for Global Smart Spaces. In *MDM'03 proceedings of the 4th international conference on Mobile Data Management*, 153–164. London: Springer. ISBN 3-540-00393-2.

Dey, A.K. 2001. Understanding and using context. *Personal Ubiquitous Computing* 5(1): 4–7. doi:10.1007/s007790170019.

Dodds, T.J., B.J. Mohler, and H.H. Bülthoff. 2011. Talk to the virtual hands: Self-animated avatars improve communication in head-mounted display virtual environments. *PLoS ONE* 6(10): e25759.

Dolan, R.J. 2002. Emotion, cognition, and behavior. *Science* 298(5596): 1191–1194.

Eysenck, M.W., and M.T. Keane. 2005. Cognitive Psychology: A Student's Handbook, Psychology Press, 1st ed. ISBN 978-1841693590.

Fisher, R., and W. Ury. 1981. *Getting to yes: Negotiating agreement without giving in.* Boston: Houghton Mifflin.

Givón, T. 2005. *Context as other minds: The pragmatics of sociality, cognition and communication.* Amsterdam: John Benjamins Publishing.

Goldberg, S.B., F.E. Sander, N. Rogers, and S.R. Cole. 2003. *Dispute resolution: Negotiation, mediation and other processes.* New York: Aspen Publishers.

Graham, M., M. Zook, and A. Boulton. 2012. Augmented reality in urban places: Contested content and the duplicity of code. *Transactions of the Institute of British Geographers* 38: 464–479. doi:10.1111/j.1475-5661.2012.00539.x 2012.

Gudykunst, W.B. 2003. *Bridging differences: Effective intergroup communication*, Interpersonal communication texts, 4th ed. Thousand Oaks: SAGE. ISBN 978-0761929376.

Jordan, P.J., and A.C. Troth. 2004. Managing emotions during team problem solving: Emotional intelligence and conflict resolution. *Human Performance* 17(2): 195–218.

Katsh, E. 2005. The Online Ombuds Office: Adapting dispute resolution to cyberspace. Available online at http://www.umass.edu/dispute/ncair/katsh.htm

Khaleghi, B., A. Khamis, F.O. Karray, and S.N. Razavi. 2013. Multisensor data fusion: A review of the state-of-the-art. *Information Fusion* 14(1): 28–44; *Information Fusion* 14(4): 562.

Klaming, L., J. Van Veenen, and R. Leenes. 2004. I want the opposite of what you want: Summary of a study on the reduction of fixed-pie perceptions in online negotiations. *"Expanding the horizons of ODR"*, proceedings of the 5th international workshop on Online Dispute Resolution (ODR Workshop'08), 84–94, Firenze, Italy.

Kolodner, J.L. 1993. *Case-based reasoning.* San Mateo: Morgan Kaufmann Publishers.

Kunkler, K. 2006. The role of medical simulation: An overview. *The International Journal of Medical Robotics and Computer Assisted Surgery* 2(3): 203–210.

Ljungblad, S., M. Hakansson, M. Gaye, and L.E. Holmquist. 2004. *CHI EA '04 CHI '04 extended abstracts on human factors in computing systems*, 1191–1194. New York: ACM.

Marucci, L., G. Mori, F. Paterno, and F. Costalli. 2001. *Design criteria for usable web-accessible virtual environments.* http://www.museumsandtheweb.com/node/9254.

Mehrabian, A. 1980. *Silent messages: Implicit communication of emotions and attitudes.* Belmont: Wadsworth Publishing Company.

Munro, A., P. Welen, and A. Wilson. 2001. *Interaction archetypes.* GLOSS consortium report D4. http://iihm.imag.fr/projects/gloss/Deliverables/D4.pdf

Naaman, M., S. Harada, Q. Wang, H. Garcia-Molina, and A. Paepcke. 2004. Context data in geo-referenced digital photo collections. In *Proceedings of the 12th annual ACM international conference on multimedia,* 196–203. New York: ACM.

Notini, J. 2010. Effective alternatives analysis in mediation: "BATNA/WATNA" analysis demystified. http://www.mediate.com/articles/notini1.cfm, 2005. Last accessed October.

O'Hare, N., C. Gurrin, G.J.F. Jones, and A.F. Smeaton. 2005. Combination of content analysis and context features for digital photograph retrieval. In *2nd European Workshop on the Integration of Knowledge, Semantics and Digital Media Technology (EWIMT 2005),* 323–328, January 2005.

Raiffa, H. 2002. *The art and science of negotiation.* Cambridge, MA: Harvard University Press.

Rekimoto, J., Y. Ayatsuka, and K. Hayashi. 1998. *Second international symposium on Wearable Computers, 1998. Digest of papers.* New Jersey: Piscataway. doi:10.1109/ISWC.1998.729531.

Rifkin, J. 2001. Online dispute resolution: Theory and practice of the fourth party. *Conflict Resolution Quarterly* 19(1): 117–124.

Rogoff, B., and J. Lave (eds.). 1984. *Everyday cognition: Its development in social context.* Cambridge, MA: Harvard University Press. 314 pp.

Satyanarayanan, M. 2002. IEEE pervasive computing: From the editor in chief – Challenges in implementing a context-aware system. *IEEE Distributed Systems* Online 3(9): 2.

Sheer, V.C., and Ling Chen. 2004. Improving media richness theory: A study of interaction goals, message valence, and task complexity in manager-subordinate communication. *Management Communication Quarterly* 18: 76.

Steenbergen, W. 2005. Rationalizing dispute resolution: From best alternative to the most likely one. In *Proceedings 3rd ODR workshop,* Brussels.

Tapia, D.I., R.S. Alonso, O. García, J.M. Corchado, and J. Bajo. 2013. Wireless sensor networks, real-time locating systems and multi-agent systems: The perfect team. *FUSION* 2013: 2177–2184.

Turner, J.C., P.J. Oakes, S.A. Haslam, and C. McGarty. 1994. Self and collective: Cognition and social context. *Personality and Social Psychology Bulletin* 20(5): 454–463. doi:10.1177/0146167294205002.

Part II
Technological Framework

Chapter 6
An Agent-Based Architecture for a Second Generation ODR Tool

Abstract As seen in previous chapters, there are currently many different commercial ODR service providers and research projects. It can also be concluded that these systems are rather specific, focused on a single domain, type of conflict or conflict resolution method. These factors constitute some of the reasons that hold back further or faster development of new ODR service providers. Indeed, single-domain or highly-focused ODR tools have markedly fewer potential clients, thus making them less appealing to investors and developers alike. This chapter addresses this specific issue by proposing an architecture that provides ODR services based on abstract concepts and processes: UMCourt. Indeed, many concepts and processes are cross-domain: they have the same meaning independently of the legal domain. They are, however, implemented differently. These different implementations should, nevertheless, be transparent to the users. The architecture described here achieves these objectives by implementing a hierarchic relationship between software agents in which higher-level agents have coordination tasks and lower-level agents implement domain-specific knowledge. The architecture has also the advantage of being easily extensible to additional domains without changes to existing agents.

6.1 Introduction

Presently, many different ODR methods may be considered, ranging from negotiation and mediation to modified arbitration or jury proceedings (Goodman 2003). Indeed, under this setting, it must be considered the existence of legal knowledge-based systems, appearing as tools that provide legal advice to the disputant parties and also systems that (help) settle disputes in an online environment (De Vries et al. 2005).

In devising such systems, the Katsch/Rifkin vision of the four parties in an ODR process must be taken into consideration, i.e., the two opposing parties, the third neutral party (e.g. mediator, arbitrator) and the technology that works with the mediator or arbitrator (Katsh and Rifkin 2001). A gradual tendency to foster the intervention of autonomous software agents in order to achieve this vision is clearly assumed in this book, with these acting either as decision support systems or as "real" electronic mediators. This approach is wittingly close to second generation ODR, proposed by Peruginelli and Chiti (2002), as it is guided by three main lines:

- The aim of such systems does not end by putting the parties in contact, but it consists of actually proposing solutions for solving the disputes;
- The Human intervention is reduced and the software intervention enhanced; and
- These systems act through the use of autonomous software agents.

The consideration of this wider role for software agents is based in the use of Artificial Intelligence techniques and information and knowledge representation tools. Yet, merely representing facts and events is not enough for dispute resolution. In order to have useful actions performed by software agents, it is required that they not only know the terms of the dispute, but also the rights and wrongs of the parties and foresee the legal consequences of facts and events (Peruginelli 2002).

The complexness and width of the legal domain, as well as the particularities of each sub-field of The Law, must also be considered. Thus, the development of fully functional technology-based tools that may assist parties may be a challenge. In fact, until now, only a very limited number of ODR tools with some real degree of autonomy have been developed. Moreover, these tools are very domain-dependent, focusing on very specific and well defined issues. Therefore, there is a need to develop architectures that are based on high-level problem-solving concepts, common to every sub-field of The Law, so as to apply them to a broader range of problems. Such architectures should be abstract enough to cover multiple legal domains but at the same time possess the specific knowledge of each one.

In this chapter a proposal of such architecture is put forward, henceforth designated as UMCourt. It is based on the Jade agent platform, which aims at the simplification of the development of multi-agent systems by providing support for agent communication and registry (Bellifemine et al. 2007). The platform runs on a Java Virtual Machine, thus agents are also programmed using the Java language.

The objective of UMCourt is to enable a range of services targeted at assisting the disputant parties, independently of the domain of their dispute. The architecture is abstract in the sense that it encompasses many concepts that are common to virtually all the legal domains. Nevertheless, each domain has its particularities.

In that sense, the architecture presented here covers a broad range of domains but also contains the specificities that allow it to operate correctly in each one, in a transparent manner. This is the main goal of the work detailed in this chapter.

To accomplish it, abstract notions that exist in conflict resolution regardless of the domain of the dispute will be identified. As an example, to a certain point, a negotiation process will always be a sequence of rounds in which, in each round, each party states his opinion about the current proposal on the table, i.e., this process proceeds independently of the domain of the negotiation. The same happens with certain concepts, i.e., independently of the domain of the dispute, the concept of best or worst possible scenarios applies.

The first step in the development of this abstract architecture is thus to identify which concepts and processes apply in different legal domains and model them. However, it must be kept in mind that, although these concepts and processes have the same meaning for legal domains, they may have to be implemented differently. This should nevertheless be transparent to the user. The final step is the definition of the minimum set of software agents developed to support such architecture.

6.2 Identifying Useful Abstract Concepts

At the outset of identifying the abstract concepts for a multi-domain ODR tool aimed at assisting the parties, there is the need to determine which information would be useful. The next step consists in the formalization of such concepts.

In a first instance, it would be interesting for parties to determine to which extent it is reasonable to engage in an alternative dispute resolution process, i.e., parties should ask themselves if a better outcome will be reached using an alternative dispute resolution process instead of litigation (Klaming et al. 2004).

This concept may be defined in terms of the BATNA – Best Alternative to a Negotiated Agreement, or the possible best outcome "along a particular path if I try to get my interests satisfied in a way that does not require negotiation with the other party" (Notini 2010). This concept is abstract as it is useful for any dispute. It is also useful for parties as it will, at least, contribute to the acknowledgement that an agreement may be disadvantageous. In fact, by knowing their BATNA, parties would on the one hand become better protected against agreements that should be rejected and, on the other hand, in a better condition to reach an agreement that better satisfy their interests (De Vries et al. 2005).

On the opposite side one should also consider the notion of a WATNA, or the Worst Alternative to a Negotiated Agreement (Steenbergen 2005). The WATNA aims to estimate the worst possible outcome along the litigation path. It can be quite relevant in the calculation of the real risks that parties will face in a judicially determined litigation, imagining the worst possible outcome for the party. With these two abstract concepts, the party is aware of the best and worst scenario, if the dispute is to be solved in a court.

It is also interesting for a party to analyze the space between the BATNA and the WATNA as a useful element to be taken into account to make decisions. Of course, the less space there is between the BATNA and the WATNA, the less dangerous it becomes for the party not to accept the agreement (unless, of course, their BATNA is really disadvantageous). A wider space between the BATNA and the WATNA may indicate that it can become rather dangerous for the party not to accept the ODR agreement (except in situations when the WATNA is really not inconvenient at all for the party).

Thus, it may be argued that knowledge about the space between the BATNA and the WATNA is quite central while it is also an abstract concept, independent of the domain. This concept is close to the Zone of Possible Agreement (ZOPA) proposed by Raiffa (2002). It is the zone where an agreement can be met that is acceptable for both parties.

It would also be interesting for a party to understand the region of this space in which an outcome is more likely, i.e., if the parties are to solve the dispute through litigation, what is the most likely outcome? In fact, sticking only with the BATNA and the WATNA may not be realistic as these are usually not the most likely outcomes but merely informative values that establish boundaries. Thus, an informed party should also consider the concept of MLATNA – Most Likely Alternative to a Negotiated Agreement (Steenbergen 2005).

Using the same arguments, it can also be argued that the existence of metrics that measure the probability of each possible outcome could also be extremely useful for a party. Thus, it is also considered the concept of probable case, i.e., a possible outcome with an associated value of likeliness.

Concluding, several abstract concepts that are important for parties can be considered in the development of an ODR tool: (1) the BATNA; (2) the WATNA; (3) the ZOPA; (4) the MLATNA and (5) the probable cases. These concepts establish what is identified in this work as the minimum set of information that a party should consider prior to getting involved in a litigation or alternative conflict resolution process.

6.3   Identifying Abstract Processes

Besides abstract concepts, abstract processes in conflict resolution should also be considered. The search for processes that follow the same model, independently of the legal domain, can result in functionality reuse and in a simplification of cross-domain conflict resolution service providers. Several abstract processes are identified and are detailed in the following sub-sections.

6.3.1   Information Retrieval

The retrieval of information generally involves a given number of pre-determined tasks such as querying a database, analyzing the results or possibly filtering or sorting them (Korfhage 1997). In this sub-section the proposed abstract model for information retrieval in the legal domain is presented (Fig. 6.1), being further detailed in the chapter that follows. The aim of the process is to retrieve a number of past cases that are, to some extent, related to the current one, i.e., it computes the similarity of each past case to the current case (which tells a party the likeliness of a past outcome on their current case) as well as the utility (which tells the party how

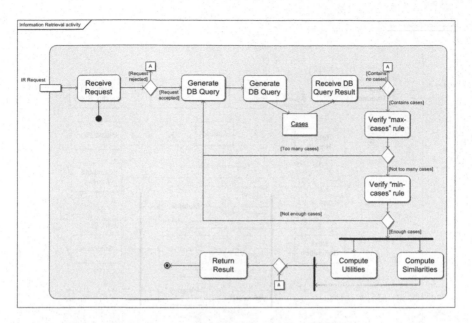

Fig. 6.1 Activity diagram depicting the sequence of main activities needed to implement the process of information retrieval

much they would win/loose if an outcome such as the one of the past case were to occur).

The Information Retrieval process starts with the reception of a request. This request is analyzed to determine if it should be considered or denied (it may be denied due to an unavailability of service, lack of permissions, among other reasons). If it is denied the process ends. If it is accepted, a query to the database is generated. This query can be seen as a pre-selection of potentially interesting cases, i.e., cases that are expected to have some degree of similarity. Given that there is no control on the number of cases that are retrieved, the pre-selection returned from the database is analyzed.

If no cases are retrieved, the process ends unsuccessfully as it cannot currently provide a solution for the problem. If, on the other hand, there are too many or too few cases, the database query is rebuilt so as to make the selection rules stricter or more relaxed, respectively. The main objective of this procedure is to obtain the optimum amount of information that parties can analyze efficiently. This has an effect on the similarity of the cases retrieved.

When a suitable selection of cases is achieved, a value of similarity and of utility is computed for each individual case. Similarity is obtained by comparing key characteristics of the cases, whose resemblance will contribute, with a given weight, to the overall measure of similarity. In order to compute the utility of a past case, the structure of the solution is changed with the values of the current case, allowing computing a value of the solution for the characteristics of the current case. This constitutes the adaptation phase.

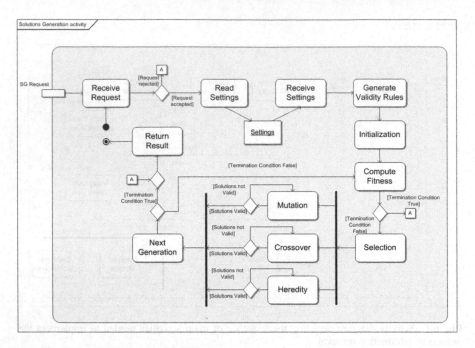

Fig. 6.2 Activity diagram depicting the sequence of main activities needed to implement the process of generating solutions, using a nature-inspired approach

Finally, when these steps are completed, a result is returned to the user that contains potentially similar past cases, a measure of this similarity and a value of utility. This will allow each party to understand to which extent a given outcome would satisfy them, as well as to understand how likely that outcome is.

6.3.2   Generation of Solutions

The process of generating solutions can be implemented in an abstract way, as long as the specific domain-dependent rules that encode the validity meaningfulness of solutions are provided. In order to develop this abstract model for generating solutions, a nature-inspired approach to problem solving was followed: that of Genetic Computation (Davis 1991). Although a much more detailed definition of the process is provided ahead in the book, the process model is depicted in this section (Fig. 6.2).

The process starts with the reception of a request for generating solutions for a given problem, with associated data describing the problem and the domain. At this point, the request may be rejected if it is malformed (e.g., necessary information missing) or refers to an invalid/unknown domain. If the request is valid, the model proceeds to read the necessary sceneries from the database, specific to the domain of the problem. With this information, the model generates the validity rules, i.e., the rules that state whether a given solution is valid in the domain, and proceeds to the initialization.

During the initialization, the model defines the settings that will control the remaining of its execution (e.g., the type and weight of the genetic operators, terminating conditions, size of the population). Moreover, it also generates a random population of a pre-determined size.

Then, the process moves on to measuring the fitness of each of the individuals. If there is a minimum number of solutions with a given level of fitness, the model terminates successfully by returning the solutions generated. Otherwise, the computational process goes on to the selection phase.

In the selection process, the main objective is to pick the most promising solutions, i.e., the ones that are likely to give birth to even better ones. Once concluded, the next step is to apply the genetic operators on the selected solutions. Each of these operators will take some solutions to generate new ones, which will be validated. When a new set of valid solutions is obtained, the terminating condition is verified. If a maximum number of generations has been reached, the process terminates by returning the best solutions obtained so far. Otherwise it returns to the computation of the fitness, repeating the whole process.

When the computational process reaches the terminating condition, it is expected to have generated a number of valid satisfactory solutions. The solutions may however have low values of utility, which is generally due to bad terminating conditions, not allowing the model to evolve during the necessary time.

6.3.3 Negotiation

Negotiation assumes a central role in any conflict resolution process. It is through negotiation that parties conjoin throughout successive proposals and counter-proposals, in order to reach a mutually satisfactory outcome. A typical negotiation process can be seen as a sequence of rounds in which parties exchange proposals, with a potential intervention of a neutral that may control the process and contribute with its own proposals to the outcome.

In that sense, an abstract negotiation model can be developed to be used in the legal domain. Figure 6.3 depicts such a model. It starts by receiving a request and verifying its validity, deciding if it can be accepted or rejected. Being accepted, the process moves on to allow all the parties to register. By doing so, each party agrees in engaging into a negotiation process providing the necessary information (e.g., personal information, personal objectives, personal appraisal of each issue).

Once all the parties are registered, the system receives a list of possible solutions (obtained from any of the two methods described before) and informs them about the issues being negotiated, detailing the number of matters, their type (e.g., monetary, real estate, divisible) and description. Then, the system, under the role

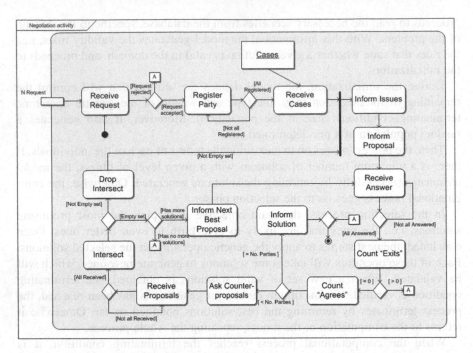

Fig. 6.3 Activity diagram depicting the sequence of main activities needed to implement the negotiation process

of an electronic mediator, proposes what is considered the best solution, i.e., the solution that maximizes the sum of the gains of the parties. After publishing the proposal the model waits for all the parties to respond. Parties can respond in several ways: ignore, reject, accept and exit the process.

Once all the answers are received, it is necessary to verify if there are parties that abandoned the process, in which case the negotiation ends unsuccessfully. Otherwise, the system checks if all the parties agreed on the proposal, in which case the process ends successfully. If this is not the case, the system asks the parties for counter-proposals, which may stand for minor modifications of the original proposal or entirely new ones. After receiving all the proposals (if any) the system tries to find intersection points in which the parties may have agreed.

If there are intersecting points, these will be marked as "agreed upon" and removed from the list of pending issues. This being the case, parties are informed of the new list of issues and the process repeats. However, if there are no intersecting points, the system itself will propose a solution of the list of the ones so far compiled. If there are none to be proposed, the process ends unsuccessfully.

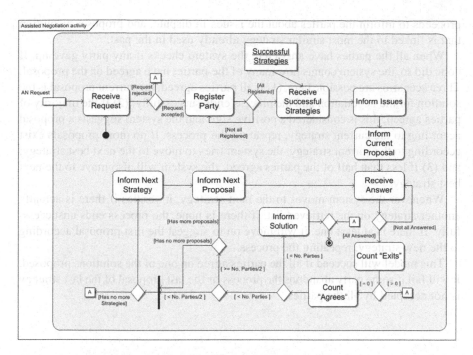

Fig. 6.4 Activity diagram depicting the sequence of main activities needed to implement the assisted negotiation process. This model is especially suited for scenarios in which parties are unable or unwilling to generate solutions

6.3.4   Generation of Strategies

One frequent challenge in ODR is concerned with the creation of effective strategies for problem-solving (generally the definition of a line of attack in a negotiated case). Frequently, parties are unable (because they lack the training or are unaware of all the details of the dispute), or are not motivated (since they avoid to deal with some sensitive issues) to think on possible solutions or strategies to solve the conflict. When this happens, the conflict resolution process risks stalling.

The main aim of this abstract model is to provide the framework for an assisted negotiation process which supports parties in going through a negotiated process (Fig. 6.4). It is similar to the model described previously in the sense that it is a negotiation model. However, while the previous one only suggests solutions, this one tries to guide the parties through a path (strategy) that has already worked in the past for similar disputes.

The system being implemented deals with some issues similarly: it analyzes the validity of the requests and registers the parties. Having concluded the registration, it receives a list of past successful negotiations that are linked to a similar case. These negotiations (here denominated "strategies") are sorted according to the degree of their similarity to the one followed in the present case. The system proceeds to inform the parties about the issues in dispute, and proposes a solution that is linked to the most similar strategy already used in the past.

When all the parties have answered, the system checks if any party gave up. If none did so, the system counts how many of the parties have agreed on the proposal. Three scenarios are possible here. (1) If all parties agreed, the current proposal is the solution for the negotiation and the process ends successfully; (2) If the majority of parties agreed, this is considered a positive sign and the system suggests a proposal according to the current strategy, repeating the process. If no more proposals exist according to the current strategy, the system tries to move to the next best strategy; and (3) If less than half of the parties agreed, the system will also move to the next best strategy.

Whenever the system moves to the next strategy, it verifies if there is actually another strategy on the retrieved list. If there is none, the process ends unsuccessfully. If there is at least one, it will move on to suggest the first proposal according to the new strategy, repeating the process.

This model will succeed if all the parties agree on one of the solutions proposed. It will fail if some party abandons the process or the last proposal of the last strategy is not accepted by all the parties.

6.3.5   Generic Conflict Resolution Model

The high-level abstract processes that were described in the previous sub-sections can now be composed in order to design a generic conflict resolution model (Fig. 6.5). This model aims to accompany the conflict resolution process since its outset to its conclusion. When the process starts, parties register providing some personal information (e.g., personal objectives, background information). Once this process is finished, parties provide and agree on the details of the case, such as the number of issues being disputed and their attributes.

Based on this model, the system evaluates a set of useful information that will allow the parties to fully understand the most important aspects of their dispute. This information includes the abstract concepts put forward in this chapter or even past similar cases. At the same time, the system generates a set of possible solutions (with the associated values of utility) and a set of strategies that may result in a successful outcome for the cases under consideration.

The information compiled is provided to the parties, so that they can be informed before the actual beginning of the negotiation. Then, parties must choose whether they intend to follow a regular negotiation process (in which the responsibility of cooperating to reach a solution is on their shoulders) or an assisted one (in which the system tries to guide the parties into a successful outcome). In the former case, if the process fails, parties can still rely on an assisted negotiation. At the end of any of these processes, independently of the result of the negotiation, the process ends, with the success being the success of any of the negotiation processes used.

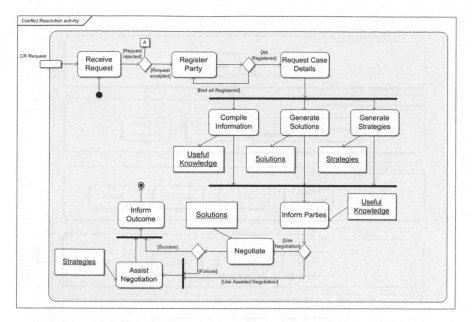

Fig. 6.5 Activity diagram depicting the sequence of main activities needed to implement a generic conflict resolution model. It can be seen as a high-level composition of the previously depicted models

6.4 Software Agents

The activities depicted in the previous section are implemented by a number of different software agents through the composition of their services. Agents are classified as *Main Agents* or *Secondary Agents*, according to their degree of autonomy.

Main Agents have an increased degree of autonomy and are based on models with a high degree of abstraction. These agents may control secondary ones and compose their services in order to implement high-level appointments or engagements. Moreover, they can take decisions at run-time, targeting the optimization of the processes implemented.

Secondary Agents are simpler and have little or no autonomy at all. Their main aim is to implement specific and relatively simpler processes. Main agents can request services from these simpler agents.

This organization results in a highly modular architecture. Moreover, it allows implementing abstract processes independently of the domain, but containing the necessary particularities to be used to solve specific problems. In the next sub-section the agents' functionalities are briefly described. Subsequently, the approach followed to use this abstract architecture to solve specific problems is detailed.

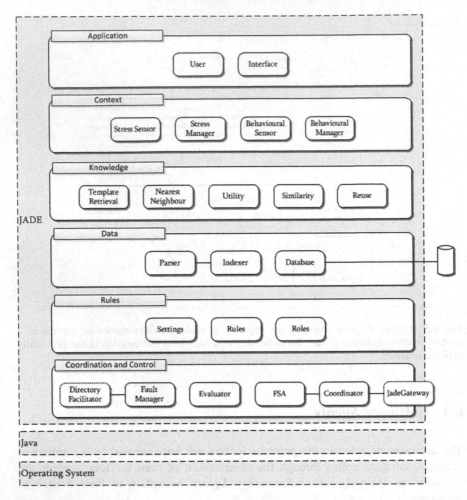

Fig. 6.6 Diagram depicting the layered nature of the architecture, with the organization of the software agents according to their functionalities. Lines between agents depict important communication paths. More than one instance of some agents may exist simultaneously

The main agent types that make up the proposed architecture and the functionalities implemented will be succinctly described. It must be stressed here that the actual architecture may encompass more than one instance of some of the agents enumerated, so as to address different specific legal domains. Figure 6.6 depicts the layered nature of the proposed architecture. A special emphasis was placed while devising this architecture on making it dynamic and modular, so as to seamlessly integrate users, devices, sensors and environment (Preuveneers and Novais 2012).

6.4.1   Coordination and Control Layer

The agents in this layer have as main purpose to control the life cycle of the platform and the correct execution of the processes:

- Coordinator – Receives task requests from a multitude of agents (e.g. external agents or interface agents) and takes the necessary steps in order to handle them. This agent maintains a list of the active tasks provided by the FSA agent;
- JadeGateway – The JadeGateway agent is a special agent that allows non-Jade and Jade-based code to communicate. It is used to allow the multi-agent system to communicate with external entities;
- FaultManager – Encompasses the necessary mechanisms to detect malfunctions in software agents. It is able to stop, restart or start the agents that constitute the environment. Its main purpose is to start the agents at startup and monitor their life-cycles;
- Evaluator – Receives messages from the software agents detailing the timestamps of certain events, in order to compute performance indicators and point out possible paths to improve the environment functioning (e.g. most common causes for case retrieval failure, average time of each activity); and
- FSA – Contains a list of Jade FSM (Finite State Machine) behaviors that describe the guidelines or steps necessary for an agent to perform given actions.

6.4.2   Rules Layer

The agents that make up this layer are intended to encode the rules that guarantee the validity of the operations of the platform, as well as the legal norms. This layer is composed of three agents:

- Settings – outlines pre-determined sceneries, mostly for case related operations (e.g. repossession, similarity or utility processes) according to which retrieved parameters may be changed;
- Roles – each software agent contains a set of roles, describing the services that each entity may or may not request. This agent also encodes the access schemes to information; and
- Rules – This agent maintains a set of rules for different purposes, ranging from legal norms to rules that establish the legitimacy of a solution.

6.4.3   Data Layer

The agents in the Data Layer have as main objective to assist in the access to data, by providing an abstraction of its files and database. The following agents constitute this layer:

- Parser – This agent receives a list of XML files unfolding cases and parses them, providing as output software objects that may be used by the remaining agents;
- Indexer – Given a list of cases, this agent indexes them in the database so that they may be easily retrieved; and
- Database – All the interactions with the database go through this agent. It provides different methods for data retrieval and storage that simplify the interaction with the database.

6.4.4   Knowledge Layer

The agents that constitute this layer aim at assembling knowledge from the information at hand in the platform, so that both parties and system may be better informed, therefore refining their decision-making practices. Five software agents support knowledge-related tasks:

- TemplateRetrieval – Encodes a pre-selection algorithm that picks a broad range of cases that match a specific set of pre-selection rules. This agent has the autonomy to change search settings, the similarity parameters and even the algorithm constraints in order to perform a better selection of cases;
- NearestNeighbour – Encodes a pre-selection procedure to retrieve cases from memory, based on the Nearest Neighbour algorithm. It has the self-sufficiency to change the search settings so that better results may be reached;
- Utility – Encodes the necessary mechanisms to compute the utility of an hypothetic outcome for a given party;
- Reuse – Holds the necessary knowledge to adapt past cases to new situations; and
- Similarity – Is able to compute a value of similarity between two cases, based on a weighted sum of their differences in key features.

6.4.5   Context Layer

The agents that constitute the context layer provide, in a seamless way, the tools to transparently access information describing the users' context. The architecture, in its current form, places particular emphasis on the analysis of behaviors and on stress detection: two aspects that are of interest in a conflict resolution process. The following four agents were implemented:

- StressSensor – An agent that provides one or more sources of information that are used to assess the user's stress level;
- StressManager – Includes the required mechanisms to assess the users level of stress (on-the-fly), based on data provided by the previous agent;

- BehaviouralSensor – Includes the sources of information that are used to evaluate the user's behavior during the conflict resolution process, which can provide valuable information considering their state; and
- BehaviouralManager – Encodes the necessary mechanisms for drawing conclusions about the users' behavior based on the information provided by the BehaviouralSensor.

6.4.6 Application Layer

This layer isolates the user from the inner complexity of the platform. The agents that compose it implement abstract interfaces that to unfold the functionalities provided by the platform:

- User – This agent embodies one party, while he/she is using the platform, encoding features such as objectives, personal information or perspectives; and
- Interface – This agent is responsible by the definition of the various interfaces with which the user may interact.

6.5 An Abstract Architecture to Solve Specific Problems

One of the main objectives of this work is to define an agent-based architecture that may be used in different legal domains, so as to increase its areas of application. In fact, many of the current ODR tools are highly domain-specific, resulting in a decreased use/acceptance on the part of the users.

Some abstract processes and concepts have already been identified that are valid in any legal domain. However, the way they are implemented differs according to the domain. As an example, let us consider the computation of the BATNA and WATNA in two different legal domains, namely in Commercial and Labour Laws. These two abstract conceptions denote, as described above, the best and worst possible scenarios in a litigation process. Nevertheless, depending on the legal domain, they may be computed differently since they are based on different aspects.

In Labor Law one has to consider issues such as worker antiquity, salary, seniority or a cause for dismissal, just to name a few. The following listing details a simplification of the rules that allow the computation of the BATNA and WATNA for the Portuguese Labor Law, as it is given in Decree of Law (DL) 7/ 2009 (Portuguese Laws). This simplified rule considers only the case in which a worker ends the contract with a just cause for dismissal.

```
Def_Rule 396
if RULE_394 then
 WATNA := 3 * (M_SALARY + SENIORITY)
 if TEMPORARY_CONTRACT then
  if WATNA < M_REMAINING * (M_SALARY + SENIORITY) then
   WATNA := M_REMAINING * (M_SALARY + SENIORITY)
 if WATNA < 15 * (D_SALARY + SENIORITY) then
  WATNA := 15 * (D_SALARY + SENIORITY)
 BATNA := 45 * (D_SALARY + SENIORITY)
 if BATNA < DAMAGE then
  BATNA := +DAMAGE
```

If rule 394 holds (i.e., if there is a just cause for dismissal), in the worst case the worker is entitled to 3 months of salary. However, it must be kept in mind that the BATNA of one party is often the WATNA of the other and vice versa, i.e., an indemnity of 3 months' salary is the BATNA of the employer and the WATNA of the employee. In the case of a temporary contract, the employee is entitled to an indemnity that amounts to the number of months still in the contract times salary and seniority. On the other hand, if the contract is not temporary, in the worst case the worker is entitled to 15 days of wage plus seniority per each year of antiquity, at a minimum of 3 months. In the best case, the employee receives 45 days of salary per each year of antiquity. This value may be higher if there has also been some damage to the employee.

On the other hand, in Commercial Law key issues are the product acquisition date, the type of the product and the warranty, or the product status. The following listing depicts a simplification of the rules that allow the computation of the BATNA for the Commercial Law, as it is given in DL 67/2003. In this example, it will be considered only the items 1–4 of Article 5th.

```
Def_Rule 5
if IS_MOBILE then
 if DEFECT_COMPLAINT_DELAY < 60 then
  if WARRANTY_DELAY < 730 then
   BATNA := { "product repair in 30 days";
     "product replacement" }
  else BATNA := { "no indemnity due" }
 else BATNA := { "no indemnity due" }
else
 if DEFECT_COMPLAINT_DELAY < 365 then
  if WARRANTY_DELAY < 1810 then
   BATNA := { "product repair in reasonable time" }
  else BATNA := { "no indemnity due" }
 else BATNA := { "no indemnity due" }
```

This rule states that: if the item is a mobile device, the complaint has been filed until 60 days from the date of detection of the defect and less than 2 years have passed since the purchased date, then the product must be repaired in 30 days or be replaced at the expenses of the manufacturer or reseller. In a dissimilar situation there is no indemnity due. On the other hand, if the item is not portable, the dates change respectively to 1 and 5 years, and the user is entitled to the reparation of the product.

Thus, as mentioned above, two perceptions that have the same meaning in different legal domains are implemented differently. The approach followed to address this issue focuses on two key points:

- Each secondary agent is divided into akin ones, which implement the same service interfaces, but implement them in different ways, according to the specific legal domain they address; and
- Each coordinator agent forwards a request to specific secondary agents according to the request's domain.

This approach holds several other advantages:

- The complexity of the process is hidden from the other agents, since the path to request a service to address a particular problem is transparent;
- It is easy to extend the architecture to other domains by adding new secondary agents;
- When new problem domains are included into the platform, no adjustment is required to the existing agents; and
- The architecture is highly modular and easily reconfigurable.

A simplified view of the architecture is depicted in Fig. 6.7. It details the agents involved in computing the BATNA value for the Labor Law domain. When the *Coordinator* agent receives a request, it acknowledges its domain and forwards it to the corresponding *domain agent* (in this case the *CoordinatorL*), which has the knowledge to carry out the task in the specific domain. In this case, only one service is needed from the BATNA agent, thus the request is forwarded to that one. However, this agent is in turn a high-level one that will, given the domain of the request, forward it to the *BATNAL* agent, which possesses the knowledge to compute the BATNA in the domain of the Labor Law. The request's result is returned via the same agents.

When forwarding messages, the following approach is followed. An agent's name details not only the service provided but also the domain of specialization. As an example, the *BATNAL* agent provides the computation of the BATNA in the Labor law domain. The domains being considered for prototyping and proof of concept purposes are *Labor Law (L), Consumer Law (C), Property Division (P)* and *Virtual Organizations (VO)*.

Subsequently, when a coordinator agent receives a request for a given service *S* in the domain *D*, it will autonomously search the agent directory for an agent identified as *SD*. If it exists the message is forwarded. Otherwise the request is rejected.

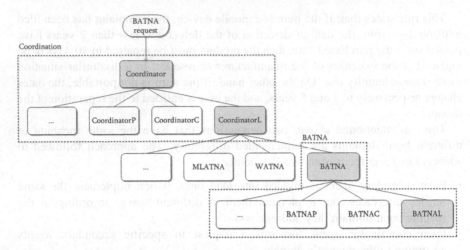

Fig. 6.7 Hierarchical nature of the architecture in which the complexity of providing specific services is hidden. Each agent forwards the request to more specific agents. Domain coordinators (e.g. *CoordinatorL*) are used to implement more complex activities involving more than one service (the computation of the BATNA requires the use of a single service from a single agent)

The added value of this approach is that new legal domains may be added to the platform and new agents encoded, without any changes being made to the existing ones.

6.6   Conclusion

One of the factors holding back a faster development and increased use of conflict resolution platforms is, without doubt, their highly domain-dependent nature. In fact, current approaches generally target a single domain. This significantly narrows the target audience, reducing eventual revenues and slowing the natural development of these environments, especially the commercial ones.

In this chapter it was analyzed the possibility of developing conflict resolution services or platforms that are, as far as possible, independent of the domain. The main objective is clearly that the same services may be used in different arenas, thus widening the potential domains of application and target audience.

In order to accomplish this vision, abstract concepts and processes were identified that encode notions that have the same meaning, independently of the legal domain. Nevertheless, their concrete implementation is specific to each domain. Thus, a unified architecture that implements such approach and hides its complexity from the user-level was presented. It results in a conflict resolution platform that provides the same services in different domains, transparently.

The layered nature of this architecture was detailed in terms of its software agents in which high-level agents act as coordinators, providing the system's functionalities through the composition of the services of the simpler, lower-level agents, that encode domain-related knowledge. These functionalities will be described in the following chapters. An architecture with such characteristics has the following advantages:

- Increased functionality reuse – process models and even specific code can be reused during development, decreasing time to market and development costs;
- Extensibility – since the name of the agents encode both their role in the architecture and their domain, no centralized agent description is necessary to forward specific domain requests. This means that no change is necessary to the existing architecture when including additional agents;
- Multi-domain and multi-approach – different functionalities can be provided in different legal domains, by a single platform. This increases the potential target audience. Different conflict resolution methods can also be followed, some of them including proactive assistance of the system.
- Transparency – the whole process of using the functionalities of the system is completely transparent to its users, i.e., a user needs no special knowledge about how the system implements a given functionality in a given domain or the steps it take to provide the same service in different domains;
- Support for innovative services – the proposed architecture includes a context layer that provides support to harness, manage and interpret information usually disregarded in traditional conflict resolution tools but that can be of major importance, especially for the mediator, such as the behavior of the parties, their level of stress or their emotional response.

References

Bellifemine, F.L., G. Caire, and D. Greenwood. 2007. *Developing multi-agent systems with JADE*, Wiley series in agent technology. Chichester: Wiley.

Davis, L.D. 1991. *Handbook of genetic algorithms*. New York: Van Nostrand Reinhold.

De Vries, B.R., R. Leenes, and J. Zeleznikow. 2005. Fundamentals of providing negotiation support online: The need for developing BATNAs. In *Proceedings of the second international ODR workshop*, 59–67. Tilburg: Wolf Legal Publishers.

Goodman, J.W. 2003. The pros and cons of online dispute resolution: An assessment of cyber-mediation. *Duke Law and Technology Review* 4: 1–16.

Katsh, E., and J. Rifkin. 2001. *Online dispute resolution: Resolving conflicts in cyberspace*. San Francisco: Jossey-Bass.

Klaming, L., J. Van Veenen, and R. Leenes. 2004. I want the opposite of what you want: Summary of a study on the reduction of fixed-pie perceptions in online negotiations. In *"Expanding the horizons of ODR", Proceedings of the 5th international workshop on Online Dispute Resolution (ODR workshop'08)*, Firenze, Italy, 84–94.

Korfhage, R. 1997. *Information storage and retrieval*, 1st ed. New York: Wiley.

Notini, J. 2010. Effective alternatives analysis in mediation: "BATNA/WATNA" analysis demystified. http://www.mediate.com/articles/notini1.cfm. 2005. Last accessed October.

Peruginelli, G. 2002. Artificial intelligence in alternative dispute resolution. In *Proceedings of the workshop on the Law of Electronic Agents (LEA02)*, ed. G. Sartor.

Peruginelli, G., and G. Chiti. 2002. Artificial intelligence in online dispute resolution. In *Proceedings of the workshop on the law of electronic agents – LEA*. Berlin: Springer.
Preuveneers, D., and P. Novais. 2012. A survey of software engineering best practices for the development of smart applications in Ambient Intelligence. *Journal of Ambient Intelligence and Smart Environments* 4(3): 149–162.
Raiffa, H. 2002. *The art and science of negotiation*. Cambridge, MA: Harvard University Press.
Steenbergen, W. 2005. Rationalizing dispute resolution: From best alternative to the most likely one. In *Proceedings 3rd ODR workshop*, Brussels.

Chapter 7
Information Retrieval

Abstract Retrieval information processes are fairly common in our knowledge-based society. While in the past information retrieval would consist in searching for a book in a library or finding a suitable train schedule, nowadays most information retrieval processes take place through computers and in an online environment. Undeniably, one of the most significant contributors to this trend was Google: a search engine that provided its users with an unprecedented access to all kinds of information. Other less generic information retrieval systems exist, targeting specific fields. In this chapter, one of these specialized information retrieval approaches is described. It targets the field of conflict resolution and provides different methods to compile a wide range of information from past cases and legal rules that include potential outcomes and a measure of their likeliness, boundary values, most likely outcomes, among others. Moreover, it also allows to take past similar cases and adapt them to the context and characteristics of the current case so that parties can have an intuitive and clear notion of what would their chances be if an outcome such as a previous one would result from their dispute.

7.1 Introduction

Information Retrieval (IR) may be seen as a generic process through which one finds and retrieves a piece of information from somewhere. Indeed, one is engaged in those processes when browsing through a library, searching for an office or even when trying to find a suitable recipe. However, in the last years, information retrieval actions became more recurrent, mostly due to search engines such as Google.

In Computer Science, IR may be defined as the process of finding material (usually documents) of an unstructured nature (usually text) that satisfies information needs (usually stored on computers) (Manning et al. 2008). While this definition focuses mostly on the search method, there are other processes involved with a direct impact on the quality and on the efficiency of the retrieval process, namely the proper indexing and storage of the information, which may later facilitate its retrieval. A more complete definition can thus be put forward, defining IR as a field concerned with the structure, analysis, organization, storage, searching, and retrieval of information (Salton 1968).

Some well-known tasks can be linked to IR. The most common and frequent one is Ad-hoc search, in which a user places an arbitrary query and proper papers or documents are retrieved. This is the most classical form of IR and may be observed when we use Google, when we search for books on our online library or when we search for news. Another task is the one of filtering, which is usually used with unstructured or semi-structured data, such as e-mail (Belkin and Croft 1992). When we search our e-mails (which contain attachments of many different types as well as structured and unstructured content) throughout a query, we are indeed filtering information that we want to access. Similarly, the *junk mail* is a filter available in most e-mail service providers that filters information we do not want to access. Another task associated to IR is the one of classification, in which the aim is to label each document in sets, such as e-mails from friends and work-related e-mails. Finally, IR tools may also be used to provide answers to questions posed in the user's native language. One of the most notable examples is WolframAlpha, a computational knowledge engine that is able to interpret questions in natural language. For example, in terms of the question *"Which is the capital of Portugal"*, the engine will recognize two key input concepts: *Portugal* and *capital city*. From that point on, the engine not only provides the correct answer to the question but also accessory information such as city population, maps, location, or information about nearby cities and weather conditions.

The IR field is also concerned with a few major issues; one of them being *relevance*: a measure of how much a retrieved document encloses the information the user is looking for. Some aspects may influence the user's notion of relevance, such as the context, the newness of the information, the time of the day or even the style of the document, which are more or less subjective. The topical relevance may also be taken into consideration, i.e., is the topic of the document the same of the query? All IR models must implement some kind of relevance metric, which will be used to sort the retrieval results.

Another issue is the one of *evaluation*, i.e., how effective was the IR method used, how satisfied the user was with the results presented (Manning et al. 2008). Essentially, evaluation methodologies look at the utility of the results, in which the key measure is *"happiness"*. Issues that affect user happiness are the speed of response and the size of the index. It is also reasonable to assume that the relevance of the results is the most important factor, i.e., the user is not interested in an extremely fast method that holds no relevant results. *Relevance* is however very user-dependent and cannot be *guessed* beforehand. There are other aspects, not necessary related to the quality of the retrieval method, that have a significant impact on the happiness of the user, namely interface design issues such as responsiveness, layout clarity or the generation of intuitive results summaries. Vital in evaluating the effectiveness of the retrieval method is to perceive what information the user really needs. In this task, merely retrieving documents that contain all the words in the query may be a poor approach. Let's take as an example a query such as *fighting AND apple AND disease*. The user might be searching for which human diseases may be fought by eating apples or he/she might be searching for ways to fight pests or diseases of apples. Thus, to effectively evaluate an IR system it is necessary to know the user's information requirements.

Information needs are indeed another big issue in IR. In fact, it is often difficult to perceive the user's information requirements from two or three words only. Previous interactions and circumstantial information about the user and their surroundings are essential for understanding the user's intent. Previous interactions allow building an account about the user's preferences, a profile that allows to infer a kind of *user-type*. Let us assume that a user is searching for the word *apple*. If he/she has past searches related to healthy food, eating habits and vegetarianism, the IR system might assume that the user is searching for the fruit apple. On the other hand, if the user has a history of searches related to technology, resembling Operating Systems, Programming Languages and Computers, the IR system may assume that the user is searching for Apple, the technological multinational corporation.

Also, the user's perspectives may acknowledge a better understanding of their intents. Specifically, aspects such as user location, time or community preferences may be used to implement multi-dimensional and context-sensitive information retrieval approaches (Church and Smyth 2008), which are particularly suited to be used in mobile devices. In fact, mobile search is a field with a significant growth. Users may search from their mobile devices, with context being harnessed and provided to the search engine in a transparent way in order to improve the search. For example, if the user is at home, and searches for *coffee*, they might just be searching for generic information related to the beverage coffee. However, if the user is downtown with their friends, they might be searching for the closest coffeehouse, open at that time off the day.

The need for more refined and powerful IR methods increases with the complexity of the information available in our environment. Indeed, the information available until recently was mainly in the form of written documents, with a more or less structured nature. Written documents are frequently *self-explainable*. Nevertheless, nowadays the information available consists in much more than written documents, including video, photos, images, audio or mixes, such as in an e-mail with different attachments. Increasingly complex IR approaches are thus needed to deal with new types of information and that may take advantage of the environment to direct the search.

7.2   Information Retrieval Approaches

Different methodologies for problem solving may coexist in IR, each one with advantages and disadvantages of their own. The classical approach is the Boolean Query (Frakes 1992). It is based on Boolean Logic and Set Theory, where the documents to be searched and the user's queries are seen as sets of rational terms. This implies that an index is built beforehand, mapping each word in the documents to the documents they appear in or, alternatively, that all the documents are sequentially scanned at the time of the search, using a technique known as *grepping* (from the Unix command-line utility for searching plain-text data sets for lines matching a regular expression, called *grep*).

Boolean models are easy to implement, intuitive and defined by clean and trivial formalisms. On the other hand, exact matching may retrieve too many or too few documents, being difficult to sort them. Moreover, it may also be difficult to translate a search intent into a Boolean query, especially for people without experience. Also, all the search terms have the same weight, whether they are domain-specific or generic. This rather simplistic approach should thus be regarded more as data retrieval than information retrieval.

An example of an IR system that still uses a Boolean approach in the legal field is Westlaw.[1] Westlaw is a major online IR for lawyers and law professionals, providing access to different databases of case law, state and federal statutes, administrative codes, newspaper and magazine articles, public records, law journals, law reviews, treatises or legal forms. The majority of users still use Boolean queries, and in particular the most experienced ones.

A slightly more complex IR approach is the one of structured retrieval. Here, a query may be structured or unstructured but the documents in the database are all structured (Kotsakis 2002). Structuring documents may allow for a more efficient retrieval since it lets one search for a specific term in a document without the need to go through it. Traditional applications of structured retrieval include libraries, patent databases or blogs. In the case of a library, information about books may be structured in fields such as *author*, *publisher* or *title*. This allows for more directed searches such as *give me all the books that contain the term 'Deoxyribonucleic acid'* in the field *title* and the term *journal* in the field *publication type*. Providing the author name, the publisher or the publishing year may further refine such queries. Many standards exist to encode structured documents, being the most widely used XML – Extensible Markup Language. In a XML document each term is described by one or more attributes. The retrieval system looks at the values of these attributes and at the values of the terms themselves to decide whether to retrieve a document or not.

There can also be a somehow intermediate model, marked by parametric and zone search. Under this scenery there will be specific fields that will describe the whole document (e.g. data modification date, file size) and zone text attributes that

---

[1] The website of Westlaw is available at www.westlaw.com. Last accessed on September 2013.

will take a piece of text as a value. The number of attributes is generally small and there is no perception of hierarchy such as in XML, i.e., the data model is flat. The main disadvantage here is that, as in the previous models, the users may not be familiar with the structure of the documents, making it difficult to specify a request in the more appropriate form.

An alternative model that deals with some of these issues is the vector space one. It is an algebraic model that represents text documents or other generic objects as vectors of identifiers (Salton et al. 1975). Essentially, documents and queries are denoted as vectors where each dimension stands for a separate item. If a given term occurs in the document, its value in the vector is different from zero. Under a binary approach this value has a value of 1, which simply denotes its existence. Under other approaches, different values might be used which are related to the term's weight.

One of the particular applications of this model is in relevance rankings. The relevance of a document to a request is obtained by comparing the deviation of angles between each document's vector and the query vector (Mihalcea et al. 2006). This model is also fairly simple, based on linear algebra, that allows to rank documents according to their possible relevance, a situation that is not accomplished with the former ones. It also caters for partial matching. The main limitation is that long documents may be poorly represented (a very long vector and a small scalar product). Moreover, and similarly to the previous methods, there is no regard to the semantic aspects. Thus, documents that fall under a similar context but with different keywords will be deemed different. Also, the order in which the words appear, which may be noteworthy, is lost in the vector space model.

In order to address the lack of semantic structures in IR and to better perceive the user's milieu and intent, new forms of IR have emerged in the last years. Traditional approaches are optimized to a generic population, trained by machine learning algorithms using either direct human relevance judgments or indirect ones obtained from click-through data from millions of users. The new personalized models are based on user profiles, which may be learned from a user's long-term history (Sontag et al. 2012). They also fall into the classification of probabilistic document relevance, with the documents being sorted by their expected relevance. Probabilistic IR models are by far the most complex ones and may also be used to build effective circumstantial retrieval models, namely by query log, which may be used to facilitate applications such as mobile search, personalized search or PC troubleshooting (Wen et al. 2004).

7.3   Information Retrieval in UMCourt

As stated previously, the estimation of possible outcomes is a central issue in conflict resolution as it is the base for a supported decision and planning process. Nevertheless, this is a complex problem involving many different variables and issues. In this chapter an information retrieval system is described that provides the user with possible outcomes for the dispute they are involved in, based on past similar cases.

There are different models that may be considered for this purpose. Utility functions have considerable applications in the legal domain (Behrman and Davey 2001; Foxall 2004; Posner 1993). A good example is the *Family Winner* system, in which Bellucci and Zeleznikow have applied this technique to family mediation (Bellucci and Zeleznikow 2006), after being observed that an important way in which family mediators encourage disputants to resolve their conflicts is through the use of compromise and trade-offs (Zeleznikow et al. 2007).

Artificial Intelligence (AI) techniques have also been used to address the same problem. James Popple used a simple Expert System to provide advice in fields of case law that have been itemized by a legal expert in a description language outlined by him (Popple 1996). Split-Up combines Rule-based Reasoning with Artificial Neural Networks in order to build a system to assist parties involved in property settlements in Australia divorce processes (Zeleznikow and Stranieri 1995).

UMCourt is framed in this group of systems, that apply AI techniques to ODR. Specifically, in UMCourt, a case-based approach is followed.

In the Case Based Reasoning (CBR) approach to problem solving, cases represent past experiences kept in memory. Each case contains the description of the past problem (the initial state of the world), the solution adopted to deal with it, and the outcome (the final state of the world). As the case memory grows, the system gains more information about the problem under study and the possible different ways to deal with it. In each new situation brought into place, past cases are analysed in search for similarities, and solutions of similar cases are adapted in order to solve the new problem. At the end of this process, it is possible to learn with its success or failure, and change the case base accordingly.

Choosing a case-based approach to problem solving in UMCourt was not an arbitrary decision. In fact, The Law itself relies on the concept of case and implements a very similar perception: the legal precedent (Landes and Posner 1976). In other words, this represents a previous case or legal decision that may or must be followed in subsequent similar cases. There are legal domains in which precedents are divided into two types, namely binding and persuasive precedents. The former type is generally the result of a process in a higher court and means that all lower courts must honour it. The persuasive precedent, on the other hand, arises from cases that are decided in lower courts and does not denote an obligation. However, in civil law, and in general, this separation does not exist, as all the precedents are simply persuasive. Judges may follow a precedent decision, but they are also entitled to decide otherwise, since judges are only bound to apply the legal norms. Indeed, different interpretations of The Law may occur (Fisher and Ury 1981; Zweigert and Kötz 1998).

A CBR model would, at first sight, be more suited to be used in common law, i.e., a law that is based on the courts' decisions. This, however, does not mean that it cannot be used in a civil law setting, such as the Portuguese one, in which laws are written by a legislature's enactment (Zweigert and Kötz 1998). It is our conviction that CBR is an appropriate method for such a problem-solving domain as the cases and their outcomes are often very similar to past ones. This conviction is shared and supported by several authors. Ashley, in particular, poses the question *"should researchers in a civil law jurisdiction pursue work on implementing AI and The Law models of case-based legal reasoning in a civil law context?"*. He then answers the question with a conclusive *"the answer may well be, Yes!"* (Ashley 2004).

Consequently, throughout this section we will be guided by five main questions synthesized by Slade (1991) and, by answering each one, we define our agent-based CBR system:

- What makes up a case? How can we represent case memory?;
- How is memory organized? What are the indexing rules?;
- How does memory change? How do the case memory and indexing rules change over time?;
- How can we adapt old solutions to new problems? What are the similarity metrics and modification rules?; and
- How can we learn from mistakes? What are the repair rules?.

We begin by developing some basic concepts that will later be useful for understanding the CBR process, and the role of each of the agents presented so far.

7.3.1   Preliminary Considerations

Let us start with a high level description of the CBR process as used in this specific domain of application. There is a database of cases which embodies information from legal disputes settled by courts, with their respective outcomes. The CBR process is mainly intended to look at these cases and infer what would happen if the parties currently involved in the dispute would have the matter set by a court. This basically consists in selecting the most similar cases and presenting their outcomes to be analyzed by the disputing parties. More than that, the system compiles information for the decision-making processes, including the previously mentioned BATNA, WATNA, ZOPA and MLATNA. With this information, parties can build their own image of the whole problem and of the possible problem solving paths and respective consequences.

At the end of this process, parties may choose to accept the proposed outcome or they may reject it. If they accept it, the added value of the proposed case is increased, denoting that it was successfully applied. Alternatively, if the parties reject the proposed outcome, that added value is negative and, should the parties advance to court, a new case is added to the system with all the information that had already been provided by the parties and the outcome from the court. Otherwise, parties can also make use of a traditional dispute resolution method (e.g. negotiation, mediation), integrated in the UMCourt platform.

7.3.2   *Parsing and Indexing*

In an indexing process, property values are assigned to cases so that they can be easily identified according to those properties. Therefore, an important part of this process is the one of selecting the right properties for indexing the cases. Evidently, this is, once more, domain-dependent. In UMCourt, cases are indexed according to:

- Background information;
- Norms addressed by parties (i.e. legal information);
- Parties Objectives;
- Case date; and
- Outcome.

This allows agents to make requests to the database such as *all the cases in which norm X is addressed, all the cases that are within a given time frame* or *all the cases with a given outcome*. The objective of indexing the cases has essentially to do with efficiency issues. It would be a rather time-consuming task to constantly search all the files for some parameters. By indexing them, this task is simplified to querying the database for the identifiers of the cases that match the desired criteria.

Indexing is often looked as a challenge to overcome in CBR systems, mainly when the indexing method is manual, as it tends to become a slow and hard task. Automated methods are thus preferred. In the case of this work, indexing is an automated process. The indexing agent monitors a predetermined folder in the system and indexes new files as they are added. However, the validity of their structure must be determined beforehand.

This agent therefore starts by using a SAX parser to parse the content of the new file and checks if it is valid according to the current schemas; if successful, the case is indexed. The indexing process is as simple as reading the appropriate contents from the parser result and add the identifier of the case to the appropriate tables in the database. However, only the information that is central for the retrieval of the cases is stored in the database, while the remaining one is kept in the files only. All the information needed for indexing the case has been previously provided by the parties, while filling in the information requested, or is automatically inferred by the system (e.g. dates, norms addressed), ensuring that the indexing process itself is a completely automated one.

Additionally, a record of failed cases is also maintained, in which each case is associated with the reasons for failure. These cases are looked at when the CBR process fails in the search for failure reasons, as it will be seen below. Moreover, when the retriever agent is retrieving the cases from memory, it may also look at this record of failed cases before taking actions that influence the parameters of the search (e.g. changing the similarity threshold), in order to prevent errors that have already occurred in the past.

Once the information is indexed, a wide range of operations becomes possible. As an example, it is possible to mine the database for association rules (Wu et al. 2007), which are then used to classify the cases (Fig. 7.1) (e.g. a case

Fig. 7.1 Indexed cases can be organized by means of association rules; i.e., all the cases for which a given rule is enforced successfully belong to the same category

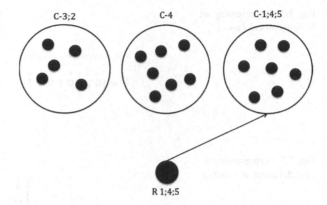

that addresses rules 1, 4 and 5 is assigned a specific label, together with other cases that address the same rules and are, for this reason, potentially similar). This is useful for retrieving cases, as will be seen below, by selecting all the cases that belong to the same category or group, i.e., all the cases for which a given mined rule is enforced successfully.

It is also possible to imagine different interpretations of the information, which will be suited for specific applications. As an example, one can picture the information as vectors of binary entries. This is a fairly simple algebraic model to represent text documents, in which instead of using textual fields, a case is represented as a vector. Specifically, in this work, a case is seen as a vector V of binary entries, in which each entry $i < N$ corresponds to a fixed descriptor from the descriptor vector D of size N. Thus, the value of each binary entry denotes the presence or absence of that descriptor in the case. Descriptors denote case components (e.g. legal norms, party objectives, case winner). Thus, one can look at a vector which represents a case and, considering the descriptors vector D, determine which information is or is not present on the case (Fig. 7.2).

Basically, this case representation allows seeing which party addresses norms, which are their objectives and what the outcome is. It is thus a very concise way of representing all this information, demanding very few resources to handle and to store. Following the same line of thought, a database with m cases in which each case is described by N descriptors can be represented as an m-by-N matrix in which each line is a vector representing a case (Fig. 7.3).

7.3.3   Case Structure

In the CBR approach to problem solving, a case is the basic unit of information. It represents a past experience and is thus a contextualized piece of knowledge. CBR allows us to estimate the outcome of a current experience by looking at past similar experiences (that took part in a comparable setting) and its respective outcome.

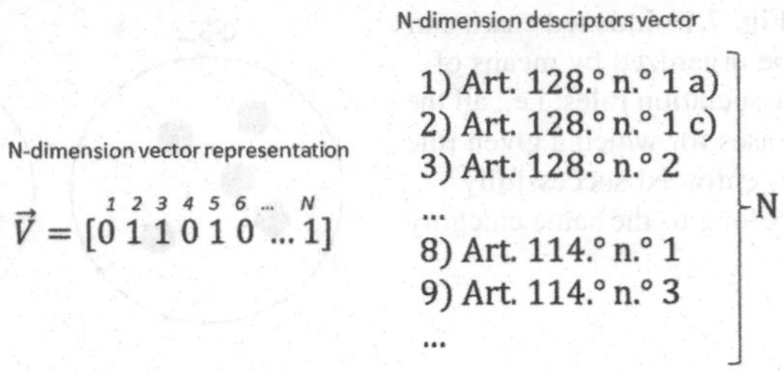

Fig. 7.2 Representing an
N-dimensional case

N-dimension descriptors vector

N-dimension vector representation

$$\vec{V} = [0\ 1\ 1\ 0\ 1\ 0\ ...\ 1]$$

$\begin{array}{l} 1\ 2\ 3\ 4\ 5\ 6\ ...\ N \end{array}$

$$\left.\begin{array}{l} 1)\ \text{Art. } 128.° \text{ n.° } 1\ a) \\ 2)\ \text{Art. } 128.° \text{ n.° } 1\ c) \\ 3)\ \text{Art. } 128.° \text{ n.° } 2 \\ ... \\ 8)\ \text{Art. } 114.° \text{ n.° } 1 \\ 9)\ \text{Art. } 114.° \text{ n.° } 3 \\ ... \end{array}\right\} N$$

Fig. 7.3 Representing a
case database as a matrix

$$DB = \begin{bmatrix} 1 & 0 & 1 & \cdots & 1 \\ 0 & 0 & 1 & \cdots & 0 \\ 0 & 1 & 1 & \cdots & 1 \\ \vdots & \vdots & \vdots & \ddots & \vdots \\ 0 & 0 & 1 & \cdots & 1 \end{bmatrix} \begin{matrix} 1 \\ 2 \\ 3 \\ ... \\ N \end{matrix}$$

$$\begin{matrix} 1 & 2 & 3 & ... & N \end{matrix}$$

The characterization of the information that should be contained in a case is therefore a major task in the development of a CBR model. Generally, the information comprised in a case may be organized into three distinct categories (Alterman 1989):

- The Problem – The problem outline, including its background, the initial world state and other data that may help to figure the problematic under consideration;
- The Solution – A description of the list of steps that were taken in order to solve the problem, which should be exhaustive enough to be applied again in an autonomous mode, and abstract enough to be adapted to new problems; and
- The Outcome – The consequences of the solution enforcement, i.e., the final state of the world.

Whereas these categories depend on the problem domain, there may be applications that consider only the problem and its solution (in which it is possible to derive solutions to new problems), while others consider the problem and the outcome (making it possible to estimate outcomes to new problems). UMCourt considers the three categories, as detailed in Table 7.1.

7.3.4   The CBR Process Model

We have, until now, described how experiences are acquired, organized and stored in the system. However, purely storing information is not enough. We need to define the processes that acquire and use this information. To take this step, we have looked at the work of Aamodt and Plaza (1994) and of Riesbeck and Bain (1987), and made the necessary revisions in order for it to be used in this particular domain.

Table 7.1 Detail of the information encoded in each case

Category	Information type	Description
Problem	Background	Basic information about the parties and the dispute, namely party's personal information and location, dispute starting date, witnesses, etc.
	Objectives	A list of the initial objectives of each party towards the dispute, i.e., the expected outcomes.
	Legal	Legal information such as the laws and norms addressed by the parties and witnesses to support their claims or the guilty statements.
	Dates	All the important dates of the case.
Solution	List of actions	A list of the actions performed by the parties in order to achieve the outcome. Generally, these actions comprise trade-offs.
Outcome	Outcome description	A list of items that describe the outcome in terms of indemnities to be paid, among others.
	Added-value	A value denoting the percentage of successful applications of this particular case to solve past disputes.

It results in a four step model organized into the Retrieve, Reuse, Revise and Retain phases (Fig. 7.4).

Retrieve

The process of retrieving may be triggered under different scenarios. It consists in selecting the cases from the case memory that may be of relevance for solving a problem, by looking at their indexes. Unlike database searches that target a specific value in a record, retrieval of cases from the case base must be equipped with heuristics that perform partial matches, since in general there is no existing case that exactly matches the new one (Watson and Marir 1994). There are several techniques for retrieving cases. The one detailed here is a hybrid one and consists of two different phases. In the first one, a pre-selection of cases is performed. Later, the pre-selection is evaluated, eventually refined by using similarity functions, and the cases are sorted. In each of these phases, two different algorithms may be combined. Each of these algorithms is analyzed below.

In the pre-selection phase, either a retrieval template or a classification algorithm may be used. The main objective of these two algorithms is to narrow the search space so that the algorithms of the evaluation phase will perform faster. Either algorithm has pre-selection rules, intended to ensure that the result of the pre-selection complies with given parameters (e.g. number of cases retrieved). In order to comply with these rules, the algorithms may run more than once per search, dynamically making adjustments to their settings.

In the Retrieve phase all the cases that are similar to the new one are pre-selected. As an example, cases that do not address the same norms cannot be similar as they address different legal domains (i.e. the retrieval algorithm uses a template search mechanism that works much like SQL queries); given a case, a set

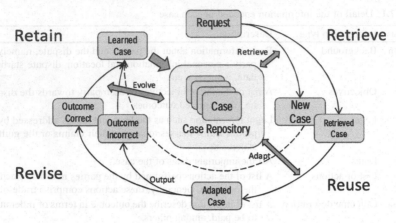

Fig. 7.4 The CBR model

of cases is retrieved from the database with the guarantee that they share features endorsed by the new one.

The classification algorithm, on the other hand, uses association rules that determine which category a case belongs to (e.g. the rule *if party1 uses norms A and B then party1 wins)*. Thus, the algorithm determines in the first place to which category the new case belongs to and then pre-selects all the cases of that category.

In the evaluation phase, additional operations are performed on the pre-selected cases, such as determining their similarity and ordering them accordingly. Considering similarity, two different approaches may be used; a first one based on a nearest neighbor algorithm, and a second one based on the cosine similarity model. The basic idea is that any of these algorithms is only applied to the reduced set of pre-selected cases, instead of applying them to the whole case base. Thus, the algorithms start by determining a similarity measure between each pre-selected case and the new one. Under the former approach, the nearest neighbor algorithm is used, detailed in Eq. 7.1.

$$\frac{\sum_{i=1}^{n} W_i * fsim_i\left(Arg_i^N, Arg_i^R\right)}{\sum_{i=1}^{n} W_i} \tag{7.1}$$

where,

- n – number of elements to consider to compute the similarity;
- W_i – weight of element i in the overall similarity;
- Fsim – similarity function for element i; and
- Arg – arguments for the similarity function representing the values of the element i for the new case and the retrieved one, respectively N and R.

Let us now detail the case information that was considered to be relevant for the similarity evaluation, with the nearest neighbor approach, i.e., the components.

According to the domain of application, three types of information were considered: the objectives of each party, the norms addressed by the eventual witnesses and the date of the dispute and the important dates of the case. Both the norms addressed and the objectives are lists of elements. The similarity function consists in comparing two lists (Eq. 7.2). The similarity is higher when the two lists have a larger number of elements in common. As for the date, the similarity function verifies if the two dates are within a given time range; the similarity is higher when the two dates are closer.

$$fsim_{list} = \frac{|L_N \cap L_R|}{n}, n = \left\{ \begin{array}{ll} |L_N|, & |L_N| \geq |L_R| \\ |L_R|, & |L_N| < |L_R| \end{array} \right\} \tag{7.2}$$

In the second approach, a similarity measure based on the notion of cosine similarity is used. This method uses a binary vector to picture the information available and is based on the assumption that the similarity between two vectors may be estimated by finding the cosine of the angle between them. Given two vectors of attributes A and B, with N entries each, the cosine similarity, θ, is determined as shown in Eq. 7.3. The similarity value is given in the interval $0 \ldots 1$, with 0 denoting the minimum value of similarity, and 1 denoting that the two vectors are the same.

$$sim = \frac{A.B}{||A|| \, ||B||} = \frac{\sum_{i=1}^{N} A_i * B_i}{\sqrt[2]{\sum_{i=1}^{N} (A_i)^2} * \sqrt[2]{\sum_{i=1}^{N} (B_i)^2}} \tag{7.3}$$

This second method of computing similarity is quite simpler and faster, as it uses vectors of binary entries. However, contrary to the previous similarity function, it does not allow assigning weights to each component of the case. This may or may not be a disadvantage, depending on the type of problem.

In the evaluation phase another operation takes place, which is independent of the method used to compute the similarity: the assessment of the utility of each case. This utility value denotes how much each case is appropriate for a party. Having access to these values, a party may assess the retrieved cases in terms of their similarity and their utility, and make a personal evaluation of potential advantages versus potential likeliness. The process of computing the utility is relatively simple. Basically, as stated before, each stored case includes a solution and an outcome. The outcome denotes the result of applying a previous solution to a new case. The application of a solution to different problems generates different outcomes. The key idea is to apply the solution of each retrieved case to the current problem and to determine its utility value. As a very simple example, one may have a past case with the following data:

Outcome = worker receives indemnity of 2,500

Solution = antiquity $*$ 25 $*$ *d_wage*

```
New Pre-Selection task arrived: < 1291886422498, 1286439756546 >
*****TemplateRetrieval: Requesting for cases that match the rules: (
      depth: article
)
2010/12/09 09:20:23 : Connected to Database
*****Database: Received request to query database from TemplateRetrieval@TIARAC1:1099/JADE
2010/12/09 09:20:23 : Connected to Database
*****Database: Returning query result...
*****TemplateRetrieval: Received a pre-selection of 77 cases
*****TemplateRetrieval: Rule violated: "Max cases". Deciding new pre-select rules...
*****TemplateRetrieval: Changed search depth to: number
*****TemplateRetrieval: Requesting for cases that match the rules: (
      depth: number
)
*****Database: Received request to query database from TemplateRetrieval@TIARAC1:1099/JADE
*****Database: Returning query result...
*****TemplateRetrieval: Received a pre-selection of 77 cases
*****TemplateRetrieval: Rule violated: "Max cases". Deciding new pre-select rules...
*****TemplateRetrieval: Changed search depth to: item
*****TemplateRetrieval: Requesting for cases that match the rules: (
      depth: item
)
*****Database: Received request to query database from TemplateRetrieval@TIARAC1:1099/JADE
*****Database: Returning query result...
*****TemplateRetrieval: Received a pre-selection of 28 cases
*****TemplateRetrieval: SUCCESS: Returning results to agent( agent-identifier :name Coordinator@T
*****Coordinator: Received results from pre-selection of task: 1291886422498
*****Coordinator: Requesting computation of similarities for task 1291886422498
*****NearestNeighbour: Received request for similarities: 1291886422498
*****NearestNeighbour: Sending list of computed similarities to: ( agent-identifier :name Coordir
*****Coordinator: Received results from computing similarity of task: 1291886422498
*****Coordinator: Returning result of Get Similarity Request
*****Coordinator: Ending sub task 1291886422498
*****Coordinator: Updating task 1291886422370
*****Coordinator: Starting a new Utilities task: 1291886425356
*****Coordinator: Requesting computation of utilities for task 1291886425356
*****Utility: Received Compute Utility request from ( agent-identifier :name Coordinator@TIARAC1:
*****Utility: RECEIVED REQUEST FOR 28
*****Utility: Sending results from Utility request to ( agent-identifier :name Coordinator@TIARAC
*****Coordinator: Received results from computing utilities of task: 1291886425356
```

Fig. 7.5 The output of a typical case retrieval process

This example denotes a case in which a worker received an indemnity of 2,500, determined by the formula depicted in the solution, defined by Decree of Law (DL) 7/2009 (Portuguese laws). As, in this case, the worker has an antiquity of 5 years and a daily wage of 20, the value of the outcome is obtained applying the formula referred to above. Now, let us consider that this case was retrieved since it is similar to the new one and that, in this new situation, the worker has an antiquity of 15 years and a daily wage of 17. For this worker, the application of the same solution would mean an outcome of 6,375.

Independently of the method used, the output of this phase is a list of similar cases ordered by their degree of similarity. This information can then be used by the disputing parties, mediators or by the platform itself in a wide range of situations. Figure 7.5 shows the textual output of a typical retrieve process, combining the template retrieval with the nearest neighbor approach. This figure highlights the process of refining the pre-select cases with successive changes in the search parameters. Figure 7.6 depicts the communication that took place between the several agents in this specific example.

The retrieval process is managed by the *coordinator* agent, which has the necessary data to interact with the remaining agents, allocate tasks and handle the results. Hence, when a request for retrieval reaches the *coordinator* agent (typically

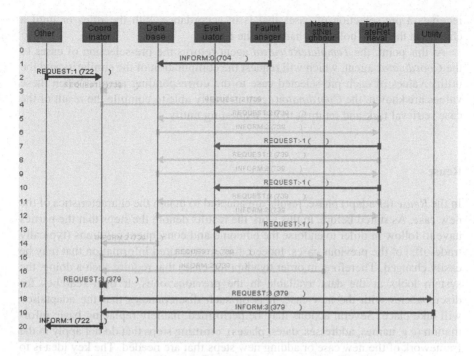

Fig. 7.6 Visualization of a typical communication between agents for retrieving similar cases

coming from a user interface or another agent), it triggers a *Complex Action* (CA), an action that uses more than one *Simple Action* (SA). In the case of the retrieval process, the *CA* includes the following *SAs*:

- Pre-Selection, handled by the *TemplateRetrieval* agent;
- Database Query, handled by the *Database* agent;
- Computation of Similarities, handled by the *NearestNeighbour* agent;
- Computation of Utilities, handled by the *Utilities* agent; and
- Return Results, handled by the *Coordinator* agent.

Note that some of these actions may be recurrent, others are sequential, and some may be executed in parallel (e.g. computation of utility and similarity). In this case, the *Coordinator* agent starts a new case retrieval requesting a pre-selection of cases from the *TemplateRetrieval* agent. In this request, the *Coordinator* agent includes only a single rule; to start the pre-selection by considering the object or article of each norm. The *TemplateRetrieval* agent then formulates a database request containing a *SQL* sentence and sends it to the *Database* agent, which returns the result. The *TemplateRetrieval* agent analyses the result and decides if the rule that establishes the maximum amount of cases to be retrieved is or is not being violated. If it is, it reformulates the request to the *Database* agent in order to reduce the cardinality of the case set being retrieved. This happens again and again until it receives a pre-selection of cases that is in accordance with the rules or until a change in the rules holds no change in the results.

At this point, the *TemplateRetrieval* agent returns the pre-selection of cases to the *Coordinator* agent, which will request the computation of the similarity and the utility values of each pre-selected case to the corresponding agents. When these values are known, the *Coordinator* agent is finally able to compile the result of the case retrieval task and return it to the requesting entity.

Reuse

In the *Reuse* (or adapt) phase, results are adapted to match the characteristics of the new case. As stated before, in this work the results denote the steps that the parties have to follow in order to endorse the outcome and consequent solutions (typically trade-offs) of the previous cases. Indeed, this is structured information that may be easily changed. Therefore, in order to adapt the cases that require such a doing, the system looks at the data available in the previous ones. It then searches for discrepancies with the new case. It is on such discrepancies that the adaptation will take place. Several actions may be performed, namely replacing basic information (e.g. names, addresses, dates, places), omitting steps that do not apply in the framework of the new case or adding new steps that are needed. The key idea is to change the cases retrieved so that the disputing parties look at what would be the outcome of their case in light of the previous ones.

Revise

In the *Revise* phase, a solution and the corresponding justification is presented to the parties, being their behavior analyzed; to accomplish this, the cases, their similarity and their likeliness are presented to the users in a graphical fashion (Fig. 7.7). In this graphical representation, parties can see the several cases that were retrieved in the form of small colored circles. By clicking on these circles, an interface pops up that shows details about the corresponding case and about the reasons for its selection. These cases span the space between the *BATNA* and *WATNA* of each party, so that they can be compared in terms of their utility to each party. In order to determine the values of the *BATNA* and *WATNA*, the system uses logic rules defined after the Portuguese Labor Law. These are rather simple rules that establish the values of eventual indemnities and other parameters of the outcome, based on concepts like worker antiquity, work hours, extra hours, night work, among others.

Let us take, as an example, the Portuguese Labor Law domain, as depicted in Decree of Law (DL) 7/2009 (Portuguese laws), considering a scenario in which a worker wants to end the labor contract claiming that the employer did not pay the last three salaries. According to Article 394th, nr. 2 a), the lack of regular payment of the salary constitutes a just cause for a worker to end the contract. Moreover,

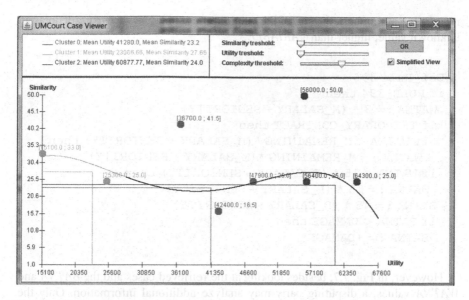

Fig. 7.7 Visual representation of the information retrieved for a given case. It includes several past cases, displayed in the space according to their degree of similarity to the current case and their utility for a given party

Article 394th, n°1 states that when there is a just cause, the worker can immediately end the labor contract.

The first question is thus to determine the existence or not of the lack of payment, and thus, of a just cause for ending the contract. Assuming that this has been proved, let us try to determine the best and worst scenarios, from the point of view of the worker. The most important norms are found in Article 396th, numbers 1, 3 and 4. Number 1 states that, if Article 394th applies (there is just cause for ending contract), the worker is entitled to 15–45 days of salary plus indemnity for each year of contract. It also states that this value varies according to the degree of wrongfulness of the employer and that the total indemnity paid to the worker should not be inferior to three salaries plus indemnity. However, number 3 states that the indemnity paid can be higher whenever the worker suffered property damage or other losses.

Finally, number 4 states that, in the cases of a temporary employment contract, the value of the indemnity cannot be smaller than the value of the salaries that would be received until the end of the contract. Thus, the resemblance between legal norms and rules, allows one to set the *BATNA* and *WATNA* in the form of *IF-THEN* rules. The deeds of this example are addressed below by presenting a simplification of the rules that allow the computation of the *BATNA* and *WATNA* values according to the Portuguese Labour Law. The code considers only the case in which a worker ends the contract with a just cause. *M_SALARY* denotes the monthly salary; *D_SALARY* denotes the daily salary; *M_REMAINING* denotes the months remaining until the end of the temporary contract; +*VARIABLE* denotes an unknown value, higher than *VARIABLE*.

```
Def_Rule 396
if RULE_394 then
 WATNA := 3 * (M_SALARY + SENIORITY)
 if TEMPORARY_CONTRACT then
  if WATNA < M_REMAINING * (M_SALARY + SENIORITY) then
   WATNA := M_REMAINING * (M_SALARY + SENIORITY)
 if WATNA < 15 * (D_SALARY + SENIORITY) then
  WATNA := 15 * (D_SALARY + SENIORITY)
 BATNA := 45 * (D_SALARY + SENIORITY)
 if BATNA < DAMAGE then
  BATNA := +DAMAGE
```

However, in Fig. 7.7, besides looking at the retrieved cases and the *BATNA* and *WATNA* values, a disputing party may analyze additional information. Only the cases more similar to the target case are selected. The horizontal axis represents the utility while the vertical one denotes the similarity. Each colored dot represents a case and different colors indicate that cases belong to different clusters. Clusters are created to show some grouping between the cases, allowing a first analysis from an abstract point of view. The interface also shows, for each cluster, the average of values for similarity and utility. A linear regression is also drawn, which may help the disputing party to determine in which region an outcome is more likely or more valuable, according to the utility values. This regression is also used to depict the *MLATNA*, i.e., the region in which the line of the linear regression is green instead of black denotes the most likely region of the outcome. Finally, using this interface it is also possible to delimit the *ZOPA*, or the *Zone of Potential Agreement*. Finally, in order to facilitate the visualization of the data, several controls are available that allow to change, in real-time, minimum levels of similarity and utility for the cases depicted in the interface. The complexity threshold allows to increase or decrease the number of cases that are depicted close to each other, being especially useful when several cases exist with very close values of similarity and utility.

Retain

This *CBR* process may be used as it was until now (as a "simple" tool to compile information from past cases) or it may be part of a higher-level dispute resolution process, as the one depicted in Fig. 7.8, in which *rectangles* represent processes, *parallelograms* denote information structures, and *rhombuses* decisions. Thus, at the end of the last phase, one may be faced with different scenarios. On the one hand, parties may accept the planned outcome, by committing to implement the

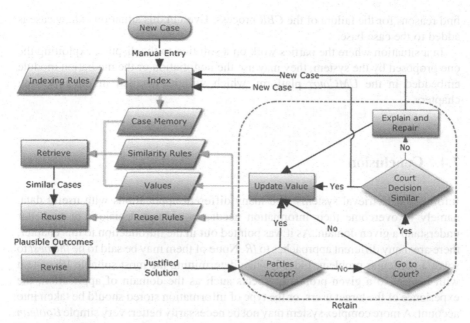

Fig. 7.8 The *CBR* process as part of a higher-level dispute resolution process

solutions proposed. In this case, the system raises the case's added value denoting its positive contribution. On the other hand, parties may not agree with the proposed solution. This being the case, parties may resort to a negotiation and search for alternative solutions in order to maximize the hypothesis of agreement. Moreover, parties may decide to end the alternative dispute resolution process, either by advancing to court or by choosing a different dispute resolution method.

If the parties decide that going to court is not the right path to follow (e.g. by choosing other methods for conflict resolution), the usefulness of the proposed case is decreased, denoting that it was not the more appropriate one, and the process ends. Therefore, and in order to gather other data that may help to improve the system's performance, parties may be asked to complete a questionnaire where they state why the process failed. This information will be useful to improve UMCourt.

Alternatively, if the parties choose to go to court, the process continues outside of the scope of the conflict resolution platform. Nevertheless, it waits for a court decision. If the decision coincides with the solution that was proposed by the dispute resolution system, the usefulness of the case selected from the case base is increased, and a new case, the one that result from the court decision, is added to the case base. This, in fact, constitutes another innovation of the UMCourt platform, as the only information needed to complete the case data is the outcome. All the remaining information has already been provided by the parties when using the system. This makes the addition of cases to the case base a simple and fairly automated process. If, however, the outcome of the trial differs from the proposed solution, the system will decrease the usefulness of the proposed case and will try to find reasons for the failure of the *CBR* process. Even in this situation, a new case is added to the case base.

In a situation where the parties work on a solution to the dispute, exploiting the one proposed by the system, they may use the negotiation or the mediation module embedded in the *UMCourt* platform, which will be detailed in the following chapters.

7.4 Conclusion

Information Retrieval systems feed many different applications with useful data, namely to overcome their information needs, to support decisions or to better understand a given domain. As it was pointed out in the introduction to this chapter, there are many different approaches to *IR*. None of them may be said to be *the best* to solve a particular problem. Indeed, when determining the most suitable IR system with respect to a given problem, aspects such as the domain of application, the experience of the target users, or the type of information stored should be taken into account. A more complex system may not be necessarily better: very simple *Boolean* models may work quite well in delimited domains and with experienced users.

In this chapter focus was on an IR system for the domain of conflict resolution, aiming at the development of methods for IR that parties may use to better understand their disputes and, hence, to take better decisions. The resulting IR system is a case-oriented one, i.e., it retrieves information from past known cases that share similar traits with the present case. This simplifies the comprehension of the recovered information or data.

Through such approach, parties can better understand their problems, assess the likeliness of the expected outcomes, and, most important of all, gain a notion of how realistic their expectations and the demands of the other parties are. It may even lead the parties into reconsidering their objectives, facilitating the convergence into a mutually agreeable solution. The approach developed and described in this chapter may be not only be used by the parties for these purposes but may also be used by the *UMCourt* platform to implement higher-level services. These include the support to negotiation between the parties and the estimation of their personal conflict handling styles. These services will be addressed in the subsequent chapters.

References

Aamodt, A., and E. Plaza. 1994. Case-based reasoning: Foundational issues, methodological variations, and system approaches. *AI Communications* 7(1): 39–59. IOS Press.

Alterman, R. 1989. Panel discussion on case representation. In *Proceedings of the second workshop on case-based reasoning*, Pensacola Beach.

Ashley, K.D. 2004. *Case-based models of legal reasoning in a civil law context.* International Congress of comparative cultures and legal systems of the Instituto de Investigaciones Jurídicas.

Behrman, B.W., and S.L. Davey. 2001. Eyewitness identification in actual criminal cases: An archival analysis. *Law and Human Behaviour* 25(5): 475–491.

Belkin, N.J., and W.B. Croft. 1992. Information filtering and information retrieval: Two sides of the same coin? *Communications of the ACM* – Special issue on Information Filtering CACM Homepage archive 35(12): 29–38. New York: ACM. doi:10.1145/138859.138861.

Bellucci, E., and J. Zeleznikow. 2006. Developing negotiation decision support systems that support mediators: A case study of the Family Winner System. *Journal of Artificial Intelligence and Law* 13(2): 233–271.

Church, K., and B. Smyth. 2008. Who, what, where & when: A new approach to mobile search. In *IUI '08 proceedings of the 13th international conference on intelligent user interfaces*, 309–312. New York: ACM. doi:10.1145/1378773.1378817.

Fisher, R., and W. Ury. 1981. *Getting to yes: Negotiating agreement without giving in.* Boston: Houghton Mifflin.

Foxall, G. 2004. What judges maximize: Towards an economic psychology of the judicial utility function. *Liverpool Law Review* 25: 177–194.

Frakes, W.B. (ed.). 1992. *Information retrieval: Data structures & algorithms.* Delhi: Pearson Education India.

Kotsakis, E. 2002. Structured information retrieval in XML documents. In *SAC '02 proceedings of the 2002 ACM symposium on applied computing*, 663–667. New York: ACM. doi:10.1145/508791.508919.

Landes, W.M., and R.A. Posner. 1976. Legal precedent: A theoretical and empirical analysis. *Journal of Law and Economics* 19: 249.

Manning, C.D., P. Raghavan, and H. Schütze. 2008. *Introduction to information retrieval.* New York: Cambridge University Press. ISBN 0521865719.

Mihalcea, R., C. Corley, and C. Strapparava. 2006. Corpus-based and knowledge-based measures of text semantic similarity. In *Proceedings, the twenty-first national conference on artificial intelligence and the eighteenth innovative applications of artificial intelligence conference*, 16–20 July 2006. Boston: AAAI Press.

Popple, J. 1996. *A pragmatic legal expert system*, Applied legal philosophy series. Aldershot: Ashgate/Dartmouth.

Posner, R.A. 1993. What do judges and justices maximize. *Supreme Court Economic Review* 3: 1–41.

Riesbeck, C., and W. Bain. 1987. *A methodology for implementing case-based reasoning systems.* Lockheed.

Salton, G. 1968. *Automatic information organization and retrieval.* New York: McGraw-Hill.

Salton, G., A. Wong, and C.S. Yang. 1975. A vector space model for automatic indexing. *Communications of the ACM* 18(11): 613–620.

Slade, S. 1991. Case-based reasoning: A research paradigm. *AI Magazine* 12: 42–45.

Sontag, D., K. Collins-Thompson, P.N. Bennett, R. White, S. Dumais, and B. Billerbeck. 2012. Probabilistic Models for Personalizing Web Search. In *WSDM 2012: Fifth international conference on web search and data mining.* New York: ACM.

Watson, I., and F. Marir. 1994. Case-based reasoning: A review. *Knowledge Engineering Review* 9: 327–354.

Wen, J., N. Lao, and W. Ma. 2004. Probabilistic model for contextual retrieval. In *SIGIR '04 proceedings of the 27th annual international ACM SIGIR conference on research and development in information retrieval*, 57–63. New York: ACM. ISBN 1-58113-881-4.

Wu, X., V. Kumar, J.R. Quinlan, J. Ghosh, Q. Yang, H. Motoda, G.J. McLachlan, A. Ng, B. Liu, P.S. Yu, Z. Zhou, M. Steinbach, D.J. Hand, and D. Steinberg. 2007. Top 10 algorithms in data mining. *Knowledge and Information Systems* 14(1): 1–37. New York: Springer. doi:10.1504/IJBM.2008.018665.

Zeleznikow J., and A. Stranieri. 1995. The split-up system: Integrating neural networks and rule-based reasoning in the legal domain. In *Proceedings of the 5th international conference on Artificial Intelligence and Law*, 185–194. New York: ACM.

Zeleznikow, J., E. Bellucci, U.J. Schild, and G. Mackenzie. 2007. Bargaining in the shadow of the law – Using utility functions to support legal negotiation. In *Proceedings of the 11th international conference on Artificial Intelligence and Law*, 237–246. New York: ACM.

Zweigert, K., and H. Kötz. 1998. *An introduction to comparative law*, 3rd ed. Oxford: Clarendon.

Chapter 8
The Conflict Resolution Process

Abstract In a conflict resolution process, several key tasks can be identified that
have a preponderant role on its success or failure. Of these, the generation of valid
solutions is among the most important. Indeed, parties are often unwilling (as in
when they are avoiding the conflict) or unable (when they lack the required skills) to
do it. Moreover, in order for the process to be successful, solutions must not only be
valid: they must also be consensual, fair and appealing for all the parties. This
makes the task harder since parties often disregard each other's expectation or find
it difficult to put themselves in the place of the other and evaluate their proposal
from the other's point of view. This chapter addresses this problem by proposing
two different methods to provide support during the actual conflict resolution
process by generating solutions. The first one relies on a case-based approach that
looks at similarities between past known cases and the current one in order to
suggest possible and likely solutions. The second one is meant to be used if the
case-based approach fails (e.g. when there are not enough past cases). It is based on
genetic algorithms that evolve solutions over successive rounds through the application of genetic operators. It is a much more flexible and domain-independent
approach, which allows to explore sometimes unexpected areas of the search space.
All in all, these approaches can be incorporated in the midst of a conflict resolution
platform such as UMCourt to facilitate the development of dynamic and autonomous conflict resolution processes.

8.1 Introduction

The most common way of implementing ODR tools is by means of Expert Systems.
Two main trends can be identified: Rule-based and Case-based ones (Waterman
et al. 1986). The use of Rule-Based Systems (RBS) aims to encode the problem
solving expertise of human experts, which may be seen as a set of procedures

D. Carneiro et al., *Conflict Resolution and its Context*, Law, Governance and
Technology Series 18, DOI 10.1007/978-3-319-06239-6_8,
© Springer International Publishing Switzerland 2014

guided by rules (Hayes-Roth 1985). The use of Case-based Reasoning (CBR), on the other hand, aims at capturing and using knowledge from past experiences, allowing known solutions to be applied to solve similar problems, either in the present or in the future (Kolodner 1993).

RBS models were first used to develop Expert Systems for the legal domain. Generally, a rule describes the conclusions that the expert draws from a set of facts. The whole set of rules constitutes the knowledge base about the domain. Then, when the system is provided with facts, it searches the knowledge base for the relevant rules and applies them in order to reach a conclusion. This kind of systems builds on the idea that chains of rules may define the reasoning processes of human experts (Waterman and Peterson 1981). Early well-known projects following this trend include *TAXMAN* (McCarty 1977); *LDS* (Waterman and Peterson 1980), and the *JUDITH* system (Popp and Judith 1975).

In the last years, however, the trend has been changing towards the use of the CBR approach. The fundament of CBR is to store and index key information of known cases. These indexes may then be used to search for past cases that may be of relevance to solve an existing problem. The key idea is that similar solutions applied to similar problems in a similar context will lead to similar and predictable outcomes (Atkinson and Bench-Capon 2006). CBR may be used to improve problem-solving tasks in quite a few different ways. Namely, it may provide interpretation shortcuts, warn for potential errors or suggest lines of thought (Kolodner and Simpson 1989). There is extensive work in the field of CBR applied to the legal domain. Some of the most well-known projects include *MEDIATOR* (Kolodner and Simpson 1989), *PERSUADER* (Sycara 1992), or James Popple's *SHYSTER* (Popple 1996).

However, both rule-based and case-based approaches to problem solving in the legal arena face criticism, given their prospective disadvantages. Indeed, most of the systems developed so far are restricted to specific domains of The Law. This makes it hard to reproduce the results of a given undertaking in other domains.

Considering RBS, the main disadvantages of this approach are linked with the human experts that formulate the rules. In fact, a big challenge is effectively to determine the Quality-of-Information (QoI) of the rules. To ensure it is as high as possible, experts from both the Legal and the Computer Science arenas should be involved in the task of rule definition. Moreover, a RBS are not an optimal solution for all problems. Consequently, considerable knowledge is needed not to misemploy these systems. Finally, it is a fact that the ease of rule creation and edition may be an advantage. However, this may be also seen as a potential disadvantage as a non-knowledgeable user may easily sabotage the system. Typical reasons for the failure of RBS include the negligence to employ simple tools for system audit that may detect incompatibilities inside or among rules.

Considering CBR, its main disadvantage stems from its potential complexness. In fact, in a multifaceted knowledge-based domain, the simple definition of the content of a case may be an overwhelming task, involving many different experts from different fields of expertise. Moreover, this also implies the use of significant amount of resources to store and deal with such cases. This means that case-based approaches are generally more intricate and resource-demanding. Additionally, most of the analyzed systems are static rather than adaptive, i.e., once a strategy is defined, generally at the outset of the process, it will be followed disregarding probable changes in the environment that sets the interaction context. It is therefore possible to enumerate the main drawbacks of both RBS and CBR approaches:

- Laws change constantly thus implying updates to rules in RBS. This frequently results in inconsistencies and/or redundancy. Moreover, this might be a quite complex task (depending on the complexity of the legal domain) that may have to be performed manually;
- The quality of an ODR tool based on a RBS is directly dependent on the quality of the work of the humans translating the legal norms into rules. The quality of information of the rules may be hard to quantify;
- RBS are static and will not shape changes in the legal domain, unless these are coded manually by a human expert;
- The quality of an ODR tool based on CBR is directly dependent on the quality, similarity and amount of past known cases;
- The fact that legal norms change frequently also has a negative impact in CBR approaches, rendering past cases potentially useless under the light of the new norms; and
- Both CBR and RBS approaches are domain dependent, i.e., rules are aimed at a legal domain, and cases from a particular domain may hardly be reused in a different one.

Another disadvantage of current ODR tools is the loss of background information regarding the interaction environment. This information may be described as the parties' mood and includes indicators such as the level of stress or escalation, or even their emotional state. All this information is taken into account by a judge or a jury in the courtroom, or by a mediator when following an alternative approach. Nevertheless, it is lost when using an ODR tool. Although it may be argued that legal disputes are more about reason and evidence and less about emotions, these ultimately influence all our decisions and actions and should be regarded as critical. As an example, a party that is stressed or feeling extremely anger at a given time in a dispute resolution affair should not make binding pronouncements as they might regret them later. Instead, they should be advised to make a pause and think about it later on. The development of ODR systems that are able to apprehend the emotional state of each party may be considered with interest.

Soft Computing techniques have been used to address similar complex problems where, among others, one may cite the works described in (Sedano et al. 2010; Corchado et al. 2010), to detect the lifetime of building thermal insulation failures, or to identify distinctive meteorological days. More specifically, evolutionary computation has been successfully used to deal with problems that involve a significant amount of complex issues, in which traditional approaches to problem solving would not be suited (Corchado and Herrero 2011; Neves et al. 2012).

Given the mentioned disadvantages of case-based and rule-based methodologies for problem solving, and the potential advantages of soft computing techniques to overcome similarly complex problems, this chapter presents two approaches that aim to improve current conflict resolution tools. The first one implements negotiation and mediation processes to improve case-based approaches. Indeed, often the parties will not agree on a solution proposed by a human expert or by an automated system, and will negotiate to reach an agreement. However, as seen previously, the number of available cases in the database may limit the efficacy of CBR. The second approach looks at evolutionary computation to improve this aspect. Namely, a tool to generate solutions for a conflict is presented that is not limited by knowledge of previous cases or by domain-specific knowledge, such as in RBS.

8.2   Using Negotiation and Mediation to Improve CBR Efficiency

As it was stated above, CBR models may be used to retrieve past cases and to point out likely solutions for a problem, by comparison. However, it may happen that the parties do not agree with the proposed solution. In these situations, approaches based on negotiation or mediation may be used to guide the parties into a solution that may be deemed fair and acceptable by either of them (Carneiro et al. 2011).

Indeed, this section describes two approaches to automated negotiation and mediation aimed precisely at guiding the parties into such an agreement. The CBR process presented in the previous chapter supports these two approaches. They are based on the notion of blackboard, i.e., a shared space in which the parties publish and debate proposals. This is implemented by a specific software agent, which is able to receive and interpret messages from the parties, and take decisions according to the content of those messages in order to guide the process to a successful conclusion (Fig. 8.1).

The CBR processes detailed in the previous chapter supports both the mediation and negotiation developments described in this section. It does so by compiling information, which encompasses the already mentioned BATNA and WATNA values, for both parties. Indeed, in the course of the conflict resolution process, these concepts are evidently significant to help the parties have a clear picture of the possible outcomes of the dispute. Moreover, parties may also use this information to put pressure on the other party in the negotiation session to come, especially in dispute resolution procedures that allow the choice of going to court. Other aspects mentioned before are also compiled at the outset of the process, namely the ZOPA and the MLATNA that help the parties in building a complete and objective view of their problem.

Finally, a list of similar cases, retrieved from the case base, is also compiled. Parties can look at these cases and their outcomes in search for potential solutions for their differences. Upon retrieval, the cases are adapted. This means that when parties look at one of these cases they will not actually see the outcome of the past case, but will instead see the outcome as if it had happened in their own case, with

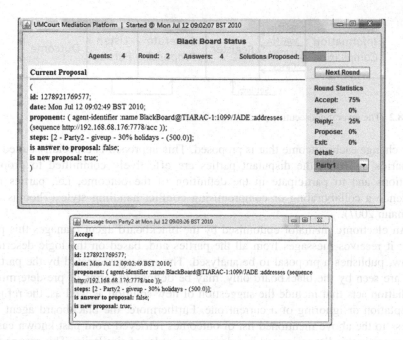

Fig. 8.1 A simple visual interface of the blackboard status (*upper image*), and the content of a reply (*lower image*)

their information and their details. As an example, let us consider a past case whose outcome entailed the employer to pay to the employee five times the monthly salary, which in the case amount to 2,500, i.e., the employer had to pay the employee a sum of 12,500. Let us assume that the salary of the employee in the present case is of 1,500. If the parties see the solution derived from this past case, they will be put forward to an outcome of 7,500, which is an adaptation of the past case with respect to a new salary. Using the procedure described in the previous chapter, this list of similar cases is sorted according to the similarity of the past cases to the current one. All this is done at the beginning of the conflict resolution process. This aims not only to inform the parties but also to build the necessary information to feed the two algorithms described in this section, aimed at guiding the parties throughout an successful process.

8.2.1   Mediation

The objective of the mediation process described in this section is to suggest alternative solutions to the parties in order to overcome impasses in scenarios in which the parties cannot agree on a given solution. The parties, throughout an iterative process that allows them to draw the most mutually satisfactory solution,

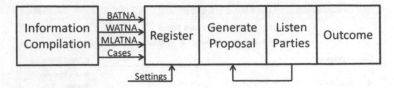

Fig. 8.2 The several consecutive phases of the mediation process

may change each outcome that is proposed. This approach is especially suited for scenarios in which the disputant parties are effectively committed to propose solutions and to participate in the definition of the outcome, i.e., parties that evidence a collaborating or compromising conflict handling style (Thomas and Kilmann 2007).

An electronic mediator epitomised by the blackboard agent manages this process: it receives messages from all the parties and, based on the logic described below, publishes a proposal to be analysed. The messages created by the parties, that are seen by the blackboard only, may be defined in terms of pre-determined mediation acts that include the suggestion of new solution as well as, the refusal, acceptance or ignoring of a current one. Furthermore, the blackboard agent has access to the above mentioned list of outcomes retrieved from past known cases. The cases in this list are sorted in a decreasing order of similarity. This means that the outcome of the first case is the most similar one, i.e., the first case constitutes the MLATNA.

Once all the parties are logged in, the process starts with the blackboard publishing a proposal for a solution. This is the first in the sorted list of similar cases, i.e., the MLATNA. Whenever the blackboard agent publishes a new proposal each party may take one of several actions. The proposal may be accepted (denoting that they agree with it) or it may be rejected. On the other hand, parties may also propose a new solution by modifying the present one, or suggest an entirely new solution by drawing it from scratch. Finally, parties may also choose to ignore the current proposal or leave the mediation process. If, in any round, one or more parties leave the process, it ends.

The lifecycle of this iterative process is entirely controlled by the blackboard agent and is organized into sequential rounds (Fig. 8.2). Each round starts with the blackboard agent publishing a new proposal. This proposal may have two different origins: it may come from the list of similar cases or it may be computed from previous answers of the parties. In the second case, if only one party answered with either a new proposal or a modified one, that will be the next solution to be proposed by the blackboard agent. Otherwise, the blackboard agent will search for similarities among the proposals, and compute a new solution based on those resemblances; the points in which the parties agree are carried to the next proposal. If, however, the proposals are divergent, the blackboard agent will propose the next solution from the list of past similar cases, if any. This process ends when all the parties agree on a proposal, at least one party leaves the process or when the system runs out of known solutions and the parties did not agree on any of the suggested ones.

An algorithm that implements the guidelines referred to above is presented below.

```
Algorithm Mediation is
    input:  List of cases with solutions, C
            List of parties, P
    output: A solution for the dispute

    round := 0        (identifies the round)
    msgSet := []      (a list of received messages)
    agree := 0        (the number of agents that agree)
    exit := 0         (the number of agents that exit)
    proposal := []    (the current proposal)
    i := 0            (the case C being currently proposed)

    while (agree < length(L) and exit < 1)
        if (round = 0)
            proposal := Cᵢ
        else if (msgSet contains "ReplyTo" or msgSet contains "Propose")
                set := ReplyTo in msgSet ∪ Propose in msgSet
                proposal := intersect set
            else i++
                    if (i = Length(C))
                        return null
                    else proposal := Cᵢ
        publish proposal
        msgSet := []
        for each party in L
            msg := receive from party or timeout
            msgSet := msgSet ∪ msg
        agree = count "agree" in msgSet
        exit  = count "exit" in msgSet
    if (exit > 0)
        return null
    else
        return proposal
```

Algorithm 8.1 The mediation algorithm

8.2.2   *Guided Negotiation*

This process shares the same objective of the previous one but tries to achieve it in a different fashion. It has been especially developed for scenarios in which one or more parties exhibit an avoiding conflict style (Thomas and Kilmann 2007), i.e., one or more parties are reluctant or find it difficult to create possible solutions. In that sense, the responsibility of generating solutions falls entirely on the system. In

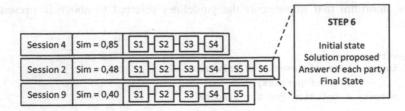

Fig. 8.3 The information needed to guide a negotiation process

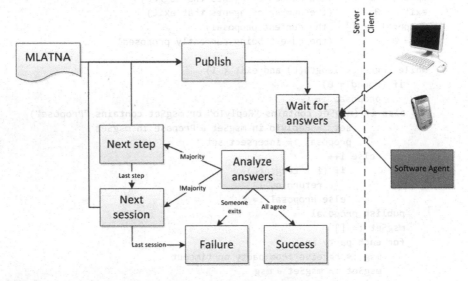

Fig. 8.4 A negotiation process coordinated by the blackboard agent

this approach, parties may answer in three ways to a new proposal: they may ignore, agree or disagree.

The negotiation process develops around a list of previous negotiation sessions provided by the CBR mechanism that are used to guide the parties through their current conflict resolution process (Fig. 8.3). Each negotiation session is defined by a list of events or steps, with each one representing a sequential stage in the negotiation process.

At each negotiation stage one has to contemplate the initial state of the problem (the initial conditions), a prospective solution (i.e., a list of the arrangements that one or more parties have to consider, usually trade-offs), the parties' answers to the suggested solution, as well as the final state of the problem (denoting the problem closing settings).

The process starts with the blackboard agent publishing the solution of the most similar past negotiation session, after which the parties reply. With a positive answer, the parties confirm that they will go through the negotiation phases described in the past session, and that they will accept the corresponding outcome. With a negative answer, they will be stating that they do not agree with the proposed solution or with the outcome.

At the end of each round, i.e., when the blackboard agent receives all the messages from the parties, the content of these messages is analysed. At this point, the negotiation may proceed according to different lines of action. If all the parties agreed on the current proposal, the negotiation process ends since a solution that satisfies all parties has been found. Otherwise, if the majority of the parties agree with the current proposal, the blackboard agent will then propose the following step of the negotiation session being used. Alternatively, if the majority of the parties do not agree with the present suggestion, the blackboard agent will fall back and select the following negotiation session in the list of past sessions, and repeats the process. This process repeats until either all the parties agree on a solution, or the system reaches the end of the list of past sessions without agreement on the part of the parties. The whole negotiation process is depicted in Fig. 8.4.

```
Algorithm Mediation is
    input:  List of previous mediation processes, L
            List of parties, P
    output: A solution for the dispute

    round := 0        (identifies the round)
    msgSet := []      (a list of received messages)
    agree := 0        (the number of agents that agree)
    exit := 0         (the number of agents that exit)
    proposal := []    (the current proposal)
    i := 0        (the mediation process being currently used)
    j := 0            (the current step being proposed)

    while (agree < length(L) and exit < 1)
        mediation := L_i
        solution := mediation_j
        publish proposal
        for each party in P
            msg := receive from party or timeout
            msgSet := msgSet U msg
        agree = count "agree" in msgSet
        exit  = count "exit" in msgSet
    if (exit > 0)
        return null
    if (agree = Length(P))
        return solution
    else if (agree > Length(P)/2)
            j++
        else i++
            j := 0
    if (j = Length(mediation))
        j := 0
        i++
    if (i = Length(L))
        return null
    round++
```
Algorithm 8.2 The guided negotiation algorithm

8.3   An Evolutionary Approach to Conflict Resolution

Until now, it was shown how case-based methodologies for problem solving may be used to compile information in order to improve decision-making procedures or techniques. Moreover, it was also described how case-based approaches to conflict resolution might be enhanced with a posterior phase of negotiation or mediation aimed at supporting the parties in reaching a mutually satisfactory outcome. So far, this is in line with most of the existing conflict resolution platforms, which are either case-based or rule-based. However, most of these classical approaches still hold disadvantages, which have been summarized at the beginning of this chapter. In this section a new view on the problem is explored, in which we look at evolutionary algorithms to generate solutions to conflict resolution processes (Carneiro et al. 2012a). The main objective is to assist parties and mediators in generating and modifying consensual solutions to the problem, namely via an agreement. The presented approach holds some advantages when compared to its two more classical counterparts:

- It stands for a more comprehensive solution when compared with case-based approaches, as it may cover virtually the entire search space of the problem. Case-based approaches, on the other hand, may fail due to a lack of suitable or similar cases. One particular problem in conflict resolution is that conflicts can be generated in many different domains, and cases from one domain may not be adapted to others;
- The number of generated solutions depends only on the initialization settings, as opposed to case-based solutions which are limited by the number of cases in the database; and
- It is domain-independent, contrary to case-based and rule-based approaches, in which information can generally only be reused in the same legal domain.

8.3.1   A Closer Overview of Evolutionary Algorithms

Evolutionary algorithms find its inspiration in the Darwinian notion of natural evolution (Darwin 1998):

- Individuals between species are variable, i.e., each individual has specific properties besides the ones that make him part of the species, that make it unique;
- Some of the specific properties of each individual are passed on to their offspring;
- In every generation not all the individuals are going to be able to live long and reproduce; and

- The survival and reproduction of the individuals is not entirely random, i.e., the individuals that survive and go on to reproduce are those with the most auspicious characteristics.

Indeed, evolution acts on the individual (and not on the group or on the population) but its effects are reflected on the population. In *nature*, the results of evolution are often creative, surprising and even unexpected. An arbitrarily large number of individuals is suffering changes that may potentially benefit the species, and spreading those changes through reproduction.

The interest in bringing these advantages into the field of Computer Science gave birth to Evolutionary Computation: the use of ideas and inspirations from natural evolution and other biological systems to solve one's problems (Holland 1992).

Evolutionary algorithms are generally used to solve problems concerning optimization, search, machine learning or automatic design (Goldberg 1989). It is a field that is naturally linked to the Artificial Intelligence arena.

A few basic concepts must be introduced at this point, that are central in evolutionary computation. The *search space* is the space of all possible solutions to a problem. The dimensions of this space may not be known beforehand. *Representation* is the strategy used to represent an individual, i.e. a candidate solution, in a simple way. Generally, individuals are represented as strings of characters or numbers, with each character or number in a given position representing a specific characteristic of the solution. The *fitness function* is the mechanism that allows evaluating how good a given solution is for the problem at hand. It takes as input the representation of the solution and returns a number that indicates how good the solution is. In evolution, the objective is to maximize some facets of the population; in particular one seeks to maximize the value of fitness of the population. Tendentiously, better solutions will be found faster with a larger population, although not necessarily.

The basic lifecycle of an evolutionary algorithm entails five main stages. The first one is the creation of the initial population. Different strategies may be used to do it, ranging from the random generation of individuals to the use of rules that may let the population in the next phases of the process converge faster to fittest individuals. The next stage consists in evaluating the population at hand by computing the objective values for each individual, i.e., what are the values of the properties that are being considered in the evolution process. The third one comprises the computing of a value of fitness for each individual, which is weighted one according to the properties' values set in the previous stage (e.g. in an environment without predators, it may be more important for a bird that feeds on seeds do develop a mutation on the beak, than to develop a mutation on the plumage, aiming at a better camouflage). The fourth stage consists on selecting the best individuals to be reproduced, i.e., the individuals with the highest fitness. These individuals are then reproduced in the fifth stage, making a new population.

Evolutionary algorithms have a number of characteristics that make them appealing to address complex problems, namely those in which one seeks to accomplish some form of optimization, and where multiple solutions are required. However, there are also some disadvantages worth being pointed out. Almost every aspect of the evolutionary algorithm can be configured, from the reproduction operators or the selection strategies to the size of the population or the maximum number of generations. This is undoubtedly an advantage. But, it may also make it difficult to fine-tune the algorithm to perform well on specific applications. Other aspects that add to the complexity of the problem are bad decisions on the definition of the fitness function or data representation model. Bad decisions on any of these aspects can make the algorithm perform poorly. Unfortunately, there is no way to know, beforehand, which decisions are good and which are bad. The general approach lies on a trial and error practice that goes on until the algorithm performs "good enough". Defining what level of performance is *good enough* may also be difficult, since one does not know the best solution beforehand. Thus, one generally runs the algorithm several times with several different settings. The best overall solution is selected from among the best solutions of these rounds. There is also no mathematical guarantee that the population will converge, although the fine-tuning of the settings (namely the ones related to the degree of randomness of the reproduction and selection operators) may increase those chances.

Several approaches exist within evolutionary algorithms, including genetic programming, genetic algorithms, evolutionary programming, or differential evolution. Particularly, in this section we look at Genetic Algorithms as a way of searching for multiple solutions for a given problem, in this case in the domain of conflict resolution.

8.3.2   Using Genetic Algorithms to Create Solutions for Conflict Resolution

Engendering solutions for the resolution of a conflict is generally a challenging task, although different methods may be used. The employment of case-based models may be a good solution as conflict resolution experts themselves rely on past experiences to make their judgments. However, a poor or unfit case-base may disrupt the system. On the other hand, relying on the parties themselves to perform this task is, in general, not a good alternative, since they may be unwilling or unable to do so. In order to deal with this drawback, we propose the use of genetic algorithms to create solutions for conflict resolution.

Under this approach, each chromosome will represent a possible solution for a conflict, i.e., a possible distribution of the items in dispute. The population evolves from generation to generation by means of genetic operators that change the items' distribution, and thus have an effect on the fitness of the solutions. This fitness is computed from the point of view of each party, i.e., a solution that is good for one party may not be so good to the others, given that they have conflicting objectives. With the successive generations, some chromosomes tend to be more fit to one

$$P = \begin{array}{|c|c|c|c|c|} \hline Ch_1 = \begin{bmatrix} V_{1,1} & \cdots & V_{1,n} \\ \vdots & \ddots & \vdots \\ V_{m,1} & \cdots & V_{m,n} \end{bmatrix} & Ch_2 = \begin{bmatrix} V_{1,1} & \cdots & V_{1,n} \\ \vdots & \ddots & \vdots \\ V_{m,1} & \cdots & V_{m,n} \end{bmatrix} & \cdots & Ch_s = \begin{bmatrix} V_{1,1} & \cdots & V_{1,n} \\ \vdots & \ddots & \vdots \\ V_{m,1} & \cdots & V_{m,n} \end{bmatrix} \\ \hline \end{array}$$

Fig. 8.5 Under this approach a population of size s is represented as a set of chromosomes with a cardinality of s

party. As in nature, there are lines of evolution that emerge naturally towards the maximization of the fitness of a given party. In this work, a species is thus defined as the group of chromosomes that stand for good solutions for a given party. Thus, there will be a species for each party. Moreover, a chromosome may belong to more than one species if it denotes a solution that is good for more than one party. Evidently, chromosomes that belong to more than one species are more attractive, since they correspond to solutions that will be more easily accepted by the parties.

Chromosome

A population P of size s is defined by a set of chromosomes Ch (Fig. 8.5). Each chromosome $Ch_i, i \in \{1, 2, \ldots, s\}$ stands for a possible solution for the problem: it represents a distribution of the items in dispute or, in other words, who gets how much of what. For a dispute involving n parties and m issues, a chromosome Ch may be denoted as an m-by-n matrix (Eq. 8.1).

$$Ch = \begin{bmatrix} V_{1,1} & \cdots & V_{1,n} \\ \vdots & \ddots & \vdots \\ V_{m,1} & \cdots & V_{m,n} \end{bmatrix} \tag{8.1}$$

where the value $V_{m,n}$ conveys the amount of issue m that the party n receives in terms of a solution Ch. The actual content of the chromosome depends on the domain of the dispute. Moreover, each domain also has specific rules that ensure the solution's correctness.

As an example, let us consider the general model of distributive negotiation, in which a group of resources has to be divided (e.g. in divorces or in winding up a company). Under this setting each entry stands for a value between 0 and 1 (Eq. 8.2), and the sum of the values of each line equals 1 (Eq. 8.3). The total amount of resources received by party n, R_n, is defined as the sum of the values of column n (Eq. 8.4).

$$V_{m,n} \in A, \quad A = \{x \in \mathbb{R} \mid 0 \le x \le 1\} \tag{8.2}$$

$$\sum_{i=1}^{n} V_{m,n} = 1, \quad \forall m \in \{1, 2, \ldots, m\} \tag{8.3}$$

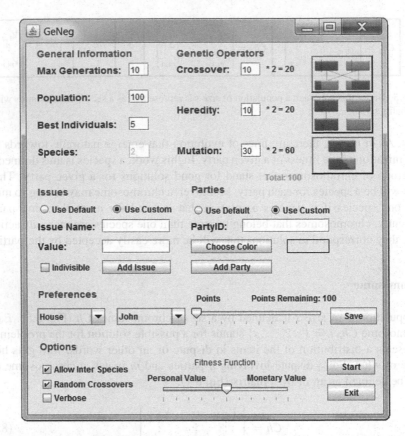

Fig. 8.6 A prototype of the interface used to configure the genetic algorithm, including information about the parties, the issues and the weight of each genetic operator

$$R_n = \sum_{i=1}^{m} V_{m,n} \qquad (8.4)$$

In this approach it was also considered the existence of indivisible goods. This is common in scenarios such as divorces, in which there are assets (e.g. car, house) that parties are not willing to sell, and must be assigned, only, to one of them. Thus, for every indivisible issue m, Eq. 8.5 must hold.

$$V_{m,i} = 1 \Rightarrow V_{m,x} = 0, \quad \forall x \in \{1, 2, \ldots, n\}, \quad x \neq i \qquad (8.5)$$

Initialization

Initially, some information must be provided to the system in order for it to be initialized (Fig. 8.6). Concerning issues related to the conflict resolution process itself, the name, value and type of each issue under negotiation must be provided, as well as an identifier and a color for each party. Moreover, each party must state its preferences concerning each item in dispute by distributing 100 points amongst them. This will allow the system to determine how much each party values each item, from a personal and subjective perspective, and not from a monetary one.

In terms of the genetic algorithm, some information is also needed for the initialization process. A predefined number of runs set the termination condition. The size of the population results in the number of chromosomes at each running cycle. Checking the *verbose* option will make the algorithm detail all its steps. The algorithm may also be configured in terms of how many individuals are considered from each species to apply the genetic operators to, being that a higher number of individuals will result in increased diversity. Concerning the genetic operators, it is also possible to define the weight of each one in the making of new populations, i.e., it is possible to decide how many individuals of the new population will be generated by each operator. Finally, it is also possible to configure the fitness function in terms of the weights of the personal and monetary values in the computation of the overall fitness of each solution. Once this information is provided, the algorithm may be initialized. In this process, a population of the specified size is generated, where each chromosome is set in terms of a random distribution of the items, i.e., a solution generated randomly.

Selection

At each running cycle there is a part of the population that is selected from each species to give birth to a new generation. Given that only the best individuals are selected to breed the new population, a fitness-based process must be defined to set which of the fitter solutions of each species may be pointed out. As each solution has a different fitness for each party, the fitness of each solution for each party must be computed. This means that for a conflict resolution involving n parties and for a population of size s, $n * s$ values of fitness will be computed at each running cycle.

The fitness function looks at each solution and assigns it a value that depends on the amount of items that each party receives, being quantified in terms of the economic value of the items and the value that each party assigned to each item (the personal value). In this work, two fitness functions were devised (Eqs. 8.6 and 8.7), where:

- tmv denotes the case economic value, i.e., the total amount of money that the issues in dispute are worth with, being defined as $tmv = \sum_{i=1}^{I} mv_i$;
- I defines the number of issues;
- mv_i stands for the monetary value of issue i;
- $fit_{j,p}$ represents the fitness of chromosome j for party p;
- W_m denotes the weight of the monetary value of the items while W_p stands for the weight of the personal value; and
- $prefs_i$ denotes the preferences of a given party regarding issue i.

The use of Eq. 8.6 will tend to result in solutions in which each party receives approximately what they valued the most, i.e., Eq. 8.6 minimizes the difference between the individual preferences for each item and the value assigned to it.

$$fit_{j,p} = W_m * \frac{\sum_{i=1}^{I} Ch_{j,p} * mv_i}{tmv} + W_p * \left(1 - \sum_{i=1}^{I} \frac{|Ch_{j,p} - prefs_i|}{I}\right) \quad (8.6)$$

On the other hand, Eq. 8.7 focuses on maximizing the individual gain of each party, i.e., Eq. 8.6 will tend to generate populations that may be described as fairer, while the ones generated by Eq. 8.7 will be greedier.

$$fit_{j,p} = W_m * \frac{\sum_{i=1}^{I} Ch_{j,p} * mv_i}{tmv} + W_p * \sum_{i=1}^{I} \frac{|Ch_{j,p} - prefs_i|}{I} \quad (8.7)$$

The system is currently using Eq. 8.6 as it generates solutions that, by being more balanced, are more likely to be accepted by the parties. At each cycle, the fitness of the population is computed as described and the best individuals from each species are selected to generate a new population.

Reproduction

In genetic algorithms, reproduction looks at the engendering of new populations, making the heuristic search move towards the maximization of the fitness function. In this work three different genetic operators are used: *mutation, crossover* and *heredity*. They are applied to each generation according to what was defined at initialization.

In genetics, a mutation is defined as a spontaneous and random change in a genomic sequence. In the particular case of this work, a mutation is a random change at the chromosome level, i.e., in terms of the issues' distribution. The issues mutated are given in terms of a mutation threshold, here designated as μ. To implement the mutation, a random issue is selected as well as two random parties. The allocation of the issue is then changed for the selected parties, according to the mutation threshold. If the issue is divisible, the amount of the issue is subtracted from one party according to μ and added to the other party. If the issue is indivisible, there is a probability that a change in ownership may occur, according to the mutation threshold.

For example, let us consider a scenario with a given μ in which two parties are disputing four issues. Assuming that issue 2 is divisible and is selected to be changed between party 1 and party 2, the result is shown in Eq. 8.8, where Ch and Ch' present a picture of a chromosome, respectively, before and after the mutation operation.

$$Ch = \begin{bmatrix} V_{1,1} & V_{1,2} & V_{1,3} \\ V_{2,1} & V_{2,2} & V_{2,3} \\ V_{3,1} & V_{3,2} & V_{3,3} \\ V_{4,1} & V_{3,2} & V_{4,3} \end{bmatrix} \quad Ch' = \begin{bmatrix} V_{1,1} & V_{1,2} & V_{1,3} \\ V_{2,1}+\mu & V_{2,2}-\mu & V_{2,3} \\ V_{3,1} & V_{3,2} & V_{3,3} \\ V_{4,1} & V_{3,2} & V_{4,3} \end{bmatrix} \quad (8.8)$$

The mutation, as defined here, has an effect on the fitness of the solution for each party, i.e., the new solution will be more favorable to party 1 and less favorable to party 2. The mutation algorithm is shown below.

```
Algorithm Mutation is
Input: List of parties, L
       List of issues, I
       Parent chromosome, C
Output: A new chromosome, C'
Do
    i  := select random issue from I
    p1 := select random party from L
    p2 := select random party from L such that p1 != p2
    C' := C
    if (i is divisible)
       C'i,p1 := C'i,p1 + μ * C'i,p1
       C'i,p2 := C'i,p2 - μ * C'i,p2
    else if (randomNumber > μ)
             temp := C'i,p1
             C'i,p1 := C'i,p2
             C'i,p2 := temp
While (C' is invalid solution)
Return C'
```

Crossover, on the other hand, is a binary genetic operator by means of which two offspring are generated from two parent chromosomes. In this work, a two-point crossover technique is used. Basically, these two points define the beginning and the end of an issue for both parents, meaning that everything between the beginning and the end of the issue will be swapped to create two offspring. Thus, crossover consists in swapping two distributions of the same issue, generating two new solutions. Two options may be used in this technique that will influence the variety of the new offspring: *inter species* and *random parents*. If the *inter species* option is checked, chromosomes from different species are crossed, generating a more diverse population. The *random parents* option allows one to decide on which parents should be used. If it is checked, random parents will be selected. On the other hand, the best parents of each species will be selected for the crossover operation. Equation 8.9 depicts an example of crossing two parent chromosomes *Ch1* and *Ch2* to generate two offspring *Ch1'* and *Ch2'*. In this case, the distribution of issue 2 was swapped.

$$Ch1 = \begin{bmatrix} A & B & C \\ D & E & F \\ G & H & I \\ J & K & L \end{bmatrix} \quad Ch2 = \begin{bmatrix} M & N & O \\ P & Q & R \\ S & T & U \\ V & W & X \end{bmatrix}$$

$$Ch1' = \begin{bmatrix} A & B & C \\ P & Q & R \\ G & H & I \\ J & K & L \end{bmatrix} \quad Ch2' = \begin{bmatrix} M & N & O \\ D & E & F \\ S & T & U \\ V & W & X \end{bmatrix} \tag{8.9}$$

Given that this technique changes the distribution of each solution, it will have effect on the fitness function. Below it is given a description of the generic algorithm that implements the crossover technique.

```
Algorithm Crossover is
Input: List of parties, L
       List of issues, I
Output: New chromosomes, C1', C2'
i   := select random issue from I
if (interspecies)
   s1 = select random species
   s2 = select random species such that s1 != s2
   if (randomparents)
      C1 := select random ch from s1
      C2 := select random ch from s2
   else
      C1 := select best ch from s1
      C2 := select best ch from s2
else
   s1 = select random species
   if (randomparents)
      C1 := select random ch from s1
      C2 := select random ch from s1 such that C1 != C2
   else
      C1 := select best ch from s1
      C2 := select second best ch from s1
   swap issues and generate C1', C2'
   return C1', C2'
```

Finally, *heredity* may be defined as the passing of traits from parent to offspring. Once this process is finished, the offspring acquires characteristics that may be compared to the ones of the parent. The evolution of the species is thus achieved by accumulating variations exhibited by different individuals. In this work, heredity is the simplest genetic operator to be considered, in the sense that the new offspring have exactly the same distribution that its parents have, i.e., this operator generates

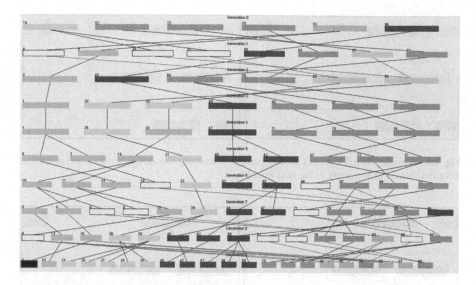

Fig. 8.7 The first ten generations of a run of the algorithm, showing only the best solutions generated

no diversity at all, and should be used when one wants to avoid *losing* the best individuals of a population, ensuring that the best traits will be passed to the next generation.

Termination

The process of selection and reproduction is repeated until the termination condition is accomplished, i.e., the maximum number of generations stated in the initialization phase is reached. At this point, the system provides a picture of the state of the evolutionary process, in terms of the solutions so far attained, and their lines of evolution (Fig. 8.7), where each rectangle denotes a different solution. Different colors stand for solutions of different species, i.e., the solutions that are better to a given party.

Moreover, each solution is represented in one or more colors. A solution with a specific color means that it belongs to the species (party) of that color. This will allow one to clearly see the natural emergence of species, i.e., the lines of evolution that tend towards the maximization of the fitness value for a specific party. Colorless individuals denote solutions that are not among the most fit for a particular population, but generated offspring that are among the best of future ones. It is also possible to look at a chromosome's content, as well to its fitness, and it's meaning, by clicking on it. The lines between individuals stand for the parent-offspring relationships. A unary genetic operator generated an individual that has a

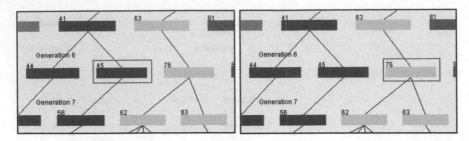

Fig. 8.8 A jump: when the state of another party is worsening, the mediator may select a solution from the species of that party in the next round

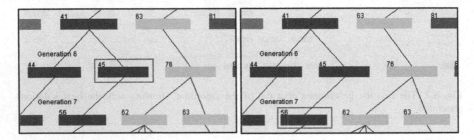

Fig. 8.9 A walk: when the state of the party improves or worsens slightly or when the negotiation is proceeding acceptably, the mediator is able to move up or down the tree in order to select solutions that are similar in terms of fitness

single line connecting to the previous making, while an individual that has two lines has been generated through crossover.

When the process ends, a relatively large number of solutions is available to be used in an attempt to solve the conflict. An autonomous negotiation system such as the one depicted above or a human mediator can use these solutions to conduct the conflict resolution. In this work we are particularly interested in developing dynamic processes that may adapt autonomously and in real time to new circumstances, namely using information concerning the parties' state. In the following chapters we consider information that the mediator may use to guide the conflict resolution process, namely the parties' level of stress or personal conflict handling style. This will allow the mediator to adapt the strategy devised at the outset of the process, to respond to significant changes in the parties' state.

To support this, the system allows to perform two main operations on the tree of solutions, namely jumps and walks. In a jump, the system selects a solution from different species (Fig. 8.8). This may happen under a situation in which the mediator realizes that a given party is being penalized, or when it is close to leave the process, i.e., the system may jump to the species that have more favorable solutions for that party. Walks, on the other hand, are used to move within the same species (Fig. 8.9). This usually takes place when the state of one or more parties changes slightly, i.e., when the system moves down the tree in searching for solutions that are better for the present party (the fitness of solutions improve as the generations increase) and vice versa. The definition of what constitutes the party's state and how the mediator may efficiently use that information, is addressed in the following chapters.

8.4 Conclusion

This chapter was dedicated to detail different methods to provide support during the actual conflict resolution process. These different approaches are all motivated by one of the main challenges that emerge when attempting to solve a conflict: the generation of valid and consensual solutions. Indeed, parties are often unwilling (when they are uncooperative) or unable (when they lack the required skills or have an unrealistic notion about their problems) to come up with solutions that may also be deemed fair and realistic by all the stakeholders. The two approaches presented focus on the generation of solutions following two different paths.

The first one looks at past similar cases. This approach is based on the notion that similar cases that happened in similar circumstances are likely to have similar outcomes. This argument may be used to convince the parties to accept a particular solution, it is what may occur if they go to court. However, case-based approaches are often limited by the cardinality of the database and other issues. Thus being, a second approach was presented that addresses such disadvantages. It is based on genetic procedures, a nature-inspired methodology for problem solving to handle complex multi-variable problems. It may cover virtually the whole search space of the problem, where case-based approaches may barely perform. It may even give birth to unexpected and out-of-the-box solutions, which may shed new light on the problem and reveal interesting alternative possibilities.

These two approaches, different in nature but similar in their objectives, are framed in a higher-level tool. They support the implementation of a dynamic negotiation algorithm whose main objective is to be able to interpret circumstantial information in order to adapt strategies in real time in a conflict resolution process. The contextual aspects that feed the adaptation mechanism are described in the following chapters. Nonetheless, adaptation requires the choice of different solutions or strategies for problem solving in real-time. The burden of the generation of these creative and valid solutions is lightened by the approaches presented in this chapter.

Indeed, conflict resolution methods that are run by human experts in the presence of the parties are generally dynamic in nature, as experts have the ability to understand the changes that occur in the interaction between the parties (e.g. a party is getting stressed, a party does not like the current state of affairs), and change the strategy before it is too late (e.g. by making a pause in the process). The problem is that under ODR settings, such information is not available for the mediators as the parties are, generally, *hidden* behind a web interface.

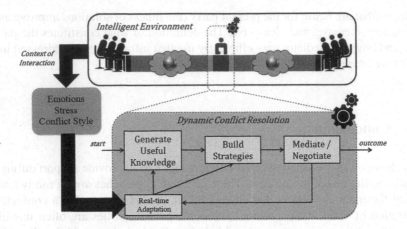

Fig. 8.10 A dynamic negotiation model; this picture depicts a high level view of a dynamic negotiation setting that is able to adapt strategies and propose different solutions according to changes in the process of negotiation. The input for the adaptation is information describing the state of the parties (e.g. emotional arousal, level of stress and personal conflict handling style)

The UMCourt framework aims to empower such actions in an online setting, by giving access to circumstantial information that is generally not available (Fig. 8.10). The mediator has access to, not only, the operational data of the negotiation setting, such as the proposals and messages exchanged, but also to background information such as the level of stress, the attitudes or the conflict handling style of the parties. This allows the mediator to detect changes in these aspects, and to adapt its strategy and problem-solving strategies. This adaptation may consist on making pauses, making some party aware of their behavior or attitude, or on proposing a different outcome from the list of solutions compiled by the conflict resolution platform. Moreover, the parties may themselves look at the solutions engendered to acquire a more realistic notion about their case, and to better prepare their strategy during the negotiation process.

The envisioned dynamic virtual environment for negotiation is implemented in four main phases. Under the first one, useful information is generated that sets the ground for the conflict resolution process, i.e., parties and mediator alike become aware of the most likely outcome in a courtroom, of the best and worst possible solutions and of solutions of past similar cases. With this information the parties are in a better position to advance to the next phase: the definition of realistic and potentially successful strategies, bearing in mind that in such a process it is easier to reach a settlement, if everyone wins something. In the third phase, parties engage on a process of negotiation or mediation, exchanging messages and proposals in iterative rounds; while these rounds advance, it is natural that their state, their expectations or their objectives may change. The mediator nurses an onus in being sensitive to these changes and to react accordingly. This may call for an adaptation phase that includes the revision of the parties' objectives, the re-definition of the strategies or the continuation of the negotiation or mediation from a different perspective. In this, the solutions generated using any of the approaches presented in this chapter may have a preponderant role.

References

Atkinson, K., and T. Bench-Capon. 2006. Legal case-based reasoning as practical reasoning. *Artificial Intelligence and Law* 13(1): 93–131. doi:10.1007/s10506-006-9003-3.

Carneiro, D., P. Novais, F. Andrade, and J. Neves. 2011. Improving mediation processes with avoiding parties. In *New frontiers in Artificial Intelligence – JSAI-isAI 2010 workshops, LENLS, JURISIN, AMBN, ISS*, Tokyo, Japan, November 18–19, 2010, Revised selected papers. Lecture notes in computer science 6797, ed. Takashi Onada, Daisuke Bekki and Eric McCready, 117–128. Berlin/New York: Springer. ISBN 978-3-642-25654-7.

Carneiro, D., P. Novais, and J. Neves. 2012. Using genetic algorithms to create solutions for conflict resolution. *Neurocomputing*. Elsevier, http://dx.doi.org/10.1016/j.neucom.2012.03.024

Corchado, E., and A. Herrero. 2011. Neural visualization of network traffic data for intrusion detection. *Applied Soft Computing* 11(2): 2042–2056.

Corchado, E., A. Arroyo, and V. Tricio. 2010. Soft computing models to identify typical meteorological days. In: Dov Gabbay (ed.), *Logic journal of the IGPL*. Oxford: Oxford University Press.

Darwin, C. 1998. *The origin of species*, Oxford world's classics. Oxford: Oxford University Press. ISBN ISBN 978–0192834386.

Goldberg, D.E. 1989. *Genetic algorithms in search, optimization, and machine learning*. Reading: Addison-Wesley. ISBN ISBN 978–0201157673.

Hayes-Roth, F. 1985. Rule-based systems. *Communications of the ACM* 28(9): 921–932. New York: ACM. doi:10.1145/4284.4286.

Holland, J.H. 1992. Genetic algorithms. *Scientific American* 267(1): 66–72.

Kolodner, J.L. 1993. *Case-based reasoning*. San Mateo: Morgan Kaufmann Publishers.

Kolodner, J.L., and R.L. Simpson. 1989. The MEDIATOR: Analysis of an early case-based problem solver. *Cognitive Science* 13: 507–549.

McCarty, L.T. 1977. Reflections on TAXMAN: An experiment in artificial intelligence and legal reasoning. *Harvard Law Review* 90: 837–93.

Neves, J., J. Ribeiro, P. Pereira, V. Alves, J. Machado, A. Abelha, P. Novais, C. Analide, M. Santos, and M. Fernández-Delgado. 2012. Evolutionary intelligence in asphalt pavement modeling and quality-of-information. *Progress in Artificial Intelligence* 1(1): 119–135. Springer, ISSN 2192–6352.

Popp, W.G., and S. Judith. 1975. A computer program to advise lawyers in reasoning a case. *Jurimetrics Journal* 15(4) (Summer 1975): 303–314. American Bar Association.

Popple, J. 1996. *A pragmatic legal expert system*, Applied legal philosophy series. Ashgate: Dartmouth.

Sedano, J., L. Curiel, E. Corchado, E. Cal, and J. Villar. 2010. A soft computing method for detecting lifetime building thermal insulation failures. *Integrated Computer-Aided Engineering* 17(2): 103–115. IOS Press.

Sycara, K. 1992. The persuader. In *The encyclopedia of artificial intelligence*, ed. D. Shapiro. New York: Wiley. January.

Thomas, K.W., and R.H. Kilmann. 2007. *Thomas Kilmann conflict mode instrument*. Mountain View: Xicom, a subsidiary of CPP, Inc.

Waterman, D.A., and M. Peterson. 1980. Rule-based models of legal expertise. In *Proceedings of the First National Conference on AI*. Stanford: Stanford University.

Waterman, D.A., and M.A. Peterson. 1981. *Models of legal decision-making, R-2717-ICJ*. Santa
    Monica: Institute for Civil Justice, Rand Corp.
Waterman, D.A., J. Paul, and M. Peterson. 1986. Expert systems for legal decision making. *Expert
    Systems* 3: 212–226. doi:10.1111/j.1468-0394.1986.tb00203.x.

Part III
Context Acquisition in Online Dispute Resolution

Part III

Chapter 9
A Framework for Developing Sensible Environments

Abstract In interpersonal relationships, information about each individual's state is paramount for a correct interpretation of everyone's actions and reactions. Some of this information is available to our "eyes" in a face-to-face interaction, including the posture of the body, particular gestures, speech rhythm or the volume of the voice. Other, possibly more accurate information, is slightly more hidden and includes the temperature of our body, the amount of perspiration or the rhythm of our hearth. Alternatively, we can always ask people how they "feel" in each moment. These are the two big approaches available so far to assess one's state: physiological sensors and questionnaires. In this chapter, we detail the development of an environment that is sensible to its user's state. It has, however, one particular requirement: access to this information must be non-invasive and non-intrusive. None of the two approaches mentioned are suited. This chapter thus details the development of an environment that fulfills these requirements by integrating concepts from behavioral analysis. The key idea is that if the environment knows how each individual user behaves in a given state, the environment will know how the state of the user from their behaviors. Following this approach, this chapter describes an environment that is not only sensible to the users' state but that can also influence it to attain some goal of the environment.

9.1 Introduction

Up until now, the focus of this book was on different ways to support conflict resolution, ranging from the generation of valuable information to support the negotiation process to the making of possible solutions to solve the problem. This chapter takes this level of support a little further, by introducing and detailing the vision of an intelligent environment for conflict resolution, i.e., an environment that may be aware of its users and their background, taking or allowing for better and contextualized decisions. Indeed, in more traditional approaches in this field, contextual information is gathered via self-report mechanisms or invasive sensors. Here it will be put forward a new approach in which such contextual information is collected from the users through the analysis of their behavioral patterns. Definitely, *behavior* is one of the mirrors of our inner state, accurately reflecting changes on that state.

As addressed in Chap. 3, Virtual Environments (VEs) aim to reproduce the conditions of real environments in digital settings. These may be used to train professionals such as doctors, airline pilots, military personnel or emergency response teams in a risk-free and realistic environment (Stanney 2002). VEs can also be used to implement online communication mechanisms, namely for teaching or solving conflicts. However, as already discussed, although these environments try to mimic reality, they tend to be poorer spaces. Specifically, they lack many of the features that constitute our complex communication mechanisms, which are based on much more than words alone. Indeed, when communicating face-to-face, we make use of our body language, our tone of voice, hand gestures, speech rhythm, and even physiological responses of our body to better send and perceive information. Although this is done mostly in an unconscious way, it has a truly important and measurable role in this process (Mehrabian 1980).

Indeed, the lack of many of these features in online environments may represent a drawback in what concerns the efficiency of the communication process. It would thus be interesting to consider environments that could convey the state of the parties, together with the words of the communicative act. This would allow the interveners to more accurately perceive the messages exchanged and the intentions of the participants (e.g. distinguishing between sarcasm and a joke). Particularly interesting in this milieu is the information regarding the individuals' emotional state, or their levels of stress and fatigue. Indeed, such aspects significantly influence our mood, our actions, our reactions or our decisions. Knowing and understanding such aspects about individuals, may certainly help to better understand them and their actions.

Countless different approaches may be used to acquire such contextual information from the users. The section that follows deals with some of the more traditional ones, including physiological sensors or questionnaires, with advantages and disadvantages of their own. Then, a more innovative approach is put forward that focuses on the analysis of the behavior of the individuals, to harness equivalent information.

9.2 Traditional Approaches on Context Acquisition

Stress, fatigue or emotional state are extremely important in describing the inner state of an individual, which ultimately affects all their conscious and unconscious decisions. These personal, subjective and conscious experiences have known effects at the level of psycho-physiological expressions, biological reactions, mental states, mood, temperament, disposition, personality, motivation and, ultimately, health and well-being. Hence the significance of their study, which is very complex, involving fields such as psychology, philosophy, neurology, physiology, or medicine.

Traditionally, two main approaches may be followed to study such phenomena. The field of psychology relies more on the use of questionnaires or surveys, whereas the field of medicine relies on different kinds of sensors. Each of these approaches has advantages and disadvantages of their own.

Various different surveys were conducted over the last decades to study stress, fatigue or emotions. Essentially, they tend to ask how the individual *feels* certain symptoms, which may include indicators describing habits, behaviors or physical/emotional responses. Concerning stress, some of the most widely used include Sheldon Cohen's Perceived Stress Scale (Cohen et al. 1983), or the Copenhagen Psychosocial Questionnaire (Kristensen et al. 2005). Two examples of known surveys to assess fatigue can be found in (Chalder et al. 1993), which describes a self-rating scale to measure the severity of fatigue, and in (Wilson 2001), a work focused on adrenal fatigue. Concerning emotions, several surveys may also be taken into consideration, particularly focused on emotion-awareness, i.e., how far and how accurately we perceive our emotions (e.g. Rieffe et al. 2008, developed a survey that is particularly aimed to determine how children and adolescents feel or think about their feelings).

Surveys are generally seen as a cost-effective way of gathering large amounts of information. They do not require much effort from the researcher and often have standardized answers that make it simple to compile data (Ackroyd and Hughes 1981). They are eminently practical and may be carried out by the researcher or by any other person, not affecting significantly its validity and reliability. However, surveys also suffer from a number of problems that go beyond the traditional ones related to question constructing and wording (Popper 1959). Namely, surveys are particularly inadequate to understand some complex issues such as emotions, behaviors or feelings. They are based on the individual's perception of rather subjective perceptions such as *good, poor, high* or *low*. People can also hide information, lie voluntarily, or unconsciously depreciate/overvalue certain signs (Milne 1999). It is nearly impossible for the researcher to detect such behaviors. Finally, when developing the questionnaire or survey, researchers make their own decisions and assumptions as to what is or is not important. Even if the individual finds some aspect of importance, they may not express it if it is not mentioned in the questionnaire or if it is not mentioned appropriately.

The medical field also developed its highly accurate approach on the problem, based on a wide range of different sensors that measure changes on physiological or neurological features of the human body, affected by fatigue, stress or emotions. Currently, one of the most accurate indicators in use is cortisol (Staufenbiel et al. 2013), measured in the saliva, hair or blood. It is particularly useful to measure the level of stress of human beings, since this hormone is released in response to this symptom.

Other approaches on the problem may also be followed using other sensors or combinations of sensors. The Galvanic Skin Response measures the electrical conductance of the skin, which varies with its moisture level. This is of interest since the sweat glands are controlled by the sympathetic nervous system, so skin conductance is used as an indication of psychological or physiological arousal, which may happen due to stress or fatigue (Sharma and Kapoor 2013). The temperature of the skin, the hearth rate, or the respiratory rate are also key indicators for the study of stress or emotions (Barreto et al. 2007; Healey and Picard 2005; Jovanov et al. 2003). In particular, hearth rate variability, the physiological phenomenon of variation in the time interval between heartbeats (Brüser et al. 2011), has been used increasingly to study stress as it is highly related to it (Bernardi et al. 2000).

The significant emergence of biofeedback tools in the last years is also noteworthy. They provide combined feedback about many of the body's functions, using instruments that analyze brainwaves, muscle tone, skin conductance, heart rate or pain perception (Schwartz and Andrasik 2003). The study of brainwaves is particularly interesting as it provides clues about the inner state of an individual, in aspects such as fatigue, stress level, arousal or emotional state. Additionally, biofeedback tools can be used to improve certain aspects or habits of the daily living, as they allow perceiving changes in the body and mind affected by such habits (Lubar 1991).

In general, such sensor based-approaches can be deemed highly accurate and are used not only to assess the state of individuals, but also as a base to perform medical treatments and interventions. Their use is thus unquestionable and unparalleled in the medical arena.

Nevertheless, in this chapter we must look at both approaches, questionnaires and physiological sensors, from the point of view of someone who intends to build a non-intrusive environment for data acquisition. Specifically, this chapter deals with the issue of user context assessment in a VE. Thus, one must ask to which extent are questionnaires or physiological sensors suitable approaches to assess the user's state in a VE.

We argue that they do not constitute suitable approaches. Let us look in detail to each one of them, and imagine their use with the stated purposes in a scenario in which two or more individuals are using such an environment to resolve their differences. They agree to use means to convey contextual information while they communicate within the VE. Let us consider two scenarios, namely A and B. In scenario A, such means rely on questionnaires or surveys. In scenario B, physiological sensors are used for the same purpose.

Under scenario A, individuals fill in a questionnaire at the beginning of the process, declaring their way of dealing with stress, problem solving styles or methodologies or reaction to fatigue. It may include questions such as *how often do you feel like giving up on your current task?*, or *how long would you endure a conversation with an impolite person?*, which have to be rated.

In some of the cases, the individuals don't fit in any of the four answers of a multiple choice question. They may choose not to answer, or select the option they may think to be closest to what they would do. Moreover, they have doubts quantifying some of the other answers. While some of the concepts used, such as *never* or *always,* are easy to understand, others such as *often* or *occasionally* are unclear. Additionally, the individuals that undertake this process end up behaving differently when the process is under its way. Indeed, they may assume that they are going to act in a given way while they are filling in the questionnaire, but, under the pressure of the proceedings, individuals may behave in a different way.

Under scenario *B* we look at the low reliability of scenario *A,* by using physiological sensors. Now, parties would not be able to (consciously or unconsciously) lie in a questionnaire. Furthermore, even if they change their problem solving style or methodologies during the procedures, the physiological sensors will detect such fluctuations and provide the new information to the conflict mediator, making them aware of the level of stress or fatigue of each party, or their emotional state, allowing to take better decisions concerning the management of the conflict.

However, the disputants may have some complaints about this approach. They do not like or are even refusing to use sensors to which they are connected constantly, seriously limiting their movements. Moreover, they may not be entirely sure about which information will be collected and what it will be used for. Hence, they are reluctant and the sheer use of such devices seems to stress them and to deflect their attention from the conflict resolution itself.

It is clear, through the analysis of these two scenarios, that none of these approaches looks reasonable to study the state of individuals in a VE. Hence, in this work we put forward a new idea in which the behavior of the individuals is analyzed in order to infer information about their inner state. Indeed, phenomena such as stress, fatigue or emotions affect not only our physiology but also our behaviors. If we have a way of identifying and measuring behaviors, and if we have a way to relate given behaviors to given states, we may be able to infer the inner state of an individual through the observation of their conduct.

9.3   A Systematic Behavioral Analysis of a Living Organism

The behavior of a living or artificial organism includes all the activities that the organism would not perform if it were not *living*, where *living* is interpreted not only in the classical sense, but also in terms of the lifecycle of a piece of software.

These activities are always the response of the system to some stimuli, or lack of them. Stimuli are said to be internal, when they are originated inside the *body* of the system (e.g. thought, pain, change of state), or they are said to be external, when originated outside of the *body* of the system and perceived by some receptor cell (e.g. a change in the temperature, the reception of a given message).

The system may be conscious or unconscious of the perceived stimuli. Independently of this, the system may respond. This response is said to be voluntary, when the system undergoes some reasoning process before acting, or involuntary, when the system reacts spontaneously, without *thinking* about it.

Nothing characterizes a system better than its behavior. Knowing how the system reacts to a stimulus allows one to predict future states. Therefore, controlling stimuli allows one to, indirectly, control the system. This is the base of behaviorism. Thus, in psychology, behavior is analyzed and influenced in order to address some behavioral issue of the individual, ranging from psychological disorders to other matters, such as smoking habits or eating disorders, just to name a few.

In terms of this work, the interest is on knowing how a given party reacts under specific scenarios, namely in terms of how a party behaves when under stress, or how a party acts during a negotiation. If the mediator has access to this information, he/she will be able to make better judgments. As an example, if a mediator knows that a given party generally assumes a highly competitive attitude during a negotiation, they may try to show to that party that such a position might be an obstacle for a successful outcome of the negotiation.

The approach described focuses on acquiring background information about the environment of the dispute, which will typify the behavior of the human beings when using the ODR tool. Moreover, it does it in an absolutely transparent and non-invasive way, i.e., rather than relying on traditional self-reporting mechanisms such as questionnaires in order to infer behaviors, it analyses the actions and reactions of the parties. It may thus be placed beneath the umbrella of Behavioral Biometrics (Yampolskiy and Govindaraju 2008).

In order to implement such processes, we look at a method defined by Cooper et al. (2007), which provides a complete description of the procedures and principles necessary to:

- Correctly identify the foundations of an individual given behavior;
- Understand the relationship between the individuals reasons and behaviors, and;
- How to change them in order to influence an individual behavior as desired.

According to the authors, all the behavioral studies should consider some specific issues, namely:

- At least one individual;
- At least one behavior (which is the dependent variable);
- At least one setting or environment;
- A system for measuring the behavior and ongoing visual analysis of the individual data;
- At least one treatment or intervention condition;
- Manipulations of the independent variable, so that its effects on the dependent variable may be quantitatively or qualitatively analyzed; and
- An intervention that will benefit the individuals in some way.

Following this approach, several studies were made with the objective of perceiving how the user's behavior may change under different ODR scenarios. The aspects considered involve the use of technological devices (e.g. how fast an individual types, how the individual moves the mouse, how does the individual holds a handheld device), which are translated in the ODR system in terms of dependent variables. The independent variables include the levels of stress or fatigue, or even the conflict handling style. The aim of these studies, addressed in the following chapters, is to study the differences among the dependent variables, taking into consideration the effect of the independent ones (e.g. how does stress affect the interaction of the individual with the computer). If this relationship is known, then the opposite is possible, i.e., to quantify an individual level of stress from looking at their interactions patterns.

9.3.1 Acquiring Contextual Features from Behavioral Analysis

The study of stress or fatigue, including their causes and symptoms, has been a topic of disciplines such as Medicine or Psychology. Traditionally, data about users is acquired either through self-reporting mechanisms (generally questionnaires), or through the use of physiological sensors. As seen above, the first has known disadvantages, namely:

- People often lie or exaggerate on their answers;
- Questionnaires are static (answers of a past questionnaire will not change if the environment or the user's state changes);
- Questionnaires are inadequate to represent certain types of complex information (e.g. emotions, behaviors, feelings), and;
- Questionnaires are dependent on the formalization and interpretation of the issues under analysis.

The second is a much more precise approach, having nonetheless disadvantages of its own, namely:

- Physiological sensors are generally invasive, with the user physically connected to one or more devices; and
- Invasive sensors may have an effect on the results, possibly invalidating them (the sheer consciousness of being measured may affect the behavior).

The development of an environment that may adjust by itself according to a mutating context may rely on non-invasive and dynamic methods of data acquisition. Moreover, given the subjective nature of the subject under study, such methods should also be personalized. In order to attain such intents, a computational environment was set up at the Intelligent Systems Lab at the University of Minho, in Braga, Portugal. Here, individuals can be isolated from external stimuli and observed while they look at different tasks that may induce stress or fatigue at different levels.

Specifically, we aim at context-aware conflict resolution environments with better communication support, motivated by the conviction that if the disputant parties and mediators are aware of the state of one another, they may better perceive

Fig. 9.1 Some of the devices that make up the environment

Table 9.1 A brief description of the devices' functionalities

Device	Brief description	Main features
HP Touchsmart	All-in-one PC	Touchscreen, web cam, large screen
Samsung Galaxy Tab	Tablet PC	Touchscreen, web cam, accelerometer, relatively large screen, mobile, Android OS
HTC PDAs	Smartphones	Touchscreen, camera, accelerometer, mobile, Android OS
Sony FCBEX780BP	25x Super HAD PAL Color block camera with external sync	25x optical zoom, image stabilizer, day/night mode, privacy, zone masking

each other's words or actions. All this is transparent to the users of the platform, i.e., the data about their context is collected, processed and added to the operational data and conveyed as part of the communicative act. Some of the devices that may be available in such an environment and that were used in this study are depicted in Fig. 9.1, being its functionalities described in Table 9.1.

The approach to collect information about the individual's behaviors can be put beneath the umbrella of Behavioral Biometrics (Yampolskiy and Govindaraju 2008), and results in a multi-modal approach on the problem of behavioral analysis, where individuals' symptoms are taken as input. Such approaches yield accuracy rates that exceed their unimodal counterparts (D'Mello and Kory 2012).

Moreover, the behavior of an individual is indeed affected by their level of stress or fatigue, i.e., the inner state of an individual is reflected not only at a physiological level but also at a behavioral level. This notion, which is central in this work, is well detailed by Dobson (1982), who makes an analysis of both the physiological and behavioral effects of stress. Smith and Principato (1982) also studied the effects of stress on the behavior and physiology of people, in the particular context of conflict resolution, to support several hypotheses. It was shown, not only, that both stress and conflict influence arousal, measured in terms of phasic electrodermal responsivity, but also that this influence is proportional to the degree of stress and conflict. It was also shown that the degree of conflict influenced the speed of the conflict resolution and that increased level of stress resulted on increased error.

More recently, Haraway and Haraway (2005) study the effect of providing conflict-management and resolution training to workers towards the reduction of stress in the workplace to conclude that even brief interventions can have positive influences.

It is thus possible to conclude, as Psychology and Medicine show, that the behavior of an individual is effectively affected by processes such as stress or fatigue. Here we present the features that will allow us to characterize some aspects of the behavior of an individual and do the opposite, i.e., detect and quantify changes in the mentioned processes through changes in the behaviors. Essentially, the same we do when we are face-to-face when someone and, from the way they talk or the gestures they use, perceive their inner state.

From video cameras and handheld devices, the following features can be acquired:

- Touch pattern – this information is acquired from touch screens with support for touch intensity. It represents the way the pressure changes over time, during a touch;
- Touch accuracy – the relationship between touches in active controls versus touches in passive areas (e.g. areas without controls or empty ones), where touches are pointless. This information is acquired from touch screens;
- Touch intensity – the amount of pressure exerted by the finger on the touch screen. It is analyzed in terms of the maximum, minimum and average intensity of each touch;
- Touch duration – the time span between the beginning and the end of the touch event. This data is acquired from devices with touch screens;
- Amount of movement – its evaluation is provided by the INT3-horus framework (Fig. 9.2). A communication module was implemented to integrate this framework with UCMourt. The image-processing stack uses the principles established by Castillo et al. (2011), and uses image difference techniques to evaluate the amount of movement between two consecutive frames (Fernández-Caballero et al. 2010);
- Acceleration – the acceleration is measured from accelerometers integrated or fitted into the mobile devices;
- Score – this feature quantifies how well the individual performs on the several tasks he was assigned; and
- Stressed touches – this feature describes which touches are classified as stressed, according to the shape of the intensity curve.

Concerning the All-in-One computers being used, and in order to compute the individual's features described below, we look at particular events published by the operating system, namely:

- MOV, timestamp, posX, posY – an event describing the mouse's movement to the coordinates (posX, posY), from its present location;
- MOUSE_DOWN, timestamp, [Left/Right], posX, posY – this event describes the initial part of a click (i.e. when the mouse button is pressed down). It also

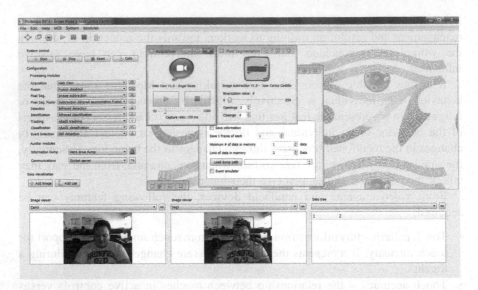

Fig. 9.2 Interface of the INT3 framework, a multilevel framework for intelligent multisensory monitoring and activity interpretation

describes which of the buttons were pressed (i.e. left or right) and the position of the mouse in that instant;

- *MOUSE_UP, timestamp, [Left/Right], posX, posY* – an event similar to the previous one but describing the second part of a click, i.e., when the mouse button is released;
- *MOUSE_WHEEL, timestamp, dif* – this event describes a mouse wheel scroll of extent *dif*, at a given instant;
- *KEY_DOWN, timestamp, key* – it identifies the *key* in the keyboard that is being pressed down, at a particular moment; and
- *KEY_UP, timestamp, key* – it describes the release of a given *key* in the keyboard, at a given instant.

The list of events described allows one to attain information about the following features:

- *Key Down Time* – the timespan between two consecutive *KEY_DOWN* and *KEY_UP* events, i.e., for how long was a given key pressed;
- *Time Between Keys* – the timespan between two consecutive *KEY_UP* and *KEY_DOWN* events, i.e., how long did the individual take to press another key;
- *Mouse's Velocity* – the distance travelled by the mouse (in pixels) over the time (in milliseconds). The velocity is computed for each interval defined by two consecutive *MOUSE_UP* and *MOUSE_DOWN* events. For example, let us consider two consecutive *MOUSE_UP* and *MOUSE_DOWN* occurrences, *mup* and *mdo*, respectively, at coordinates (x_1, y_1) and (x_2, y_2), that occur, respectively, at instants $time_1$ and $time_2$, where the vectors pos_x and pos_y, of size n, hold

the coordinates of consecutive *MOUSE_MOV* events between *mup* and *mdo*. The mouse's velocity between the two clicks is, therefore, given by $\frac{r_{dist}}{(time_2 - time_1)}$, where r_{dist} denotes the distance travelled by the mouse, and is computed according to Eq. 9.1.

$$r_{dist} = \sum_{i=0}^{n-1} \sqrt{(posx_{i+1} - posx_i)^2 + (posy_{i+1} - posy_i)^2} \qquad (9.1)$$

- *Mouse's Acceleration* – the increase in velocity of the mouse (in pixels/milliseconds) over the time (in milliseconds). A value of acceleration is computed for each interval defined by two consecutive *MOUSE_UP* and *MOUSE_DOWN* events, using the intervals and data computed for the *Mouse's Velocity*;
- *Time Between Clicks* – the timespan between two consecutive *MOUSE_UP* and *MOUSE_DOWN* events, i.e., how long did it took the individual to perform another click;
- *Double Click Duration* – the timespan between two consecutive *MOUSE_UP* events, whenever this time span is inferior to 200 milliseconds. Wider timespans are not considered double clicks;
- *Average Excess of Distance* – the excess of distance, in average, that the pointer travels between two consecutive *MOUSE_UP* and *MOUSE_DOWN* events. For example, let us consider two consecutive *MOUSE_UP* and *MOUSE_DOWN* events, *mup* and *mdo*, respectively, at coordinates (x_1, y_1) and (x_2, y_2). To compute this feature, first of all it is necessary to calculate the distance, in straight line, between the coordinates of *mup* and *mdo*, which is given by $s_{dist} = \sqrt{(x_2 - x_1)^2 + (y_2 - y_1)^2}$. Then, it is measured the distance traveled by the mouse, by summing the distance between each two consecutive *MOV* events, where vectors *posx* and *posy*, of size *n*, hold the coordinates of the consecutive *MOV* events between *mup* and *mdo*, being the distance travelled by the mouse, r_{dist}, given by Eq. 9.1. The average excess of distance between two consecutive clicks is, in turn, given by $\frac{r_{dist}}{s_{dist}}$;
- *Average Distance of the Mouse to the Straight Line* – it measures the average distance of the mouse to the straight line defined by two consecutive clicks. For example, let us consider two consecutive *MOUSE_UP* and *MOUSE_DOWN* events, *mup* and *mdo*, respectively, at coordinates (x_1, y_1) and (x_2, y_2), where vectors *posx* and *posy*, of size *n*, hold the coordinates of the consecutive *MOUSE_MOV* events between *mup* and *mdo*. Therefore, the sum of the distances between each mouse's position and the straight line, given in terms of the coordinates (x_1, y_1) and (x_2, y_2), is given by Eq. 9.2, where *ptLineDist* returns the distance between the specified point and the closest point on the infinitely-extended line defined by (x_1, y_1) and (x_2, y_2). The average distance of the mouse to the straight line, depicted in terms of the coordinates of two consecutive clicks, is, in turn, given by $\frac{s_{dists}}{n}$, where

$$S_{dists} = \sum_{i=0}^{n-1} ptLinedist(posx_i, posy_i) \qquad (9.2)$$

- *Distance of the Mouse to the Straight Line* – this feature is similar to the previous one, in the sense that it will compute the s_{dist} between two consecutive *MOUSE_UP* and *MOUSE_DOWN* events, *mup* and *mdo*, according to Eq. 9.2. However, it returns the total of the distance travelled by the mouse rather than a computed average of the mouse's trajectory;
- *Signed Sum of Angles* – here the aim is to determine if the movement of the mouse tends to *turn* more to the right or to the left. As an example, let us consider three consecutive *MOV* events, respectively *mov1*, *mov2* and *mov3*, at coordinates (x_1, y_1), (x_2, y_2), and (x_3, y_3). The angle between the first line (defined by (x_1, y_1) and (x_2, y_2)), and the second line (defined by (x_2, y_2) and (x_3, y_3)), is given by $degree(x1, y1, x2, y2, x3, y3) = \tan(y3 - y2, \quad x3 - x2) - \tan(y2 - y1, \quad x2 - x1)$. If now we consider two consecutive *MOUSE_UP* and *MOUSE_DOWN* events, *mup* and *mdo*, where vectors *posx* and *posy*, of size *n*, hold the coordinates of the consecutive *MOUSE_MOV* events, between *mup* and *mdo*, the sum of angles marked between these two clicks is given by Eq. 9.3;

$$S_{angle} = \sum_{i=0}^{n-2} degree(posx_i; posy_i; posx_{i+1}; posy_{i+1}; posx_{i+2}; posy_{i+2}) \qquad (9.3)$$

- *Absolute Sum of Angles* – this feature is quite similar to the previous one. However, it seeks to find how much the mouse *turned*, independently of the direction to which it was. In that sense, the only difference is the use of the absolute value returned by the function $degree(x1, y1, x2, y2, x3, y3)$, as shown in Eq. 9.4; and

$$S_{angle} = \sum_{i=0}^{n-2} |degree(posx_i; posy_i; posx_{i+1}; posy_{i+1}; posx_{i+2}; posy_{i+2})| \qquad (9.4)$$

- *Distance Between Clicks* – it stands for the distance travelled by the mouse between two consecutive clicks, i.e., between two consecutive *MOUSE_UP* and *MOUSE_DOWN* events. As an example, let us consider two consecutive *MOUSE_UP* and *MOUSE_DOWN* events, *mup* and *mdo*, at coordinates (x_1, y_1) and (x_2, y_2), where vectors *posx* and *posy*, of size *n*, hold the coordinates of the consecutive *MOV* events between *mup* and *mdo*. Therefore, the distance travelled by the mouse is given by Eq. 9.1.

Figure 9.3 depicts the architecture envisioned to tackle the proposed challenge. It is formed by six interrelated layers, where the upper layers are built on top of the lower ones. The environment is, in itself, composed of users and devices. Users are the key part of the Ambient Intelligence archetype (Aarts and Grotenhuis 2011),

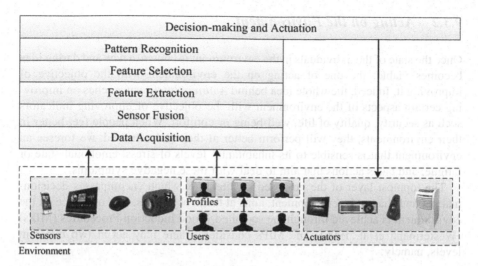

Fig. 9.3 The layered architecture of the environment

defined in terms of their profiles. Users may interact with devices and feel the results of their engagement with the environment, i.e., they may provide some information about the environment (in which case they become sensors), or they may act on the environment (in which case they become actuators).

In terms of the architecture, the lower layer is the *Data Acquisition* one, which acts as the input of information about users' behavioral patterns. Essentially, it receives data from multiple sources (e.g. computers, handheld devices, video cameras) and creates the respective software objects, which may be accessed by the upper layers.

The *Sensor Fusion* layer is responsible for synchronizing the data from the lower layer. Synchronization is performed via timestamps. From this layer, it is possible to know the state of the environment and their components in a given instant.

Going up one level, we find the *Feature Extraction* layer. This layer takes the output from the previous one and generates the features described above.

Afterwards, the *Feature Selection* layer takes the features and selects the most suited ones. This process of selection is based on the availability of the sources of the data, the quality of the data and the problem being dealt with.

After the interesting features have been selected, the *Pattern Recognition* layer will compute interpretable knowledge about the environment. This knowledge actually quantifies concepts such as stress, fatigue or personal conflict handling style in a way that allows humans and machines to use them as inputs in their decision-making processes.

9.3.2 Acting on the Environment

Once the state of the individuals in the environment is known, a new and daring idea becomes viable: the one of acting on the environment with the objective of improving it. Indeed, the whole idea behind *Ambient Intelligence* relies on improving certain aspects of the environment with the objective of improving indicators such as security, quality of life, well-being or comfort. When people feel better in their environments, they will perform better at their tasks. Indeed, we foresee an environment that is sensible to its inhabitants' levels of stress, emotional state or fatigue, and takes actions that aim to deal with these negative symptoms.

The topmost layer of the proposed architecture, which encompasses decision-making and shapes the environment, aims at these objectives. The influence on the environment is achieved through the so-called Mood Induction Procedures (MIPs) (Westermann et al. 1996). The MIPs considered here may act at two different levels, namely:

- At an *User Level*, including actions that may impact singular users (e.g. calming him/her down); and
- At *a Group Level*, including decisions that may influence a group of users simultaneously (e.g. control of temperature or noise).

In terms of *User-area MIPs*, the following are considered:

- *Autobiographical Recall Layer* – each user has in their own space a *USB* digital photo frame. They may look at pictures of specific objects, memories and emotions, people or past personal experiences, that may induce a constructive change on their mood;
- *Color Schemes Layer* – this layer may produce changes on the color scheme of the system in order to induce particular user's states (e.g. dark tones of blue and green tend to relax people);
- *Musical Selection Layer* – music may be used in order to induce specific feelings on the user; and
- *Individual Recommendations Layer* – individual recommendations may be issued in the form of notifications that aim to improve the user's mood (e.g. take a break, play a game for a while).

In terms of *Group-area MIPs*, the following are considered:

- *Environmental Actuators* – this group of devices controls environmental parameters such as temperature or luminosity, which are closely related to stress and fatigue (e.g. open windows to increase creativity, or close them to make people to focus on their tasks);
- *Environmental Sounds* – the system may use the installed sound system to induce specific moods on a group of users (e.g. agitation, calm), by playing specific types of music or sounds;

- *Level of Noise* – when the level of noise is too loud on the part of the users, the system may react by issuing a notification or by turning the music lower or down; and
- *Video Projectors* – video projectors may be used to display specific colors, shapes, images or videos on the unobstructed white walls of the environment, in order to frame the users' mood.

With such an approach, VEs are able to induce specific moods on the users, with the objective of maximizing common goals, namely to get a more harmonious and relaxed environment (which is desirable, for example, in a long-term working environment), or it may be used to induce agitation, creativity or even conflict (as could be desirable in brainstorming sessions). Indeed, we look at people's performance, through a sense of comfort and well-being.

9.4 Conclusion

At the outset of Ambient Intelligence, the general expectation was that it would allow to improve people's performance and productivity by providing constant support in people's tasks, allowing them to do better, faster and more. This rather industrial view on the field later changed to give way to a new and more balanced one: Ambient Intelligence would focus on improving people's environments in terms of comfort and well-being. Aarts and Grotenhuis (2011) call this new vision *Synergetic Prosperity*, referring to meaningful digital solutions that balance mind and body, and society and earth, thus contributing to a prosperous and sustainable development of mankind. Rather than having high-performance and highly productive environments, focus was placed on the development of harmonious and pleasant spaces. Rather than focusing on supporting daily tasks, focus slowly changed to sensing peoples' needs, preferences and desires, with the aim of shaping the environment according to those preferences.

The environment developed and described in this chapter is intended to be used in the domain of conflict resolution. Its aims to quantify one's level of stress, fatigue or emotional arousal and to feed this information to conflict managers so that they can better understand the state of the parties and take better decisions.

A particularly interesting subject was addressed in this chapter: the one of acquiring information that can allow one to build knowledge about the features enumerated. Indeed, as it was pointed out, current methods for studying stress or emotions are not the best suited to the tasks being considered in this work. Questionnaires, on the one hand, are static self-reporting mechanisms, dependent on subjective considerations and on the researcher's interpretation of what is and is not important in a given problem. Physiological sensors, on the other hand, are far more accurate and reliable as a form of reading emotional states or arousal. They are, nevertheless, invasive pieces of technology, as they must be placed in precise places of the body, often by specialized personnel, and have to be always connected to the body of the wearer. This makes this approach unsuited.

An alternative approach was described in this chapter, one based on behavioral analysis. In a few words, it looks at how people change their behaviors when under stress or significant cognitive load. The central idea is that if we know how someone changes their behavior when under stress, then we may infer their level of stress from observing behavioral changes. We focused particularly on the user's behaviors when interacting with the technological devices used currently in most online conflict resolution platforms: computers and handheld devices such as smartphones. Indeed, such devices can provide a significant amount of information regarding its use (e.g. velocity of the mouse, typing speed, amount of movement of the handheld device).

The main advantage of this approach is that it is non-invasive. Unlike physiological sensors, there is no requirement for sensors or devices to be placed on the body of the user or around it: the presented method is based solely on the observation of the user. Moreover, by being based on behaviors, it also presents advantages when compared to questionnaires. People can easily lie in a questionnaire but they cannot so easily fake their own behaviors that are, in most of the cases, involuntary and unconscious. This approach thus addresses some of the most significant disadvantages of both physiological sensors and questionnaires when considering a scenario of application such as the one of this book: the classification of the state of a user of an online conflict resolution platform.

References

Aarts, E., and F. Grotenhuis. 2011. Ambient intelligence 2.0: Towards synergetic prosperity. *Ambient Intelligence and Smart Environments* 3(1): 3–11.

Ackroyd, S., and J.A. Hughes. 1981. *Data collection in context.* London/New York: Longman.

Barreto, A., J. Zhai, and M. Adjouadi. 2007. Non-intrusive physiological monitoring for automated stress detection in human-computer interaction. In *HCI 2007*, LNCS 4796, ed. M. Lew et al., 29–38. Berlin/Heidelberg: Springer.

Bernardi, L., J. Wdowczyk-Szulc, C. Valenti, S. Castoldi, C. Passino, G. Spadacini, and P. Sleight. 2000. Effects of controlled breathing, mental activity and mental stress with or without verbalization on heart rate variability. *Journal of the American College of Cardiology* 35(6): 1462–1469.

Brüser, C., K. Stadlthanner, S. de Waele, and S. Leonhardt. 2011. Adaptive beat-to-beat heart rate estimation in Ballistocardiograms. *IEEE Transactions on Information Technology in Biomedicine (IEEE)* 15(5): 778–786. doi:10.1109/TITB.2011.2128337. PMID 21421447.

Castillo, J.C., A. Rivas-Casado, A. Fernández-Caballero, M.T. López, and R. Martínez-Tomás. 2011. A multisensory monitoring and interpretation framework based on the model-view-controller paradigm. In *IWINAC'11 proceedings of the 4th international conference on interplay between natural and artificial computation*, vol. Part I, 441–450. Springer, Berlin/Heidelberg.

Chalder, T., G. Berelowitz, T. Pawlikowska, L. Watts, S. Wessely, D. Wright, and E.P. Wallace. 1993. Development of a fatigue scale. *Journal of Psychosomatic Research* 37: 147–53.

Cohen, S., T. Kamarck, and R. Mermelstein. 1983. A global measure of perceived stress. *Journal of Health and Social Behavior* 24: 386–396.

Cooper, J.O., T.E. Heron, and W.L. Heward. 2007. *Applied behavior analysis.* Upper Saddle River: Prentice Hall. ISBN ISBN 978–0131421134.

D'Mello, S., J. Kory. 2012. Consistent but modest: A meta-analysis on unimodal and multimodal affect detection accuracies from 30 studies. In *Proceedings of the 14th ACM international conference on Multimodal interaction*, 31–38. ICMI'12, ACM, New York, http://doi.acm.org/10.1145/2388676.2388686

Dobson, C.B. 1982. The physical and behavioural effects of stress. In *Stress: The hidden adversary*, 169–200. Dordrecht: Springer. ISBN ISBN 978-94-010-9800-7.

Fernández-Caballero, A., J.C. Castillo, J. Martínez-Cantos, and R. Martínez-Tomás. 2010. Optical flow or image subtraction in human detection from infrared camera on mobile robot. *Robotics and Autonomous Systems* 58(12): 1273–1281.

Haraway, D.L., and W.M. Haraway. 2005. Analysis of the effect of conflict-management and resolution training on employee stress at a healthcare organization. *Hospital Topics* 83 (4): 11–17.

Healey, J.A., and R.W. Picard. 2005. Detecting stress during real-world driving tasks using physiological sensors. *IEEE Transactions on Intelligent Transportation Systems* 6(2): 156–166.

Jovanov, E., A. O'Donnell Lords, D. Raskovic, P.G. Cox, R. Adhami, and F. Andrasik. 2003. Stress monitoring using a distributed wireless intelligent sensor system. *Engineering in Medicine and Biology Magazine, IEEE* 22(3): 49–55.

Kristensen, T.S., H. Hannerz, A. Høghl, and V. Borg. 2005. The Copenhagen psychosocial questionnaire – A tool for the assessment and improvement of the psychosocial work environment. *Scandinavian Journal of Work, Environment & Health* 31(6): 438–449.

Lubar, J.F. 1991. Discourse on the development of EEG diagnostics and biofeedback for attention-deficit/hyperactivity disorders. *Biofeedback and Self-regulation* 16(3): 201–225.

Mehrabian, A. 1980. *Silent messages: Implicit communication of emotions and attitudes*. Belmont: Wadsworth Publishing Company.

Milne, J. 1999. Questionnaires: Advantages and disadvantages. In *Evaluation cookbook*. Edinburgh: LTDI Publications, Heriot Watt University.

Popper, K. 1959. The logic of scientific discovery. Reprinted (2004) by Routledge, Taylor & Francis.

Rieffe, C., P. Oosterveld, A.C. Miers, M. Meerum Terwogt, and V. Ly. 2008. Emotion awareness and internalizing symptoms in children and adolescents; the Emotion Awareness Questionnaire revised. *Personality and Individual Differences* 45: 756–761.

Schwartz, M.S., and F.E. Andrasik. 2003. *Biofeedback: A practitioner's guide*. New York: Guilford Press.

Sharma, T., and B. Kapoor. 2013. Emotion estimation of physiological signals by using low power embedded system. In *Proceedings of the conference on advances in communication and control systems*. Atlantis Press, April.

Smith, B.D., and F. Principato. 1982. Effects of stress and conflict difficulty on arousal and conflict resolution. *British Journal of Psychology* 73(1): 85–93.

Stanney, K.M. (ed.). 2002. *Handbook of virtual environments: Design, implementation, and applications. Human factors and ergonomics*. Mahwah: Lawrence Erlbaum Associates Publishers. xxxix 1232 pp.

Staufenbiel, S.M., B.W.J.H. Penninx, A.T. Spijker, B.M. Elzinga, and E.F.C. van Rossum. 2013. Hair cortisol, stress exposure, and mental health in humans: A systematic review. *Psychoneuroendocrinology* 38(8): 1220–1235. ISSN 0306–4530, http://dx.doi.org/10.1016/j.psyneuen.2012.11.015.

Westermann, R., K. Spies, G. Stahl, and F.W. Hesse. 1996. Relative effectiveness and validity of mood induction procedures: A meta-analysis. *European Journal of Social Psychology* 26(4): 557–580.

Wilson, J. 2001. *Adrenal fatigue: The 21st century stress syndrome*. Petaluma: Smart Publications. ISBN 978–1890572150.

Yampolskiy, R.V., and V. Govindaraju. 2008. Behavioural biometrics: A survey and classification. *International Journal of Biometrics* 1(1): 81–113. http://dx.doi.org/10.1504/IJBM.2008.018665.

Chapter 10
Inferring Conflict Resolution Styles

Abstract Each one of us has a particular way to behave before a conflict. We can assume a cooperative and collaborative attitude or we can behave in a more selfish or competitive way. Given our personality traits or our past experiences, each one has a tendency to behave more towards one or the other. Nonetheless, there are also external factors that influence our conflict handling style including the individuals we are conflicting with, our level of stress or fatigue, the level of escalation of the conflict or even the context or the setting in which it is being settled. Undeniably, the personal conflict resolution style of the parties is preponderant for the outcome of the conflict resolution process. The mediator, while knowing the style of each party, may better conduct the process, namely by pointing out and changing unrealistic, selfish or overly competitive behaviors. Traditionally, the mediator makes use of questionnaires to assess the conflict resolution style of the parties. In this chapter we detail a new view on the problem in which this knowledge is built in real-time, in a non-invasive way, based on the behavior evidenced by the parties during the conflict resolution process. The level of escalation of the conflict is also analyzed similarly, through the non-invasive analysis of the level of stress of the parties during the actual negotiation process. The relationship between stress and the personal conflict handling style is also studied.

10.1 Introduction

Conflicts are common and bound to take place whenever two or more individuals come together. On the one hand they may be seen as opportunities to mature together, to learn about one another, and to improve relationships. On the other hand, when poorly managed, they may be detrimental and harmful. The outcome is indeed dependent on different issues, one of them being the style that people have to deal with the conflict. If the parties are cooperative and maintain a positive attitude, the resolution of the conflict might also prove positive. Otherwise, parties may engage in a negative process that might, at the end, put them in a worst position than the one they were at the beginning.

While the notion of conflict has already been detailed in Chap. 2 of this book, this chapter is dedicated to the topic of conflict resolution styles that define how each individual will behave when faced with a conflict.

Mary Follett, a pioneer in the fields of organizational theory and organizational behavior, presented one of the earliest models of conflict resolution styles. According to Follett, there are three main ways to react when one is confronted with a conflict, namely domination, compromise and integration. Follett was also the first to point out the need and the advantages of an integrative approach to negotiation, in which parties cooperate and understand each other's needs and objectives. On this topic she stated: "*If we get only compromise, the conflict will come up again and again in some other form, for in compromise we give up part of our desire, and because we shall not be content to rest there, sometime we shall try to get the whole of our desire. Watch industrial controversy, watch international controversy, and see how often this occurs. Only integration really stabilizes. But the stabilization I do not mean anything stationary. Nothing ever stays put. I mean only that that particular conflict is settled and the next occurs on a higher level*" (Metcalf and Urwick 2003).

Later, Blake and Mouton outlined a first model based on five styles, namely *forcing, withdrawing, smoothing, compromising*, and *problem solving* (Blake and Mouton 1964). These styles, defined in terms of the parties' behaviors are somehow similar to the ones expressed by more recent representations, based on the parties' concerns. Indeed, several different examples were proposed that look at the combination of the parties concerns and their own interests (i.e. assertiveness), or their worries about the interests of those across the table (i.e. cooperativeness).

One of these models was defined by Robert Maddux, based also on five styles, with different degrees of assertiveness and cooperation (Maddux and Wingfield 2003), namely *Avoidance, Accommodating, Win/Lose, Compromising,* and *Collaborative* (Fig. 10.1).

The *Avoidance* style is a non-confrontational one. The person may ignore the issue or ignore the individual with whom he/she is in conflict. We may hear people that avoid dealing with conflicts expressing themselves through sentences such as "*it is not worth arguing*", or "*let us wait and see how things go*". This style is the one with the lowest level of cooperation and assertiveness.

On the opposite side we have the *Collaborative* style. This style is characterized with a high degree of cooperation and assertiveness. People under this setting really want to solve the problem at hands and have a high degree of respect in terms of one another and each other's needs and rights. Instead of thinking alone about how to solve the problem, these individuals will rather talk to their counterparts in search of mutually satisfying solutions.

When the individual has a high degree of assertiveness but a low degree of cooperation, Maddux calls it the *Win/Lost* style. These individuals are confrontational and even aggressive and will do whatever they can to win as much as

Fig. 10.1 The distribution of the different styles in terms of their degree of assertiveness and cooperation

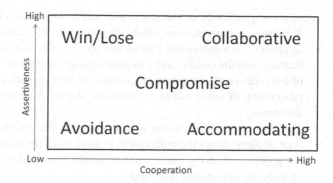

possible. There is a complete disregard with respect to the other's positions. There is also little respect for the other's opinions, and insult may be frequent and part of the strategy to weaken the opponents.

On the contrary, if the individual has a high degree of cooperation but a low degree of assertiveness, the style is designated as *Accommodating*. Individuals with this behavior will be agreeable and nonassertive, and might cooperate even at the expenses of personal goals. A commonly observed conduct is that of one individual that acknowledges the importance of the other's goals and steps aside.

Finally, in an intermediary degree of assertiveness and cooperation, we may find the *Compromise* style. Under this setting, individuals will give up some of their claims, but will expect something in return, i.e., at the end they will be somewhat satisfied but, nonetheless, approve the outcome.

Other authors defined similar models. Pruitt (1983) see these five styles as *yielding* (low assertiveness/high cooperativeness), *problem solving potential* (high assertiveness/high cooperativeness), *inaction* (low assertiveness/low cooperativeness), and *contending* (high assertiveness/low cooperativeness).

Kenneth Thomas and Ralph Kilmann set the way we react when faced with a conflict, using different modes or styles (Thomas and Kilmann 2007). They take into consideration the individuals assertiveness, which denotes how much each party tries to satisfy his/her own interests, and the cooperativeness, which denotes to which extent the parties are willing to satisfy the other's interests. Each item is described as follows:

- *Competing* – A party that shows this uncooperative style aims at maximizing his/her own gain, with a consequent minimization of the other's expectations. Usually, competing individuals will use their ability to argue, rank, social status or whatever advantageous position they may hold to express dominance over the other parties. This is clearly a power-oriented style;
- *Accommodating* – An accommodating party has a behaviour that may be classified as the opposite to a competing one. It may happen that accommodating parties will even neglect their own gain, in order to reach a solution. Thus, it may be said that there is a certain degree of altruism. Generally, such a party will tend

to show generosity or tolerance, will understand and will focus on the other's directives or desires, even when this results in self damage;

- *Avoiding* – An individual that shows an avoiding behaviour is most likely not dealing with the conflict as he usually satisfies neither his own interests nor those of the other party. Common behaviours include diplomatically sidestepping, the postponing of some issues, or even the depart from threatening or unpleasant situations;
- *Collaborating* – Contrasting with avoiding is the collaborative behaviour. This type of party shows the willingness to work with the other one in order to clarify the problem, showing interest in finding the fears and desires of the opponent so as to better understand him; and
- *Compromising* – A compromising party will attempt to find a firm and satisfactory solution for the problem that may be subscribed by both. This conflict style may be seen as an in-between the competing and the accommodating ones. A compromise is in general a way to split the differences between two views on the problem, to make some concessions or to seek middle-ground solutions.

There are also authors that follow different approaches. Kuhn and Poole (2000), for example, look at how the conflict resolution process is conducted. If a solution to the problem is approached as a distribution of an unchanging amount of assets, where one side ends up winning and the other one losing, the conflict resolution style is said to be distributive. On the other hand, if parties see conflict as a chance to integrate the needs and concerns of both and look at the best outcome, the conflict resolution style is said to be integrative.

It is known that people may follow different conflict resolution styles, depending on factors such as past experiences, temperament, or the structure of a given situation. Therefore, it is not possible to characterize one individual as having a single conflict-handling style. Still, people tend to use some styles more than others, generally due to personality traits. The knowledge about the conflict-handling style may be of interest, either from the point of view of a human mediator or even from the point of view of a conflict resolution platform as it allows predicting, to some extent, the evolution of the conflict resolution process.

Indeed, the work presented here is committed to assess the parties' conflict handling styles. Similarly to what was argued on the previous chapter, all current approaches on the problem are based on questionnaires. These surveys are generally based on a series of multiple-choice questions, such as *"I need to attain excellent results and cannot be limited by others"*, *"I am always willing to listen to other's opinions, but I also want to give them mine"*, or *"I often make slight modifications in my goals to meet other people's needs"*. To answer these questions one may have options such as *"Definitely true"*, *"True"*, *"Tends to be true"*, *"Tends not to be true"*, *"Not true"*, or *"Definitely not true"*. The disadvantages of using questionnaires have already been discussed in the previous chapter and, therefore, will not be debated here again.

The truth is that all the existing approaches to assess people's conflict resolution styles have their roots in social and organizational sciences. They are, therefore, questionnaire-based. Despite some reticent examples, remarkable advances on the topic by computer scientists are still scarce. Nandalal and Simonovic (2003) describe a conflict support system for water resources planning. However, this work presents a rather static perception of the conflict. No inventory conflict resolution style is used, despite the approach proposed to solve the conflict be based in two styles of handling it. Yiu (2005) developed an agent-based assistant for electronic negotiation, using the Thomas-Kilmann Conflict Model (Thomas and Kilmann 2007), and negotiation data from an experiment conducted by human mediators. In this approach the process of capturing the participant's behavior uses assumptions based on preferences, obtained through questionnaires. The Rahim Organizational Conflict Inventory (Rahim 1983) has also been used to classify five negotiation/conflict resolution styles, but the approach has a similar problem to the one of Ludwig (2008), since both rely on self-report instruments to measure the personal conflict handling styles. Jain and Solomon (2000) highlight the unaddressed issue of the participants' predisposition to conflict on negotiation outcomes, and conclude that future research may focus on the effects of the representative elements of a negotiations, such as task complexity and participants' predisposition to conflict.

On the other hand, Holt and DeVore (2005) point out the need for a rigorous conflict resolution instrument that may measure conflict behaviour rather than the self-report instruments used in the past decades. In line with this idea, this chapter presents a new approach on the problem, based on technological artefacts rather than on self-reporting mechanisms. The key idea in this chapter is that these issues should be addressed with dynamic and automated conflict resolution styles classification methods, incorporated in a conflict resolution platform or framework.

10.2 From the Computation of the Utility to the Classification of the Personal Conflict Resolution Style

The style of dealing with a conflict must be seen as having a preponderant role in the outcome of a conflict resolution process, especially on those in which the parties interact directly, either face-to-face or through a communication tool (e.g. negotiation, mediation). Ultimately, it is acceptable to state that the outcome will largely depend on the conflict resolution style of each party, as well as on the interaction of the styles of the parties. Undeniably, as seen in the introductory section of this chapter, different approaches may be followed to validate the way we respond to conflicts. For the remaining of the chapter, the model presented by Thomas and Kilmann will be used.

This chapter explores the potential relationship between the personal conflict resolution style, and the utility of the proposals exchanged by the parties when solving the conflict. Under this setting, the utility quantifies how good a given

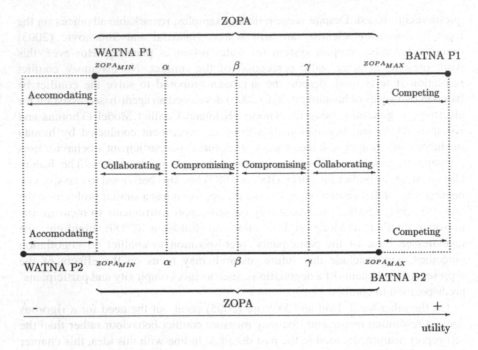

Fig. 10.2 The space that defines the personal conflict resolution styles in function of the utility of the proposals and the values of the BATNA, BATNA and ZOPA

outcome is (e.g. in monetary or in subjective terms) for a given party. In that sense, it is acceptable to argue that a competing party will generally propose solutions that maximize his/her own utility, at the expenses of the other one, while a compromising party will, generally, search for solutions in a more intermediary region of the utility curve. Essentially, the conflict resolution style of the parties is classified by constantly analysing the utility of the proposals they produce. The relationship between the utility of the proposals and the conflict resolution style, which will be detailed ahead, is depicted in Fig. 10.2. It is defined in terms of the utility of the proposal and the concepts outlined in Chap. 5, which include the BATNA, WATNA or MLATNA.

Another factor relies on the evolution of the parties' behaviour, i.e., if the conflict resolution tool has the ability to make a prediction about the evolution of the parties' behaviour, it may take better decisions that foresee potential future states. As we see it, the parties' conduct towards the conflict may be determined following two different approaches: by questioning them or by analysing their behaviour. The former approach will provide information previously to the initiation of the process, being therefore possible to plan ahead. However, the main disadvantage here is the possibility to lie and to fake behaviours in an attempt to undermine the process. Moreover, once the (potentially stressful) conflict resolution starts, parties are likely to change their attitude and behave in ways they did not expect themselves. The second approach, on the other hand, will gradually provide information as the process evolves. Although it may be a slower way of getting evidence about the individual conflict resolution style, it will expose it in a more reliable way and, more important than that, will detect eventual changes in real time.

In this work it is explored the potential of the second approach, i.e., the actions of the parties are analysed in each stage of the conflict resolution process in a non-intrusive way. Indeed, in each turn of the negotiation a party may ignore, accept or refuse a proposal, may reply with a new proposal or may leave the process. Moreover, the nature of the solutions proposed is also taken into consideration to build this information (e.g. *is a party being too greedy?*, *is a party being realistic?*). We make a combined analysis of this information together with the BATNA and the WATNA of each party as well as the ZOPA (Zone of Potential Agreement), in order to classify the behaviour of each party. The detailed definition of these concepts is provided in Chap. 5.

To implement this methodology for problem solving, it will be used a conflict resolution algorithm that was developed for the legal domain, as is defined in Chap. 8. During the process, parties make successive proposals and counterproposals in order to achieve a mutually agreeable compromise. Consequently, it is possible to make an analysis of the proposals of each party and, using additional background information (e.g. the space defined by the BATNA and WATNA with respect to each party), sort the party's behaviour.

Each action on the part of a party contributes to the overall characterization of their conflict resolution style. Under this approach, two main scenarios are possible: a party either ignores the proposal or gives an answer to it. If parties, upon receiving a proposal, simply ignore it, they are clearly not satisfying their own interests, nor the ones of the counterpart. In such a situation, the conflict resolution style evidenced is the *Avoiding* one.

When parties make a proposal or a counter-proposal, they are looked as being cooperative. However, the nature of the proposal has to be analysed, namely in what respects to its advantage to each party. When the utility of the proposal is higher than the BATNA of the other party, they are evidencing a *Competing* style, once they are trying to maximize their own gain, in a way that is potentially unrealistic and disregards the interests of the other party. On the other hand, if the utility of the proposal is lower than the WATNA of the counterpart, they are neglecting their own gain or even maximizing the gain of the other. Under such a scenario, it is reasonable to state that the party is recommending *Accommodating* conduct.

When the utility of the proposal falls within the range of ZOPA, it indicates that the party is being reasonable and realistic, and is trying to propose a settlement in which both contenders will not either win everything, or lose all. Under this settlement, the conflict style is firmed according to the distance to the ZOPA midpoint, as it is defined in Eq. 10.1.

$$\beta = \left(\frac{ZOPA_{MIN} + ZOPA_{MAX}}{2}\right) \tag{10.1}$$

Two additional points are defined that allow the classification of the remaining conflict styles, as depicted in Eqs. 10.2 and 10.3, by defining additional intervals.

$$\alpha = \left(ZOPA_{MIN} + \frac{\beta - ZOPA_{MIN}}{2}\right) = \left(\frac{ZOPA_{MIN} + \beta}{2}\right) \tag{10.2}$$

$$\gamma = \left(ZOPA_{MAX} - \frac{ZOPA_{MAX} - \beta}{2}\right) = \left(\frac{ZOPA_{MAX} + \beta}{2}\right) \tag{10.3}$$

When the utility of a proposal falls in the range $[\alpha, \gamma]$, a contender is trying to negotiate in ZOPA middle points, i.e., they are trying to compromise, which entails a loss to both opponents. Under such a scenario, the party's behaviour is considered to be *Compromising*. On the other hand, if the value of the utility belongs to the range $[ZOPA_{MIN}, \alpha[\cup]\gamma, ZOPA_{MAX}]$, a party is proposing a solution that is closer to the ZOPA boundaries, i.e., a party is trying to work out a mutually agreeable solution, although they may be trying to explore the weaknesses of the counterpart, attempting to force them to accept a given solution. These scenarios are classified as *Collaborating*.

Nevertheless, as depicted in the literature and as evidenced by our own daily interactions, we do not make use of a single conflict resolution style throughout a conflict resolution process. More likely, we evidence a combination of conflict styles. In that sense, in order to more accurately define the boundaries, we propose an approach in which a main conflict style is inferred, potentially accompanied by a trend style. The notation used to denote a *main* conflict style with a trend to a *secondary* one is presented in the form $Main_{\rightarrow secondary}$. If φ denotes the utility's value of a proposal, the following intermediary styles are defined:

$$Collaborating_{\rightarrow Accom} \qquad if \; \varphi \in \left[ZOPA_{MIN}, \frac{ZOPA_{MIN} + \alpha}{2}\right[$$

$$Collaborating_{\rightarrow Compr} \qquad if \; \varphi \in \left[\frac{ZOPA_{MIN} + \alpha}{2}, \alpha\right[$$

$$Compromising_{\rightarrow Coll-Accom} \qquad if \; \varphi \in [\alpha, \beta[$$

$$Compromising_{\rightarrow Coll-Compe} \qquad if \; \varphi \in [\beta, \gamma[$$

$$Collaborating_{\rightarrow Compr} \qquad if \; \varphi \in \left[\gamma, \frac{ZOPA_{MAX} + \gamma}{2}\right[$$

$$Collaborating_{\rightarrow Collab-Compe} \qquad if \; \varphi \in \left[\frac{ZOPA_{MAX} + \gamma}{2}, ZOPA_{MAX}\right]$$

Evaluating the conflict resolution style of each party at each round makes it possible to analyse its evolution throughout the conflict resolution process

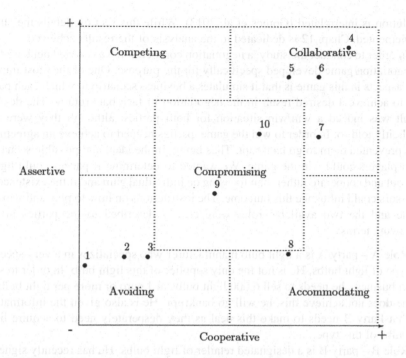

Fig. 10.3 The evolution of the conflict resolution style of a party in 10 rounds following the approach presented and the styles depicted by Thomas and Kilmann

(Fig. 10.3). When the conflict resolution platform has a temporal representation of the evolution of the contender's conflict styles, it may implement dynamic conflict resolution methodologies and techniques for problem solving, i.e., it may adapt problem solving strategies in real time, as it is depicted in Sect. 10.4.

10.3 Studying the Relationship Between Stress and Conflict Resolution Style

Besides personal conflict resolution styles, there are other aspects that assume a significant importance in the course of a conflict resolution process. One of them is the level of escalation of the conflict, in which the stress of the disputants has a significant role. The study of stress on the users of technological devices is indeed another interesting topic in this field, addressed in detail in the following chapters.

In this section a particular study carried out in the Intelligent Systems Lab of the University of Minho is described, aimed at determining the relationship between stress and personal conflict resolution styles. This study aimed to determine how both stress and conflict resolution style evolve during a negotiation and also if this evolution is interrelated (Gomes et al. 2013). While this section details the study implemented, Chap. 12 is dedicated to the analysis of the results achieved.

In order to conduct the study, a negotiation competition was carried out based on a negotiation game developed specifically for the purpose. One of the most important aspects in this game is that it simulates a business scenario in which each party has to achieve a desired result in the negotiation or face bankruptcy. The desired result was indeed a win/win situation for both parties, although they were not explicitly told so. In order to win the game, parties needed to achieve an agreement that prevented them to go bankrupt. Thus being, in the ideal and possible scenario, both players could win the game. We wanted to determine if parties could figure this out and cooperate rather than focusing on individual gain and if the existence of stressors could influence this outcome. The instructions on how to play and win the game and the two available roles were clearly described to the parties in the following terms:

- Role A – party A is a light bulb manufacturer who specializes in a very specific type of light bulbs. He is not the only supplier of this light bulb. In order to stay in business, he needs to sell 6,000 light bulbs at 1 euro or more per light bulb. If he does not achieve this, he will go bankrupt. He is also given the information that Party B needs to make this deal as they desperately need to acquire light bulbs of this type.
- Role B – party B is a designated retailer of light bulbs. He has recently signed a contract to supply a hotel chain 6,000 of these specific light bulbs. The hotel is prepared to pay 2 euros per light bulb. If Party B does not manage to buy the light bulbs at 1.20 euros or less he will go bankrupt. Party B is told that this specific manufacturer is in financial trouble and that a transaction of this volume may be very important for them.

At the end of the game parties know that they need to make a deal to win but they also have the notion that they can put some pressure on the other side to get a *better* deal. Each pair of participants plays the game two times. The first one without any stressors, with 10 rounds at most, in which the parties only get used to the negotiation game. They have plenty of time to exchange messages and get to know the interface. The second time the participants play the game, they are told that it is for real now and that their score will be reflected on their performance in the competition. Nonetheless, stress is induced this time with time limit, ambient noise, people walking by and observing the negotiation as well as with annoying sounds and behaviors of the devices. Parties are also told that if they do not manage to reach an agreement before the time limit, both players lose

During the study, the information about the user's level of stress was provided by the environment detailed in Chap. 9, using the approach described in Chap. 11. Among other features, this environment collects information from a camera located in front of the user and from the handheld devices in order to build information about the user's behaviors, which are then correlated to a stress level. The group of sensors and associated features used is described in detail in Chap. 11. Indeed, when people are nervous or stressed, the touch or click accuracy tends to decrease and

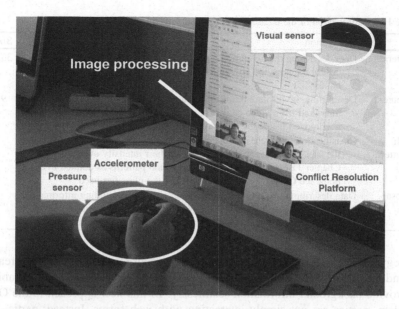

Fig. 10.4 The setting in which the participants took part in the negotiation competition

they tend to perform more abrupt and sudden movements, which can be detected from the video camera or the accelerometers on the handheld devices. These are only two examples of the behaviors that the environment used allows to analyze. Figure 10.4 depicts the setting in which this study took place. To deduce the parties' personal conflict style at each negotiation round, later correlated to stress, the information from the interaction of the parties is analyzed through the use of the approach mentioned in Sect. 10.2.

This study resulted in a relatively large dataset describing the different important aspects considered. These include the values of the acceleration measured on handheld devices, the amount of movement of the user in the environment, the classification of the touch pattern as stressed or not stressed and the details of each of the proposals exchanged. Table 10.1 describes the dataset.

10.4 A Sensible and Dynamic Conflict Resolution Model

The insights learned from the study described in the previous section were integrated into a higher-level conflict resolution archetypal based on perceptions borrowed from recent trends in Intelligent Environments, in which computer systems seamlessly merge into the environment (Aarts and Grotenhuis 2011). We look at a dynamic model, similar to the ones used by human experts, who are able to perceive changes in the environment of interaction (e.g. a party is getting stressed, or he/she does not like the current state of affairs), and change the problem solving

Table 10.1 Description of the dataset collected in the study

Data	Description	Size
Acceleration	Data describing the acceleration measured on the handheld device, describing how and how much the user gesticulated or moved their hands	33,366
Movement	Description, in absolute terms, of the amount of movement of the users measured from video cameras and detailing how and how much the user moved inside the environment	9,137
Touch pattern	Classification of touches in touch screens in terms of the level of stress of the user, according to the variation of their intensity over time. Chapter 11 describes the concept of touch patterns as defined in this book and Chap. 12 detail the results of the classifier used	590
Proposals	Data describing in detail the proposals exchanged, including information such as the identification of the players, the round, the issues being negotiated and their value or the current distribution being proposed	60

strategy before it is too late (e.g. by introducing a pause in the process). The reason behind the following of a line based on Intelligent Environments lays on its ability to provide background information seamlessly. In this new approach to the ODR problem, parties are not simply interacting with web forms. Instead, parties use ODR tools under an intelligent setting that supports conflict resolution programmes with access to information like the level of stress, the conflict handling style, or even the parties' emotional state.

One of such trends, extracted from the study carried out and detailed further in Chap. 12, is the one in which parties exhibit an avoiding behaviour in the earlier stages of the conflict resolution process, then evolving to a more cooperative one when the confidence on the process grows. Moreover, it is also frequent to have parties that in the beginning of the process present themselves as competitive and having high expectations, but tend to be more realistic as the process evolves. Nonetheless, the opposite may also happen.

This new approach on the problem may be seen, from a high-level point of view, as depicted in Fig. 10.5. It may begin by assembling of data and information describing the problem objectively, such as the BATNA, WATNA, and ZOPA. With these assets at hand a realistic problem solving strategy is built, where a set of possible outcomes will be successively suggested to the contenders. A case-based approach to problem solving can be used, such as the one described in Chap. 7. During the actual negotiation phase, the strategies for problem-solving can be adapted in real-time, based on significant changes in the context of interaction. One particularly interesting aspect for this adaptation is the conflict handling style. It is realistic to assume a scenario with two parties in which party A is consistently exhibiting a collaborative behaviour, while party B is moving towards a competitive one and the mediator, upon acknowledging this fact, advises party B to change their behaviour or they may jeopardize the process. This is just an example of a possible adaptation based on contextual information.

In order to put these ideas into practice and integrate the proposed functionalities in the UMCourt conflict resolution platform, stress-aware interfaces were

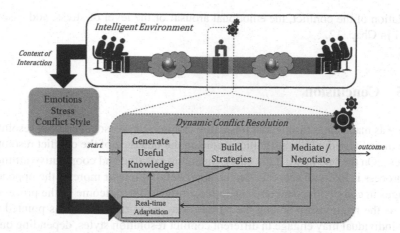

Fig. 10.5 A high level view of the dynamic conflict resolution archetype. With information detailing the emotional arousal, level of stress or conflict handling style, the mediator is able to adapt his posture in real-time, resulting in a dynamic process that uses as input the state of the parties

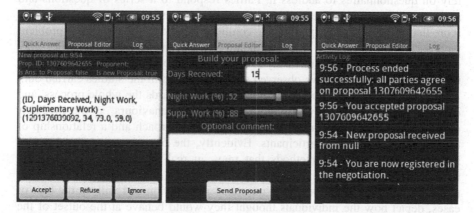

Fig. 10.6 Screenshots of Android interfaces that provide interaction with the conflict resolution platform while, at the same time, providing information about interaction patterns

developed for handheld devices (Fig. 10.6 shows an example of this) and for computers. In the case of handheld devices, stress is estimated from the way users touch and hold them. In the case of computers, stress is estimated from the way the mouse and the keyboard are used. All in all, this approach allows to empower the mediator with very powerful knowledge about the parties and their state, with which to take better decisions concerning the management of the conflict.

Nonetheless, we acknowledge that information about the personal conflict handling style alone may not be sufficient to accurately adapt the conflict resolution process. Additional sources of information may be considered, namely the escalation of the conflict, the emotional arousal or the level of stress, addressed in detail in Chap. 12.

10.5   Conclusion

As it was made clear throughout this entire chapter, the personal conflict resolution style of an individual has a significant role on the outcome of the conflict resolution process. On the one hand, if the parties maintain positive and cooperative attitudes, the process is likely to succeed. On the other hand, if one or more of the opponents engages in competitive and uncooperative attitudes, the outcome of the process, as well as the relationship among the parties, may be at risk. As it was pointed out, each individual may engage in different conflict resolution styles, depending on the type of the conflict, on the state of the relationships among the opponents, on their individual objectives, or on the domain of the dispute. For these reasons, determining one's conflict resolution style may be challenging.

Traditionally, existing approaches from the social and organizational sciences rely on questionnaires to address it. Parties respond to a series of questions and researchers or team managers will sum up their answers, and come up with a final score that represents their approximate conflict resolution style. The main problem with such approaches lies, from our point of view, in the fact that parties may change their conflict resolution style during the resolution process. Indeed, as Chap. 12 points out, we have observed such behaviours in the studies carried out.

People may start uncooperative and suspicious towards the whole process, and only slowly may move towards more cooperative behaviours, as the mediator exposes the potential advantages of an integrative approach and a relationship of trust is built among the participants. Evidently, the opposite may also happen; hence the importance of methods that may, in real-time, provide the conflict manager with information about the parties' conflict resolution style. Questionnaires will only provide potentially out-dated information and will, in the best of cases, depict how the individuals thought they would behave at the outset of the process.

To some extent, the conflict resolution style may be understood as our behaviour towards a negotiation; it is our way of acting and reacting when facing events that take place during the conflict resolution process. In this chapter an innovative approach to the problem was proposed, based on the analysis of the parties' behaviour: we classify the conflict handling style from the characteristics of the case and the proposals exchanged by the parties. The use of such computer-interpretable approaches allows the development of conflict resolution systems that may, indeed, be more than a mere support tool for communication, allowing the mediator to take decisions using knowledge that is generally not available, at least formally. The most interesting possibility proposed in this chapter is indeed the one of analysing the evolution of the conflict resolution style of the parties in real time. By doing so, the mediator may detect and interpret significant changes in the state of the parties, taking action when necessary in order to avoid undesired behaviours such as an overly competitive negotiation style.

References

Aarts, E., and F. Grotenhuis. 2011. Ambient intelligence 2.0: Towards synergetic prosperity. *Ambient Intelligence and Smart Environments* 3(1): 3–11.

Blake, R.R., and J.S. Mouton. 1964. *The managerial grid*. Houston: Gulf.

Gomes, M., T. Oliveira, D. Carneiro, P. Novais, and J. Neves. 2013. Extracting behavioural patterns from a negotiation game. In: Barbosa, S., Chen, P., Cuzzocrea, A., Du, X., Filipe, J., Kara, O., Kotenko, I., Sivalingam, K.M., Slezak, D., Washio, T., Yang, X. (eds.), *Highlights on practical applications of agents and multi-agent systems*, Communications in computer and information science, vol. 365, 304–315. Berlin: Springer.

Holt, J.L., and C.J. DeVore. 2005. Culture, gender, organizational role, and styles of conflict resolution: A meta-analysis. *International Journal of Intercultural Relations* 29(2): 165–196.

Jain, B.A., and J.S. Solomon. 2000. The effect of task complexity and conflict handling styles on computer-supported negotiations. *Information and Management* 37(4): 161–168.

Kuhn, T., and M.S. Poole. 2000. Do conflict management styles affect group decision making? *Human Communication Research* 26: 558–590.

Ludwig, S.A. 2008. Agent-based assistant for e-negotiations. In *Proceedings of the 17th international conference on Foundations of intelligent systems, ISMIS'08*, 514–524. Berlin/Heidelberg: Springer.

Maddux, R.B., and B. Wingfield. 2003. *Team building: An exercise in leadership*, 4th revised ed. Mississauga: Course Technology Inc.

Metcalf, H.C., and L. Urwick. (eds.). 2003. *Dynamic administration: The collected papers of Mary Parker Follett*, vol. 3. Routledge: Taylor & Francis.

Nandalal, K.D.W., and S.P. Simonovic. 2003. *Conflict resolution support system: A software for the resolution of conflicts in water resource management*, Water resources research report. London: University of Western Ontario.

Pruitt, D.G. 1983. Strategic choice in negotiation. *American Behavioral Scientist* 27: 167–194.

Rahim, M.A. 1983. A measure of styles of handling interpersonal conflict. *The Academy of Management Journal* 26(2): 368–376.

Thomas, K.W., and R.H. Kilmann. 2007. *Thomas-Kilmann conflict mode instrument*. Mountain View: Xicom, A Subsidiary of CPP, Inc.

Yiu, T.W. 2005. *A behavioral analysis of construction dispute negotiation*. City University of Hong Kong.

Chapter 11
Stress in Conflict Resolution

Abstract Stress is nowadays one of the most serious health-related issues, being even deemed by some as the health epidemic of the century. Many studies have approached stress from different angles, being stress in the workplace and its associated economic costs one of the most studied topics. Nonetheless, stress has consequences that go much further than the economic ones, impacting decision making skills, mood, social relationships, productivity, performance or health. In this line of work, we look at stress as one of the most preponderant factors in decision-making. Excessive stress may lead to poor judgment or hasty decisions while lack of stress may lead to inaction and indecision. For these reasons, stress emerges as an important factor to consider in a conflict resolution scenario, in which the pressure of the proceedings, the unknown potential outcomes or the escalation of emotions may easily result in significant stressful moments. At the same time it must be emphasized the importance of weighted decisions and interpersonal relationships towards a successful outcome: two of the issues that are definitely affected by stress. With such a motivation in mind, in this chapter we describe the approach followed to study stress on the users of technological devices, in a non-intrusive way. We aim to understand how people behave when under stress so that we can incorporate such knowledge in a next generation conflict resolution framework such as UMCourt.

11.1 Introduction

Stress is one of the important factors to consider in conflict resolution, much like in any other activity in our lives. In fact, even in an unconscious way, stress (or the lack of it) influences all our decisions and actions. It is a multi-modal phenomenon: it influences peoples' lives in many different dimensions, from the physical to the psychological. Moreover, there is no one-size-fits-all solution: each individual is affected in different ways and each one has a natural level of stress that brings balance to his life. More stress will make the individual take hasty decisions, be weary, strained or less tolerable to stressors. Less stress will make the individual's life dull, decrease productivity and ultimately lead to depressive states.

In the particular domain of conflict resolution, stress is also one of the key factors conditioning decisions. Specifically during the negotiation phase, the levels of stress may make people take wrong decisions that they may regret later. Mediators have a major role in avoiding this: they should reveal the necessary skills to interpret the state of the parties and intervene when necessary in order to prevent an escalation of the emotions.

When negotiations take place with all the parties in the physical presence of each other, this is fairly easy for a skilled mediator (Herrman et al. 2001). However, when negotiations take part in virtual environments, in which parties usually communicate through text-based messages only, it becomes very difficult for a mediator to accurately evaluate the state of the parties.

The work described in this chapter aims at tackling this challenge. Specifically, it describes a context layer that can acquire information about the parties' level of stress, allowing mediators to have a richer view on the environment. With the integration of such functionality, UMCourt results in a conflict resolution platform that is constantly sensible to the state of the parties. While the previous chapter described the effects of stress during an actual session of negotiation, this one analyses how stress also has effects on the same variables outside of the actual negotiation process. Thus, a classification of the level of stress exists even before or after the negotiation process (e.g. while the user is communicating with other parties, while accessing or managing information), allowing the mediator to understand the state of the parties at any time and especially at the beginning or at the end of the proceedings. This information may reveal very useful at the time of defining the strategy for conducting a negotiation or mediation or at the time of evaluating its success.

The context layer developed is completely non-intrusive and relies on the analysis of the individual's behavior, as described in Chap. 9. This chapter starts by describing the multi-modal view on stress adopted in this book, that considers both predictive and diagnostic aspects. Afterwards, a non-exhaustive list of common stressors that every individual deals with on a daily basis is put forward. The remaining of the chapter describes the experiments set up to study behavioral responses to stress, ultimately allowing to develop conflict resolution platforms that are sensible to the stress of their users.

11.2 A Multi-modal View on Stress

One of the first definitions of stress was proposed by Hans Selye (1978). According to the Austrian-Canadian endocrinologist, stress can be seen as a non-specific response of the body to external demands. These demands (the load or stimulus that triggered a response) are denominated *stressors* while the internal body changes that they produce constitute the actual *stress response*. Selye was also the first to document the chemical and hormonal changes that occur in the body due to stress.

Nevertheless, the definition of stress is still not consensual in the scientific community, remaining as an open topic of discussion. In fact, stress involves a multiplicity of factors, many of them subjective, leading to multiple interpretations that make it difficult to objectively define it. Thus being, some researchers argue that such a concept is elusive because it is poorly defined (Cox 1985) while others prefer not to provide an actual definition of the concept until a more accurate and consensual view of the phenomenon is achieved.

In an attempt to address this issue, researchers started dealing with stress from an empirical point of view. In this sense, a strong focus was put on its cognitive and behavioral effects and it started to be viewed as a mind-body, psychosomatic or psycho-physiologic phenomenon. A more up-to-date view of stress thus looks at it as a physic-physiologic arousal response occurring in the body as result of stimuli. It should also be added that these stimuli only become stressors by virtue of the cognitive interpretation of the individual, i.e., the effects of stressors depend on the individual. This is the interpretation of stress considered in this book and is the starting point for the definition of a stress model.

Given the multiplicity of factors that influence stress and the different modalities of the behavior and cognition that are affected, a single-modality approach for measuring the effects of stress would not be suited, as some experimental results demonstrate (Wenhui Liao 2006). In fact, for a sufficiently precise and accurate measurement of stress, a multi-modal approach should be considered. The diagram depicted in Fig. 11.1 represents the multi-modal approach described in this book to measure stress. This diagram has two main parts. The upper part concerns the predictive aspects of stress, i.e., aspects influencing stress that can be estimated from the background or context of the user. The lower part concerns the diagnostic aspects of stress, i.e., it deals with the effects of stress on the several spheres of the individual.

The Predictive part of the model considers the following aspects:

- Context – Includes meaningful information to describe the different dimensions of the individual, including the historical, economic, social or geographical contexts. Numerous studies exist that map such information to a base level of stress. Soylu et al. (2000) evaluate the effect of socioeconomic status on blood pressure of children living in areas with different degrees of development. Evans et al. (1998) look at the context in which people live as a source of stress, namely in what concerns environmental stressors such as noise. The important role of the economic situation of the individual on his level of stress has also been studied by Elder and Caspi (1988). Meyer (2003) evaluates the weight of social stress, i.e., the stress that society makes each individual feel for their choices, limitations or conditions. As a last example, Stockdale et al. (2007) analyze the importance of the social context for stress, namely in what concerns

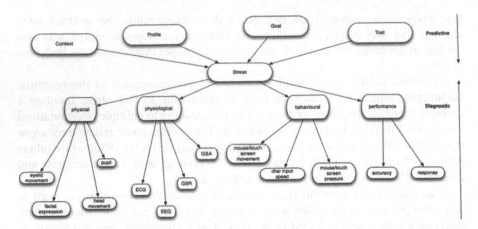

Fig. 11.1 The stress recognition model described in this chapter. It includes two main groups of aspects: predictive and diagnostic. Predictive aspects are the ones that can be estimated from the background or context of the individual. Diagnostic aspects are the ones that can be observed and measured and have a relationship with the level of stress

neighborhood stressors. Commonly known notions include: living in a metropolitan area is more stressful than living in a rural area; a poor bank account or a debt to the bank is more stressful than a rich account or no debts; an active social life helps to relief stress.

- Profile – The profile of the individual includes more personal information such as the age, gender, marital status, number of children, type (or lack) of employment, job category, among others. The relationship between these factors and stress has been thoroughly studied by researchers of different fields. Fagin (1985) evaluates the role of unemployment on stress. Parental stress is thoroughly analyzed by Berry and Jones (1995), with the definition of a stress scale. A good review of empirical research on job stress is also carried out by Beehr et al. (1999).
- Goal – While the previously mentioned aspects can be considered more generic, this one is more intrinsically related with the scope of this book. The goal of the individual in the conflict resolution process is related to his level of stress: an individual that aims at maximizing his gain at all cost is generally under a higher level of stress than an individual that wants only to reach an agreement, despite of the losses, as the work of Tidd and Friedman points out (Tidd and Friedman 2002).
- Trait – The trait is related with the personality of each individual, i.e., habitual patterns of behavior, thought or emotion. Some specific traits can be related to stress. As an example, an impulsive individual is generally a stressed one, with stress driving his hasty decisions. Specifically interesting here are the personal conflict handling styles described in the previous chapter, that can be seen as traits of individuals before a conflict and can also be related to the level of stress (Tidd and Friedman 2002).

The Diagnostic components of the model include:

- Physical – The physical aspects include, in a general way, body movements or postures that have some particular meaning that can be related to stress. Specifically interesting are aspects such as eyelid movement, facial expressions, body movements (e.g. specific gestures, head movements, repetitive movement patterns) or pupil movement and dilatation.
- Physiological – Physiological aspects are the ones that provide an easier diagnose of stress. In fact, several approaches exist nowadays that can evaluate the level of stress of an individual from the Galvanic Skin Response (the electrical conductivity of the skin, influenced by sweating, which is caused by stress), from Electroencephalography (a measure of one's brain electrical activity) or from Electrocardiography (a measure of the electrical activity of the heart) (Picard 2000). Other physiological indicators include the respiratory rate, heart rate or body temperature. All these aspects are reliable indicators of the level of stress.
- Behavioral – As addressed before in this chapter, the behavior of an individual is the visible end of his inner self. In that sense, besides other things, behaviors (and especially changes on the behaviors) may also be a good indicator of the level of stress. Given the scope of this book, particularly interesting are the behaviors related to the interaction patterns with technological devices (e.g. how an individual types, how an individual interacts with a smartphone, how an individual moves when in front of a computer).
- Performance – The performance of an individual is significantly affected by stress. The optimum level of stress will maximize performance. A higher level of stress may increase performance temporarily but will soon tire the individual. A lower level of stress will decrease productivity and lead the individual into increasing lethargy. Thus, tests that evaluate the performance of the individual in given tasks for which standard performance measurements are known can be a good indicator of the effects of stress on the individual.

From a high-level point of view, different types of stress can also be identified, namely acute and chronic stress. Acute stress comes from recent demands and pressures and from anticipated demands in the near future. On the other hand, chronic stress is a long-term one, due to social or health conditions, dysfunctional families, among many other issues. This type of stress will have nefarious effects on the body and mind of the individual, slowly wearing him away day after day. On the other hand, acute stress, because it is short-term, won't do the extensive damage associated with chronic stress. Nevertheless, it will instantaneously influence the performance of the actions being performed. The interest here is clearly in the analysis of acute stress and its effects, given that they may be more determining for the outcome of a conflict resolution process.

11.3   Common Stressors

A stressor can take many different forms including a chemical or biological agent, environmental condition, external stimulus or an event that forces an organism to adapt to new conditions. Human stressors, in particular, may include environmental stressors such as noise or over-illumination, daily stress events such as traffic or lack or physical activity, dramatic life changes such as the death of a relative or a divorce, workplace stressors such as job demands or unrealistic objectives, chemical stressors such as alcohol or drugs consumption or social stressors such as family demands. Other less obvious stressors have been identified and studied by researchers in the last years.

In a study conducted in 1995 by researchers of the State University of New Jersey, it was analyzed the impact of electronic performance monitoring and its social context on the productivity and stress of the users. Its purpose was to analyze the impact of electronic performance monitoring and social context on productivity and stress of employees (Aiello and Kolb 1995).

Electronic Performance Monitoring (EPM) systems are one of the many technological developments employees face in today's workplaces. These systems provide managers a wide range of information about employees' routines including real-time information such as the pace of employees' work, their degree of accuracy, log-in and log-out times, and even the amount of time spent on bathroom breaks. This study examined how productivity and subjective experiences are affected by EPM systems and how the social context of the workplace moderates that influence.

In a survey involving the monitored workers, 81 % of the respondents declared that electronic observation made their jobs more stressful (Gallatin 1989). Other study, from 1986 compared the behavior of monitored and non-monitored workers who performed similar jobs, and found that monitored workers felt more stressful (Davis et al. 1986).

The changes in job design introduced concurrently with electronic monitoring have been identified as the cause for the increase of stress. The introduction of EPM systems can transform ordinary jobs into high-stress jobs. It can also reduce the opportunities for employees to socialize with each other at work, what could lead to a loss of social support partially responsible for the stress associated with EPM (Smith et al. 1992; Amick and Smith 1992).

Researchers from the School of Psychology of the University of Liverpool have also analyzed the relationship between stress and productivity in the workplace. The researchers investigated the predictors of productivity with A Shortened Stress Evaluation tool (ASSET) (Donald et al. 2005).

The economic and social effects of the existence of stressors have also been studied. A study from 1999 estimated that each worker experienced a monthly productivity loss of approximately $200–$400 due to depression (Kessler et al. 1999). Similarly, another study estimated that the loss of productivity due to depression has cost American corporations $12.1 billion in 1990 alone (Greenberg et al. 1990).

The psychologist community clearly acknowledges the existence of a relationship between workspace stressors and mental and physical health outcomes. However, little research is devoted to the effects of stressors on health outcomes or their impact on productivity.

Albeit sparse, there are some evidences that establish an association between stress and productivity. In 1986, Yeh, Lester, and Tauber performed a study on real estate agents that revealed a negative relationship between stress and productivity (Yeh et al. 1986). In 1992, Jamal and Baba, using data collected from blue-collar, managerial and nursing employees showed a direct, linear and negative stress-productivity relationship: the greater the stress was, the less productive the workforce was (Jamal and Baba 1992).

11.4 A study on the Effects of Stress

The main objective of this line of research is to identify which factors of the human physiology influenced by stress can be pointed out using a non-invasive approach.

The following research questions and hypothesis are analyzed in this study:

(a) Does stress actually influences, in a significant manner, our interaction patterns while using common technological devices?
(b) Is it possible to accurately measure this influence in a non-invasive and non-intrusive way?

With regard to the first question, it is hypothesized that stress does influence interaction patterns in a significant manner. The work of other researchers, who proved that stress does influence people's behaviors and physical responses in a significant way, serves both as a motivation and as a pre-validation of the approach. For some examples see (Healey and Picard 2005; Vizer et al. 2009; Rehm et al. 2008).

Concerning the second question, it is hypothesized that it is possible to measure, using non-invasive and non-intrusive methods, the level of stress of the users by analyzing key features in their interaction with technological devices.

There are also some sub-questions that, although not compulsory, will contribute to the achievement of better results. Namely:

1. Determine how the interaction patterns of each user are affected by stress and develop personalized stress models that will maximize the accuracy of the approach.
2. Find groups of people that are affected in similar ways (e.g. same parameters show similar tendencies when subject to stress) in order to develop more accurate generic stress models, to be applied when a personalized model is not available.

Table 11.1 Description of the dataset generated during the study, with data detailing the behavioral features of the participants

Data	Brief description	Size
Acceleration	Data concerning the acceleration felt on the handheld device while playing the game	27,291
Maximum intensity of touch	Data about the maximum intensity of each touch in a touchscreen	1,825
Mean intensity of touch	This dataset contains data about the mean intensity of each touch event in a touchscreen	1,825
Amount of movement	A dataset containing information about the amount of movement during tests	25,416
Touches on target	This dataset contains information about the accuracy of the touches	1,825
Stressed touches	A dataset containing information that allows to classify each touch as stressed or not stressed	1,825
Score	A dataset describing the performance of the user playing the game, during the tests	321
Touch duration	A dataset containing the duration of each touch event	1,825

In order to test these hypotheses, a study was conducted in the Intelligent Systems Lab of the University of Minho, in which the environment described in Chap. 9 is implemented, allowing to collect data about how people interact with technological devices, when calm and when under stress. The collection of the data was organized in two phases. In a first phase, individuals were required to perform these tasks in a stress-free environment. In a second phase, the same individuals performed the same tasks subject to stressors such as the vibration of the devices, loud and annoying sounds, unexpected behaviors of the devices, time constraints, among others.

The empirical data gathered in both phases about the user interaction patterns and physical response is described in Table 11.1. Each of these datasets consists of a list of values describing the respective feature as well as a time stamp and a user name. This data was synchronized and transformed/normalized to allow its joint analysis. The participants of the proposed experiment were volunteer students and professors from the University of Minho. Nineteen male and female individuals participated in the experiment aged between 20 and 57. All these individuals are familiar with the technological devices used and the interaction with them was not an obstacle.

The data gathered was analyzed in order to determine statistically significant differences between phase 1 and phase 2 of the data collection. Measures of central tendency and variability were calculated for all variables of interest. The Mann-Whitney-Wilcoxon Statistical test was used to test whether there are actual differences in the distributions of the data. A 0.05 level of significance was considered. The data analysis was performed using Wolfram Mathematica, Version 8.0.

This analysis of the data allowed to determine which features, for each individual, were effectively affected by stress and to which extent. This information allows to develop personalized models for stress estimation in real time. Moreover, a more generic model can also be developed taking into consideration the data of several or all the users. This generic model can be applied in the cases in which a personalized one is not available. The models developed are used to develop a real-time stress estimation software layer to be used in a VE or in other domains.

In order to identify which factors vary with stress and in what magnitude, a game with the following features was developed: a mentally challenging objective and stressors. The main objective of the game is that the user performs mental calculations using the four basic arithmetic operations and a group of numbers given randomly in order to get as close as possible to a target number. The user must also memorize any intermediary result. The score is given in function of the distance of the result to the target number: the closer to a given target number, the higher the score, up to a maximum of 100 points when the result is equal to the target number. There are however some constraints. In each round, it is only possible to use each number and each operator once. As an example, let us say that the target number is 198 and you have four random numbers such as 50, 45, 3 and 8. A fairly good solution would be $3 * 50 + 45$.

In each consecutive round of the game the user has to perform one of such calculations. There are however stressors that make the effects of stress felt, including a time limit, vibrations and sounds on the handheld devices. The time limit decreases as the number of rounds increases. Moreover, the longer the user takes to answer in a round, the smaller the time limit in the following round. Thus, there is a pressure on the user to answer quickly. At the same time, there is also the pressure to make the best possible score. Vibration and sounds are used to increase the level of stress when the time is almost over at each round. When only a few seconds remain, the handheld device starts vibrating and making a disturbing beeping sound whose frequencies are higher when the time limit is smaller. All this increases the physiological effects of stress on the users, as the results show. Two screenshots of the game are shown in Fig. 11.2.

As stated, the game is developed to induce stress in the individual and to determine in which way each one is affected in terms of cognitive performance and interaction patterns. To study this, eight of the features mentioned in Chap. 9 were selected and analyzed for each user.

11.4.1 Real-Time Assessment of Stress

The final step in this process is to develop a solution that allows to assess the level of stress of each individual, in real-time, so that the mediator can take real-time decisions as well. Two approaches that address this objective are described in this section. The first one is based on the analysis of the data for each feature individually. The second one looks at the touch patterns of the users, i.e., it looks at the shape of the touches' curve of intensity.

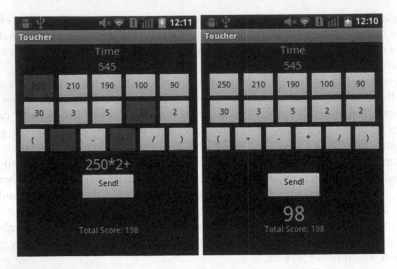

Fig. 11.2 Screenshots of the game interface in which the user must perform mental calculations and memorization of intermediary results while under stress

Feature Analysis

From a high-level point of view, the first approach consists in collecting data in real-time about the features studied, and comparing it to the data that was already collected for the individual in the study. In a few words, if the data being collected is very similar to the data collected when the user was calm, it can be concluded that user is in a calm state. Alternatively, if the data is similar to the data collected when the user was stressed, it can be concluded that the user is stressed. The main challenge here is thus the one of finding the similarity between distributions of data. Moreover, if it is possible to evaluate the degree of similarity, it will be possible to provide a quantitative value of *how stressed* or *how calm* an individual is, by determining *how similar* the data being collected is to each of the known distributions.

Two approaches have been implemented to address this problem and are described in this subsection. The results of their use are described in the following chapter. The first one is based on the notion of Confidence Intervals while the second is based on a statistical classifier.

The Confidence Interval is a term used in statistics that measures the probability that a population parameter will fall between two set values. As an example: given a 95 % confidence interval, an individual's maximum touch intensity falls between 0.08 and 0.14 when the individual is stressed. What this means is that we are 95 % confident that when the individual is stressed, the values for the maximum intensity of his touches on a touch screen will fall between 0.08 and 0.14.

The first approach thus compares two distributions of data by comparing their confidence intervals. Figure 11.3 depicts how this is achieved. The lower part

Fig. 11.3 Quantifying the similarity between two distributions of data by measuring the overlap of their confidence intervals

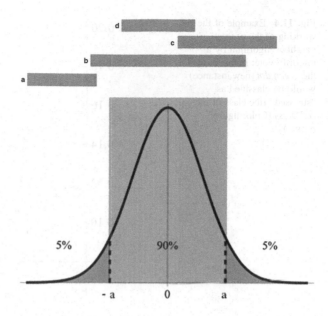

depicts a distribution of data, with the 90 % confidence interval highlighted by a blue rectangle. This represents a known distribution. The upper part of the figure (the orange rectangles) depicts several confidence intervals of another distribution (the one being generated in real-time), under different scenarios. Specifically, four examples are provided. In scenario (a), the new distribution is not similar to the new one as their confidence intervals do not overlap at all. Under scenario (b) there is some significant degree of similarity as their confidence intervals overlap considerably. Scenario (c) presents a similar situation. Finally, scenario (d) shows some similarity as well, although smaller, given that the overlap area is smaller.

Hence, under this approach, the similarity between two distributions is given in terms of the percentage of overlapping area of the confidence intervals of the two distributions. Distributions are constructed in real-time for each feature and compared with the known stressed and calm distributions, at regular time intervals. Thus, in each time interval, the system outputs a measure of how similar the behavior of an individual is to the known stressed and calm behaviors, for each feature studied.

Under the second approach, a standard and well known pattern recognition tool is used: the k-nearest neighbor algorithm, specifically, the weka.classifiers.lazy.IBk (Aha et al. 1991) implementation for java, provided by the Weka workbench (version 3.6.3) (Holmes et al. 1994). It is a method for classifying objects based on closest training examples in the feature space: an object is classified by a majority vote of its neighbors, with the object being assigned to the class most common amongst its k nearest neighbors (k is a positive integer, typically small). If $k = 1$, then the object is simply assigned to the class of its nearest neighbor.

Fig. 11.4 Example of the working of the nearest neighbor algorithm by a majority vote: in this case the *green dot* (new instance) would be classified as "stressed" (the class of the *red dots*) (Color figure online)

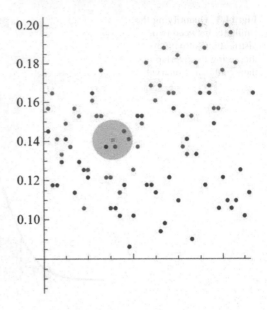

Figure 11.4 depicts the working of this algorithm with a real example. The data detailed describes several instances of the maximum intensity of touch: the red dots correspond to the data collected under stress while the blue dot to the data collected without stress. This data shows a tendency that will be analyzed in detail in the following chapter: under stress the intensity of touch is higher. Given the new instance to be classified represented by the green dot (a new touch), and $k = 4$, the algorithm would classify it as stressed given that there are more neighbors from the class "stressed" (3) than from the class "not stressed" (1). The working of the algorithm is the same for each of the other features and for each new instance that must be classified. A classifier was trained for each feature and for each individual that participated in the experiment, using the data collected.

The analysis of the classifiers' performances for each feature is performed in detail in the following chapter. This analysis is validated by the Cohen's kappa coefficient, which is a statistical measure of inter-rater agreement that tells how much of the accuracy is due to chance. Afterwards, for each feature the average performance of all the classifiers in terms of their average sample accuracy is also considered. Box-and-whisker diagrams are plotted with the values of the sample accuracies of all the classifiers. For each feature we also look at the median, and at the upper and lower quantiles. Finally, the average values of the kappa coefficient of all the classifiers trained for each feature are also considered.

Independently of the approach used, the system will compute a value of stress for each feature, in each instant. These values are normalized and the final value of stress is a weighted sum of the level of stress corresponding to each feature. The weight is given in terms of the results of the significance tests (e.g. the touch intensity has a bigger weight than the acceleration if the individual is more significantly affected by stress on the touch intensity than on the acceleration). More details on this process are given in the following chapter.

Touch Patterns

The second approach mentioned at the beginning of this subsection looks at the shape of the touch patterns of the users in order to provide an additional feature for assessing stress. The hypothesis being assessed is that stressed users will have different touch patterns (e.g. longer, shorter, steeper). This approach is clearly targeted at data collected from devices with touch screens, particularly the Android smartphones and tablets used to build the environment detailed in Chap. 9.

Thus, to assess the level of stress of each touch, this approach relies on the event listeners provided by the Android framework. An event listener is an interface in the View class that contains a single callback method that will be called by the Android framework when the View to which the listener has been registered is triggered by user interaction with the item in the UI. For this purpose, the onTouch() callback method is used, which is called when the user performs an action qualified as a touch event, including a press, a release, or any movement gesture on the screen (within the bounds of the item). Thus, in each touch of the user on an item of the UI several touch events are fired: one when the finger of the user first touches the screen (identified by the action event ACTION_DOWN), several while the user is touching (depending on the duration of the touch) and one when the finger releases the screen (identified by the action event ACTION_UP).

Each of these events has information about the intensity of the touch (via the getPressure() method) and about the position of the event. Moreover, when each event is fired, it is registered together with a timestamp. This allows to visualize the evolution of a touch in terms of its intensity over time. From this information it is also possible to extract the duration and intensity features:

- Duration feature – is defined as the difference between the timestamps of the action events ACTION_UP and ACTION_DOWN. One of the hypotheses being tested is that the stress of a user will have an influence on the duration of the touch, hence our interest. The duration of the touch can however be influenced by factors other than the stress. Namely, the type of item of the UI being touched. In that sense, events fired by items such as sliders or by scrolling pages are not considered. For the purpose of the study carried out, the interest lies in the standard touches used to interact with buttons, inputting text and similar actions.
- Intensity feature – The intensity of a touch event depicts the force exerted by the finger of the user while touching the device. Given that each touch event includes a pressure and that each touch fires several touch events (as described above), it is possible to analyze the variation of the intensity throughout all the touch, from the moment the finger first touches the screen to the moment it releases it.

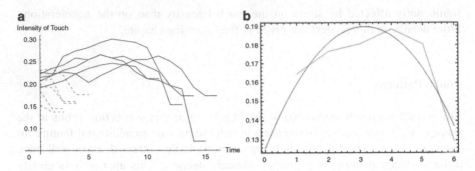

Fig. 11.5 (a) Ten different touch patterns from users: touches can be composed of a different number of touch events. The *orange lines* depict touches classified as "calm" whereas the *blue lines* belong to touches classified as "stressed". (b) Fitting a polynomial curve (*blue curve*) to a given touch (*orange line*) (Color figure online)

The main goal of this approach is thus to investigate if it is possible to build a classifier for touch patterns that can be used in real-life applications to provide some information about the level of stress of the user. Two standard and well known machine learning tools are used for this purpose: a decision tree constructor and a support vector machine. As the decision tree constructor the J48 algorithm is used – the java implementation of the C4.5 (Quinlan 1993). As support vector machine, the SMO function was selected, which implements John Platt's sequential minimal optimization algorithm for training a support vector classifier (Platt 1999). These experiments were also performed using the Weka workbench (version 3.6.3).

The results of the two classifiers will be compared in the following chapter by looking at some performance measures such as the percentage of correctly classified instances, the Kappa statistic (which is a chance-corrected measure of agreement between the classifications and the true classes) and the ROC area.

As previously described, each touch in the screen results in several touch events that are fired during the time of the touch. This number varies according to the duration of the touch. In that sense, the data for each touch, as it is, cannot be used to build a classifier (each touch would have a potentially different list of values of intensity, one for each touch event). Figure 11.5a highlights this by depicting different types of touches.

To tackle this problem it was observed that the intensity of touches follows a similar shape: a convex curve that grows to a maximum point and then decreases. Thus, the approach followed consisted in fitting a second degree polynomial curve to each touch pattern. To perform this fitting in real-time the proposed approach uses J/Link, the Mathematica's Java interface that allows for controlling Mathematica Kernels from Java programs. Specifically, the Fit[*data, funs, vars*] function is used which finds a least-squares fit to a list of data as a linear combination of the functions *funs* of variables *vars*. To implement this, Mathematica v8.0 was used. An example of this approach is depicted in Fig. 11.5b. Given that the second degree polynomial curves are of the type $y = ax^2 + bx + c$ it is possible to compare the parameters of the curve of each touch pattern: similar values of *a, b* and c indicate similar curves, thus similar touch patterns. Hence, the input for the classifier are three numeric attributes a, b and c (the independent variables) and a nominal attribute that describes the state of the user at the time of the touch as "stressed" or "not stressed" (the dependent variable).

In a few words, this last approach characterizes the behavior of an individual based on the way he touches the screen of the handheld device. Each touch is classified as "stressed" or "not stressed", allowing a temporal analysis of the type "number of touches classified as stressed per unit of time".

These two approaches (analysis of each feature individually and analysis of touch patterns) allow the development of a real-time solution for estimating the level of stress of an individual in a non-invasive way. All the results concerning this subject are provided in the following chapter.

11.5   Conclusion

This section has been dedicated to the importance of stress, its causes and its effects. Undeniably, stress is nowadays one of the main factors affecting aspects such as health, quality of life, productivity or quality of work. The participation in a conflict resolution process, by being potentially stressful, may constitute a stressful event, with consequences on the people's decision making mechanisms or judgment. As addressed, people should be relaxed in order to think their problems thoroughly, avoiding hasty decisions. With the objective of devising a technology-supported stress-aware conflict resolution process, this chapter detailed a study on stress, conducted at the Intelligent Systems Lab of the University of Minho, in which the environment described in Chap. 9 is implemented.

From this study, several challenges can be put forward at the time of developing a practical human stress monitoring system, namely:

- The expression and the measurements of human stress are very much person-dependent and even time or context-dependent for the same person;
- The sensory observations are often ambiguous, uncertain, and incomplete;
- Human stress is dynamic and evolves over time;
- The lack of a clear criterion for the feasible classification of stress states greatly increases the difficulty of validating stress recognition systems.

In order to tackle these challenges, a multi-modal and personalized approach was followed. Its multi-modal nature allows it to consider inputs from the different spheres of an individual that are affected by stress, making it exhaustive. Its personalized nature stems from the models developed, in which data from each user is analyzed individually. Moreover, a systematic approach has been implemented, inspired by the applied behavior analysis methodologies of Social Sciences.

Thus, each of the seven points enumerated in Chap. 9 were addressed in the following way:

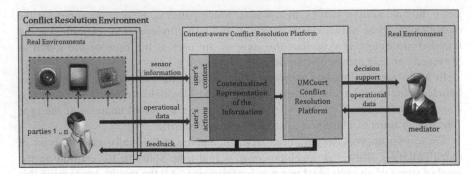

Fig. 11.6 The proposed concept of a Conflict Resolution Environment is central in this book: the user's context is acquired from sensors placed in the environment of the user. This allows to build a contextualized representation of his actions, supporting the conflict resolution and the mediator in taking better actions

- At least one participant is needed to study a given behavior. The study detailed in this chapter involved 19 participants from the faculty;
- There must be at least one behavior being studied. In this study, eight features were considered that depict how individuals behave using technological devices in face of stress;
- An environment was developed to implement the experiment. This environment allowed to control stressors that induced stress on the participants and to collect information about behavioral features being studied;
- A system for measuring the behavior of the participants was developed, based on the statistical analysis of the data gathered. Specifically, a measure of the similarity between distributions of data was developed. This included real-time and visual analysis of data;
- A small difference from the classical approaches exists at the level of the intervention condition. It does not exist during the experiment but only posteriorly, during the actual conflict resolution process, i.e., the intervention takes place by the mediator or the conflict resolution platform, when the level of stress escalates, and not during the collection of the data;
- Stressors (the independent variable) may be manipulated in order to study their effect on the behavioral features (the dependent variables). This is done by changing their intensity (e.g. changing the time limit, increasing the volume/frequency of the sounds, increasing the rate of vibrations on the handheld device);
- The participant will benefit from the experiment in the sense that the mediator or the conflict resolution platform will be able to take better-framed decisions, ultimately leading to better and more mutually satisfactory outcomes;

The final goal of this approach inspired on applied behavioral analysis research is the development of stress-aware conflict resolution environments (Fig. 11.6).

Under this new view, each individual participates in the conflict resolution from his/her own *real* environment, which is equipped with sensors and devices that acquire different kinds of information in a non-intrusive way. While the individual conscientiously interacts with the system and takes his/her decisions and actions, a parallel and transparent process takes place in which this information is sent in a synchronized way to the conflict resolution platform. The platform, upon converting the sensory information into useful data, allows for a contextualized analysis of the operational data of the individuals. This contextualized analysis is performed by the platform itself (e.g. for performing decision-support related tasks) and by the mediator. Then, the parties receive feedback from the platform (e.g. a new proposal, information updates, notifications), which may also include some kind of feedback from the state of the parties (e.g. an avatar showing the state of the parties).

The following chapter details the results achieved during the study detailed here. It shows how stress influences people's behavioral patterns, specifically when interacting with technological devices.

References

Aha, D.W., D. Kibler, and M.K. Albert. 1991. Instance-based learning algorithms. *Machine Learning* 6(1): 37–66.

Aiello, J.R., and K.J. Kolb. 1995. Electronic performance monitoring and social context: Impact on productivity and stress. *The Journal of Applied Psychology* 80(3): 339–353.

Amick, B.C., and M.J. Smith. 1992. Stress, computer-based work monitoring and measurement systems: A conceptual overview. *Applied Ergonomics* 23(1): 6–16.

Beehr, M., M. d'Inverno, N.R. Jennings, M. Luck, C. Preist, and M. Schroeder. 1999. Negotiation in multi-agent systems. *Knowledge Engineering Review* 14(3): 285–289.

Berry, J.O., and W.H. Jones. 1995. The parental stress scale: Initial psychometric evidence. *Journal of Social and Personal Relationships* 12(3): 463–472.

Cox, T. 1985. The nature and measurement of stress. *Ergonomics* 28(8): 1155–1163.

Davis, G.B., R.H. Irving, C.A. Higgins, and F.R. Safayeni. 1986. Computerized performance monitoring systems: Use and abuse. *Communications of the ACM* 29(8): 794–801.

Donald, I., P. Taylor, S. Johnson, C. Cooper, S. Cartwright, and S. Robertson. 2005. Work environments, stress, and productivity: An examination using ASSET. *International Journal of Stress Management* 12(4): 409–423.

Elder, G.H., and A. Caspi. 1988. Economic stress in lives: Developmental perspectives. *Journal of Social Issues* 44(4): 25–45.

Evans, G.W., M. Bullinger, and S. Hygge. 1998. Chronic noise exposure and physiological response: A prospective study of children living under environmental stress. *Psychological Science* 9(1): 75–77.

Fagin, L. 1985. Stress and unemployment. *Stress Medicine* 1(1): 27–36.

Gallatin, L. 1989. *Electronic monitoring in the workplace: Supervision or surveillance?* Boston: CNOT.

Greenberg, P.E., L.E. Stiglin, S.N. Finkelstein, and E.R. Berndt. 1990. The economic burden of depression in 1990. *The Journal of Clinical Psychiatry* 54(11): 405–418, 1993.

Healey, J.A., and R.W. Picard. 2005. Detecting stress during real-world driving tasks using physiological sensors. *IEEE Transactions on Intelligent Transportation Systems* 6(2): 156–166.

Herrman, M.S., N.H. Jerry Gale, and M. Foster. 2001. In practice: Defining mediator knowledge and skills. *Negotiation Journal* 17(2): 139–153.

Holmes, G., A. Donkin, and I. Witten. 1994. WEKA: A machine learning workbench. In *Proceedings of ANZIIS'94 – Australian New Zealand intelligent information systems conference*, 357–361. IEEE.

Jamal, M., and V.V. Baba. 1992. Stressful jobs and employee productivity: Results from studies on managers, blue-collar workers and nurses. *International Journal of Management* 9: 62–67.

Kessler, R.C., C. Barber, H.G. Birnbaum, R.G. Frank, P.E. Greenberg, R.M. Rose, G.E. Simon, and P. Wang. 1999. Depression in the workplace: Effects on short-term disability. *Health Affairs* 18(5): 163–171.

Meyer, I.H. 2003. Prejudice, social stress, and mental health in lesbian, gay, and bisexual populations: Conceptual issues and research evidence. *Psychological Bulletin* 129(5): 674–697.

Picard, R.W. 2000. *Affective computing*. Cambridge, MA: MIT Press.

Platt, J.C. 1999. *Fast training of support vector machines using sequential minimal optimization*, 185–208. Cambridge, MA: MIT Press.

Quinlan, J.R. 1993. *C4.5: Programs for machine learning*. San Francisco: Morgan Kaufmann Publishers Inc.. ISBN 1-55860-238-0.

Rehm, M., N. Bee, E. André. 2008. Wave like an Egyptian: Accelerometer based gesture recognition for culture specific interactions. In *Proceedings of the 22nd British HCI Group annual conference on people and computers: Culture, creativity, interaction*, vol. 1, 13–22

Selye, H. 1978. *The stress of life*. New York: McGraw-Hill.

Smith, M.J., P. Carayon, K.J. Sanders, S.Y. Lim, and D. Legrande. 1992. Employee stress and health complaints in jobs with and without electronic performance monitoring. *Applied Ergonomics* 23(1): 17–27.

Soylu, A., S. Kavukcu, M. Turkmen, N. Cabuk, and M. Duman. 2000. Effect of socioeconomic status on the blood pressure in children living in a developing country. *Pediatrics International* 42(1): 37–42.

Stockdale, S.E., K.B. Wells, L. Tang, T.R. Belin, L. Zhang, and C.D. Sherbourne. 2007. The importance of social context: Neighborhood stressors, stress-buffering mechanisms, and alcohol, drug, and mental health disorders. *Social Science and Medicine (1982)* 65(9): 1867–1881.

Tidd, S.T., and R.A. Friedman. 2002. Conflict style and coping with role conflict: An extension of the uncertainty model of work stress. *International Journal of Conflict Management* 13(3): 236–257.

Vizer, L.M., L. Zhou, and A. Sears. 2009. Automated stress detection using keystroke and linguistic features: An exploratory study. *International Journal of Human-Computer Studies* 67(10): 870–886.

Wenhui Liao A, W.Z.A. 2006. Toward a decision-theoretic framework for affect recognition and user assistance. *International Journal of Human-Computer Studies* 64(9):847–873.

Yeh, B.Y., D. Lester, and D.L. Tauber. 1986. Subjective stress and productivity in real estate sales people. *Psychological Reports* 58(3): 981–982.

Part IV
Conclusions and Future Directions

Chapter 12
Analysis of Practical Results

Abstract This chapter describes both the performance of the several practical approaches described in the last chapters and the results of the studies conducted to assess individual's behavior under stress. The chapter starts with an evaluation of the performance of the several information retrieval methods implemented in terms of its efficiency (how fast they perform) and their efficacy (how well they perform). Afterwards it presents some results on the relationship between stress and personal conflict handling style. A significant part of the chapter is then devoted to detailing the results of the studies conducted on stress and its effect on interaction patterns, focusing on several especially interesting features. The performance of the classifiers developed, used to quantify a level of stress in real time, is also detailed. At this point it is still not a critical analysis of the results, which is performed in the following chapter, but rather an objective and statistical view on the data collected. It is concluded that the most affected features are the ones that people do not conscientiously control, such as the acceleration of our gestures or the intensity of the touch. On the other hand, the parameters that are more rational are not influenced in such a significant manner. This can be seen as positive, in the sense that unconscious behaviors and reactions are more difficult to forge and are usually true reactions of the human body. Thus, the results that stem from their analysis are more reliable.

12.1 Concerning Information Retrieval

In this first section of the chapter, the performance of the information retrieval methods described is analyzed. To do it, a test case was implemented in the field of Portuguese Labor Law. However, given the complexity of this legal domain, a restrict set of norms was used. In that sense, a group of 36 norms of the Decree of Law 7/2009, from February 12th, 2009 were considered. These norms were selected because they are generally present in most of the disputes in Labor Law and address the following domains: (1) functions performed by the employee; (2) effects of the lack of professional title; (3) employee's rights; (4) employee's obligations and (5) general obligations of the parties. The database used in these tests contains a total of 127 indexed cases. The representation of these cases in vectors of binary entries was generated previously and was made available, in the form of a file.

12.1.1   Efficiency

The focus of this performance assessment process was on collecting data about two main issues: efficiency of the different algorithms and UMCourt self-assessment. Concerning the first issue, multiple iterations of the algorithms were executed, under different settings, and their times of execution measured. This is useful to compare them in terms of their execution times. These tests thus evaluate the efficiency of each algorithm presented. One of the factors that influences the performance of the algorithms in a more significant way is the size of the database. The more cases there are the higher the efficacy of the algorithms. However, the efficiency will necessarily decrease as more cases need to be analyzed and compared. Given that the algorithms presented here have linear complexity, the efficiency of these algorithms will generally decrease proportionally to the size of the database.

Pre-select (Classification)

The data depicted in Fig. 12.1 describes 100 iterations of the pre-selection algorithm that uses the association rules to retrieve cases according to their classes. To test it, in each iteration a random case was provided to the algorithm. The algorithm thus had to analyze the case, determine which rules were true and then pre-select, from the file containing the vectors of all the cases, the ones that belonged to the same category of the case provided. Analyzing Fig. 12.1, it is possible to conclude that this is a considerably efficient process. This is essentially due to the fact that: (1) the representation of the data as vectors had been previously performed and (2) cases are already indexed according to the rules they comply with. Therefore, once all this information is made available, this is a highly efficient algorithm for information retrieval. Another factor contributing to this is that the data is stored locally. This is possible given the small size of the data when stored according to the Vector Space model, constituting another advantage of this method.

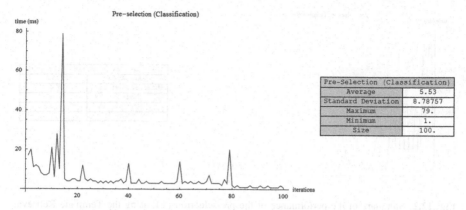

Fig. 12.1 Summary of the performance of the pre-selection task using association rules for 100 requests generated randomly

Pre-select (Template Retrieval)

To test this algorithm, several pre-selection tasks were requested, using a random case. To perform the pre-selection, the algorithm had to analyze the case and then interact with the database, requesting all the cases that matched a given criteria. This algorithm was tested using a local instance of a database and a remote one. Looking at Fig. 12.2, the first 30 values correspond to the tests in which a remote instance was used while the remaining correspond to the use of the local instance. There is a visible difference between the two scenarios. This difference is aggravated by the fact that: (1) the database is not a dedicated one, (2) being distributed, the system depends on external factors like the speed of the internet connection and (3) in order to satisfy the pre-selection rules, the algorithm may need to adapt strategies and make several iterations (requests to the database). This can be improved by choosing the best pre-selection rules, minimizing the number of times that the algorithm must adapt the search queries in search for more/less/better cases. When compared with the previous algorithm, this shows significantly higher times of execution, mainly due to the interaction with a remote database but also to the potential need for multiple iterations.

Evaluation (Cosine Similarity)

This algorithm uses the cosine similarity formula described in Chap. 7 to determine the similarity between two cases. To test it, the algorithm was provided with an isolated case and a list of cases, with the objective of determining the similarity between the isolated case and each one of the cases in the list. The results depicted in Fig. 12.3 show that this is a relatively fast way of computing the similarity, mainly because it only deals with binary values. However, a major disadvantage of

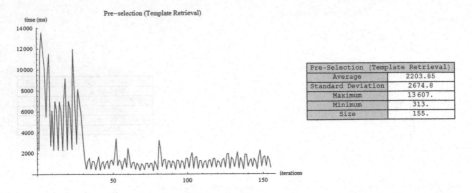

Fig. 12.2 Summary of the performance of the pre-selection task using the Template Retrieval technique for 155 requests generated randomly

this algorithm is that it does not allow assigning weights to the different components of a case.

Evaluation (Nearest Neighbor)

To test this algorithm, an approach similar to the previous one was followed. When analyzing the collected data depicted in Fig. 12.4, it is possible to conclude that the Nearest Neighbor algorithm performs slightly slower. As both algorithms have linear complexity, this poorer performance can be attributed to the fact that this algorithm deals with more complex types of data (e.g. integers, strings, floating points) rather than binary ones. However, this algorithm allows for weights to be assigned to the different components of the similarity function, allowing an evaluation that might be closer to the one performed by a human expert.

Get Complete Info

In this test, the objective was to determine the efficiency of a request of all the information regarding a case, i.e., given a random new case, how much time does it take to compile all the possible information for the user. This includes, as described before, pre-selecting and evaluating cases, computing the BATNA, WATNA, MLATNA, ZOPA as well as building the visual representation of the information. For this purpose, the algorithms described above were randomly selected to be used. Both local and remote requests were made, which is reflected in the execution times, similarly to the previously presented results. Thus, the execution time of a complete info request depends mostly on which algorithms are selected. The resemblance of the graph depicted in Fig. 12.5 with the one depicted in Fig. 12.2 is also not a coincidence as, given the potentially high execution times of the Template Retrieval algorithm, it has a considerable influence on the overall

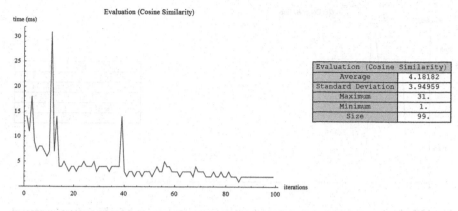

Fig. 12.3 Summary of the performance of the evaluation task using the Cosine Similarity technique for 99 requests generated randomly

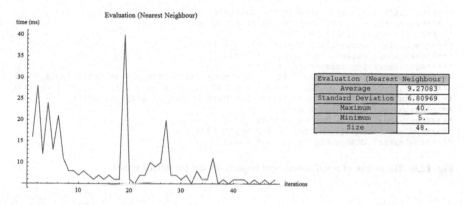

Fig. 12.4 Summary of the performance of the evaluation task using the Nearest Neighbor algorithm for 48 requests generated randomly

performance. Depending on location of the database used and the algorithms, the entire process may take between 5 to 20 s to compute. Given that this process may be carried out "offline", when parties finish providing the information about their case and stored for future use, we find these times adequate for the purposes of UMCourt.

12.1.2 *Efficacy*

More than the efficiency of the algorithms, their efficacy must also be considered, i.e., it is not enough to perform a given task quickly, it must also be performed as correctly as possible. In this sense, the platform keeps record of some key

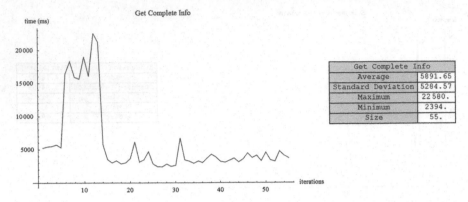

Fig. 12.5 Summary of the performance of the "Get Complete Info" task for 55 requests generated randomly

```
*****Evaluator: Indexed cases in the database: 127
*****Evaluator: Evaluation of System Performance:
*****Evaluator: Action: preselect
*****Evaluator: Successfull iterations: 33% (271)
*****Evaluator: Failed iterations: 66% (543)
*****Evaluator: Top reasons for failure
*****Evaluator: Code: 1; Description: Too many cases were pre-selected ; 61% (501)
*****Evaluator: Code: 0; Description: Not enough cases were pre-selected ; 2% (23)
*****Evaluator: Code: 2; Description: Not possible to satisfy all rules ; 2% (19)
*****Evaluator: Recommended actions:
*****Evaluator: Change Max Cases rule (33%)
*****Evaluator: Change initial search depth (33%)
*****Evaluator: Change Min Cases rule (33%)
```

Fig. 12.6 The output of a self-assessment request for the pre-select action

actions/decisions as well as their results. This allows, in a first instance, to determine which actions fail the most. Then, together with a description of the possible problems, eventual causes and eventual solutions, the platform is able to provide advice about what parameters to change in order to potentially improve its efficiency. The objective is that, in the long term, the platform is able to apply these recommendations autonomously, self-improving over time.

A typical output of a self-assessment request is shown in Fig. 12.6, in which the platform is assessing the performance of the preselect algorithm. First of all, it provides information about the amount of times that the action failed or succeeded. Here, failing means that the pre-selection violates some rule (e.g. regarding the number of cases) and must be reformulated and re-run. Succeeding means that the pre-selection respects all the rules. In the example, this action is failing in 66 % of the times, corresponding to a total of 543 cases.

Following, the platform points out the top reasons for failure as well as their frequency. In this example, the pre-selection fails mostly because too many cases are being pre-selected. Other minor reasons include not enough cases being pre-selected or reaching a state in which it is not possible to satisfy all rules. This happens when it is not possible to manage the pre-selection settings with enough precision or when the pre-selection rules are too strict.

Finally, given this, the platform points out several possible actions that might be used to address the described problems. In this case, three actions are suggested: (1) changing the rule that establishes the maximum amount of cases that should be pre-selected (this would actually decrease the number of errors but might not be good for who deals with all the cases later); (2) changing the initial search depth (this is more advisable as changing the initial search parameters might lead to a better result faster) and (3) changing the rule that establishes the minimum cases that should be selected.

12.2 Concerning Conflict Handling Styles

In this section an analysis of the effect of stressors on the personal conflict handling style of the parties is performed. In order to do it the data collected in the two phases of the game (with and without stressors) described in Chap. 10 was compared for the same pairs of players in search for statistically significant differences due to the action of the stressors. The main aim of the study is to assess the influence of stress on the behavior of the parties and on the outcome of the negotiated process. This experiment involved 14 users playing the game, in a total of 60 negotiation rounds. The data gathered included behavioral features provided by the environment, which were used to estimate the level of stress of each user using the personalized stress models developed, described in the next section. These models were used to determine how the level of stress relates with the behavior of the participants in a negotiation.

In order to statistically deal with this data, a numeric scale was used to describe the conflict handling styles. Table 12.1 depicts the conflict handling styles considered, the number of times that each style was evidenced by each participant (classified as described in Chap. 10) and the ordinal rank attributed (necessary to use this data in data-mining algorithms). The exact numeric quantity of a particular value has no purpose beyond its ability to establish a ranking over a set of data points. Therefore, rank-ordering was used which describes an order but does not establish relative size or degree of difference between the items measured. This was a mandatory step to make the data suitable for statistical and machine-learning techniques.

One of the first conclusions achieved when analyzing this data is that parties show a competitive style of negotiation most of the times, both in stressed and calm settings. However, when calm, the use of more cooperative style is slightly larger. The histograms depicted in Fig. 12.7 depict exactly this: the green curve refers to the distribution of the conflict handling styles in the calm phase while the red line refers to the distribution in the stressed phase. However, the differences are not statistically significant (MannWhitneyTest $= 0.33$). On average, the style of a party

Table 12.1 Summary of the conflict handling styles, the number of times that each style was evidenced and the rank-ordering of each style

Style	# times detected	Ordinal rank
Competing	30	1
Collaborating	12	2
Compromising	8	3
Accommodating	10	4
Avoiding	0	5

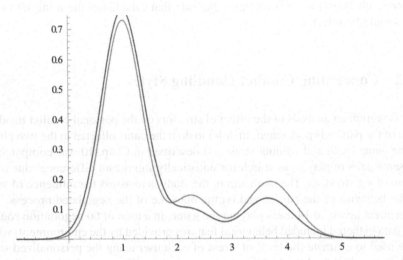

Fig. 12.7 Histograms depicting the distribution of the styles used by the parties: the *red line* represents data from the stressed phase while the *green line* represents data from the calm phase. The X axis represents the ordinal rank of the conflict handling styles as defined in Table 12.1. In a calm state the users evidence more cooperative styles (color figure online)

when stressed is 1.525 (closer to competing) and when calm is 1.74 (closer to collaborating).

The evaluation of the progress of the conflict styles during the negotiation process was centered on the average slope of its numeric values. In other words, the object of study was the variation of the conflict styles used by each party within the negotiation game. It was concluded that in a stressful state the parties tend to vary their conflict handling style more (on average 0.71 points between the beginning and the end of the game) than when they are calm (on average 0.61 points). This is in line with other results that point out to more sudden and less weighted decisions under stress. Besides that, it was also concluded that the 'manufacturer' role presents a higher average slope, i.e., a faster change in the conflict style (on average 0.83) than the 'retailer' (on average 0.51 points).

Concerning the values of the proposals exchanged by the parties during the negotiation, it can be concluded that both parties change more the values of the proposals (on average 0.19) when under stress than during the calm phase (on average 0.14). Moreover, the 'manufacturers' present a more dynamic proposal evolution (changing 0.19 in average) than the 'retailers' (average slope is 0.11).

The Euclidean distance to the optimum value was also analyzed, i.e., it was studied the deviation given the most desirable negotiation outcome (the value that prevented both parties from entering into bankruptcy). Under a stressful situation both parties were at a distance of, in average, 0.154 euros from the optimum value while in stress-free situation the distance decreases to 0.071 euros, in average. Therefore, it can be concluded that in a stressful situation it is more likely that the parties propose more uncooperative values. This can be explained as a consequence of acting too quickly or relying too much on coercion. When parties are under pressure they can commit strategic mistakes or give in unwanted concessions. It may also lead to bad agreements.

Acting too quickly is also a known response to external and internal stressors. Indeed, considering the duration of the rounds, it is possible to conclude that 90 % of the negotiation rounds had a shorter duration under a stressful environment than under a stress-free one. However, only in 30 % of these cases was the different statistically significant (at a level of 0.05).

Concerning the evolution of the conflict handling style in each game played, it is possible to conclude that 80 % of the participants used a competitive conflict style, which is assertive and uncooperative, in the early rounds. During the game 55 % of the players improve their styles (shifting towards more cooperative solutions), 35 % remain on the same style and 10 % become more competitive. It is known that 'competitors' often use power as the primary tool for handling conflict, and work to prove the importance of one side of the argument in order to win. This can be one explanation. Moreover, they are usually more concerned with winning the game than finding the best solution. Taking into consideration the pre-conditions of the game, the second hypothesis is more plausible.

In order to provide a more specific view of the results, one actual case is highlighted. It shows the evolution of the values proposed during the negotiation with stress (Fig. 12.8a) and without stress (Fig. 12.8b). The blue line represents the values proposed by the 'retailer' and the red one by the 'manufacturer'. It is possible to conclude that the 'manufacturer' is more flexible (changes more often). This is a recurrent behavior and can be explained by the fact that the seller (in this case, the 'manufacturer' role), in a buyer's market, needs to be more flexible and expect more negotiation about contingencies. Comparing the lines, in a calm state the 'manufacturer's' average slope is 0.31 and the 'retailer's' is 0.056. When under stress, the values rise to 0.5 and 0.1, respectively (approximately twice as much). Similar results are also observed in other pairs of players and are in line with the previously described conclusions: stressed participants take hastier and less weighted decisions.

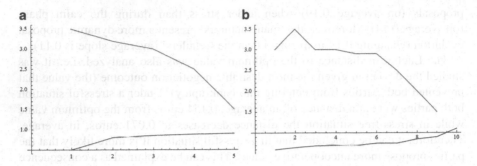

Fig. 12.8 Evolution of the values proposed during the negotiation when under stress (**a**) and without stress (**b**). The *red line* depicts the values proposed by the manufacturer while the *blue line* depicts the values proposed by the retailer. It is possible the see that under stress the values proposed vary faster: the parties achieve a similar result in only half the rounds (color figure online)

12.3 Concerning Stress

This section details the results from the studies on stress and its effects on the interaction patterns. Particularly, a preliminary analysis of the data is performed in which the datasets from stressed and calm states for each feature studied are analyzed in search of measurable significant differences. This is done using the Mann-Whitney statistical test. Afterwards, the performance of the classifiers developed with such datasets is assessed.

12.3.1 Preliminary Data Analysis

Each individual that participated in the study detailed in Chap. 11 was requested to play the game for some rounds without any source of stress. In this version, the game has no time limit and no vibration or annoying beeping sounds. In that sense, the user calmly plays the game, with enough time to think on the different possibilities. This phase allows collecting some data about how the individual normally behaves when he/she is not under stress (e.g. how he touches the screen, how he holds the smartphone, how well he fares in the game). This enables establishing a baseline for comparison. Afterwards, the same data is collected when the individual is playing the game with the stressors. The data gathered without stress is from now on designated as *baseline data*, whereas the data gathered with the influence of the stressors is from now on designated as *stressed data*.

Given that the data about the state of the user comes from different sources (e.g. handheld device, video camera) and is synchronized by a timestamp, the clocks of the devices are previously synchronized. The collected data is organized into five groups. The first one contains the baseline data. The second one contains

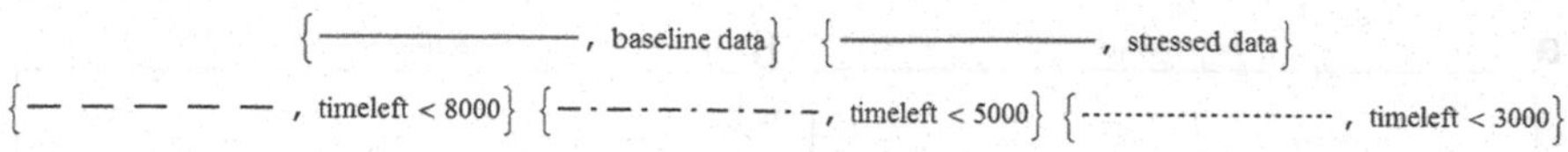

$$\{ \text{———————} , \text{ baseline data} \} \quad \{ \text{———————} , \text{ stressed data} \}$$

$$\{ - - - - - - , \text{ timeleft} < 8000 \} \quad \{ - \cdot - \cdot - \cdot - \cdot - \cdot - , \text{ timeleft} < 5000 \} \quad \{ \cdots\cdots\cdots\cdots , \text{ timeleft} < 3000 \}$$

Fig. 12.9 Different styles of the lines used to depict the different groups of the data collected. These styles will be used in the remaining of this book

the stressed data. The other three are subgroups of the stressed data created according to the time that was left for the end of the round at the instant of the event. Three groups were created: one for events that took place when there were less than 8 s left for the end of the round, another for events that took place when there were less than 5 s and the last one for events that took place when there were less than 3 s remaining. The notation depicted in Fig. 12.9 is used for the graphical representation of the data from this point on in the book, in order to distinguish between the different groups of data. Each of these three sub-intervals can be seen as depicting an increased stress level.

To determine to which extent each feature considered is or is not influenced by stress, the baseline data is compared with each of the remaining four groups. Provided that most of the distributions are not normal, the Mann-Whitney test is used to perform the analysis. This test is a non-parametric statistical hypothesis test for assessing whether one of two samples of independent observations tends to have larger values than the other. The null hypothesis is thus: $H_0 = $ *The medians of the two distributions are equal*. For each two distributions compared, the test returns a p-value, with a small p-value suggesting that it is unlikely that H_0 is true. For each feature, the training data is compared with the remaining four groups. In all the tests, a value of $\alpha = 0.05$ is used. Thus, for every Mann-Whitney test whose p-value $< \alpha$, the difference is considered to be statistically significant, i.e., H_0 is rejected.

A significant difference between the baseline data and the stressed data means that the feature is effectively influenced by stress for this specific user. This is the most desirable result as it indicates a higher level of confidence. This type of analysis is from now on designated as *first order*. If this is not the case, the baseline data is compared with each of the three subgroups of the stressed data (subgroups describing increased levels of stress), in search for significant differences. If statistically significant differences between one of these groups and the baseline data are found, it may still be concluded that the individual is affected by stress in this feature, although not in such an explicit manner. From now on, this kind of analysis is designated as *second order*.

Acceleration

The information about the acceleration is provided by the handheld devices. The interest in this parameter lies in a potential relationship between Human movements and the level of stress, specifically in what concerns the way that the user holds and

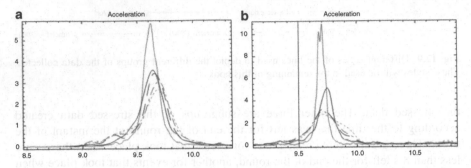

Fig. 12.10 Histograms of data from the module of the acceleration concerning two different users (**a** and **b**). The difference between the baseline data and the stressed data (and its subgroups) is clearly visible: the data from stressed users has more variability, i.e., stressed users move their hands more or in more sudden ways

interacts with the handheld device. The initial assumption is that a stressed user generally exhibits sudden hand gestures and movements and may also touch the device in a more harsh way.

Considering the first order analysis (as defined above), 80 % of the users show a significant difference between the baseline and stressed data. Moreover, when comparing the baseline data with the data from higher levels of stress (second order analysis), the results are even more expressive: 93.3(3)% of users show a statistically significant difference between the histograms. In that sense, the acceleration felt in the handheld devices is effectively different between calm and stressed users.

Moreover, it should also be concluded that, for most users, the amount of acceleration measured tends to increase. Figure 12.10 shows two examples in which the baseline values of the acceleration are more centered in a given value (less deviation) while the stressed data is slightly shifted to the right. The three subgroups of the real data are even more shifted, although the standard deviation also increases. For these two examples, the p-value returned by the Mann-Whitney test for the first order analysis is $5.9975 * 10^{-7}$ (for the data in Fig. 12.10a) and $2.75591 * 10^{-14}$ (for the data in Fig. 12.10b).

Maximum Intensity

From the touchscreen of the handheld device it is possible to acquire data about how the user touches it. In this case, the maximum intensity of the touch is analyzed. The initial assumption is that a more stressed user touches the screen with more intensity. The results obtained prove the assumption (see Fig. 12.11a, b that provide two example histograms). In both cases there is a clear shift in the values of the intensity towards higher values. Moreover, the differences observed between the distributions of the baseline data and the stressed data are statistically

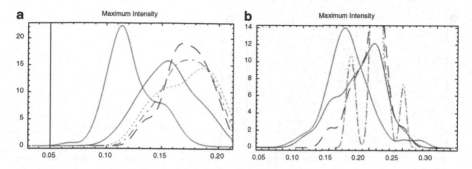

Fig. 12.11 Histograms of two different individuals (**a** and **b**) concerning the maximum intensity of the touch. These two histograms show the tendency observed in most of the data: stressed individuals touch the screen with more intensity

significant: p-value $= 1.94289 * 10^{-11}$ for Fig. 12.11a and p-value $= 0.00169036$ for Fig. 12.11b. And, if taking into consideration the second order analysis, we notice that the higher the level of stress the more the distributions are shifted to the right (black lines in Fig. 12.11).

This is, in fact, the general tendency: for all the participants who show a statistically significant difference, higher levels of stress are associated to increased touch intensity. From a global point of view, considering a first order analysis, 53.3 (3)% of the users under stress exhibit important differences in their touch intensities. If considering the second order analysis, this value increases to 60 % of the users. Thus being, it is concluded that for approximately half of the users, the maximum intensity of the touch is indeed significantly related to stress.

Average Intensity

A conclusion similar to the one of the previous section is achieved when the object of the analysis is the average value of the intensity during the touch. As depicted in Fig. 12.12, the average value of the intensity tends to increase as greater levels of stress are considered. These two particular examples have a p-value $= 0.00265927$ for Fig. 12.12a and p-value $= 6.5901 * 10^{-11}$ for Fig. 12.12b, which means that the differences observed are statistically significant. Moreover, when analyzing data from all the users, the results seem to be slightly better than the ones of the maximum intensity. In fact, in a first order analysis 60 % of the users show a considerable difference, while in a second order analysis this number increases to nearly 73.3 %. In this sense, the average intensity of the touch can also be used to detect the effects of stress.

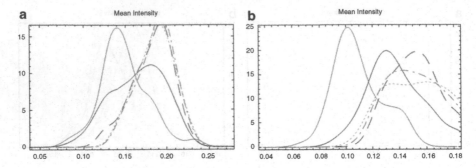

Fig. 12.12 Histograms of two participants (**a** and **b**) of the study concerning the average intensity of the touch. As with almost every participant, the average intensity of the touch increases with increased levels of stress

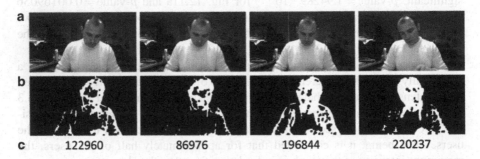

Fig. 12.13 Results of movement detection on a non-stressed user. Row (**a**) shows input images, row (**b**) shows binarized and filtered movement and row (**c**) shows the amount of movement detected

Amount of Movement

The amount of movement represents a measure of the movement in front of the camera. The process is carried out from the information captured by cameras placed in the users' environment and using computer vision techniques to extract features regarding the users' states. The initial hypothesis is that a stressed user moves more and in more sudden ways when under an increased level of stress. However, the results obtained point the other way around: when users are under increased levels of stress they tend to move less. In fact, it was observed that users become tenser, more rigid and highly focused on the tasks they are doing. This can even be observed visually on the participants, with the decreasing of behaviors such as gesticulating, messing with the hair or looking around.

Qualitative examples are depicted in Figs. 12.13 and 12.14. The differences between the amount of movement detected in the two scenarios are noticeable. The first excerpt belongs to a non-stressed user while the second one belongs to the same user in a more stressed state. Furthermore, a quantitative example is offered in

Fig. 12.14 Results of movement detection on a stressed user. Row (**a**) shows input images, row (**b**) shows binarized and filtered movement and row (**c**) shows the amount of movement detected

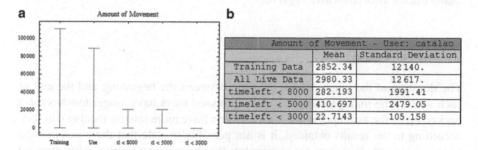

Amount of Movement - User: catalao		
	Mean	Standard Deviation
Training Data	2852.34	12140.
All Live Data	2980.33	12617.
timeleft < 8000	282.193	1991.41
timeleft < 5000	410.697	2479.05
timeleft < 3000	22.7143	105.158

Fig. 12.15 An example of how the amount of movement generally varies with the amount of stress: higher stress is related to a smaller amount of movement. (**a**) Range of the values of movement for each dataset. (**b**) Average and standard deviation for the different datasets for a specific user

Fig. 12.15. Given the nature of the data concerning the amount of movement, histograms are not the best way to depict it graphically. Instead, a Box-and-Whisker plot shows how the values are distributed for each of the five different analysis. The results show how the user moves more during the calm phase. On the contrary, when the level of stress increases, the user moves less (Fig. 12.15a). More accurate values for this specific example are shown in Fig. 12.15b. It is possible to see that, not only the average value of the amount of movement decreases but also the values of the standard deviation.

From a general point of view, the analysis of the amount of movement shows statistically significant differences for around 47 % of the users in a first order analysis. In a second order one, this value increases to 60 %. We were surprised that the results achieved with this parameter point out to a different conclusion than the expected. Nevertheless, the feature can be considered for the estimation of the levels of stress.

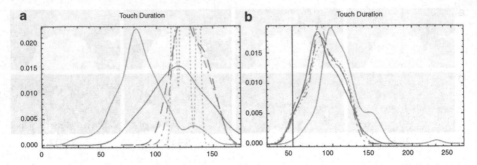

Fig. 12.16 Histograms of two different participants (**a** and **b**) concerning the duration of their touches. This feature does not have a homogeneous behavior: some stressed participants have shorter touches while others have longer ones

Duration of Touch

The duration of the touch defines the time between the beginning and the end of each touch. The initial assumption is that stressed users have longer touches (also backed up by the assumption that stressed users have more intense touches). In fact, according to the results obtained, it is not possible to state that there is a marked tendency towards this: there are participants that have longer touches when stressed while others have shorter ones. Figure 12.16 depicts two examples of these opposing behaviors: (a) shows data from a participant whose touch duration increases with stress, while (b) shows data from a participant whose touch duration decreases. The fact that there is a time limit in each round may also have an influence on the results, as participants must finish the calculation rapidly, making use of shorter touches.

Nevertheless, both examples depict statistically significant differences: p-value $= 2.70933 * 10^{-8}$ for (a) and p-value $= 9.54313 * 10^{-6}$ for (b). In fact, when analyzing data from all the participants, nearly 47 % show significant differences in a first order analysis and around 60 % show significant differences in a second order analysis. Thus being, although different users react differently for this parameter, it still provides valuable data about how the individual user is affected.

Scores

In analyzing the scores of the users, the main objective is to determine to which extent the cognition of the users is affected by stress. As it would be expected, the scores achieved by the users tend to decrease as the level of stress increases. Figure 12.17a shows this tendency for a specific user: without stressors, it is fairly easy and common to achieve good scores, with the average scores decreasing when

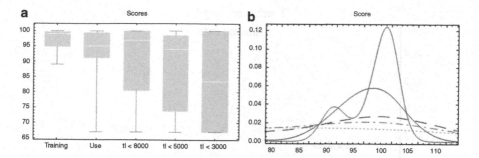

Fig. 12.17 Box-and-Whisker plot denoting the distribution of the scores for a given participant, in different levels of stress (**a**). The same data is shown in (**b**). Although the several distributions are visually different, these differences are not statistically significant. However, the general tendency is that participants under stress tend to have worse performances

under stress. The histogram depicted in Fig. 12.17b depicts the distribution of the same data. For this specific user, although a visual analysis may point otherwise, the differences are not statistically significant: the Mann-Whitney test returns a p-value $= 0.398694$.

In fact, when analyzing all the users, the score does not appear as a parameter that can be said to be related to stress. In a first order analysis, only around 7 % of the users show statistically significant differences between the scores in the baseline data and in the stressed data. Moreover, in a second order analysis this number only increases to 13 %. In that sense, the score does not seem to be very preponderant in analyzing the effects of stress in an individual. Nevertheless, score is solely used in these experiments as one way to induce an objective "worth fighting for", thus making the participants commit to the experiment and actually feel the stress. In any case, the concept of score is most likely not present in a real conflict resolution scenario or, if it is, it is certainly estimated differently. Thus being, the fact that a low number of significant differences in analyzing score was found constitutes no drawback.

Accuracy

Here, the accuracy of the touches of the participants is analyzed. Accuracy defines the relation between the touches on active versus passive areas. The type of data from this feature is different from the previous ones. In fact, instead of having a list of continuous values, there is a list of *true* or *false* values, indicating whether touches did or did not occur in an active area. Thus being, this parameter is not analyzed with the Mann-Whitney test but by looking at plots such as the one depicted in Fig. 12.18, that shows how the accuracy varies when considering the data collected from all the users.

It can be concluded that the accuracy of the touch remains relatively high, even for increased levels of stress (above 95 %). However it is possible to identify the expected decreasing tendency.

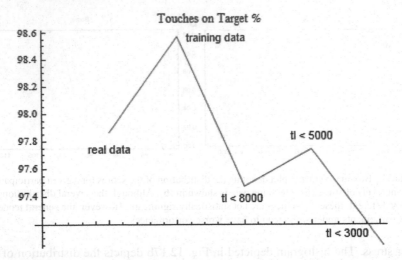

Fig. 12.18 This plot shows the percentage of touches on target in the five different analysis for all the participants

12.3.2   Classifiers

The main goal of this section is to analyze the datasets built in order to determine if it is possible to train classifiers for the purpose of analyzing the participants' behaviors. A feature-by-feature analysis is performed, in which the performance of the classifiers is analyzed according to indicators such as the correctly classified instances and kappa statistics.

Acceleration

For each participant, a classifier was trained in order to classify each instance of the acceleration measured on the handheld device as "stressed" or "not stressed". In the best case, the classifier was able to correctly classify 99.85 % of the instances (k = 0.995). The worst classifier trained for a user was successful in 95.36 % of the instances (k = 0.866). When analyzing all the classifiers built for all the participants, the average value of correctly classified instances is 98.1 %. The median is 98.01 %, the lower median is 96.92 % and the upper median 99.85 % (Fig. 12.19). For all this data, $\overline{k} = 0.94$. Given these results, it is possible to conclude that this classifier performs very well when used to classify the acceleration on the handheld device. This is in line with the very satisfying results of the significance tests on this feature.

Fig. 12.19 Box-and-whisker diagram detailing the sample accuracies of the classifiers trained for the acceleration feature

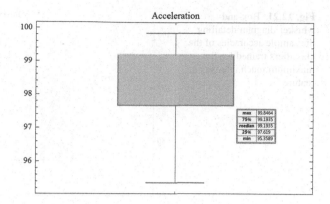

Fig. 12.20 Box-and-whisker diagram detailing the sample accuracies of the classifiers trained for the movement feature

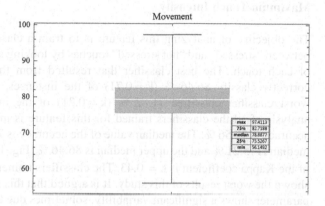

Amount of Movement

Another classifier was trained to classify the amount of movement of each user. The best classifier trained was able to correctly classify 97.41 % of the instances (k = 0.86). On the other hand, the worst classifier trained from the data gathered resulted in a sample accuracy of 56.15 % (k = 0.03). When a global analysis is performed of all the classifiers built for this feature, it is possible to conclude that the average sample accuracy is of 78.84 %. Looking at the distribution of the accuracy results, the median is 78.89 %, the lower median 75.53 % and the upper median 82.72 % (Fig. 12.20). The average value of the Cohen's kappa coefficient for this data is $\bar{k} = 0.23$.

The results point out that it is possible to train such classifiers that look at the amount of movement of the participants to categorize it as "stressed" or "not stressed". However, this data has not shown as good results as the acceleration on the handheld device. Especially negative is the lower value of the Cohen's kappa coefficient. Moreover, unlike all the remaining features, the sample accuracy of these classifiers shows a large variation. Nevertheless, the positive results of the sample accuracy are encouraging and validate the approach.

Fig. 12.21 Box-and-whisker diagram detailing the sample accuracies of the classifiers trained for the maximum touch intensity feature

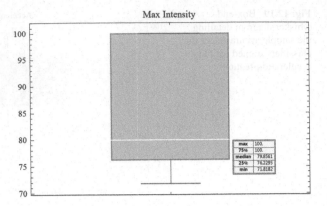

Maximum Touch Intensity

The objective of analyzing this feature is to train a classifier able to distinguish between "stressed" and "not stressed" touches by looking at the maximum intensity of each touch. The best classifier that resulted from this exercise was able to correctly classify 86.46 % (k = 0.71) of the instances. On the other hand, the worst classifier classified 71.82 % (k = 0.21) of the instances. When a broad analysis of all the classifiers trained for this feature is made, the average sample accuracy is 77.56 %. The median value of the accuracy is 76.487 % while the lower median is 75.21 % and the upper median is 86.46 % (Fig. 12.21). The average value of the Kappa coefficient is $\bar{k} = 0.43$. The classifiers trained for this parameter have shown the worst results of this study. It is argued that this is due to the fact that this parameter shows a significant variability, sometimes due to outlayer values that do not reflect the values of intensity measured during the touch. Not only are the values of the performance relatively lower than the others, but also the values of the Cohen's Kappa coefficient.

Average Touch Intensity

The aim of analyzing this feature is similar to the previous one. The only difference is that instead of considering the maximum pressure exerted on the screen during the touch, the average value during the touch is considered. The best classifier trained with this data was able to correctly classify 100 % of the touches (k = 1.0). On the opposite side, the classifier with the worst performance for this parameter classified 87.79 % of the instances correctly (k = 0.69). The average value of the sample accuracy when analyzing all the classifiers trained was of 95.13 %. The median value of the accuracy of the classifiers is 95.87 %, the lower median is 92.14 % and the upper median is 98.18 % (Fig. 12.22). The average value of the Cohen's Kappa is $\bar{k} = 0.89$. This classifier also shows some very interesting results, significantly better than the ones of the maximum touch intensity. This may be

Fig. 12.22 Box-and-whisker diagram detailing the sample accuracies of the classifiers trained for the average touch intensity feature

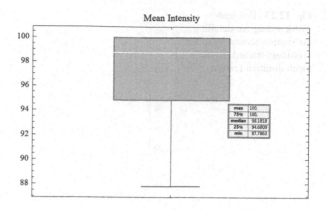

related to the fact that the maximum intensity of the touch often does not reflect the value of the pressure during the touch and may be an outlayer value. On the other hand, the average value shapes in a better way the value of the pressure exerted during the touch. This results in a classifier with a fair better accuracy.

Duration of Touch

With the analysis of this feature we want to train a classifier that looks at the duration of the touches in order to assign a label to each value, marking them as "stressed" or "not stressed". The classifier with the best performance was able to correctly classify 93.92 % of the touches (k = 0.86). On the other hand, the classifier with the worst performance classified 80.37 % of the instances (k = 0.56). In average, the sample accuracy was of 87.32 %. Looking at the Box-and-whisker diagram for the performance of the classifiers, we conclude that the median value is 86.26 %, while the lower median is 85.12 % and the upper median 89.34 % (Fig. 12.23). The average value of the Cohen's coefficient $\bar{k} = 0.71$. On the overall the results of this classifier are satisfactory, given the high sample accuracy verified and the generally high value of the measure of inter-rater agreement chosen.

Intensity Curve

The last feature considered in this study is the nature of the touches on the touchscreen. The objective is to classify the variation of intensity and time during a touch as belonging or not to a stressed user. Each touch has a shape that is very similar to a second degree polynomial curve. Hence, it can be approached by one. However, each touch has an arbitrary duration and this results in more or less intensity points being generated during the touch. Thus, given that the number of values is arbitrary for each touch, it is not possibly to simply make a classifier using

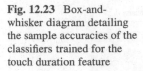

Fig. 12.23 Box-and-whisker diagram detailing the sample accuracies of the classifiers trained for the touch duration feature

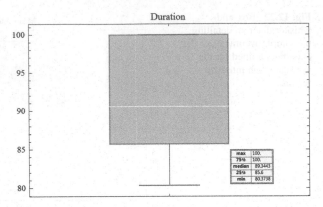

this data as it is. The approach used to deal with this issue was described in Chap. 11.

In the case of this feature, the meta-classifier weka.classifiers.meta.CVParameterSelection provided by Weka (a popular machine learning suite) was used that allows optimizing a given base-classifier. After finding the best possible configuration of parameters, the meta-classifier trains an instance of the base classifier with these parameters and uses it for subsequent predictions. The meta-classifier was used with lower bound 0.01, upper bound 0.5 and 10 optimization steps.

When using the J48 classification tree as the base classifier for the meta-classifier, the model is able to correctly classify 271 out of the 349 instances, which amounts to 77.6504 %. The Kappa statistic for this model is 0.5434 and the value of the ROC area is 0.796. The constructed tree has a size of 15 nodes and a total of 8 leaves (Fig. 12.24a). In this tree, attributes x0, x1 and x2 correspond to the values of a, b and c of the polynomial curve, respectively (as detailed in Chap. 11). Given this, it is possible to use the rules of this tree to build a classifier for distinguishing between stressed and calm touch curves.

When the SMO function is used to build a classifier, the results achieved are similar. In fact, the correctly classified instances amount to 79.9427 % (279 out of 349), the value of the Kappa statistics is 0.5809 and the value of the ROC area is 0.781. These results also show that a classifier can be trained with this data to distinguish between stressed and calm touches. Given that the results of both classifiers are similar, the decision was on using the J48 tree since the rules it generates can easily be used to classify touches in real time.

The classifier was assessed with data from 16 of the participants. Concerning this data, 13 participants show an increase in the touches classified as stressed by this classifier, when comparing the data from the baseline with the data from the highest stress. The minimum value of increase detected was of 6 %, the maximum value of increase was of 60 % and the average increase of touches classified as stressed, for all users, was of 32.3077 %. The three participants for which the classifier reported a decreasing percentage of stressed touches for increased levels of stress have shown relatively low values of decrease (−2.5 %, −5 % and −1 %). This means

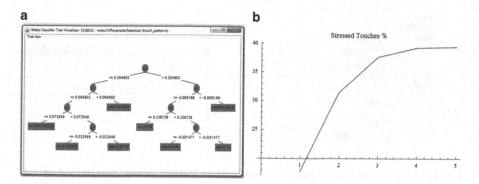

Fig. 12.24 (a) J48 pruned tree generated by the algorithm. This tree can be used to classify touches in real time as stressed ("yes" leaves) or not stressed ("no" leaves). (b) Percentage of touches classified as stressed in each of the five levels of the experiment

that the results of the classifier are consistent with the ones previously achieved in 81.25 % of the cases. Figure 12.24b depicts the average increase of the touches classified as "stressed" in each of the five levels of stress of the experiment.

12.4 Conclusion

When making an overview of the results achieved, it is possible to conclude that the feature that is most significantly affected by stress is the acceleration, with 80 % of the participants exhibiting significant differences between baseline and stressed data. On the other hand, the parameter that presents the worst results is the score. However, as stated before, the score feature is merely indicative and is not considered in the real application. It is used solely with the purpose of inducing an objective on the user: without the objective of maximizing the score, the user would not commit to the activity and *feel* the effects of stress (Fig. 12.25).

It was also concluded that, as expected, all the parameters show a better performance in a second order analysis. However, as already stated, the first order analysis is preferred as it considers all the data (and not only data from more stressed states), which means that a statistically significant difference (when it exists) is more solid. Analyzing all the data, each participant has in average 2.93 (3) features with considerable differences (out of 6). Moreover, in the worst case there are 3 participants with only 1 parameter with significant differences, and in the best case there are 4 participants with 5 features showing significant differences. Given this, it can be stated that a generic model can be applied to users for whom no baseline data exists. However, personalized models are certainly more accurate and that is the aim.

From the results, it is also concluded that the most affected features are the ones that people do not conscientiously control, such as the acceleration of our hand

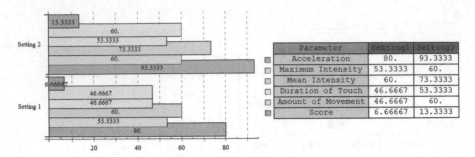

Fig. 12.25 Percentage of users that reveal significant differences between baseline and stressed data considering a first order analysis (Setting 1) and second order analysis (Setting 2)

Table 12.2 Summary of the results of the analysis of the performance of the classifiers

Dataset	Best		Worst		Average	
	%	K	%	K	%	K
Acc.	99.85	0.995	95.36	0.866	98.1	0.94
Mov.	97.41	0.86	56.15	0.03	78.84	0.23
Max.	86.46	0.71	71.82	0.21	77.56	0.43
Avg.	100	1.0	87.79	0.69	95.13	0.89
Dur.	93.92	0.86	80.37	0.56	87.32	0.71

gestures (i.e. how much they move) or the intensity of the touch. On the other hand, the parameters that are more rational (in this case the score) are not influenced in such a significant manner. This can be seen as positive, in the sense that unconscious behaviors and reactions are more difficult to forge and are usually true reactions of the human body. Thus, the results that stem from their analysis are more solid.

Concerning the performance of the classifiers developed with this data, the results are briefly summarized in Table 12.2. In each row the table describes the name of the parameter as well as the best and worst classifier trained (in terms of the percentage of correctly classified instances) and the respective kappa coefficients. Finally, for each parameter it also shows the average performance of the classifiers.

Using the classifiers described it is possible to build a solution for estimating the level of stress of users, in a personalized way, since each user has a number of classifiers that were trained using his personal interaction patterns. These can thus be used in real time to classify each instance of data being generated by the stress sensor agents. The information generated is then depicted graphically. Figure 12.26 shows a prototype of a web interface developed for such purpose. The dashed red line depicts the level of stress computed while the dashed orange line depicts the quality of that information.

The quality of the information generated is computed based on the type of inputs available and their significance, i.e., the assessment of stress is more reliable (higher quality of the information) if it is based on features that have shown very significant

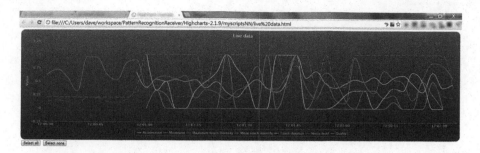

Fig. 12.26 The evolution of the level of stress for a given user. The *red dashed line* represents the level of stress, the *orange dashed line* represents the quality of the information and the remaining lines represent the contribution of each parameter for the level of stress computed (color figure online)

differences. On the other hand, if it is based on a low number of inputs or on inputs that have shown low levels of significance, the information compiled is not very reliable. This measure allows the decision-makers to have a more realistic view on the data provided. The remaining lines represent the contribution of each available stress source for the overall computation of stress. They allow to determine in which feature the user is being more or less affected by stress.

Fig. 12.28. The development of the level of stress for a given user. The red dotted line represents the level of stress, the orange dashed line represents the quality of the information and the remaining lines represent the calculation of each parameter for the level of stress computed. (color figure online)

difference. On the other hand, if it is based on a low number of inputs or on inputs that have shown low levels of significance, the information compiled is not very reliable. This measure allows the decision-makers to have a more real-time view on the data provided. The remaining lines represent the contribution of each available stress source for the overall computation of stress. They allow to determine in which feature the user is being more or less affected by stress.

Chapter 13
Concluding Remarks and Future Thoughts

Abstract As technological tools find their way into the realms of conflict resolution, the field gains increased complexity. Until a few years ago, conflict resolution would only touch fields such as Psychology, Philosophy, Economy or Law. Now, it also touches a wide range of technological fields that go much further than communication technologies to include Artificial Intelligence and many of its sub-fields. This significantly expands the possible future directions of research which, at the same time, plunges the field in a certain degree of uncertainty. One must, nonetheless, bear in mind that such uncertainty, doubt and suspicion is natural in any revolution and that, at the time, it is a Technological Revolution that we are living. Thus, a significant focus should be placed on analyzing the work carried out so far by researchers and commercial providers in an attempt to draw conclusions that can better guide the future steps. Moreover, these future steps should be guided not only by the technical challenges or the improvement of performance but also by more abstract notions such as fairness and transparency, with a marked concern on ethics. Only this way can the support and trust of significant slices of the society be harnessed, fundamental for the successful implementation and active use of the type of tools described in this book.

13.1 On the Use of Case-Based Reasoning in the Legal Context

The use of Case-based Reasoning for conflict resolution is a natural approach in common law contexts, although it's use in civil law systems also makes sense, as described in previous chapters. Moreover, negotiators and mediators alike rely on their past experiences in order to take better decisions. These were, in fact, the reasons that supported the decision to study case-based approaches.

D. Carneiro et al., *Conflict Resolution and its Context*, Law, Governance and
Technology Series 18, DOI 10.1007/978-3-319-06239-6_13,
© Springer International Publishing Switzerland 2014

Traditionally, two main drawbacks are associated to CBR (Aamodt and Plaza 1994), which could, transitively, be associated to UMCourt. Several decisions were taken in order to avoid this. On the one hand, case-based approaches may suffer from inefficiency, mostly when the size of the database grows. Concerning this issue, the decision was to develop different approaches (from pure case-based to hybrid ones) so that their performances could be assessed in order to determine the most efficient ones. Moreover, it must also be acknowledged that conflict resolution is generally an asynchronous process, which takes place over several hours or even days. Thus being, given that the methods presented have relatively small times of execution and that the context of application does not mandatorily demand for higher performance, it can be concluded that they can be used in this context.

On the other hand, the efficiency and efficacy of case-based approaches is also known to depend directly on the number and characteristics of the cases in the database. And this must be acknowledged as a more serious challenge to overcome. The number of cases influences the performance of the algorithms and its efficacy. Moreover, case-based approaches are highly domain-dependent, i.e., cases take place in a given legal framework and are not easily adapted to other domains as the norms are different. In the case-study implemented, a database with cases focusing mostly on employee's rights and obligations was used (articles 129 and 128 of the Portuguese labor law, respectively), although some cases also addressed other articles. The case-study consisted of conflict resolution scenarios in the labor law domain, set up by users, involving the issues addressed by the five articles and respective numbers and items addressed by the database (Articles 118, 117, 126, 128 and 129). The participants were students and teachers of master courses on Law and on Informatics in our institution. Disputes involving employee's rights and obligations had many more useful solutions proposed by the platform than disputes involving other issues. Diminishing the success rate of the resolution of the second ones.

In that sense, the main conclusion drawn concerning this subject is that a pure case-based approach can be quite effective in generating solutions for a conflict resolution in scenarios in which there are enough past cases. In that sense, the domain of the database should be explicitly defined in order to define the domain of the conflict resolution platform. However, a hybrid approach can be successfully used in which case-based reasoning is supported by other tools that can generate solutions when a case-based approach alone is not enough. This possibility was tackled in this work by devising an approach based on genetic algorithms. The main advantage of such approach is that it depends only on the rules of each specific domain, which are needed to ensure the validity of the solutions. Alternatively, it is also possible to rely on parties themselves to generate solutions, although this approach tends to fail when parties are unable or unwilling to do it.

13.2   On the Use of Negotiation/Mediation for Conflict Resolution

The use of negotiation or mediation for conflict resolution is indeed one of the most effective ways of solving disputes out of court. Nevertheless, from the experiments implemented it can be learned that these processes alone may not suffice. One of the first issues faced during the studies carried out was a consequence of the fact that most of the participants from the informatics field had very little to no knowledge at all about Portuguese labor law or about conflict resolution at all (as many of the parties involved in conflict resolution do). In that sense, the resolution process often failed because of a clearly unrealistic view of their chances in the dispute. Moreover, these participants generally had no idea about the possible outcomes for each side and could not realistically evaluate how good or bad a given solution was.

The first conclusion about the use of these alternative methods is that negotiation or mediation alone are not enough to ensure the success of the conflict resolution process. There is, more than anything else, the need for tools that can effectively inform the parties about the possibilities, so that they can take better and more informed decisions. Namely, it was found to be crucial for parties to know their best and worst possible scenarios, the most likely one, as well as some past cases that can be used as learning examples, providing a notion of realism.

An important conclusion is thus that methods for compiling useful information should be considered before the actual conflict resolution process starts, so that the parties can gain a realistic view about their conflict. In doing so, parties will converge faster to a solution that is realistic and in line with the solutions retrieved from the past similar cases. This increases the success rate of conflict resolution processes.

This success rate was also found to depend significantly on the attitude of the parties, i.e., when participants are actively creating solutions and collaborating for the resolution of the dispute, the process is more likely to succeed than when one or more users are not or cannot create solutions, limiting their actions to replying affirmatively or negatively to the solutions proposed.

Evidently, the challenge here is still the one of accurately determining the conflict handling style of each party. In that sense, an automated and non-invasive method that is able to classify the conflict style of a party based on their behavior during the process was developed (e.g. is the party proposing solutions?, are the solutions proposed selfish?, is the party simply answering positively or negatively?). Based on this, the mediator or the conflict resolution platform is able to determine the conflict style in real time and to adapt or point out possible adaptations to any of the parties involved.

13.3 On the Relationship Between Personal Conflict Handling Styles and Stress

Concerning the interpretation of the conflict handling styles, the results achieved were consistent for the majority of the participants. They can be summarized as follows:

- Stressed participants take hastier decisions, taking less time to think them through;
- Stressed participants are more prone to change their behavior and do it in more significant ways (we focused on the values of the proposals exchanged and on the conflict resolution style evidenced);
- Under a stressful environment, outcomes tend to be farther away from the optimum result;
- Under stress, participants tend to be more competitive.

This points out the need for seeking calm and harmonious environments for conflict resolution. As a consequence, it can be concluded that courtrooms are definitely not the ideal conflict resolution environment as these are highly competitive milieus in which parties forget each other's rightful ambitions and focus on the maximization of the own gain. Alternative environments, focused on cooperative strategies, should be preferred.

Moreover, in order for conflict managers to improve their action, access to the context information mentioned should be provided. This would allow them to detect, in due time, an escalation on the level of conflict and prevent a degradation on the relationships. This context information, that is available in face-to-face settings, must also be considered in virtual settings so that conflict managers can increase the efficiency of their decisions by considering more complete information.

However, despite its apparent advantages, this approach may also encompass risks. One of the main concerns raised is related with the risk of people trying to control the system if they know how it works. On the one hand it is known that people have tried to cheat systems as much as they try to make them cheat-proof (e.g. parties in court will also try to manipulate decision-makers leading them into believing what they want). It is argued that following this approach, this kind of behaviors may be hindered, namely because it is difficult to consistently fake expressions, gestures or other behavioral features since they constitute reflexes rather than conscious behaviors.

Given this, it is concluded that this approach may encompass several interesting advantages for mediators, specifically for the ones operating in online environments, allowing them to take more informed decisions.

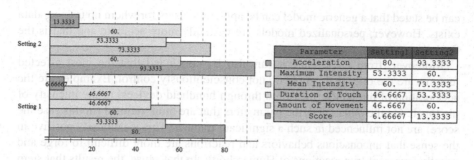

Fig. 13.1 Percentage of users that reveal significant differences between baseline and stressed data considering a first order analysis (Setting 1) and a second order analysis (Setting 2)

13.4 On the Assessment of Stress

In this work, some behavioral features and their relation to stress have been studied. One of the main objectives was to do it in a non-invasive way, so that the experiments performed would not influence the results. In that sense, focus has been set on features whose data could be transparently acquired from the environment, without the user being explicitly aware of it. Specifically, it has been studied how stress influences the acceleration of the handheld device, the maximum and mean intensity of touch, the duration of the touch, the amount of movement, the cognitive performance, just to name a few. Essentially, this work allowed to define a way to measure how each user is affected by stress.

A general overview of its effects on the participants can be performed by taking another look at Figure 13.1, retrieved from the previous chapter. It can be concluded that the feature most significantly affected by stress is *acceleration*, with 80 % of the users exhibiting statistically significant differences between baseline and stressed data.

On the other hand, the parameter that presents the less satisfying results is the *score*. However, it must be stressed that this last parameter is merely indicative and shall not be considered in eventual final application scenarios since the concept of a score may not even exist. It was however used in this study with the purpose of inducing an objective on the user: without the objective of maximizing the score, the user would not feel any stress.

It can also be concluded that, as expected, all the parameters show a better performance in a second order analysis. However, as already mentioned previously, the first order analysis is preferred as it considers all the data (and not only data from more stressed states), which means that a statistically significant difference (when it exists) is more solid.

When considering all the data, each participant has in average 2.93(3) parameters with significant differences (out of 6). Moreover, in the worst case there are 3 participants with only 1 parameter with significant differences, and in the best case there are 4 users with 5 parameters with significant differences. Given this, it can be stated that a generic model can be applied to users for whom no training data exists. However, personalized models are certainly more accurate and that is the final aim.

Moreover, from the results, it can also be concluded that the most affected features are the ones that people do not conscientiously control. Examples are the acceleration of our hands (measured through handheld devices) or the intensity of the touch. On the other hand, the parameters that are more rational (in this case the score) are not influenced in such a significant manner. This is definitely positive in the sense that unconscious behaviors and reactions are more difficult to forge and usually represent true reactions of Human body. In that sense, the results that stem from their analysis are more solid and reliable when considered for building a stress model.

13.5   Future Lines

Since the first steps on the work detailed in this book, it was clear that it would be a multidisciplinary one, drawing mostly from Computer Science but also largely from Legal Science. From the technological point of view, it also merged many different fields, including Multi-agent Systems, Behavioral Analysis, Service-oriented Architectures, Natural Computing, among others. In that sense, it is only natural that at the closure of this endeavor, a multitude of possible future paths exists, each one following different directions under the different fields addressed.

Several especially interesting issues emerge at the time of the conclusion of this book, to be tackled by future research efforts:

- The pursuit of approaches that can minimize the classical drawbacks of Case-based Reasoning, especially the ones that matter in the legal field. In this book some positive experiences in this direction where carried out, namely the evolution of case-based approaches towards less domain-dependency, through the mixed use of nature-inspired techniques;
- The development of mechanisms that allow for an easier interpretation of norms and arguments written in natural language, its translation into rules and the verification of their validity. This is a complex field with ongoing research efforts, focusing mostly on the automatic interpretation of natural language. However, an equal effort should be placed on taking this information and using it to better inform parties, also in an automated way;
- The pursuit of computational models for legal reasoning, with an ethical background, that can not only take decisions but also argue about them. Indeed, one of the common arguments against autonomous legal reasoning is its cold and mathematical nature. Parties would trust more in such systems if they included ethical notions as well as the ability to explain and justify their decisions and suggestions. This would be a step forward in accurately informing the parties and boosting their trust in the system;

- The inclusion of the notion of fairness into conflict resolution platforms. Although algorithms for fair division have been around since the 1940s (through the work of researchers such as Hugo Steinhaus, Bronisław Knaster or Stefan Banach), there is the need to not only use them but also to expose thoroughly how decisions are undertaken and how the notion of fairness is treated computationally;

There is a particularly innovative research line that stems from this work: the non-invasive and multi-modal acquisition of contextual information. The approach implemented opens the door to define personalized models to measure the influence of stress in the users of technological devices. It could lead to further developments with high social and economic impact in a wide range of application fields.

Nonetheless, given the topic of the book, we will focus here on the potential advantages of such approach form the point of view of legal practitioners. In the first place, it must be noted the evolution of our society towards the favoring of virtual interactions in replacement of traditional face-to-face interaction. In seeking to resolving conflicts, the same trend exists. As stated multiple times throughout this book, virtual interactions are far poorer, lacking a significant amount of contextual information that is used to accurately sending and perceiving communicative acts. These cues include our body language, our posture, the tone of our voice, the rhythm of the speech, among many others. Despite their apparent accessory nature, that most likely stems from the fact that we do not use them consciously, these non-verbal cues are very important to accurately send and perceive messages. Without them, communicative acts can easily result in misunderstandings. As an example, unless we know our interlocutor very well, it results challenging to identify a joke, sarcasm or an offense in a sentence just by looking at its words. Alternatively, if one would consider the tone of voice or the facial expression of the interlocutor while saying such sentence, it would result easier to correctly interpret it. The lack of such information constitutes an obstacle for effective communication in general. However, when considering more sensible domains such as the one of conflict resolution, the consequences may go much further as simple misunderstandings may undermine the confidence of the parties and jeopardize the whole process.

It is our conviction that, in light of this recent evolution, communication tools and approaches should also evolve to provide support for better and more realistic interactions. Particularly, in this book we addressed this topic considering the point of view of mediators and disputant parties involved in a technology-supported conflict resolution process. Undeniably, it becomes increasingly difficult for a mediator and the parties to understand each other's state just by the words exchanged in an e-mail or chat message. And the state of a party, which includes his level of stress, his mood, his level of fatigue and many other aspects, is essential to contextualize the party's actions. Failing to do so may result in inaccurate perceptions about each other, which may lead to misunderstandings that will jeopardize relationships, which are in turn essential to a positive and successful conflict resolution process.

In light of this, our vision is that, in a short-term future, the existence of environments for conflict resolution becomes a reality. The main change in the current paradigm is that such environments will include, besides the computer itself, additional mechanisms for harnessing contextual information in a transparent way. This will allow improving communication between the parties and empower their decision-making in an unprecedented way, bringing the whole process closer to the richer traditional interactions, without the added pressure of face-to-face.

An environment such as this is nowadays feasible. Nevertheless, where can we go from there? What other doors does this open? In a slightly more futuristic view, but still feasible in a short-term, we envision the development of such environments endowed with proactivity. Indeed, the environment developed and described so far considers only the issue of harnessing information about the parties and providing it to support decision-making. We foresee an environment that is not only sensible to its user's context but is also able to proactively influence it. The main aim is that such environments take actions aimed at improving its users' state, in an autonomous way. Undeniably, we are considering here the hypothesis of inducing moods.

Inducing specific moods in human beings has been a topic of research of psychology. However, the relationship between cognition and emotions has not been studied in detail until recently. The interest in this relationship lies in the hypothesis of influencing mental processes that, in turn, affect mood. Such mental processes include, but are not limited to, attention, memory or decision-making.

There are many different ways to induce mood (Jallais and Gilet 2010), with varying effects on the type of mood induced, its positiveness or negativeness, its duration and its intensity. Some of the most frequent ones include the use of uplifting music, upsetting or relaxing images, critical feedback or storytelling.

The effects of these techniques can act on several spheres of the individual. Experiments have been conducted to induce mood on users in order to increase their creativity and originality (De Dreu et al. 2008). Activating moods (e.g., angry, fearful, happy, elated) lead to more creative fluency and originality than do deactivating moods (e.g., sad, depressed, relaxed, serene). Baños et al. (2012) conducted a study in this field in which the satisfaction of elderly in Virtual Environments was improved by inducing joy and relaxation through the use of exercises for generating positive-autobiographic memories, mindfulness and slow breathing rhythms.

We foresee a similar approach in which the experience of parties in a conflict resolution process can be felt as more positive, thus increasing their satisfaction and interest. Indeed, maintaining people interested in the process is the first step to ensure that they are actually committed to actively search for a solution. In an approach such as the one proposed, this can be achieved by building harmonious and positive environments that reduce the stress felt, prevent the escalation of the conflict, are physically comfortable and avoid burnouts and fatigue.

This will, essentially, consist of three parts: sensing, decision making and actuation. So far, and as detailed in this book, we have addressed the aspects related to sensing the environment and the state of the parties. So, future steps towards this vision will include the decision-making processes that will determine when it is time for taking a given action. The actual actions are, at this time, clear. They will include playing specific types of music, the projection of colors, images or videos on the walls, the control of luminosity or temperature and suggestions such as taking a walk, making a pause, taking a coffee or tea or resuming the process on the next day.

From a technological standpoint, this vision is at the moment perfectly feasible. However, other points of view should be taken into account, being ethical considerations probably the most important ones. Indeed, many questions arise when considering such an innovative approach. Would people agree to be monitored this way? Is it necessary for people to agree? Would they consent in using a system that formalizes information about their state in an explicit and easily accessible manner?

Our first thought on this is that we are considering information that people already share in their daily interactions. So, the proposed system does not come up with something new, it just formalizes and quantifies it. But, the truth is that this may make all the difference. Indeed, we often fail to acquire all the contextual cues, given their diversity. We may even choose an ODR service to actually keep our feelings and emotions to ourselves. In such cases, the formalization of context may significantly change the course of the conflict resolution process.

We do not deny this. However, we are convinced that it can change its course for better. We also believe that these concerns will not be an obstacle to the acceptation of Intelligent Environments for Conflict Resolution if people can understand the potential benefits. Actually, many other fields have faced similar problems in which concessions must be made to gain something in return. The building of profiles of users while surfing the web is, most likely, the most startling example: we give away information about our preferences, our routines and other information about our individuality to gain in exchange a personalized recommendation system.

In one of the most recent books on the topic, edited by Kenneth Pimple, these issues are analysed in detail (Pimple 2014). Specifically, several chapters are devoted to the important trade-off mentioned above: how much are we willing to give up in order to receive something in return. The book analyses specific cases: public health surveillance without patient consent, the constant monitoring of people in their daily routines as they appear in video cameras of airport terminals, interact with ATMs (Automatic Teller Machines) or make electronic transactions or even when elderly give up their privacy to preserve their independent lifestyle.

Our feeling as we end this book is that this trend, in which our privacy seems to be diminished in favour of enhanced services, is unstoppable. Although there are those who actively oppose such practices, there are also those who are willing to pay the price. In every similar *crisis* that existed in the past around this duality, the numbers of the ones that belong to the second group seem to grow with time. In other words, we could use a famous saying by an equally famous Portuguese poet, Fernando Pessoa, when coming up with a slogan for the debut of Coca-Cola in the Portuguese market: *"primeiro estranha-se, depois entranha-se"*, which roughly translates to *"at first you find it strange, but then it becomes a part of you"*.

There is no doubt in our mind that systems such as the one detailed in this book will be a reality in the future. The only doubt lies in the manner and speed of this evolution. Indeed, many aspects need to be addressed so as to make such systems reliable, transparent and clearly useful.

One of the most important is *trust*. On this topic, Ben Shneiderman provides a list of principles and guidelines to enhance cooperative behaviours and win user/customer loyalty by giving assurances, references, certifications from third parties, and guarantees of privacy and security (Shneiderman 2000). Such principles should be seen as fundamental at the time of devising an ODR platform.

In (Pimple 2014), other important ethical principles are put forward. Intrinsically related to trust is the *Respect for People*. Researchers, developers and marketers should clearly expose all the important and sensitive details of the system and receive informed consent from the potential users. Then, these same stakeholders, should acknowledge and inform about the whole range of potential consequences of the system. That is, it is not enough to say what the system aims to do or what it was designed to do but everything that it can be used to do, beneficial or maleficent. Stakeholders should also implement, as far as possible, techniques that prevent the system to be used with malice by criminals, terrorists or other groups with nefarious aims.

One of the most challenging aspects to consider in this particular work is the one of transparency. Ideally, users should be fully aware of what the system does and how it does it. Nonetheless, in this work as in other approaches to Context-aware Computing, one of the main objectives is to acquire information and take appropriate actions without the awareness of the user. Doing it otherwise would defeat the purpose. In our particular case, to let people know which information is collected and how it is used to classify their psychological or physical state would potentially lead to a change in their behaviours or even to attempts to cheat the system by faking behaviours. This is probably the biggest challenge in this work, opposing ethics to the accuracy of the system. It is clear to us that people must be informed about the information collected and they must consent to it prior to the use of such systems. Nevertheless, while consenting, people must at the same time be sensitized to the fact that trying to behave abnormally, in an attempt to cheat the system for example, might not result in an advantage for either side. Indeed, the key advantages of such systems stem from the analysis of the behaviours of the users. If they are not willing to consent to this, other conflict resolution tools should be used.

Then, there is also the always-concerning issue of privacy: sensitive information about people or their processes must not be shared or traded as a commodity, it cannot be collected without permission and cannot be used to other ends than the ones explicitly agreed upon.

At the end of this book it is clear that innovative systems, such as the one proposed, face a natural opposition that stems from the imperative analysis of a wide range of implications. And it could not be otherwise. At a time in which everything changes at such an unprecedented rate, one must be additionally careful about the applications and systems we interact with and about the kind and amount of information we provide them. Nonetheless, these new kinds of systems provide functionalities that were unthinkable a few decades ago. Such advanced functionalities are what make users take the decision to share their sensitive information: because they expect to receive something of higher value in return.

Thinking about the legal domain in particular, the community should aim for ODR systems with innovative and high-value functionalities that can be, at the same time, deemed reliable and trustworthy. If we manage to do so, we can finally start to see the path to the second generation ODR devised by Peruginelli and Chiti in 2002, in which computer systems finally take the reins and provide autonomous, sensible and proactive support to conflict resolution.

References

Aamodt, A., and E. Plaza. 1994. Case-based reasoning: Foundational issues, methodological variations, and system approaches. *AI Communications* 7(1): 39–59. IOS Press.

Baños, R.M., E. Etchemendy, D. Castilla, A. García-Palacios, S. Quero, and C. Botella. 2012. Positive mood induction procedures for virtual environments designed for elderly people. *Interacting with Computers* 24(3): 131–138.

De Dreu, C.K.W., M. Baas, and B.A. Nijstad. 2008. Hedonic tone and activation level in the mood-creativity link: Toward a dual pathway to creativity model. *Journal of Personality and Social Psychology* 94(5): 739–56.

Jallais, C., and A. Gilet. 2010. Inducing changes in arousal and valence: Comparison of two mood induction procedures. *Behaviour Research Methods* 42(1): 318–325.

Pimple, K.D. (ed.). 2014. *Emerging Pervasive Information and Communication Technologies (PICT): Ethical challenges, opportunities and safeguards*, Law, governance and technology series, vol. 11. Dordrecht: Springer. ISBN 978-94-007-6833-8.

Shneiderman, N. (2000). Designing trust into online experiences. *Communications of the ACM* 43(12): 57–59. New York: ACM.

Printed in the United States
By Bookmasters